A TO Z
OF AFRICAN AMERICANS

AFRICAN AMERICANS
IN THE
MILITARY

Revised Edition

Catherine Reef

Facts On File
An imprint of Infobase Publishing

Note on Photos

Many of the illustrations and photographs used in this book are old, historical images. The quality of the prints is not always up to current standards, as in some cases the originals are from old or poor quality negatives or are damaged. The content of the illustrations, however, made their inclusion important despite problems in reproduction.

African Americans in the Military, Revised Edition

Copyright © 2010 by Catherine Reef

Facts On File, Inc.
An imprint of Infobase Publishing
132 West 31st Street
New York NY 10001

Library of Congress Cataloging-in-Publication Data
Reef, Catherine.
    African Americans in the military / Catherine Reef.—Rev. ed.
        p. cm.—(A to Z of African Americans)
    Includes bibliographical references and index.
    ISBN 978-0-8160-7839-4 (acid-free paper) 1. United States—Armed Forces—African Americans—Biography—Dictionaries. 2. African American soldiers—Biography—Dictionaries. I. Title.
    U52.R42 2010
    355.0089'96073—dc22   2009031298

Facts On File books are available at special discounts when purchased in bulk quantities for businesses, associations, institutions, or sales promotions. Please call our Special Sales Department in New York at (212) 967-8800 or (800) 322-8755.

You can find Facts On File on the World Wide Web at http://www.factsonfile.com

Excerpts included herewith have been reprinted by permission of the copyright holders; the author has made every effort to contact copyright holders. The publishers will be glad to rectify, in future editions, any errors or omissions brought to their notice.

Text design by Joan M. Toro
Composition by Hermitage Publishing Services
Cover printed by Sheridan Books, Ann Arbor, Mich.
Book printed and bound by Sheridan Books, Ann Arbor, Mich.
Date printed: June 2010
Printed in the United States of America

10 9 8 7 6 5 4 3 2 1

This book is printed on acid-free paper.

CONTENTS

LIST OF ENTRIES

ACKNOWLEDGMENTS

I wish to thank General J. Gary Cooper, U.S. Marine Corps, retired; General Fred A. Gorden, U.S. Army, retired; and Dr. Roscoe C. Brown, Jr., for their assistance and interest in this book. All three were generous with their time.

INTRODUCTION

In 1898, the actor Mason Mitchell became a national celebrity when he left the New York stage to enlist in the Rough Riders, Teddy Roosevelt's regiment of cowboys and aristocrats that fought in the Spanish-American War. Mitchell was wounded in the July 1 assault on a Spanish stronghold, the village of El Caney, Cuba; but by December 26 he had recovered enough to regale an audience in Richmond, Virginia, with tales of his wartime adventures.

The crowd that packed the Academy of Music that afternoon cheered vociferously as Mitchell described his unit's gallantry at El Caney and at San Juan Hill, site of a second and more important U.S. victory. Then the actor paused in his rousing account to pay tribute to the 10th Cavalry, an African-American regiment that performed heroically at San Juan Hill, and there were no more hurrahs. Instead, hisses filled the auditorium, and there were shouts of "Stop him" and "Put him out." No longer able to make himself heard, Mitchell rang down the curtain and left the stage.

What happened in that lecture hall more than a century ago reveals much about the challenges faced by African Americans in the armed forces, not just in the 1890s, but from the time of the Revolutionary War through the middle of the 20th century and perhaps beyond. Throughout much of U.S. history, African Americans motivated by patriotism to serve their country had to fight against a biased majority for recognition. In times of war, blacks in uniform hoped that proving themselves equal to their white comrades would gain them opportunities in civilian life. Although such expectations were repeatedly frustrated, the heroism of African Americans was essential to building and defending the United States.

Americans honor a fugitive from slavery, Crispus Attucks of Boston, as the first person to die in the struggle for independence. On March 5, 1770, Attucks led an angry protest against the presence of British troops in his city. The crowd's taunting drew gunfire from the red-coated British soldiers, and Attucks and several of his followers met their death.

Despite the fact that African Americans fought at Lexington and Concord in April 1775 and helped to win other early battles, George Washington and his generals were reluctant to accept their services. On July 9, 1775, Washington's recruiting officer issued an order barring "any stroller, negro, or vagabond" from enlisting in the Continental army. Washington confirmed this policy four months later, on November 12, when he again ordered blacks excluded from enlistment. He soon learned, however, that Lord Dunmore, the governor of Virginia, was increasing the British ranks by granting freedom to slaves who fought for the Crown. On December 31, Washington therefore amended his policy and allowed free

African Americans to enlist. By 1778, most states and the Continental Congress were also welcoming enslaved African Americans into their armies with the understanding that military service would gain them their freedom.

African Americans, numbering roughly 500,000 in a population of 2,600,000, were a valuable source of manpower, and as many as 8,000 men of African descent fought for American independence, most of them serving in racially mixed units. They fought in nearly every battle of the war, from the first exchange of gunfire at Lexington to the siege of Yorktown in 1781. African-American heroes of the Revolution included Peter Salem, who is credited with killing British major John Pitcairn in the Battle of Bunker Hill on June 17, 1775. Today, the musket that Salem used in that encounter hangs on display in Boston's Bunker Hill Monument. Two more African Americans, Jordan Freeman and Lambert Latham, died defending Fort Griswold in Connecticut on September 6, 1781; and James Forten, later a well-known abolitionist, as a captured 15-year-old powder boy spent seven months interned aboard a crowded, rotting British prison ship in 1782.

Black soldiers and sailors served the United States in a second armed conflict with Great Britain, the War of 1812. The United States went to war in 1812 to protect its maritime rights as a neutral nation and especially to stop Britain from impressment, or the seizing of hands from American ships for service in the Royal Navy against France. The United States also hoped to acquire from Great Britain additional land in North America. New York formed two black regiments, but most of the blacks taking part in the war fought in the same units as whites.

African Americans accounted for one-tenth of the personnel aboard navy ships on the Great Lakes during this war. In the summer of 1813, Captain Oliver H. Perry complained to his superior, Commodore Isaac Chauncey, that the 400 sailors and gunmen placed under his command included 100 African Americans. Chauncey took him to task, telling him, "I have yet to learn that the color of a man's skin or the cut and trimmings of the coat can affect a man's qualifications or usefulness." Indeed, those 100 black seamen helped Perry defeat the British fleet in one of the most important armed conflicts of the war, the Battle of Lake Erie, fought on September 10, 1813.

In the fall of 1814, with a British force recently landed at the mouth of the Mississippi River, General Andrew Jackson appealed to the blacks of New Orleans to defend their city from capture and promised them the same financial compensation that white soldiers received. He promised them as well "the applause and gratitude of your countrymen." African Americans responded to the call, and two black regiments helped Old Hickory win the last encounter of the war, the Battle of New Orleans, on January 8, 1815. An appreciative Jackson sent a written commendation to the War Department, praising the valor of his African-American troops.

The War of 1812 ended in a stalemate. Canada remained a British possession, and the United States failed to secure the maritime rights for which it had fought, but with the end of the Napoleonic Wars, Britain was no longer impressing American seamen.

If white Americans were grateful for the contributions of blacks in the war, they had odd ways of showing it. Many men who had been promised their freedom in return for military service were returned to slavery, and the army stopped enlisting African Americans in 1820. The War Department declared that "No Negro or Mulatto will be received as a recruit of the Army." On August 5, 1842, Secretary of the Navy A. P. Upshur had "the honor to report" to Congress that the number of blacks in the navy was well within the limit allowed by law, or "not more than one-twentieth part of the crew of any vessel." There were no slaves in the navy, Upshur added, "except only in some few cases, in which officers have been permitted to take their personal servants, instead of employing them from the crews."

With the outbreak of the Civil War in 1861, thousands of African Americans offered to join the Union army—only to be told that the nation was fighting a "white man's war" and that their services were not required. With the public riding a wave of patriotism, there seemed to be an adequate supply of white volunteers to fight what was expected to be a brief and easily won contest. Rebuffed by the military, African Americans initially helped the Union cause in noncombat roles, as cooks and nurses, as builders of bridges and repairers of railroads. Some African Americans spied for the Union. For example, the noted abolitionist Harriet Tubman slipped behind enemy lines to locate Confederate encampments.

It gradually became clear to the North, as the death toll mounted, that the war would be neither swift nor easily won. The Union lost 13,000 men in Tennessee at the Battle of Shiloh in April 1862, and 5,000 at Seven Pines, Virginia, a month later. In August 1862, 25,000 Union and Confederate soldiers were killed, wounded, or captured when their armies clashed at Manassas, Virginia, in the second battle at that site. In addition, so many men were killed or wounded near Antietam Creek in Maryland on September 17, 1862, that one soldier commented, "[T]he whole landscape for an instant turned slightly red." Union casualties at Antietam totaled 12,000; Confederate casualties numbered 10,000.

No longer able to afford the manpower to conduct a white man's war, the Union called on its black citizens. The Militia Act of 1862, signed into law in the summer of that year, authorized the president to employ African Americans "for any military or naval service for which they may be found competent." The first five African-American regiments were formed in fall 1862 in Union-occupied regions of South Carolina and Louisiana, and in Kansas. The former slaves and free blacks who enlisted served under white officers.

The Emancipation Proclamation, which became effective January 1, 1863, truly opened up military service to African Americans. This document, which granted freedom to all slaves living in regions controlled by the Confederacy, permitted African Americans to serve in "forts, positions, stations, and other places, and to man vessels of all sorts."

The African-American regiments in the Union army, known as the United States Colored Troops, built forts and moved behind enemy lines to destroy Confederate installations and supplies. They took part in more than 400 armed conflicts, including the Battle of Milliken's Bend, Louisiana, which began in the early morning of June 7, 1863. In temperatures nearing 100 degrees Fahrenheit, along with 200 white comrades in arms, 1,000 raw black recruits, poorly trained and using old weapons, held off an attack by 2,000 Confederate soldiers until they could be rescued by Union gunboats. One anonymous hero had his jaw broken but stayed at his post and engaged in hand-to-hand combat. The battle was considered a Union victory, although the Confederates killed or captured one-third of the African-American fighting men. Those taken prisoner were sold into slavery or executed.

The best-known African-American regiment, the 54th Massachusetts Volunteer Infantry, led the Union assault on Fort Wagner, a Confederate installation at the entrance to the Charleston, South Carolina, harbor, on July 18, 1863. The Battle of Fort Wagner was a loss for the Union, but despite high casualties it was a victory for the men of the 54th, whose actions were widely reported in the press. These soldiers proved to a doubting public that African Americans had the courage needed to fight in war, and some among them emerged as heroes. Sergeant William Carney of the 54th became the first African American to earn the Medal of Honor, the nation's highest military decoration.

African Americans contributed substantially to the Union army's efforts at New Market

Heights, Virginia, in September 1864, and in the Battle of Nashville in December 1864. They fought to reunite the nation, free the enslaved population, and secure their rights as citizens.

Although African Americans served in the Union navy from the beginning of the Civil War and may have accounted for one-fourth of total naval enrollment, they made their greatest contribution to the army. African Americans numbered approximately 29,000 in the Union navy and 186,000 in the Union army. More than 38,000 black soldiers and sailors died in the war.

In March 1865, a new Confederate law provided for the training of 300,000 African-American soldiers who were to be drawn from the enslaved population with the consent of their masters and the states in which they resided, but the war ended before enlistment could begin. As black and white Union soldiers returned to civilian life, Major Martin R. Delany, the highest-ranking African American to lead troops in the war, addressed an audience of former slaves. "If it was not for the black man," he said, "this war never would have been brought to a close with success to the Union and the liberty of your race."

After the Civil War, for the first time, African Americans were permitted to serve in the regular, peacetime army. Needing additional troops in the West to keep the American Indian population contained and respond to hostilities, the army formed four African-American regiments, the 9th and 10th Cavalry and the 24th and 25th Infantry. Like the U.S. Colored Troops of the war years, these regiments had white officers in command. Among the initial 12,500 soldiers to enlist were Civil War veterans and young men in search of adventure. For most, though, army life guaranteed food, clothing, and shelter, and offered an alternative to farming. "I got tired of looking mules in the face from sunrise to sunset," said one recruit.

The Indians gave the name "Buffalo Soldiers" to the African Americans who staffed forts in the unsettled regions of the West. The origin of the name is unclear; it has been suggested that the black soldiers reminded the Indians of buffalo because they had dark, curly hair or because in winter they wrapped themselves in buffalo robes for warmth. According to other accounts, the Native Americans admired the soldiers' courage, just as they admired the mighty and abundant buffalo. Whatever its origin, the Buffalo Soldiers adopted the name with pride.

The Buffalo Soldiers on the western frontier protected settlers and railroad workers from Indian attacks, and they took part in numerous clashes of the Indian Wars. On August 1, 1867, for example, 34 soldiers of the 10th Cavalry fought off an armed band of Cheyenne that had attacked a Kansas railroad camp. A decade later, black cavalry regiments hunted for the elusive Apache leader Victorio in the mountains of the Southwest. "The work performed by these troops is the most arduous, horses worn to mere shadows, men nearly without boots, shoes and clothing," observed Colonel Edward Hatch, commander of the 9th Cavalry.

The African-American troops encountered prejudice and even brutality in the white settler population. A particularly ugly incident occurred in San Angelo, Texas, on January 31, 1881, when a white rancher shot and killed Private William Watkins of the 10th Cavalry for disregarding a request to sing and dance. The local sheriff let the rancher walk free until his trial; in the summer of 1882, a jury in Austin acquitted him.

Some Buffalo Soldiers faced racism within their own regiments. Most notable among these was Lieutenant Henry Flipper, the first African American to graduate from West Point, who joined the 10th Cavalry at Fort Sill, Indian Territory (present-day Oklahoma), in 1878. Although Flipper proved himself to be a capable officer at Fort Sill and later at Fort Davis, Texas, his white peers resented his status and his friendship with a white woman.

In 1881, Flipper was tried by a court-martial for allegedly stealing commissary funds that had been entrusted to him. Although he insisted that he had been framed and the court cleared him of the charge, he was found guilty of conduct unbecoming an officer and dishonorably discharged.

The Buffalo Soldiers did earn respect and gratitude in many communities, however. On April 20, 1898, the people of Lander, Wyoming, turned out to cheer the 9th Cavalry as the regiment paraded through town before departing for Cuba and the Spanish-American War. "We are sorry to see the soldier boys leave the post and hope that the war to which they marched will in some manner be averted and that there will be no need of them encountering any of the dangers of war," wrote the editor of the *Clipper,* the local newspaper.

The brief Spanish-American War was fought ostensibly over the explosion of the battleship USS *Maine* in Havana harbor on February 15, 1898 (a disaster that claimed the lives of 260 Americans, including 22 African-American sailors), but actually to liberate Cuba and end Spanish influence in the Western Hemisphere. All four regiments of Buffalo Soldiers took part, becoming the first African-American troops to fight on foreign soil. On June 23, they battled beside Teddy Roosevelt's Rough Riders at Las Guasimas, where they cleaned out nests of Spanish sharpshooters. On July 1, they helped to win the most important battle of the war, capturing San Juan Hill, a key position outside the city of Santiago. The cost of the victory was high: More than a thousand Americans died fighting for San Juan Hill, including one-fifth of the African-American soldiers. Nevertheless, "It was glorious," said Lieutenant John J. Pershing. "We officers of the 10th Cavalry could have taken our black heroes in our arms."

Pershing was given an administrative assignment after the war. He rose in rank to general and in 1916 was ordered to lead a campaign in Mexico to capture the revolutionary leader Pancho Villa. On March 9, 1916, some of Villa's followers had crossed the border into New Mexico, where they had killed several Americans and destroyed part of the town of Columbus. Remembering the skill and valor of the 10th Cavalry in Cuba, Pershing asked to have the regiment accompany him in Mexico. The mission meant a year of hardship for the Buffalo Soldiers, of riding for hundreds of miles over forbidding terrain, enduring extremes of temperature, and coping with shortages of equipment and supplies. Pancho Villa eluded capture, and with their attention drawn to the war in Europe, U.S. leaders abandoned the Punitive Expedition in February 1917. Pershing, who earned the nickname Black Jack for his service with the Buffalo Soldiers, said, "It has been an honor which I am proud to claim."

It was Germany's threat to sink any ships traveling to or from Great Britain that brought the United States into World War I in 1917. Whether to support the war was a controversial issue in the black community. A. Philip Randolph and other socialists viewed the Great War as an economic conflict and objected to members of their race fighting to protect the interests of the American shipping industry. Others questioned whether African Americans should defend a country whose marines had occupied an independent black nation, Haiti, in 1915; in which lynching was on the rise; and in which they were denied basic rights.

Most African Americans, however, agreed with the intellectual leader W. E. B. DuBois, who said, "Let us, while the war lasts, forget our special grievances and close ranks shoulder to shoulder with our white fellow citizens and the Allied Nations that are fighting for democracy." After all, it could be hoped that exemplary performance on the battlefield might lead to improved opportunities at home after the war.

Some 367,000 African Americans served in World War I. Initially, African-American soldiers in Europe belonged to labor battalions and carried out noncombat duties such as driving trucks and unloading ships. The first of four African-American combat regiments, the 369th Infantry, landed in France at the end of December 1917. Reassigned to the French, the four regiments distinguished themselves in battle on the Argonne, at Verdun, and elsewhere. Two soldiers of the 369th, Privates Henry Johnson and Needham Roberts, were the first Americans of any race to receive the Croix de Guerre, France's highest decoration for valor.

As the United States went to war, many young, educated African-American men, not content to serve in the lower ranks, petitioned their government to allow them to be trained as officers. Students staged protests on the campuses of traditionally black colleges, while the National Association for the Advancement of Colored People (NAACP) and other organizations appealed to President Woodrow Wilson. The army relented, and in October 1917, 639 African Americans were commissioned as officers to serve with black regiments. More became officers in the months that followed.

The army refused, however, to use the talents of its highest-ranking African American, Colonel Charles Young, the third black graduate of West Point. Although Young had served with the 9th Cavalry in the West and distinguished himself as military attaché to Haiti and Liberia, the army found him unfit for service in Europe due to high blood pressure.

One unit of black Canadians, the No. 2 Construction Battalion, served in Europe in World War I. African Canadians had been turned away from recruiting stations at the start of the war in 1914, often being told that Canada did not want "a chequer-board army." In May 1916, bowing to pressure from some leading citizens and acknowledging a shortage of white replacements for units overseas, the British War Office stated its willingness to accept an African-Canadian noncombat battalion. The No. 2 Construction Battalion joined the Canadian Forestry Corps in France in 1917, and its 605 enlisted men provided lumber to maintain trenches on the front lines. The regimental chaplain, Captain William A. White, was the only black commissioned officer in the Canadian armed forces at the time.

People of African descent have always constituted a small percentage of the Canadian population, but as early as 1860, blacks on Vancouver Island in British Columbia formed the Victoria Pioneer Rifle Corps, the first officially authorized military force in western Canada. An African Canadian, William Edward Hall of the Royal Marines, was the first black to win Great Britain's highest military honor, the Victoria Cross, for his actions in 1857 in the Indian Mutiny. The No. 2 Construction Battalion was disbanded in 1920, and there were to be no segregated units in the Canadian armed forces in World War II.

World War I ended in November 1918, and African Americans returned home not to greater opportunities, but to racial violence. During the months that writer James Weldon Johnson called the "Red Summer" of 1919, riots occurred throughout the United States, from Longview, Texas, to Omaha, Nebraska, as whites lashed out against perceived competition from blacks for jobs and housing. The riot of greatest consequence erupted in Chicago on July 27, 1919, and raged for 13 days, leaving 38 people dead and 537 injured. Fires and vandalism destroyed the homes of 1,000 families, most of them African American.

Remembering incidents of racial hatred such as these, the great majority of African Americans recognized the danger in the Nazi theory of ethnic superiority and understood the need to fight in World War II. Approximately 1 million African Americans served in the armed forces during this war—half of them overseas—and although they were still assigned to segregated units, they made important gains. For the first time, the Marine Corps and the Coast Guard enlisted African Americans. African-American soldiers were first permitted to operate tanks, and the celebrated 761st Tank Battalion, an African-American unit, fought in six European countries and helped to win the Battle of the Bulge.

At the Tuskegee Army Air Base in Alabama, African Americans trained as military pilots for the first time. Black America took great pride in the Tuskegee Airmen, especially the pilots of the 99th Pursuit Squadron and the 332nd Fighter Group, the two major African-American air-combat units of the war. Beginning in April 1943, the 99th flew combat missions in North Africa and Sicily and provided air cover for the Allied invasion of Italy. Stationed at Ramitelli Air Base in Italy, the 332nd completed 200 long-range bomber escort missions over central and southern Europe between June 1944 and April 1945 without losing a single bomber to enemy aircraft. Commanding the 99th through September 1943 and then the 332nd through the duration of the war in Europe was Lieutenant Colonel Benjamin O. Davis, Jr., an African-American graduate of West Point.

African Americans made progress in the navy as well during World War II. Prior to the war, most African Americans in the navy, including Dorie Miller, a hero of Pearl Harbor, were messmen. Protests by black citizens persuaded the secretary of the navy, in April 1942, to permit the enlistment of African Americans for general service and as noncommissioned officers. Nearly two years later, in March 1944, the navy commissioned its first African-American officers, a group that came to be known as the Golden Thirteen.

As in World War I, however, the United States declined to place its highest-ranking black officer in command of combat forces. Benjamin O. Davis, Sr., had become the nation's first African-American general on October 25, 1940, but for the duration of the war he performed administrative tasks in Washington, D.C., and in Europe.

During World War II, racial discrimination affected African-American military personnel of all ranks, from general to private. As a civilian aide to Secretary of War Henry L. Stimson, the lawyer and activist William H. Hastie investigated numerous complaints of unfair treatment and racially motivated violence within the armed forces. The incidents investigated by Hastie and his staff included the allegation that a white army captain had beat a black private with a rifle sling at Camp Atterbury, Indiana, in January 1943, and

a complaint from Clarence E. Adams, a black soldier stationed at Camp Breckinridge, Kentucky, that a white officer had ordered him not to read a book of poems by African-American writers. "Yes we are Negro Soldiers, giving our sweat, blood and lives for what is known as IDEALISTIC DEMOCRACY, and here in the midst of a world crisis we are told not to read books as that one by men of our own race," Adams wrote.

Hastie and his staff looked into the denial of training to four African-American privates sent to Akron, Ohio, to attend a tire-maintenance course because the commanding officer in Akron had decided that it was inadvisable for blacks and whites to attend the same classes. More disturbing were complaints of harassment from black soldiers stationed at Camp Bowie, Texas, in spring 1941. Not only were these soldiers made to ride in the rear of camp buses, but they were also subjected to insults, threats, and physical abuse. When they appealed to their white officers for help, they were merely told to ignore the taunts, walk away, and respond nonviolently to physical attacks.

Discrimination in housing for defense workers was another matter that Hastie investigated. Although this housing was to be available to all workers on an equal basis, in Washington, D.C., and elsewhere, whites routinely received preference. On November 19, 1943, the *Washington Post* reported that more than 2,000 apartments in publicly financed housing sat vacant because no whites chose to occupy them. Meanwhile, blacks who had come to the city to work in defense jobs struggled to find places to live. By this time, though, Hastie had resigned from the War Department to protest the Army Air Force's reluctance to place black officers in positions of responsibility at Tuskegee Army Air Base and its plans to open a segregated officer candidate school at Jefferson Barracks, Missouri.

Race influenced the awarding of medals as well. Thousands of African Americans displayed extraordinary valor during World War II and were decorated with medals up to and including the

Distinguished Service Cross, the nation's second-highest award for exceptional heroism in combat. Yet none was selected to receive the highest award, the Medal of Honor. On January 13, 1997, President Bill Clinton corrected that injustice by presenting the Medal of Honor to seven African-American World War II veterans. Only one of those old soldiers, former first lieutenant Vernon J. Baker of St. Maries, Idaho, was alive to accept his award.

Segregation continued in the U.S. armed forces after World War II, causing Roy Wilkins of the NAACP to state in 1946, "A Negro American soldier is still first a Negro and then a soldier." A. Philip Randolph, who had gained prominence as a labor leader and spokesperson for his race, formed the League for Nonviolent Civil Disobedience Against Military Segregation and sought an executive order to integrate the armed forces. Responding to President Harry S. Truman's 1947 call for a peacetime draft, Randolph urged African Americans to go to jail rather than serve in segregated units. "Negroes will not take a jim crow draft lying down," Randolph warned. Although African Americans were divided in their support for draft resistance, Randolph took his cause to Philadelphia in 1948, and picketed the Democratic National Convention. Fearing the loss of African-American votes, Truman issued Executive Order 9981, calling for an end to discrimination in the armed forces "as rapidly as possible."

The United States sent integrated units into combat for the first time in the Korean War, which began in June 1950. Although the branches of the armed forces responded dissimilarly to the executive order, with the air force striving rapidly to be fully integrated and the other branches moving more slowly, by the war's end in 1953, 90 percent of U.S. military units were integrated, and more than 90 percent of African Americans in the army were serving in integrated units. "Korea gave black Americans the opportunity to prove among other things that they could be soldiers," said

retired African-American army general Julius W. Becton, Jr., in 1980. In 1950, Becton had gone to Korea as a platoon commander.

American troops again became involved in a war in Asia in December 1961, when President John F. Kennedy sent 400 uniformed army personnel to South Vietnam to advise that nation as it defended itself against attacks from communist North Vietnam. U.S. military strength in Vietnam increased dramatically in the following years: By late 1962, there were 11,200 uniformed Americans in Vietnam, and by the end of 1965, there were 184,000, most in combat units. Of that total, 21,519 were African Americans. Of the 1,363 American soldiers who had been killed in Vietnam by the close of 1965, 237 were black.

Already African Americans, who made up 12 percent of the U.S. population, were dying in Vietnam at a disproportional rate. During one period in 1965 and 1966, one-fourth of all soldiers killed in Vietnam were African American. At the same time, African Americans were unfairly represented on the front lines, where soldiers were most likely to be exposed to enemy fire. Several units in the forward line of battle were as much as 40 percent African American. (Some of these combat units, such as the 173rd Airborne Brigade, were among the top performers.)

In response to public concern about bias in troop assignments, in 1967 the army and the Marine Corps began assigning more African Americans to noncombat units. Yet in January 1969, African Americans still made up about 20 percent of combat troops and accounted for 14 percent of battlefield casualties.

Troop assignments were one example of alleged racism in the armed forces of the 1960s; the draft was another. In one year of the war, 1968, 31 percent of eligible whites and 64 percent of eligible blacks were drafted. This inequality has been blamed on local draft boards that did not reflect the racial makeup of the communities that they represented and on a Selective Service law that made it easier for young men from affluent families to qualify for deferments than those from low-income families.

There was a dearth of African-American leadership in the armed forces as well. In 1968, the United States had only two African-American generals: Benjamin O. Davis, Jr., of the air force and Frederic E. Davison of the army. Of more than 400,000 officers in all branches of the uniformed services, only 8,325 were African American.

The Vietnam War was fought against a backdrop of protest on the home front. Not only were college students and others demonstrating against U.S. military involvement in Southeast Asia, but many Americans not taking part in the protests objected to the war as well. In 1969, nearly 70 percent of African Americans opposed the Vietnam War because they disagreed with its objectives, because young blacks were being called upon unfairly to fight, and because the war took federal funds away from needed domestic programs. Especially between 1965 and 1967, growing frustration about social conditions led to rioting in African-American sections of major cities. Violence erupted again following the assassination of the Reverend Martin Luther King, Jr., in April 1968.

The assassinations of King and Robert Kennedy, disillusionment with the war, and awareness of black militancy in the United States gave rise to racially motivated fighting among servicemen in Vietnam. The most serious incident took place on August 30, 1968, at the Long Binh Detention Center, 19 miles north of Saigon. Built to hold 400, at the time of the uprising this federal prison housed 720, more than half of whom were African American. The riot at Long Binh, which the U.S. command determined was triggered by racial incidents, left one prisoner dead and 58 others injured. Black and white troops also clashed at U.S. military bases. One such incident, occurring at Kaneohe Marine Corps Air Station in Hawaii on August 10, 1969, resulted in 16 injuries. Meanwhile, thousands of African-American fighting men had sufficient confidence in their nation's

cause in Vietnam to reenlist. In 1966 and 1967, nearly half of all African Americans eligible for discharge reenlisted.

The United States withdrew its troops from Vietnam within 60 days of signing a peace agreement on January 27, 1973. In the years that followed, African Americans made gains in the U.S. military. In 1975, for example, Daniel "Chappie" James, Jr., of the air force became the first African-American four-star general. In 1978, the year General James died of a heart attack, there were 1,159 generals and admirals in the U.S. fighting force, of whom 24, or about 2 percent, were African American. There were 14 African-American officers of flag rank in the army, seven in the air force, and three in the navy, but none in the Marine Corps.

The government had ended the draft in 1973, and by the end of the 1980s, African Americans accounted for 28 percent of total enlistment in an all-volunteer army. The percentage of African-American officers continued to rise as well, reaching approximately 7 percent in 1994. African Americans increasingly sought careers in the uniformed services because they encountered less discrimination in the military than in civilian life. Boasted General Colin L. Powell of the army, who in August 1989 became the first African-American chairman of the Joint Chiefs of Staff, "The military of the United States is the greatest equal opportunity employer around." The fact that military personnel enjoyed job security as well as health, retirement, and education benefits also appealed to many African Americans.

A number of critics voiced concern that if the United States went to war, too many African Americans would be called upon to fight. Their predictions seemed valid in 1991, when Powell supervised the conduct of the Persian Gulf War, which was mounted in response to Iraq's invasion of Kuwait. African Americans constituted approximately 12 percent of the U.S. population but 26 percent of the American military presence in the Persian Gulf. According to the Department of

Defense, 30 percent of the army, 21 percent of the navy, 17 percent of the Marine Corps, and 14 percent of the air force in the region were African American. Contrary to what was expected, however, only 15 percent of the 184 Americans killed in the Persian Gulf War were black. Many veterans of the war in the Middle East were left with disabling ailments, which might have resulted from exposure to chemical warfare, or lingering psychological distress, however.

In fall 2002, as the United States geared up for a possible war with Iraq and Defense Department officials predicted that African-American soldiers would make up a large part of any invading ground force, military service, traditionally viewed as a way to demonstrate one's ability and move up economically and socially, had lost its appeal to many African Americans. In 2000, the number of African Americans enlisting in the armed forces, and especially the army, began a record decline. In fiscal year 2000, more than 42,000 African-American men and women applied to enlist in the army, and African Americans represented 23.5 percent of recruits. In fiscal year 2005, 17,000 army recruits, or 13 percent, were African American. Nevertheless, the percentage of African Americans in uniform remained slightly higher than the percentage in the population as a whole. In 2005, African Americans accounted for 14.5 percent of the military and 12.8 percent of the U.S. population.

Enlistment of other groups fell as well over the same period, but the decline measured for blacks was greater than that for any other racial or ethnic group. White enlistment dropped 10 percent, and Hispanic enlistment fell 7 percent. In 2005, the army fell 7,000 short of its goal of recruiting 80,000 new soldiers.

A principal reason for the reduction in enlistment among African Americans was the war in Iraq. Eighty-three percent of African Americans responding to a 2008 CBS News poll said that the 2003 invasion of Iraq had been a mistake. President George W. Bush had assured the nation that the war would be brief and that it was necessary because Iraqi dictator Saddam Hussein was building and storing "weapons that could enable him to dominate the Middle East and intimidate the civilized world." Even after intelligence reports confirming the existence of Iraqi weapons of mass destruction proved false, however, the war dragged on. In January 2007, Bush dispatched thousands more soldiers to Iraq.

African Americans also mistrusted the Bush administration for its handling of the disaster caused by Hurricane Katrina in 2005, but many chose not to enlist for other reasons. Concern lingered from the time of the Vietnam War that African Americans would be disproportionately represented among combat troops in Iraq, although defense department statistics indicated that black recruits were more likely to receive clerical or support assignments than to be ordered to the front lines. In addition, wider professional and educational opportunities in civilian life had robbed military service of some of its appeal or at least attracted African-American recruits to fields such as communications or logistics, which were likely to lead to careers outside the military. For all these reasons, parents, teachers, members of the clergy, and coaches—adults who traditionally offer guidance to youth—were less likely than in years past to steer young blacks toward military careers, despite higher dropout and unemployment rates in the black community than among whites.

As part of its effort to comply with a congressional mandate to increase manpower by 65,000 between 2008 and 2013, the army raised enlistment bonuses, relaxed age and fitness requirements, and developed an intense recruiting campaign targeting African Americans that emphasized the educational benefits of military service.

A failure to halt the decline in African-American enlistment potentially could reverse some of the gains that black Americans have made in the armed forces, because if fewer were to enlist, then fewer would be commissioned as officers. In 2008,

60 years after President Truman ordered the integration of the armed forces, just 6 percent of general officers were African American, as was only one of the 38 active-duty four-star generals and admirals, General William E. "Kip" Ward of the army. Ward was one of 10 African-American generals and admirals ever to reach four-star rank in the history of the U.S. military. There have been five in the army, four in the air force, and one in the navy. Were this trend to continue, fewer African Americans would direct the military and humanitarian operations of the U.S. armed services or act as role models for enlisted personnel. Reduced African-American representation might also impede the effectiveness of the U.S. fighting force. The United States Military Academy at West Point is addressing the need for African-American commissioned officers by actively recruiting black cadets. African Americans currently make up about 7 percent of the corps. The freshmen entering the academy in 2009 numbered 1,248, of whom 91 were African American. The academy wants to increase the number of incoming African-American cadets to 120 by 2014, but it must compete with other prestigious universities for a limited number of qualified young blacks.

Meanwhile, the economic downturn that began in 2008, coupled with President Barack Obama's intention to withdraw combat troops from Iraq, stimulated military recruiting. In the first quarter of the 2009 fiscal year, the army exceeded its recruiting goals for the first time since the start of the Iraq War. Data from this period still need to be evaluated, but as of September 30, 2008, the last day of fiscal year 2008, African Americans accounted for 19.8 percent of active-duty personnel in the U.S. Army. This was a hopeful sign for people such as General Lloyd Austin III, an African American who rose through the ranks of the infantry to be second in command in Iraq. He has observed, "We treasure diversity because it brings in a lot of different viewpoints and blends in a lot of cultures. It makes us better."

A

Adams-Ender, Clara Leach

(1939–) *brigadier general, chief of the U.S. Army Nurse Corps*

As chief of the U.S. Army Nurse Corps, Brigadier General Clara Adams-Ender oversaw an organization of more than 40,000 healthcare workers. As the surgeon general's director of medical personnel during the Persian Gulf War, she was responsible for the more than 25,000 military medical professionals who served the combat forces. Adams-Ender said that she owes her success to following a simple rule: "Do the job that you are assigned and make sure that you do it well. And very often people will decide that you are ready for other kinds of responsibilities."

The future brigadier general was born Clara Leach in Willow Springs, North Carolina, on July 11, 1939. The fourth of 10 children in a farming family, she did chores before and after school from the age of five. Her parents valued education and achievement as well as hard work; Leach recalled that they frequently told her, "You can do anything you want if you put your mind to it." Young Clara was an avid summer reader, sometimes finishing 60 to 100 books during the vacation from school. Her parents were sharecroppers who eventually bought their own land. As an adult, Adams-Ender purchased their farm to keep it in the family.

Clara Leach graduated from Fuquay High School in 1956, at age 16, and enrolled in the North Carolina Agricultural and Technical State University at Greensboro. It was her childhood dream to be a lawyer, but "my father said, 'No,'" Adams-Ender recalled. "He wanted me to become a nurse." In 1959, she entered the Army Student Nurse Program, which financed her third and fourth years of college. She graduated in 1961 with a bachelor of science degree in nursing and entered the U.S. Army Nurse Corps as a second lieutenant.

Leach began her nursing career in the Recovery and Intensive Care Unit at Walson Army Hospital, Fort Dix, New Jersey. In 1963, she was transferred to the 121st Evacuation Hospital at Ascom, Korea, where an encounter with a wounded infantryman affected the course of her life. At the time she treated the soldier, who had been shot while on a reconnaissance mission in the Demilitarized Zone, she was anticipating a return to civilian life. The young man's dedication to his unit and its task caused her to reevaluate her plans. "It made me stop and think about the important work that our soldiers and nurses were doing," she said.

She demonstrated her commitment to military service by enrolling in the U.S. Army Nurse Corps Officer Advanced Course at Fort Sam Houston, Texas, in July 1964. After teaching at the Army Medical Training Center at Fort Sam Houston

Brigadier General Clara L. Adams-Ender was the second African American to head the Army Nurse Corps. *(Army Nurse Corps)*

from 1965 to 1967, she began studies at the University of Minnesota that led to a master of science degree in medical-surgical nursing. From June 1969 through July 1972, she taught medical-surgical nursing at the Walter Reed Army Institute of Nursing in Washington, D.C. On July 12, 1969, Leach married Kelso Adams of Willow Springs. The couple divorced in 1974.

Promotions came with regularity: Clara Adams was promoted to captain on September 17, 1964, and to major on February 23, 1968. In 1967, she became the first woman in the army to be awarded the Expert Field Medical Badge. Nine years later, she was the first woman, the first African American, and the first nurse to earn a master of military art and science degree from the U.S. Army Command and General Staff College at Fort Leavenworth, Kansas.

After a two-year assignment with the Health Services Command at Fort Sam Houston as inspector general of services provided in army hospitals worldwide, Adams was transferred to the Army Regional Medical Center at Frankfurt, West Germany, as assistant chief of the Department of Nursing. In 1979, she became the department's chief.

The years in Germany were a fulfilling time for Adams. She immersed herself in German language and culture and took part in a collaborative program that brought together American and German health care professionals. Through this program she met Heinz Ender, a German orthodontist and oral surgeon, whom she married in 1981. On July 10, 1979, while still in Germany, she was promoted to the rank of colonel.

Adams-Ender continued to chalk up "firsts." In 1980, she was the first woman to lead Europe's largest international marching festival, the Nijmegan March in Nijmegan, the Netherlands, in which the participants, most of whom are military personnel, cover 100 miles in four days. In 1982 she was the first African-American Army Nurse Corps officer to graduate from the U.S. Army War College, and in 1984 she was the first African-American nurse to be named chief of the Department of Nursing at Walter Reed Army Medical Center.

Her promotion to brigadier general occurred in September of 1987, the year in which she became the second African American to head the U.S. Army Nurse Corps. (HAZEL WINIFRED JOHNSON-BROWN was the first, in 1979.) Adams-Ender had long professed that "persistence is the greatest quality that anybody can ever have," and now she said that persistence had taken her from "rags to respect." In 1990 she was placed in charge of all medical servicemen and women on active duty in the Persian Gulf War.

Most chiefs of the Army Nurse Corps have retired upon completion of their tours of duty, but after her tenure ended on August 31, 1991, Adams-Ender served as commanding general of U.S. Army Fort Belvoir, Virginia, and deputy commanding general of the U.S. Army Military District of Washington, D.C. She retired from the army in 1993 to become president and chief executive officer of Caring About People with Enthusiasm Associates, Inc., a consulting firm specializing in leadership development and healthcare management and reform. She wrote an autobiography entitled *My Rise to the Stars: How a Sharecropper's Daughter Became an Army General,* which was published in 2001.

Adams-Ender's military honors include the Legion of Merit, the Distinguished Service Award, the Meritorious Service Medal with three Oak Leaf Clusters, and the Army Commendation Medal. She is a recipient of the Roy Wilkins Meritorious Service Award from the National Association for the Advancement of Colored People (NAACP) and was named a Regents' Distinguished Graduate by the University of Minnesota. She has been a member of the American Nurses Association, the American Red Cross Nurses, the National Council of Negro Women, and the National Association for Female Executives. She is a lifetime member of the NAACP and has served on the board of the Northeast Illinois Council of the Boy Scouts of America.

Further Reading

Adams-Ender, Clara L. *My Rise to the Stars: How a Sharecropper's Daughter Became an Army General.* Lake Ridge, Va.: CAPE Associates, Inc., 2001.

Cheers, D. Michael. "Nurse Corps Chief." *Ebony* 44, no. 8 (June 1989), pp. 64–68.

Hine, Darlene Clark, ed. *Black Women in America.* 2nd ed. Vol. 3. New York: Oxford University Press, 2005, pp. 278–279.

Smith, Jessie Carney, ed. *Notable Black American Women.* Detroit: Gale Research Inc., 1992, pp. 1–2.

Alexander, Clifford Leopold, Jr.

(1933–   ) *first African-American secretary of the U.S. Army*

Clifford Alexander's contributions as secretary of the U.S. Army under President Jimmy Carter con-

stitute one phase of a career devoted to serving society and his race.

Born in Harlem in New York City on September 21, 1933, Alexander was the only child of parents devoted to self-improvement. They instilled in him a deep respect for his race's qualities and merits. "My folks were always pointing out with pride the things that blacks had done in this society," he said. Clifford Alexander, Sr., a native of Jamaica, had begun his working life as a waiter and had moved up to positions of responsibility. For a time he was business manager of the Harlem YMCA; later he managed an apartment building and a bank.

Alexander's mother, Edith McAllister Alexander, had been born and raised in Yonkers, New York. She, too, was an achiever. She was an employee of the New York City Welfare Department before heading a biracial committee formed by Mayor Fiorello H. La Guardia to investigate a race riot that occurred in Harlem in August 1943. In 1948, Edith Alexander was the first African-American woman selected for the Democratic Party's electoral college, and in 1954 New York mayor Robert Wagner chose her to head a citizens' advisory committee.

"Both of my parents, but particularly my late mother thought of education as an extraordinary part of life," Alexander said in 2000. The Alexanders sent young Clifford to private schools—the Ethical Culture School and the Fieldston School—where he was often the only African American in his class.

Alexander continued his education at Harvard University, where he was the first African-American president of the student council. He distinguished himself not only in student government but in athletics as well. A star basketball player, the six-foot, three-inch Alexander considered a career in professional sports until a broken foot forced him to abandon that dream. Basketball has remained a lifelong interest, however.

Despite having graduated cum laude from Harvard in 1955 with a degree in American government, Alexander went to work for the United Mutual Insurance Company handling customer complaints. He quickly realized that "in the time I was coming out of school, opportunities in the private sector for professional corporate jobs were not there for Black people." Rather than remain in a dead-end job, he enrolled in Yale Law School, earning a bachelor of laws degree (LL.B.) in 1958.

Alexander next enlisted in the 369th Field Artillery Battalion of the New York National Guard and in February 1959 completed a six-month tour of duty as a private at Fort Dix, New Jersey. On July 11, 1959, he married Adele Logan, a former classmate at the Fieldston School. He spent the following two years as assistant to the district attorney of New York County, New York, the county that encompasses Manhattan.

In 1961, Alexander was named executive director of the Manhattanville-Hamilton Grange Conservation Project. His primary duty was to make property owners in this section of Manhattan's Upper West Side comply with the city's housing code and thereby improve living conditions for residents. He claimed that during his nine-month administration, neighborhood landlords corrected more than 3,000 violations.

Alexander went on to head Harlem Youth Opportunities Unlimited (HARYOU), a program dedicated to bettering life for Harlem's young people by improving schools and reducing the dropout rate, delinquency, and youth unemployment.

In 1963, Democratic National Committee deputy chairman Louis Martin summoned Alexander to Washington, D.C. Martin was looking for highly qualified African Americans to work in the Kennedy administration, and he offered Alexander a staff position with the National Security Council (NSC). For the NSC, Alexander monitored cable reports from Vietnam and other Asian countries.

On June 18, 1964, Alexander joined President Johnson's White House staff as a deputy special assistant for personnel and administration. In

1965 he was named an associate special counsel to the president, and in 1966 he was promoted to deputy special counsel. In 1967 Johnson asked Alexander to be his personal consultant on civil rights problems; as a direct result of Alexander's input, Johnson appointed more African Americans as judges and commissioners, more African Americans advised the president, and more attended White House social gatherings.

On August 4, 1967, Alexander became the first African American to chair the Equal Employment Opportunities Commission (EEOC). The EEOC was created by Title VII of the Civil Rights Act of 1964 to combat job discrimination. Although not empowered to take legal action, the commission investigated alleged discrimination and made recommendations for change. As EEOC chairman, Alexander examined employment practices in textile manufacturing and other industries, in utilities, and in labor unions. In 1968, he held four days of hearings on the hiring practices of 4,200 major corporations headquartered in New York City. The inquiry revealed that in a city with a population that was 28 percent African American and Puerto Rican, more than 40 percent of these firms had no African Americans in white-collar jobs and more than 33 percent had no Puerto Ricans in such positions. Alexander stayed on as EEOC chairman following the election of President Richard M. Nixon in 1968, but resigned in April 1969 due to disagreements with Republican leadership over his investigative approach.

Alexander went from government to private law practice, but he continued to aid minorities. While a partner with Arnold and Porter in Washington, D.C., he convinced the firm to hire law school graduates from traditionally black Howard University. Between 1971 and 1974, he hosted the television program *Cliff Alexander: Black on White* on WMAL-TV, Washington.

In May 1974, the voters of Washington, D.C., approved a home-rule charter giving them an elected mayor and city council. Prior to the vote, a commissioner appointed by the president had governed the city. In 1974, Alexander ran for mayor of Washington in the first municipal election held in that city in more than a century but lost by a narrow margin to Walter Washington, the incumbent city commissioner.

Alexander returned to public life on January 19, 1977, when President Carter made him the first African-American secretary of the army. At the time the department had a budget of $28.8 billion. There were approximately 1.3 million army regulars, reservists, and National Guardsmen and 370,000 civilian army employees. Alexander was responsible for operations and training and for developing and managing the army's budget. He also served as chairman of the board of the Panama Canal.

His goal as secretary was to increase "the emphasis that is placed on *people* in the Army— recognizing their needs and stressing their importance," he said. He took charge at a time when critics were raising questions about military preparedness. After the Vietnam War, the armed forces had replaced the draft with an all-volunteer system, and there was concern that the quality of recruits had declined. Alexander defended the volunteer army, stating repeatedly that incoming soldiers were as fit intellectually and physically as those inducted under the draft. He also combated racism in the army. The volunteer system had attracted a large number of minority recruits, and African Americans, who made up 11 percent of the U.S. population, accounted for 22.2 percent of army enlisted personnel. Alexander acknowledged that many blacks were joining the army because good jobs were unavailable to them in civilian life, but he also insisted that most were motivated by patriotism and the desire to serve.

After stepping down as secretary of the army in 1981, Alexander founded a consulting firm, Alexander and Associates of Washington, D.C., to help businesses strengthen their workforces by recruiting and promoting minorities and women.

Alexander and Associates also aided Major League Baseball, the umbrella organization for professional baseball in the United States, in its effort to improve the hiring of minorities.

Clifford Alexander continues to be active professionally. In 1999, when Volney Taylor retired as chairman and chief executive officer of Dun and Bradstreet Corporation, Alexander was hired to oversee operations temporarily and to head the search for a new chairman and CEO. (Dun and Bradstreet is the world's largest provider of business information.) The candidate who was selected, Allan Z. Loren, joined Dun and Bradstreet on May 30, 2000.

Alexander has served on the boards of Radcliffe College, Atlanta University, TLC Beatrice International Holdings, MCI WorldCom, Inc., and other corporations. He received the Ames Award from Harvard University (1955), the Washington Bar Association Award (1969), and the Distinguished Public Service Award from the Department of Defense (1981). In 1980, the Department of the Army named him Outstanding Civilian.

Adele Alexander is a writer and professor of history at George Washington University. The Alexanders have two grown children: Elizabeth Alexander, a poet, and Mark C. Alexander, a professor of law at Seton Hall University.

Further Reading

Hawkins, Walter L. *African American Biographies: Profiles of 558 Current Men and Women*. Jefferson, N.C.: McFarland and Co., 1992, pp. 7–8.

Palmer, Colin A., ed. *Encyclopedia of African-American Culture and History*. Vol. 1. Detroit, Mich.: Thomson Gale, 2006, p. 69.

Smith, Jessie Carney, ed. *Notable Black American Men*. Detroit: Gale Research, 1999, pp. 15–17.

Stapleton, Katina. "Interim CEO of Dun & Bradstreet." Black Collegian Online. Available online. URL: http://www.black-collegian.com/issues/1stsem00/dunbrad2000-1st.shtml. Downloaded on July 30, 2008.

Alexander, John Hanks
(1864–1894) *second African American to graduate from the U.S. Military Academy*

Because of his early death, John Hanks Alexander often receives only brief mention in histories of African-American service in the armed forces, but as one of the first black graduates of West Point and a pioneering army officer, he was among the outstanding young black Americans of his time.

Alexander was born in the Mississippi River town of Helena, Arkansas, on January 6, 1864, the fifth of eight children. His parents, Fannie and James, had spent most of their lives in slavery. James Alexander appears to have enjoyed a mobility and opportunity that were unusual among the enslaved. In the late 1840s he operated a thriving barbershop and soon began purchasing himself and his family out of slavery. By 1862, James Alexander owned a general store, selling groceries and dry goods. This business prospered until March 1867, when the flooding Mississippi extensively damaged his store and stock. Lacking the resources to rebuild, he returned to barbering, and Fannie Alexander took in boarders.

James Alexander, who expressed pride in John's ability to learn, died suddenly in 1871, at age 56. Left to support her family, Fannie Alexander worked as a maid and cook and was determined, despite her low income, to see her children educated. John Alexander said about his mother, "She can not blame her children for being as proud and manly as the most aristocratic on earth, for that is the way she raised them." John graduated first in his class from Helena's African-American high school; he taught briefly near Carrollton, Mississippi, before enrolling in Oberlin College in Ohio in the fall of 1880.

After two years at Oberlin, inspired by the story of HENRY OSSIAN FLIPPER, who in 1877 became the first African American to graduate from the United States Military Academy at West Point, New York, Alexander entered a competition for an appointment to the academy to be made by Congressman George W. Geddes of Ohio. Two finalists emerged from the preliminary examination: the son of Ohio's chief justice and Alexander. Alexander scored higher on the admission test administered at West Point and therefore won the appointment.

Earlier blacks at West Point, including Flipper, endured verbal and physical abuse from the white cadets. For Alexander, the years at the academy were a time of ostracism and loneliness. No white cadet would speak to him. He and CHARLES YOUNG, an African American accepted by the military academy in 1884, sat apart from the others in chapel. Alexander said that he felt he was "in the confines of the highest and most secluded peak of the Himalaya Mountains." He saved his money to pay for his mother to attend commencement exercises, and in 1887 she saw him graduate as a second lieutenant in the U.S. Army, 32nd in a class of 64.

On September 30, 1887, Alexander reported to Fort Robinson, Nebraska, for duty with the 9th Cavalry, one of the African-American units known as Buffalo Soldiers serving on the frontier. He was the only African-American army officer in a position of command. In March 1888, Alexander and his troops were transferred to Fort Washakie, Wyoming, and on June 11, 1888, he embarked with Troop M of the 9th Cavalry on a 17-day march across rugged, mountainous country to Fort Duchesne, Utah.

Alexander returned to Fort Robinson in late 1891 to serve as assistant commissary officer in charge of the post exchange. His performance earned praise from his superiors, and indeed his entire service record was exemplary. Nevertheless, after six years of active duty he had yet to be promoted.

On his 30th birthday, January 6, 1894, Alexander was assigned to Wilberforce University in Ohio, a historically black school, as professor of military science and tactics. On March 26, 1894, while on a visit to Springfield, Ohio, he died suddenly and unexpectedly of a ruptured cerebral blood vessel. Springfield's white military guard escorted his remains to Wilberforce, where a funeral was held.

In 1918, the army honored John Hanks Alexander, a "man of ability, attainments, and energy—who was a credit to himself, to his race and to the service," by naming an encampment in Virginia after him.

Further Reading

Gatewood, Willard B., Jr. "John Hanks Alexander of Arkansas: Second Black Graduate of West Point." *Arkansas Historical Quarterly* 41, no. 2 (summer 1982): pp. 103–128.

"John Hanks Alexander (1864–1894)." *The Encyclopedia of Arkansas History and Culture.* Available online. URL: http://www.encyclopediaofarkansas. net/encyclopedia/entry-detail.aspx?entryID=46. Downloaded on July 31, 2008.

Katz, William Loren. *The Black West.* Rev. ed. New York: Harlem Moon, 2005, pp. 213–214.

Lowery, Charles D., and John F. Marszalek, eds. *Encyclopedia of African-American Civil Rights: From Emancipation to the Present.* New York: Greenwood Press, 2003, pp. 10–11.

Allensworth, Allen
(1842–1914) *army chaplain, educator, founder of Allensworth, California*

Allen Allensworth dedicated himself to the educational and social betterment of his race, both as chaplain of the 24th Infantry in the West and as a civilian.

Allensworth was born in slavery in Louisville, Kentucky, on April 7, 1842, the son of Levi and Phyllis Allensworth. Like many enslaved boys and girls, he played with white youngsters, including the children of his owner. Hungering for knowledge even as a child, he attempted to learn to read and write from his white playmates. It was illegal in Kentucky and throughout the South to teach a slave to read, and when the master learned of the children's activities he punished 12-year-old Allen by selling him to a cotton planter in the Deep South.

There Allensworth remained through the start of the Civil War. Then, as white southern men left home to join the Confederate forces, the system of slavery began to break down. Allensworth was among the thousands of enslaved African Americans who slipped away from the plantations of the South and sought protection from the Union Army. He briefly worked for an army unit before enlisting in the navy as a seaman on April 3, 1863.

Lieutenant Colonel Allen Allensworth, an army chaplain from 1886 until 1906, founded the community of Allensworth, California. *(California Historical Society, North Baker Research Library; FN-32157)*

He rose to the rank of chief petty officer and was honorably discharged at the war's end.

It took some time for Allensworth to find direction in civilian life. After spending about two years as a commissary worker at a Mound City, Missouri, naval yard, he opened a restaurant with his brother in 1867. Then, still desiring an education, he enrolled in the Nashville Institute, a Baptist school for African Americans (on the site of the present-day Peabody College for Teachers). He was ordained a Baptist minister on April 9, 1871, around the time he married Josephine Leavell, a teacher. The couple would have two children. From 1871 until 1886, Allensworth served as pastor to Baptist congregations in Kentucky and Ohio.

On April 1, 1886, Allensworth entered the army as a captain when President Grover Cleveland appointed him chaplain of the 24th Infantry. It was Allensworth's duty to minister to the spiritual needs of these African-American soldiers serving in the West, but he made it his business to educate them as well.

Most of the African-American soldiers had entered the army illiterate. As a lieutenant in the 9th Cavalry observed, "Few indeed could read and scarcely any were able to write their own names." Certain that schooling would make the men more capable soldiers and improve their prospects after they left the army, Allensworth offered instruction in English grammar and U.S. history at Fort Supply, Indian Territory (present-day Oklahoma). Later, at Fort Bayard, New Mexico, he oversaw a post school with an enrollment of 118 that employed four teachers. Once the school was well-established, regimental commanders promoted only soldiers who could read to the rank of noncommissioned officer.

An innovative teacher, Allensworth supplemented his lectures with stereopticon images (transparent glass slides that, when viewed in pairs, give an impression of depth). At times he used his own money to meet the school's expenses. Building on the success of his academic classes, he established vocational courses to train soldiers as bakers, printers, and teachers. His efforts helped to persuade the federal government in 1889 to make schooling compulsory for all enlisted men.

Allensworth sailed to Cuba with the 24th Infantry in 1898, when the African-American soldiers fought in the Spanish-American War, and to the Pacific in 1899, when the unit was sent to defeat insurgents and assert U.S. dominance in the Philippine-American War. He retired from the army in 1906 as a lieutenant colonel, at the time the highest ranking African-American ever to serve in the army. He then embarked on a speaking tour of the East and Midwest, lecturing to African Americans on self-improvement.

Allensworth's message was consistent with the philosophy of Booker T. Washington (1856–1915), the well-known black educator who advocated vocational training for his race and gradual progress toward economic and social equality with whites. At the Alabama school that he founded and supervised, the Tuskegee Institute, Washington trained African Americans in a broad range of employable skills, including food preparation, carpentry, mattress making, and farming.

The Allensworths settled in Los Angeles, California, but unhappy with the racial discrimination that his family encountered there, Allen Allensworth joined with three other men, including William Payne, formerly a professor at the West Virginia Colored Institute, to form the California Colonization and Home Promotion Association, with the goal of establishing a black utopia. In 1908, the group purchased land in California's fertile San Joaquin Valley and founded the town of Allensworth for ex-slaves and their descendants.

Allensworth, California, quickly grew into a small but prosperous farming community with several stores, a library, church, school, and hotel. In 1912, at its height, 300 families called Allensworth home. Allen Allensworth dreamed of starting a vocational school modeled on the Tuskegee Institute in the new town, but he never realized that plan. He died on September 14, 1914, after being struck by a motorcycle while visiting Los Angeles.

The town of Allensworth declined, especially after 1966, when California officials detected unsafe levels of arsenic in the town's water supply. Around that time, as the Civil Rights movement generated interest among scholars in African-American culture, historians began an effort to preserve the only California town founded and governed by African Americans. Allensworth became a state park in 1978, and restoration of its buildings began in 1980.

Further Reading

Alexander, Charles. *The Battles and Victories of Allen Allensworth.* Boston: Sherman, French and Co., 1914. (The University of North Carolina at Chapel Hill, through a grant from the National Endowment for the Humanities, has made the complete text of this book available online at *Documenting the American South.* URL: http://docsouth.unc.edu/neh/alexander/menu.html.)

Radcliffe, Evelyn. *Out of Darkness: The Story of Allen Allensworth.* Menlo Park, Calif.: Inkling Press, 1998.

Royal, Alice C. *Allensworth, the Freedom Colony: A California African American Township.* Berkeley, Calif.: Heyday Books, 2008.

Wheeler, B. Gordon. "Allensworth: California's African American Community." HistoryNet.Com. Available online. URL: http://www.historynet.com/allensworth-californias-african-american-community.htm. Downloaded on July 31, 2008.

Anderson, James, Jr.

(1947–1967) *first African-American marine to be awarded the Medal of Honor*

The name of the first African-American marine to earn his nation's highest military decoration, James Anderson, Jr., is engraved on the Vietnam Veterans Memorial in Washington, D.C., Panel 15E, Row 112.

Private James Anderson, Jr., USMC, won the Medal of Honor for valor in Vietnam. *(National Archives)*

A native of California, Anderson was born in Los Angeles on January 22, 1947, and raised in the suburb of Compton. He was inducted into the army in Los Angeles and in December 1966 went to South Vietnam as a rifleman assigned to Company F, 2nd Battalion, 3rd Marine Division.

Private First Class James Anderson, Jr., had not been in the country three months when, on February 28, 1967, his company was ordered to rescue a reconnaissance patrol that was under attack in the dense jungle northwest of Cam Lo in the Quang Tri province. From 1966 to 1968, this region near the Demilitarized Zone was the scene of heavy fighting. Anderson's platoon, which was leading the rescue mission, had progressed only about 200 meters into the jungle when it came under enemy fire. Seemingly from all directions came the sounds of small arms and automatic weapons firing. Grenades rained down on the advancing column, killing the battalion commander and a sergeant major.

Anderson's platoon took cover and began returning fire. The men were packed tightly together in the thick forest, barely able to move. A mere 20 meters from the enemy, Anderson lay on his belly shooting through the branches, when a grenade rolled along the ground and landed next to his head.

With only seconds before the grenade would detonate, Anderson thought only of the others and not of himself. He picked up the grenade, held it against his chest, and curled his body around it. Shrapnel wounded several marines, but Anderson's body absorbed most of the force of the explosion. His remains were recovered and laid to rest at Lincoln Memorial Park Cemetery in Carson, California.

On August 21, 1968, Navy Secretary Paul R. Ignatius presented the Medal of Honor to Anderson's parents, Mr. and Mrs. James Anderson, Sr., at a full-dress ceremony in Washington, D.C. General Leonard F. Chapman, Jr., commandant of the Marine Corps, read the citation, which stated that Anderson's "personal heroism, extraordinary valor, and inspirational supreme self-sacrifice reflected great credit upon himself and the Marine Corps and upheld the highest traditions of the U.S. Naval Service. He gallantly gave his life for his country." Anderson's was the 42nd Medal of Honor awarded for heroism in Vietnam and the 12th to a marine. Three other African Americans had previously received the medal for their actions in Vietnam.

The United States has continued to honor the first black Medal of Honor winner in the Marine Corps. On March 26, 1985, the navy launched a ship named for him. USNS *Pfc. James Anderson Jr.* (T-AK-3002) can carry the full range of cargo needed to support a Marine Ground Task Force for 30 days and is certified to land some classes of helicopters. Also, on Memorial Day 2000, the Anderson family joined officials of Carson and Compton, California, for the unveiling of a monument to Anderson at his gravesite. The ceremony included a Marine Honor Guard salute and the release of white doves, symbolizing peace.

Further Reading

Lee, Irvin H. *Negro Medal of Honor Men.* New York: Dodd, Mead and Co., 1969, pp. 154–156.

Murphy, Edward F. *Vietnam Medal of Honor Heroes.* New York: Ballantine Books, 1987, p. 78.

"Private First Class James Anderson, Jr. United States Marine Corps." *Military Sealift Command.* Available online. URL: http://www.msc.navy.mil/inventory/citations/anderson.htm. Downloaded on August 1, 2008.

United States of America's Congressional Medal of Honor Recipients and Their Official Citations. Columbia Heights, Minn.: Highland House II, 1994, pp. 18–19.

"U.S. Gives First Medal of Honor to a Negro Marine." *New York Times,* August 2, 1968, p. 3.

Westheider, James E. *The African American Experience in Vietnam: Brothers in Arms.* Lanham, Md.: Rowman and Littlefield, 2008, pp. 52, 102.

Anderson, Michael Philip

(1959–2003)   *lieutenant colonel in the U.S. Air Force, astronaut*

For mission specialist Michael P. Anderson, to fly in space was to realize a lifelong dream. He understood that, although never free of danger, space exploration contributes to scientific knowledge, and he concluded that "the benefits are worth the risks." Anderson, who was aboard the space shuttle *Columbia* when it exploded on February 1, 2003, died doing something in which he believed.

Michael Philip Anderson was born on December 25, 1959, near Plattsburgh Air Force Base in New York, where his father, Bobbie Anderson, worked on the flight lines, servicing jets. Bobbie Anderson's air force career soon took his family to

Fairchild Air Force Base, near Spokane, Washington, the city that Michael Anderson would call his hometown. While Michael was growing up, Bobbie Anderson often brought him to the air base to show him the instruments in the cockpits of jets and aircraft taking off and landing. At home, Michael pretended to be a plane in flight, running with his arms extended and dipping from side to side.

Barbara and Bobbie Anderson predicted that their son would be a pilot, but Michael dreamed of becoming an astronaut. "I can't remember ever thinking that I couldn't do it," he said. As a nine-year-old child in July 1969, he was thrilled to see the televised moon landing. He learned the names of all the astronauts in the space program, and he watched numerous episodes of *Star Trek*. The Andersons were a religious family and regularly attended Morning Star Missionary Baptist Church in Spokane, and they valued education. Michael took advanced classes in science and mathematics at Cheney High School and graduated in 1977, one of four African Americans in a class of 200.

Michael Anderson earned a bachelor's degree in physics and astronomy from the University of Washington and upon graduating in 1981 was commissioned a second lieutenant in the air force. He completed a year of technical training at Keesler Air Force Base in Mississippi before going to Randolph Air Force Base in Texas, where he served as chief of communication maintenance for the 2015th Communication Squadron and then as director of information system maintenance for the 1920th Information System Group.

Because many astronaut candidates are military pilots, Anderson moved a step closer to his goal in 1986, when he was selected for pilot training at Vance Air Force Base in Oklahoma. He was subsequently assigned to the 2nd Airborne Command and Control Squadron at Offutt Air Force Base in Nebraska. Flying for the Strategic Air Command, he piloted the EC-135 Looking Glass, which was used to patrol the skies during the cold war.

In 1990, Anderson earned a master's degree in physics from Creighton University in Omaha. In January 1991, he became an aircraft commander and instructor pilot with the 920th Air Refueling Squadron at Wurtsmith Air Force Base in Michigan. Anderson returned to his birthplace in September 1992 to serve as an instructor pilot and tactics officer with the 380th Air Refueling Wing.

By December 1994, when he was one of 19 candidates selected by NASA for astronaut training from 2,962 applicants, Anderson had logged more than 3,000 hours of flight time. He reported to the Johnson Space Center in Texas in March 1995, and after a year of training and evaluation qualified as a mission specialist on space-shuttle flights. Initially, however, NASA assigned him technical duties in the Flight Support Branch of the Astronaut Office.

On January 22, 1998, Anderson was aboard the space shuttle *Endeavour* when it lifted off from Cape Canaveral, Florida, to begin an eight-day mission. *Endeavour* docked with the space station *Mir* to retrieve astronaut David A. Wolf, who had spent 119 days aboard the Russian craft, and to leave mission specialist Andrew S. W. Thomas. Anderson conducted experiments during the flight and oversaw the transfer of more than 9,000 pounds of scientific equipment and other hardware to *Mir*.

At the time, Anderson was one of seven African Americans in the space program, the ninth to fly on a shuttle, and the first to visit a space station. He understood that he was a role model for minority children, and he often visited their schools to encourage them to aim high. He was also devoted to his wife, the former Sandra Lynn Hawkins, whom he had met at Morning Star Missionary Baptist Church, and their two daughters.

On January 16, 2003, Anderson began his second shuttle mission, aboard the *Columbia*. The crew for this 16-day scientific mission also included an Israeli military pilot, Ilan Ramon. Anderson, Ramon, and the others performed 80 competitively selected and commercially sponsored experiments that shed light on such phenomena as crystal formation, blood flow, the physics of combustion, and the effects of space flight on the body. Anderson said that some of the experiments might be of particular benefit to African Americans. "We have a bioreactor which is growing prostate cancer cells, and prostate cancer has a high rate of return in African American males," he said. In microgravity, free from the limits imposed by Earth's gravity, scientists can learn a great deal about the function of cells. Anderson also remarked on the beauty of Earth as seen from space, noting, "[I]t's hard to take your eyes off it."

On the morning of Saturday, February 1, *Columbia* was streaking across the Texas sky, heading toward a landing at the Kennedy Space Center on the east coast of Florida, when it exploded, killing all seven crew members, including Lieutenant Colonel Michael P. Anderson. Accident investigators traced the explosion to a piece of protective foam that broke free from the shuttle's external fuel tank during launch and punctured its heat shield along the forward edge of the left wing, leaving *Columbia* vulnerable to superheated gases when re-entering the atmosphere. NASA engineers spent more than two years developing new heat-shield inspection and safety tools at a cost of $1.4 billion, and the agency resumed shuttle flights in 2005.

Further Reading

"Astronaut Bio: Michael P. Anderson." *National Aeronautics and Space Administration.* Available online. URL: http://www.jsc.nasa.gov/Bios/htmlbiosanderson.html. Downloaded on August 1, 2008.

Egan, Timothy. "Lt. Col. Michael P. Anderson: A Source of Hope for Children." *New York Times,* February 2, 2003, p. 22.

Sanchez, Rene. "'It Was Always His Strong Desire to Fly.'" *Washington Post,* February 4, 2003, p. A12.

Smith, Jessie Carney, ed. *Notable Black American Men.* Book II. Detroit, Mich.: Thomson Gale, 2007, pp. 14–16.

Walsh, Edward. "Michael P. Anderson: Scientist and Pilot Followed a Straight Path to Stars." *Washington Post,* February 2, 2003, p. A31.

Archer, Lee A., Jr.
(1919–2010) *Tuskegee Airman, World War II flying ace*

Lee "Buddy" Archer was the only ace among the Tuskegee Airmen, the African-American military pilots of World War II. In his career with the air force after the war, he worked on behalf of international military cooperation.

Lee A. Archer, Jr., was born in New York City on September 16, 1919. As a child in Harlem, he gazed beyond the tops of the city's tall buildings into the sky, and read everything he could find about the Red Baron, Eddie Rickenbacker, and other World War I flying aces. He earned high grades in high school and subsequently enrolled in New York University to study international relations. In early 1941, foreseeing that the United States would be drawn into the war in Europe, he applied to the U.S. Army Air Corps for pilot training. He met all of the qualifications but one: He had the wrong skin color. Archer was rejected because African Americans were not admitted into the Air Corps. Let down but believing it his duty to "hold the hand" of his country in times of emergency despite discrimination, he withdrew from school and enlisted in the army.

In May 1942, Archer was serving as an instructor at Camp Wheeler, Georgia, preparing soldiers to be infantry replacements, when he heard about an experimental program in Tuskegee, Alabama, in which the army was training African Americans as military pilots. He immediately reapplied to the Army Air Corps and was accepted.

Graduating first in his class, Buddy Archer earned his wings and was commissioned a second lieutenant in July 1943. He was assigned to the 302nd Fighter Squadron of the 332nd Fighter Group, which joined the war in Italy in January

1944. Piloting the P-39 Aircobra, a single-seat fighter-bomber, Archer completed convoy escort and reconnaissance missions. He also flew strafing missions in support of the Allied ground forces invading Italy.

In March 1944, Archer's fighter group was reassigned to the 306th Fighter Wing at Ramitelli Air Base in Italy. In the P-47 Thunderbolt, a rugged, heavyweight fighter, Archer flew 169 combat missions, twice returning to base after having shot down a German plane. On another memorable mission he counted three more "kills," giving him the five needed to be designated an ace, but the Air Corps credited him with only four. "They said three plus one plus one is four," Archer remarked, hinting that the denial of proper credit resulted from reluctance to acknowledge an African-American ace. "It's obvious what it was all about," he said in 2001.

Despite the deliberate or inadvertent oversight, Archer elected to remain in uniform after the war. He returned to the United States to act as chief of the Instrument Instructors School at Tuskegee Army Air Field. He completed his education at the University of California at Los Angeles and later attended the Air Command and Staff College at Maxwell Air Force Base in Alabama.

As an air force officer, Archer held positions of international importance. He commanded the U.S. Air Force Base at Bordeaux, France, and was chief of the Air Force Latin American Postal Service. Stationed in Paris, he was chief of protocol for the French Liaison Office of Supreme Headquarters Allied Powers Europe (SHAPE). This international military organization protects the security and territorial integrity of NATO member nations in Europe. Archer also served as executive officer of the 36th Division of the North American Aerospace Defense Command (NORAD). Both U.S. and Canadian military forces participate in NORAD to monitor manmade objects in space and warn of attack against North America by aircraft, spacecraft, or missiles. In addition, Archer commanded Headquarters, U.S. Air Force Southern Command, in Panama.

Lieutenant Colonel Lee A. Archer, Jr., retired from the air force in 1970, after 29 years of service, and embarked on a business career. He was manager of urban affairs for the General Foods Corporation before being promoted to director in 1971. Four years later, he was elected corporate vice president. He has held executive positions with Hudson Commercial Corporation, TLC Beatrice, Independent Tobacco Leaf Sales, and other business concerns. In 1987, he formed Archer Associates, Ltd., a venture capital holding corporation.

In the 1990s, cadets at the Air Force Academy researched Archer's war record and determined that he had indeed downed five German warplanes. This finding established Archer's status as an ace, making him the only ace among the distinguished pilots known as the Tuskegee Airmen.

In November 2001, along with General JULIUS W. BECTON, JR., and others, Archer was named to the council directing the Veterans History Project for the Library of Congress, the library effort to collect first-person accounts from men and women who defended the United States in wartime.

Archer's awards include eight Air Medals, the Distinguished Flying Cross, and citations from Presidents Eisenhower, Kennedy, and Johnson and the director of the CIA. He also received the Accueil de Paris from the mayor of Paris in recognition of his activities that furthered U.S.-French relations. Lee A. Archer, Jr., died in 2010 and was buried at Arlington National Cemetery.

Further Reading

Cluff, James R. *Lieutenant Colonel Lee Andrew "Buddy" Archer, Jr.: A Lifetime of Servant Leadership.* Maxwell Air Force Base, Ala.: Air Command and Staff College, Air University, April 2006.

"Lee Archer Collection (AFC/2001/001/44004)." Veterans History Project, American Folklife Center, Library of Congress. Available online. URL: http://lcweb2.loc.gov/diglib/vhp/bib/loc.natlib.

afc2001001.44004. Downloaded on August 1, 2008.

Lewin, Arthur N. "The Black Ace of World War II." *Black WebPortal News Wire.* Available online. URL: http://www.blackwebportal.com/wire/DA. cfm?ArticleID=418. Downloaded on August 1, 2008.

Armistead, James
(James Lafayette)

(1760–1832) *Revolutionary War spy whose reports made possible the American victory at Yorktown*

Many blacks acted as spies in the Revolution, but none made a greater contribution to American independence than James Armistead.

Only a few facts have been unearthed about Armistead's life prior to 1781. It is known, for example, that he was a slave owned by William Armistead of New Kent County, Virginia. In March 1781, his master granted James Armistead permission to serve with the Marquis de Lafayette, the French statesman and military leader who had been commissioned a major general in the Continental army in 1777.

At the time Lafayette was quartered near Richmond, with his men stationed at New Kent County Court House and Williamsburg, Virginia. His adversary, General Charles Cornwallis, second in command of British forces in North America, fresh from victories at Camden, South Carolina, and Guilford Court House, North Carolina, had moved his soldiers into Virginia. Cornwallis was encamped at Portsmouth, near the entrance to the Chesapeake Bay. The occupying British army was more than twice the size of the American force, and to be victorious, Lafayette needed timely and accurate information on British personnel, troop movements, and equipment.

The French general had tried several times to place spies in Cornwallis's camp, but the information he received from them had proven unreliable.

In spring 1781, he sent Armistead to infiltrate the British headquarters, and by July 7, the former slave had secured employment as a servant to Cornwallis. In this privileged position, Armistead gathered crucial data on British supplies of weapons and horses, the movements of British ships in coastal waters, and the positions of Cornwallis's forces. Ironically, the British general grew to trust his African-American servant enough to enlist him to spy on the Americans. Thus, for a time Armistead acted as a double agent, passing along false information to Cornwallis as he prepared accurate reports for Lafayette. The fact that Armistead sent Lafayette written communiques indicates that he was literate.

In August, Armistead informed Lafayette that 60 British ships were anchored in the York River,

James Armistead, who acted as a double agent during the American Revolution, changed his name to James Lafayette to honor his hero, the Marquis de Lafayette. The marquis issued a certificate to the value of Armistead's contribution. *(Virginia Historical Society)*

and that the British were fortifying downstream at Yorktown and Gloucester. Based on this knowledge, Lafayette advised General Washington to send a French fleet to the mouth of the York River and blockade the British. The positioning of French ships and American and French infantrymen in the region set the stage for the last major action of the war, the siege of Yorktown, which ended with British surrender on October 19, 1781. Following his surrender, Cornwallis was astonished to see his former servant and spy in Lafayette's headquarters.

Lafayette was sufficiently grateful for Armistead's reports to issue a certificate of recommendation dated November 21, 1784, stating that Armistead's "intelligences from the enemy camp were industriously collected and more faithfully delivered. He properly acquitted himself with some important communications I gave him and appears to be entitled to every reward his situation can admit of." Armistead, in turn, paid tribute to the French nobleman by adopting his name.

A 1783 act of the Virginia legislature granted freedom to slaves in the state who had fought in the Revolution, but its provisions failed to include spies. In 1786, the legislature passed a separate motion declaring James Lafayette a free man. In 1816, James Lafayette bought 40 acres nine miles south of New Kent County and settled down to farm and raise a large family. In 1819, the Virginia legislature awarded him a yearly pension of $40. In 1824, when the Marquis de Lafayette made a celebrated return visit to the United States, he met again with his namesake and former spy and greeted him warmly.

Further Reading

Gottschalk, Louis, ed. *The Letters of Lafayette to Washington, 1777–1779.* Philadelphia: American Philosophical Society, 1976.

Gray, Madison. "James Armistead: Patriot Spy." *Time: Unsung Heroes.* Available online. URL: http://www.time.com/time/2007/blackhistmth/bios/01.html. Downloaded on August 1, 2008.

Intelligence in the War of Independence. Washington, D.C.: Central Intelligence Agency, 1998, p. 22.

Kaplan, Sidney, and Emma Nogrady Kaplan. *The Black Presence in the Era of the American Revolution.* Amherst: University of Massachusetts Press, 1989, pp. 37–41.

Kranz, Rachel, and Philip J. Koslow. *The Biographical Dictionary of African Americans.* New York: Facts On File, 1999, pp. 10–11.

Logan, Rayford W., and Michael R. Winston, eds. *Dictionary of American Negro Biography.* New York: W. W. Norton and Co., 1982, pp. 16–17.

Armour, Vernice

(1973–) *first female African-American naval aviator and U.S. military combat pilot*

Vernice Armour joined the Marine Corps asking herself, "If I don't do it, who will?" This eagerness to embrace challenges allowed her to excel and become the first African-American woman to pilot naval aircraft and to fly military aircraft in combat.

Armour was born in Chicago but was raised in Memphis, Tennessee. Throughout her childhood and teens, older family members instilled in her a pride in military service. Her father, Gaston C. Armour, Jr., was a retired major in the U.S. Army Reserve; her stepfather, Clarence Jackson, was a retired Marine Corps sergeant; and a grandfather had also been a marine. Yet Vernice Armour's childhood dream was to join the police force.

She was a member of the National Honor Society and the math honor society while a student at Overton High School. While attending Middle Tennessee State University (MTSU), she joined first the Army Reserves and later the Army Reserve Officers' Training Corps (ROTC). Armour took a break from college in 1996 to join the Metropolitan Nashville Police Department, and she became the first African-American woman on the force's motorcycle squad. After returning to MTSU and graduating in 1997, she worked in law enforcement in Tempe, Arizona.

In 1998, when opportunities for women in the U.S. military were expanding, Armour learned that the Marine Corps wanted to train its first African-American female combat pilot. This knowledge inspired her to enlist in the marines as an officer candidate, despite her stepfather's warning that she would be treated poorly. Armour assured him that the role of women in the armed services had changed since he fought in Vietnam.

Armour was commissioned a second lieutenant on December 12, 1998. She attended flight school at Naval Air Station Corpus Christi, Texas, and Naval Air Station Pensacola, Florida. She earned her wings on July 13, 2001, finishing not only first in her class of 12, but also first among the most recent 200 graduates. She had the distinction of becoming the first female African American to fly naval aircraft.

Her training continued at Marine Corps Base Camp Pendleton, near San Diego, where she learned to fly the AH-1W Super Cobra, a twin-engine, missile-equipped attack helicopter. She excelled in athletics at Camp Pendleton, earning the title Female Athlete of the Year in 2001 and twice winning the Strongest Warrior Competition. She also played running back for the San Diego Sunfire, a women's football team.

In March 2003, Marine Captain Vernice Armour flew the AH-1W Super Cobra during the U.S. invasion of Iraq, becoming the first female African-American pilot in any branch of the service to see combat. In 2003 and 2004, through two tours in support of Operation Iraqi Freedom, the U.S.-led offensive in Iraq, she engaged the opposing forces in combat and provided air support for U.S. personnel on the ground.

Armour was next assigned to Marine Corps Headquarters in Arlington, Virginia, as a liaison officer in the Equal Opportunity Branch, Manpower and Reserve Affairs. In 2007, she returned to civilian life and formed VAI Consulting and Training, in Stafford, Virginia, where she worked as a motivational speaker and life coach and tried especially to reach young people. "I do feel a responsibility and an obligation to be a role model, mentor and leader," she has said. "That's paramount for the success of the coming generations."

Further Reading

Holmstedt, Kirsten. *Band of Sisters: American Women at War in Iraq.* Mechanicsburg, Pa.: Stackpole Books, 2007, pp. 154–183.

Mann, Howard. "Vernice Armour: The First African-American Woman Combat Pilot." *Black Collegian Online.* Available online. URL: http://www.black-collegian.com/issues/2ndSem08/vernice_armour.htm. Downloaded on June 2, 2008.

Williams, Sha'ahn. "First Black Female Pilot Honored in Memory of Bessie Coleman." *Henderson Hall News.* Available online. URL: http://www.dcmilitary.com/stories/082406/hendersonhall_20060824002.shtml. Downloaded on June 2, 2008.

Attucks, Crispus

(ca. 1723–1770) *seaman, first American to die in the American struggle for independence*

Crispus Attucks, the first fatality of the 1770 skirmish between American colonists and British soldiers that is remembered as the Boston Massacre, was born in Framingham, Massachusetts, of African and Native American lineage. Slavery was permitted in the 13 British colonies in North America, and Attucks was the property of Deacon William Brown of Framingham.

Little is known of Attucks's life prior to 1750, the year he fled to freedom. Not even his exact birth year is known. In September 1750, Brown advertised for the return of a missing slave in the *Boston Gazette*. Brown's notice stated that he was looking for a man 27 years old and six feet, two inches tall. The runaway, named "Crispas," wore

Paul Revere of Boston printed and sold this image of the "massacre" of March 5, 1770, in which Crispus Attucks became the first person to die for American independence. *(Library of Congress)*

"a light colour'd Bearskin Coat." Identifying features included "short curl'd Hair" and "Knees nearer together than common." Brown offered a reward of 10 pounds for Attucks's return.

No one ever collected that reward. Using the name Michael Johnson, Attucks found work and safety from recapture aboard a sailing ship. By March 1770, however, he was back on land, living in the tense city of Boston.

The North American colonists were increasingly angry at the mother country because of English laws and taxes that restricted colonial trade and cut into profits. For example, the Navigation Acts, which were enacted by Great Britain in the 17th and 18th centuries, had restricted colonial trade with other nations and imposed duties that the colonists considered unfair. More recently, the Townshend Acts of 1767, named for

British minister of finance Charles Townshend, imposed duties on glass, lead, and tea and permitted colonial warehouses and homes to be searched for smuggled goods. These and other assessments had been levied by a Parliament that included no American members. Furious at this "taxation without representation," Bostonians had resolved at a town meeting to import no goods on which the duties of the Townshend Acts had been placed, and Great Britain had responded by quartering two British infantry battalions in their city. The colonists equated the soldiers' red uniforms with British tyranny and resented their presence, and repeated clashes between the colonists and infantrymen had left several people injured.

Crispus Attucks was supping in a waterfront inn on the evening of March 5, 1770, when word reached the docks that a British sentry had injured a boy. Soon, a crowd was pushing its way through the cold streets, armed with sticks and clubs. With Attucks at the forefront, the irate colonists swore that they would drive the British from their city.

They reached the site of the disturbance to learn that a sentinel had struck a jeering youth with the butt of his firearm. The colonists sounded battle cries: "Kill the dogs"; "knock them over"! Some in the mob began to throw snow and ice at Captain Thomas Preston and his red-coated force. "Be not afraid," Attucks is reported to have called out. "They dare not shoot." In fact, the British were under orders not to fire their weapons unless instructed to do so by the city magistrate. Then someone—an eyewitness said it was that stout fellow, Attucks—struck at a soldier's musket with a piece of cordwood.

Suddenly, one soldier acted without orders and fired, hitting Attucks in the chest and killing him. More shots were heard, and before the violence ended, 11 people had been hit; two more colonists lay dead, and two more were dying. Also killed were Samuel Gray, a rope maker; Samuel Maverick, a joiner's apprentice; James Caldwell, a ship's mate; and Patrick Carr, an Irish leather worker.

This incident, in which Americans first shed their blood for independence, would be known as the Boston Massacre.

Thousands attended the funeral of the five martyrs to freedom, who were buried in a common tomb. The British soldiers were tried for their role in the massacre and acquitted, but it was the fallen Americans who were remembered as heroes. Crispus Attucks inspired pride in the African-American militia companies of the antebellum period that called themselves Attucks Guards, and in the black citizens of Boston who from 1858 to 1870 observed the date of his death, March 5, as Crispus Attucks Day.

Further Reading

"The Boston Massacre and Crispus Attucks." *Negro History Bulletin* 33, no. 3 (March 1970): pp. 56–57.

Kaplan, Sidney, and Emma Nogrady Kaplan. *The Black Presence in the Era of the American Revolution.* Amherst: University of Massachusetts Press, 1989, pp. 6–11.

Lanning, Michael Lee. *The African-American Soldier: From Crispus Attucks to Colin Powell.* New York: Citadel Press, 2004, pp. 1–3.

Palmer, Colin A., ed. *Encyclopedia of African American Culture and History.* Vol. 1. Detroit, Mich.: Thomson Gale, 2006, pp. 163–164.

Quarles, Benjamin. *The Negro in the American Revolution.* Chapel Hill: University of North Carolina Press, 1996, pp. 4–7.

Augusta, Alexander Thomas

(1825–1890) *Civil War surgeon, first African-American commissioned officer in the U.S. Army, highest-ranking African American to serve with the U.S. Colored Troops*

A physician with a successful private practice in Canada, Alexander T. Augusta persuaded the U.S. Army Medical Board in 1863 to permit him to be the first black surgeon serving with the U.S. Colored Troops.

Augusta, who was born to free black parents in Norfolk, Virginia, on March 8, 1825, learned to read as a young man in Baltimore, where he worked as a barber. Wanting to do more with his life than cut hair, he began studying the practice of medicine with local physicians. Unable to obtain a formal medical education in the United States because of his race, he moved to Toronto, Canada, where he earned a bachelor of medicine degree from Trinity Medical College in 1856. He wrote, "I was compelled to leave my native country, and come to this on account of prejudice against colour, for the purpose of obtaining a knowledge of my profession. . . ."

Skin color mattered less in Canada than it did in the United States, and Augusta built a busy medical practice in Toronto, primarily treating white patients. Having established himself in Canada, which until 1867 was a colony of Britain, he became a British subject.

Augusta followed closely events in the United States leading up to the American Civil War. The formation of the first African-American regiments in fall 1862 inspired in him a desire to return to the nation of his birth and aid in the war against slavery. He addressed a letter to President Abraham Lincoln in which he offered his services as a physician, explaining, "I . . . would like to be in a position where I can be of use to my race. . . ."

Lincoln passed along Augusta's letter to the Army Medical Board. At the time the board was having trouble finding enough qualified physicians to serve in the army and with African-American troops in particular. Nevertheless, the board rejected Augusta, giving two reasons: first, he was a British citizen, and enlisting him might violate Britain's proclamation of neutrality; second, he was "a person of African descent. . . ." There was concern that white soldiers might object to receiving treatment from a black doctor, and even if Augusta were assigned to a black regiment, he would treat the unit's white officers.

Unwilling to let the board's decision go unchallenged, Augusta made the long trip from Toronto

Alexander T. Augusta, M.D., served in the Civil War as a surgeon with the U.S. Colored Troops. *(Courtesy of the Moorland-Spingarn Research Center, Howard University Archives)*

to Washington to plead his case in person, and his persistence paid off. He was permitted to take the qualifying exam, which he passed. On April 14, 1863, he was commissioned a major, thus becoming the first of eight African-American physicians to receive commissions during the war, and on October 2, 1863, he was appointed regimental surgeon of the 7th U.S. Colored Troops, which was part of a larger force being sent to Beaufort, South Carolina. His appointment drew complaints from white surgeons unwilling to serve under him, which resulted in Augusta spending much of his period of enlistment overseeing the Freedman's Hospital in Washington, D.C., a facility that treated many of the refugees from slavery who were arriving daily in the District of Columbia. In this way he became the first African American to head a hospital anywhere in the United States.

The prejudice that Augusta faced as an African-American officer was at times blatant and brutal. A month after joining the army he was assaulted by a railroad guard and eight or more thugs as he boarded a train in Baltimore. With his uniform torn and fearing for his safety, he left the station and returned with a military and police escort. Despite this protection, he suffered a hard blow to the face and took his seat on the train only after his bodyguards drew their revolvers. On another occasion, he reported for duty at Camp Stanton, Maryland, to find that the white assistant surgeons there refused to serve under him. When he appealed to Lincoln to intervene, he—and not the assistant surgeons—received a transfer.

As an added insult, Augusta's rate of pay was based on his race rather than on his rank and responsibilities. At the time, all blacks in the army received $10 a month, regardless of rank. White enlisted men were given $13, and white officers earned more. A white army surgeon with a major's rank would receive $169 per month. Augusta first received his rightful salary in April 1864, after Maryland congressman Ephraim King Wilson appealed to Secretary of War Edwin M. Stanton. Four months later, in August 1864, the government paid black and white enlisted men equally for the first time.

On March 13, 1865, for meritorious and faithful service, Augusta was brevetted a lieutenant colonel. As such, he was one of the few African-American field officers to serve in the Civil War. Augusta was mustered out of the army on October 13, 1866, and resumed the practice of medicine.

In 1868, when Howard University in Washington, D.C., opened its medical school, Augusta was one of the first faculty members and the only one who was African American. He remained at historically black Howard until 1877, when he returned to private practice in the District of Columbia. He was one of the founders in 1870 of the National Medical Society of the District of Columbia, a professional organization formed because African Americans were barred from membership in the district's existing medical society.

Alexander T. Augusta died on December 21, 1890, and was buried at Arlington National Cemetery. On June 30, 1896, he received (posthumously) the first honorary doctorate awarded by Howard.

Further Reading

Henig, Gerald S. *Civil War Firsts.* Mechanicsburg, Pa.: Stackpole Books, 2001, pp. 208–209.

Holzer, Harold, ed. *The Lincoln Mailbag: America Writes to the President, 1861–1865.* Carbondale: Southern Illinois University Press, 1998.

Lloyd, Sterling M., Jr. "A Short History of the Howard University College of Medicine." Howard University College of Medicine. Available online. URL: http://www.med.howard.edu/nuHoward/history.html. Downloaded on August 5, 2008.

Logan, Rayford W. *Howard University: The First Hundred Years.* New York: New York University Press, 1969.

Quarles, Benjamin. *The Negro in the Civil War.* New York: Da Capo Press, 1989, pp. 203–204, 234.

Austin, Lloyd James, III

(1953–) *lieutenant general, commander of Multinational Corps Iraq*

An infantryman who feels more at home in the field than behind a desk, Lieutenant General Lloyd J. Austin III assumed leadership of Multinational Corps Iraq in February 2008, thus becoming second in command in the ongoing military effort to bring stability to this middle eastern country.

Austin grew up in Thomasville, Georgia, the fifth of six children. He grew to six feet, four inches, in height and was a basketball star in high school. After graduating, he enrolled in the U.S. Military Academy at West Point, New York, following in the footsteps of a distant cousin, Second

Lieutenant HENRY O. FLIPPER, who in 1877 was the first African-American graduate of the academy. Austin earned a bachelor of science degree from the academy in June 1975 and was commissioned a second lieutenant in the U.S. Army.

His early army assignments included rifle and scout platoon leader, 3rd Infantry Division, U.S. Army Europe and Seventh Army; company commander, 2nd Battalion, 508th Infantry, 82nd Airborne Division at Fort Bragg, North Carolina; and company commander, U.S. Army Recruiting Battalion, Indianapolis. From June 1991 through October 1992, he was company tactical officer at the U.S. Military Academy. At the same time, he was executive officer of the 1st Infantry Brigade, 10th Mountain Division (Light), which was stationed at Fort Drum, New York. (The 10th Mountain Division is a unit trained to fight in all kinds of harsh terrain throughout the world.)

Austin also continued his education, earning a master's degree in education administration from Auburn University in Alabama and a master's degree in management from Webster University in St. Louis. In addition, he completed the Infantry Officer Basic and Advanced Courses at the U.S. Army Command and General Staff College at Fort Leavenworth, Kansas, and the U.S. Army War College in Carlisle, Pennsylvania.

As he rose through the ranks of the infantry, Austin held command and staff positions with the 82nd Airborne Division at Fort Bragg and in Panama, as part of Operation Safe Haven, the 1994 effort to give temporary shelter to Cubans who had tried to enter the United States illegally and were awaiting passage to Cuba. In June 1999, Austin became chief of the J-3 Operations Directorate, Joint Staff, at the Pentagon. This office coordinates the movement of U.S. military forces around the world, briefs the nation's leaders on military operations, and acts as a link between commanders in the field and the national command authority. Austin was selected to be an assistant division commander with the 3rd Army Division (Mechanized) at Fort Stewart, Georgia

in July 2001, and his promotion to brigadier general came on January 1, 2002.

In 2003, General Austin was deployed to Iraq as a member of the U.S.-led invasion force that intended to disarm weapons of mass destruction and free the Iraqi people from a dictator who supported terrorism. In April 2003, he became the first African American to maneuver an army division in combat when he led the forward headquarters of the Third Army Division, which spearheaded the march of coalition forces into Baghdad that brought about the fall of Saddam Hussein's government. His combat leadership earned him a Silver Star.

By September 2003, Austin was in Afghanistan, commanding the 10th Mountain Division as part of Operation Enduring Freedom, another aspect of the War on Terrorism, one which the United States launched in reaction to the September 11, 2001, attacks on the World Trade Center and Pentagon. On January 1, 2005, Austin was promoted to major general.

Austin went on to serve, from September 2005 through October 2006, at MacDill Air Force Base, Florida, as chief of staff for U.S. Central Command (CENTCOM), which is responsible for all U.S. forces deployed in the Middle East, Central Asia, and the Horn of Africa. On December 8, 2006, he was promoted to lieutenant general. In the same month he took command of the XVIIIth Airborne Corps, headquartered at Fort Bragg. Its 35,000 soldiers made up the 82nd Airborne Division and other units.

On February 15, 2008, in Baghdad, Austin assumed command of Multinational Corps Iraq, the tactical branch of the 26-nation force conducting military operations throughout Iraq. As second in command, reporting to General David Petraeus, commander of Multinational Force Iraq, Austin was responsible for the command and control of those operations, for prioritizing the use of combat personnel, aircraft, unmanned drones, and other resources to achieve U.S. objectives. His goals, he said, were to "help the Iraqi government integrate local volunteers into the Iraqi security force and other employment opportunities that will promote progress for this great country."

Further Reading

Bigenho, Laura M. "Austin Assumes Command of Multinational Corps Iraq." U.S. Department of Defense. Available online. URL: http://www.defenselink.mil/news/newsarticle.aspx?id=48978. Downloaded on August 19, 2008.

"Lieutenant General Lloyd J. Austin III." Fort Bragg. Available online. URL: http://www.bragg.army.mil/18ABN/CommandGroup.cg.htm. Downloaded on August 18, 2008.

Tyson, Ann Scott. "Hands-on General Is Next No. 2 in Iraq." *Washington Post,* January 13, 2008, p. A4.

B

Baker, Vernon Joseph

(1919–   ) *World War II veteran, Medal of Honor winner*

On April 5 and 6, 1945, Second Lieutenant Vernon Baker demonstrated extraordinary heroism in an attack on German installations at Viareggio, Italy. More than 50 years later, the United States honored him with the Medal of Honor he had long deserved.

On December 17, 1919, Baker was born into one of a handful of African-American families living in Cheyenne, Wyoming. When his parents died in an automobile accident four years later, Vernon and his two older sisters went to live with their paternal grandparents, Dora and Joseph Baker. Joseph Baker, a brake inspector for the Union Pacific Railroad, taught young Vernon to hunt. In the Wyoming wilderness, the boy learned to stalk game and handle a rifle, skills that would serve him well as a soldier.

Vernon sought more freedom as an adolescent than his grandparents permitted, and he and his grandfather frequently clashed. In 1931, his grandparents sent Vernon to Father Flanagan's Boys Town, and he lived for two years at the famous orphanage in Omaha, Nebraska. He next stayed with cousins in Iowa, where he graduated from high school. He worked as a railroad porter for a year before returning to Cheyenne, where he held a series of odd jobs.

Foreseeing a limited future in civilian life, Baker enlisted in the army on June 6, 1941. After boot camp, he was assigned to Fort Huachuca, Arizona, where knowing how to type earned him the company clerk's job. By December 1941, when the United States entered World War II, he held the rank of sergeant. Regimental command ordered him to Officer Training School at Fort Benning, Georgia, although for Baker and all African-American soldiers, overseas duty was still three years away. Despite the exemplary service of black units in earlier wars, the army doubted that African Americans had the skill and courage to be effective in combat.

In 1944, caving in to pressure from African-American leaders, the army formed the 92nd Infantry, a black fighting unit nicknamed the Buffalo Division in tribute to the Buffalo Soldiers, the African-American soldiers of the frontier. Most of the regiment's officers were white men from the South, because army leaders thought that they knew best how to work with blacks. Vernon Baker, never shy about speaking his mind, saw it this way: "The Army decided we needed supervision from white Southerners, as if war was plantation work and fighting Germans was picking cotton." In August 1944, assigned to Company C, 370th Division, 92nd Infantry, Baker went to the Arno River region of northern Italy, where the Germans were well entrenched.

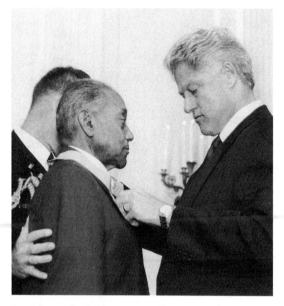

President Bill Clinton presented Vernon Baker with the Medal of Honor on January 13, 1997. *(Clinton Presidential Materials Project)*

On April 5, 1945, Second Lieutenant Baker led a 25-man platoon taking part in an assault on heavily fortified German positions at Castle Aghinolfi in Viareggio, on the Ligurian Sea. The Americans faced enemy gunfire so heavy that the commanding officer, a white captain, found an excuse to move to the rear. Meanwhile, Baker crawled forward. He reached one machine-gun nest and destroyed it, killing three German soldiers. He went on to surprise the two occupants of an enemy observation post and killed them both. Then, with one of the soldiers under his command, he attacked two more machine-gun emplacements, in the process killing or wounding four more Germans. Baker functioned by separating his fear from the demands of the task at hand. He explained: "I focused on the desperate need to survive the moment, capture a few hundred feet of hillside, a trench, a machine gun nest. If I survived one minute, I figured out how to deal with the next."

Having done everything he could offensively, Baker occupied an exposed position to draw enemy fire away from the wounded men of his company, who were being evacuated. His platoon's losses were great: Only Baker and six of his men had survived. Still, the next day Baker volunteered to lead a battalion on an advance through enemy minefields and heavy fire. Because of his heroism on April 5 and 6, his commanding officer recommended him for the Medal of Honor. Instead he was one of nine African Americans to receive the Distinguished Service Cross, the nation's second-highest decoration for bravery, for their actions in World War II.

When the war ended, Baker made the army his career. In June 1953, he married Fern V. Brown, a swimming instructor, and the couple raised three daughters. Baker retired from the army in 1965 as a first lieutenant; after Fern Baker died in 1986, he lived a solitary life in St. Maries, Idaho, and became an avid hunter. In 1993, he married Heidy Pawlik, an interior designer.

The fact that not one of the 470 Medals of Honor awarded for service in World War II had gone to an African American bothered the consciences of many Americans, black and white, especially when a Defense Department study commissioned in 1994 determined that Baker and six other African-American servicemen from the Second World War had clearly earned it. In order to recognize the men, Congress authorized a waiver of the statute of limitations for such awards that had expired in 1952.

On January 13, 1997, President Bill Clinton presented the Medal of Honor to Vernon J. Baker, the only one of the seven recipients still alive, and to family members or representatives of the other six. (Among the soldiers honored were Staff Sergeant EDWARD A. CARTER, JR., Staff Sergeant RUBEN RIVERS, and Private GEORGE WATSON.) "Now and forever, the truth will be known about these African Americans who gave so much that the rest of us might be free," Clinton said.

The ceremony brought tears to the eyes of Vernon Baker, who said that he could not help "remembering what happened on that hill." He was an uneasy hero who reflected that war "is the most regrettable proving ground." He has said, "I hope no man, black, white, or any color, ever again has the opportunity to earn the Medal of Honor."

In the spring of 1997, Baker returned to Italy, to the scene of his valor, and in December of that year, he received a check for more than $70,000, representing the monthly stipend he would have received beginning in July 1945 had he been awarded the Medal of Honor at the rightful time. Also in 1997, he published a memoir, *Lasting Valor*. Idaho's governor, Dirk Kempthorne, appointed Baker to the State Human Rights Commission in 2001.

Further Reading

Astor, Gerald. *The Right to Fight: A History of African Americans in the Military*. Novato, Calif.: Presidio Press, 1998, pp. 204, 256, 287–291.

Baker, Vernon J., with Ken Olsen. *Lasting Valor*. Columbus, Miss.: Genesis Press, 1997.

"Lt. Vernon J. Baker." Iowa Medal of Honor Heroes. Available online. URL: www.iowahistory.org/museum/exhibits/medal-of-honor-/baker_v_wwii/index.htm. Downloaded on August 1, 2008.

Olsen, Ken. "Heroism Outlasts Prejudice: North Idaho Man Honored for Acts in World War II." *Spokane Spokesman-Review*, November 29, 1996, p. A1.

Barnes, Samuel Edward

(1915–1997) *one of the "Golden Thirteen," the first African-American officers of the U.S. Navy*

The commitment to teamwork and drive to succeed that Samuel E. Barnes acquired as a high school and college athlete served him well when he trained to be one of the navy's first African-American officers in 1944. The leadership experience that he gained in the navy was invaluable in his later career as an athletic instructor and coach.

Barnes was born in Oberlin, Ohio, on January 25, 1915. His father, James D. Barnes, Sr., worked as a dormitory chef at Oberlin College. His mother, Margaret S. Barnes, was a college graduate who owned and operated a laundry. Margaret Barnes was also active in women's clubs, politics, and the Baptist church. The Barneses were a religious family, and the five children—two boys and three girls—spent long hours in church on Sundays.

Both Samuel and his older brother, James, excelled in sports. As a high school student, Samuel placed second in a state-championship track meet, behind Jesse Owens, the great African-American runner who won four gold medals at the Berlin Olympics of 1936. Samuel graduated from high school with honors in the spring of 1932 and entered Oberlin College in the fall. A physical education major, he won letters in track, basketball, and football.

After graduating from Oberlin in 1936, Barnes taught physical education and coached football and men's and women's basketball at Livingstone College, a small school for African Americans in Salisbury, North Carolina. He left Livingstone in 1941 to take a job as secretary at a Cincinnati, Ohio, YMCA. He left that job following U.S. entry into World War II to enlist in the navy. He was stationed at Fort Robert Smalls in Great Lakes, Illinois, on December 19, 1943, when he married Olga Lash, a teacher.

In 1943, navy leaders selected 16 African-American enlisted men for officer training with the expectation that four, or one-fourth of the class, would fail. Barnes learned that he was one of the chosen, and in January 1944 he began training at Great Lakes.

The 16 officer candidates adopted the motto of the Three Musketeers: "All for one, and one for all." As they endeavored to master a curriculum that included navigation, naval history and regulations, survival techniques, and gunnery, they worked as a team, sharing knowledge and helping one another along. It was important for every candidate to do his best. "We knew that we were the foot in the door for many other black sailors, and we were determined not to be the ones who were responsible for having the foot removed," Barnes explained.

All 16 officer candidates passed the course, but only 12—including Barnes—were commissioned ensigns. A 13th candidate was promoted to warrant officer. Together, these men became known as the "Golden Thirteen," the first African-American active-duty officers in the navy. (On June 18, 1942, the navy had awarded a reserve commission to Bernard Whitfield Robinson, a black Harvard medical student.) The three officer candidates passed over for promotion returned to active duty as enlisted men.

As an officer, Barnes first was assigned to supervise athletic and recreational programs for the African Americans stationed at Great Lakes. Next, he went to Camp Peary in Williamsburg, Virginia, to assume command of an African-American stevedore unit.

Barnes's 120-man company was ordered to Okinawa after the Japanese island came under U.S. control, in June 1945. The United States planned to launch an invasion of Japan from Okinawa, and the stevedores unloaded supplies from the many ships that were arriving. The atomic bombs dropped on Japan in August 1945 ended the war, and the invasion never took place. Barnes returned to the United States and was discharged at Great Lakes in early 1946.

After Barnes earned a master's degree at Oberlin in 1946, he and Olga settled in Washington, D.C., where they would raise a son and two daughters. Samuel Barnes became a physical education instructor and coach at Howard University. He received a doctorate in athletic administration from Ohio State University in 1956 and was promoted to athletic director and chairman of the Physical Education Department at Howard. Barnes spent the 1957–58 academic year on sabbatical in Iraq as part of a State Department program, teaching American coaching and physical

education practices. In 1971, he joined the faculty of District of Columbia Teachers' College (now the University of the District of Columbia). He retired in 1981 and became an active navy recruiter who was responsible for 80 enlistments.

From 1971 to 1972, Barnes was secretary-treasurer of the National Collegiate Athletic Association (NCAA), and as such was the first African-American officer of that organization. He was on the U.S. Olympic Committee in 1972 and was inducted into the Athletic Directors' Hall of Fame in 1970 and the Oberlin College Hall of Fame in 1986. He died in Washington, D.C., on January 21, 1997, and is buried at Arlington National Cemetery. In spring 2006, groundbreaking took place in Veterans Memorial Park, in North Chicago, Illinois, for a monument to the Golden Thirteen.

Further Reading

Bielakowski, Alexander. *African American Troops in World War II.* Oxford, U.K.: Osprey Publishing, 2007, pp. 13–28.

Porterfield, Harry. "U.S. Navy's Golden 13 to Be Honored." ABC7 Chicago. Available online. URL: http://abclocal.go.com/wls/story?section=news/local&id=4209363. Downloaded on August 13, 2008.

"Prof. Samuel Barnes Dies: Health, Phys Ed Instructor." *Washington Post,* January 24, 1997, p. B4.

Stillwell, Paul, ed. *The Golden Thirteen: Recollections of the First Black Naval Officers.* Annapolis, Md.: Naval Institute Press, 1993.

Beaty, Powhatan

(1837–1916) *Civil War soldier, Medal of Honor winner*

After nearly every white officer with Company G of the 5th U.S. Colored Troops was wounded or killed in the bloody charge at New Market Heights, Virginia, a black sergeant took command. The African Americans had been ordered to the front of the assault, where the danger was greatest. Beaty and his comrades knew that their risk of dying was high, and they knew as well that being captured by the Confederates would mean execution or sale into bondage. Yet they understood that demonstrating courage was the only way to advance the cause of racial equality in the army and in civilian life. Many men became heroes on that day, including Beaty, whose bravery on the battlefield earned him the Medal of Honor.

Beaty was born into slavery in Richmond, Virginia. In 1849, he moved to Cincinnati, in the free state of Ohio, to attend school. (The date when he gained his freedom is unknown.) At school he became interested in the theater, and he did his first public acting in a school production.

On September 2, 1863, more than a year after the Civil War had begun, a rumor reached Cincinnati that the Confederates were planning to attack the city. The men of Cincinnati organized themselves into units and prepared to mount a defense. Beaty reported for duty on September 5 and was assigned to a company of the Black Brigade, an African-American unit numbering roughly 700. With orders to fortify an area near Licking River, Kentucky, Beaty's company dug trenches and rifle pits and built magazines and forts before the threat of attack diminished. The brigade was disbanded on September 20.

Beaty again volunteered to serve in June 1863, when recruiters from Massachusetts came to Ohio to enlist soldiers for African-American regiments. He signed on for three years, but before he departed for Boston, news reached Cincinnati that the Massachusetts regiments had been filled. The U.S. War Department then authorized Ohio governor David Tod to form an African-American regiment, and Beaty was assigned to the 127th Ohio Volunteer Infantry (later designated the 5th U.S. Colored Infantry Regiment) and given the rank of sergeant.

On September 29, 1864, Beaty's regiment was one of several African-American units ordered to attack Confederate defenses near New Market Heights, Virginia, southeast of Richmond, beginning at dawn. The assault was part of a larger Union effort to break through the defensive line protecting Richmond and Petersburg. The Union men greatly outnumbered the Confederates guarding this line, but the Southerners were well entrenched and protected by a line of palisades (fences made from pointed posts that were designed to halt cavalry charges) and two lines of abatis (ramparts constructed from felled trees with sharpened trunks and limbs).

The Confederates met the first attacking force with intense gunfire. The African-American soldiers in the lead, who had been ordered not to shoot because firing and reloading would slow them down, braved the bullets to reach the first line of abatis. But with hundreds of men falling wounded or dead, they turned back. The 5th U.S. Colored Infantry took part in the second assault, for which the order not to fire had been lifted.

Beaty's company, Company G, began the charge with eight white officers and 83 black enlisted men. Before long, only 16 enlisted men, including Beaty, survived unwounded. At a time when only whites led troops in battle, First Sergeant Beaty then took command of Company G and ordered it forward. The second assault on the Confederate line broke through the fortifications, and many of the southerners turned and ran. As a result of the victory at New Market Heights, Union cavalry and infantry regiments were soon marching toward Richmond.

The 5th U.S. Colored Infantry Regiment fought in 13 battles and various skirmishes throughout the Richmond-Petersburg campaign. Beaty was commended for his actions at New Market Heights and in the Battles of Fair Oaks and Darbytown Road, in October 1864. Twice the regimental commander recommended him for a commission, and twice the recommendation was turned down. Beaty was given a brevet promotion to lieutenant, however, and on April 6, 1865, he was awarded the Medal of Honor for his actions at New Market Heights.

After the war, Powhatan Beaty returned to Cincinnati and to the stage. He wrote a play called *Delmar; or, Scenes in Southland,* and he acted the role of Delmar, a southern planter, when the play was presented in Cincinnati in January 1881. He also acted alongside the acclaimed African-American actor Henrietta Vinton Davis in Cincinnati, Philadelphia, and Washington, D.C. The pair performed scenes from Shakespeare as well as a play titled *Ingomar, the Barbarian,* in which Beaty played the title role, dressed in a wolf skin. Beaty was a founder of the Literary and Dramatic Club of Cincinnati and became its drama director in 1888.

In 2001, the State of Virginia honored this native son by naming the bridge that carries Route I-895 (the Pocahontas Parkway) over Virginia Route 5 for him.

Further Reading

"Black Brigade of Cincinnati." City of Fort Wright, Kentucky. Available online. URL: http://www. fortwright.com/index.asp?page=Black_Brigade. Downloaded on July 27, 2008.

Claxton, Melvin, and Mark Puls. *Uncommon Valor: A Story of Race, Patriotism, and Glory in the Final Battles of the Civil War.* Hoboken, N.J.: John Wiley and Sons, 2006.

Hill, Errol G., and James V. Hatch. *A History of African American Theatre.* Cambridge: Cambridge University Press, 2005.

Robertson, Gary. "PROFILE: Powhatan Beaty." inRich. com. Available online. URL: http://www.inrich. com/cva/ric/news/blackhistory.apx.-content-articles-RTD-special-0506.html. Downloaded on July 27, 2008.

Becton, Julius Wesley, Jr.

(1926–) *lieutenant general, federal and municipal administrator*

With an aptitude for leadership, Julius Becton rose from private to general in the course of a 36-year army career. A veteran of World War II, the Korean War, and the conflict in Vietnam, he gained prominence in the 1990s as chief executive officer of the troubled District of Columbia Public Schools.

Julius W. Becton, Jr., was born in Bryn Mawr, Pennsylvania, on June 29, 1926, the son of Julius W. Becton, Sr., a janitor, and Rose Banks Becton, a domestic worker. In 1943, he joined the Army Air Corps Enlisted Reserves, and in July 1944, he entered active duty as an army private. As a black soldier stationed in Florida, he was treated as an inferior by most of the whites he encountered, including Italian prisoners of war. Nevertheless, he attended officer candidate school, graduating in 1945. In 1948, he married Louise Thornton, with whom he would have five children.

Becton served briefly in the South Pacific in the aftermath of World War II. He was wounded twice while serving in Korea as a platoon commander with the 3rd Battalion of the 9th Infantry Regiment. In 1950, at the start of his combat duty in Korea, every soldier in the battalion, excepting the commanding officers, was African American, despite President Harry Truman's 1948 executive order calling for integration of the armed forces. Then, battlefield casualties created a demand for replacements, and new soldiers were assigned to units according to need rather than race. As Becton assumed the duties of company executive officer and, later, company commander, white soldiers accepted his authority. "Korea gave the Army the opportunity to prove that integration would work and work well," Becton said.

In the army, Becton furthered his education. In 1960, he received a bachelor of science degree in mathematics from Prairie View A & M University, a historically black school in Texas, and in 1967 he earned a master's degree in economics from the University of Maryland at College Park. He also studied at the Army Command and General Staff College at Fort Leavenworth, Kansas; Houston-Tillotson College in Austin, Texas; and Muhlenberg College in Pennsylvania.

Becton's army career included assignments throughout the United States and all over the world. He served in Vietnam with the 101st Airborne Division and was stationed in the Philippines, France, and Japan. In 1978, he was promoted to lieutenant general and given command of U.S. VII Corps, which remained prepared to defend southern Germany, should the need arise. He was responsible for a base that housed the 88,000 soldiers of VII Corps, 21,000 civilian employees, and 76,000 dependents. From 1981 to 1983, he was army inspector of training.

General Becton retired from the army in 1983 and went to work in the private sector as chief operating officer of American Coastal Industries, a Virginia corporation. In 1984, he returned to public service as director of the Office of Foreign Disaster Assistance of the U.S. Agency for International Development (USAID). In 1985, he took over the directorship of the Federal Emergency Management Agency (FEMA) at a time when the agency had been under investigation for alleged fraud and mismanagement. Becton rid FEMA of inefficiency and corruption in four years. His next challenge came in 1989, when as president of his alma mater, Prairie View A & M University, he remedied the school's financial troubles, decaying physical plant, and campus crime problem.

Those accomplishments were cause for high hopes in 1996, when Becton was named chief executive officer of the District of Columbia Public Schools, a system long plagued by falling test scores, low standards for teachers, and deteriorating buildings. Declaring his motto to be "Children First!" Becton vowed to mold the district's schools into a model system by June 30, 2000, when he would turn over leadership to a new superintendent. He brought in a staff of retired army officers and prepared to make big changes. Becton ran up against a city government and a school staff that were strongly resistant to change, however, and for the first time in his career, he met with frustration rather than success. He resigned from the school

system in 1998, two years ahead of schedule, to join the Center for Strategic and International Studies, a Washington think tank devoted to issues of national and international security.

General Becton's awards include the Silver Star with Oak Leaf Cluster, the Bronze Star with two Oak Leaf Clusters, the Republic of Vietnam Cross of Gallantry, and the Distinguished Service Award from the Federal Emergency Management Agency. In 2007, Becton received the George Catlett Marshall Medal from the Association of the U.S. Army, a private, nonprofit educational organization. This annual award recognizes "selfless service to the United States of America." In 2008, he published *Becton: Autobiography of a Soldier and Public Servant.*

Further Reading

Becton, Julius W., Jr. *Becton: Autobiography of a Soldier and Public Servant.* Annapolis, Md.: Naval Institute Press, 2008.

Greene, Marcia Slacum. "Familiar Territory for New Leader." *Washington Post,* November 16, 1996, p. A1.

Hawkins, Walter L. *Black American Military Leaders.* Jefferson, N.C.: McFarland and Co., 2007, p. 32.

Latty, Yvonne. *We Were There: Voices of African American Veterans, from World War II to the War in Iraq.* New York: Amistad, 2004, pp. 77–81.

Vogel, Steve. "Erasing the Color Line: War Forced a Reluctant U.S. Military to Accept Integration." *Washington Post,* June 20, 2000, p. B1.

Bivins, Horace Wayman

(1862–1937) *sergeant with the 10th Cavalry, sharpshooter, veteran of the Spanish-American War*

Buffalo Soldier Horace W. Bivins distinguished himself as a marksman while stationed in the West and served with valor in Cuba in 1898.

Bivins was born on May 8, 1862, in Accomack County, on the Virginia shore. His parents,

Severn S. and Elizabeth Bivins, were free African-American farmers. Horace Bivins shouldered adult responsibilities early in life, managing a farm near Keller, Virginia, when he was 15 years old. On June 13, 1885, at age 23, he entered the Hampton Institute (now Hampton University), a school for African Americans in the Tidewater region of Virginia that was founded in 1868. The curriculum included military training for young men, giving Bivins his first taste of a soldier's life.

Sergeant Horace W. Bivins of the 10th Cavalry posed for this photograph with his trusted companion, Booth. *(Library of Congress)*

On November 7, 1887, "Having a very great desire for adventure and to see the wild West," Bivins enlisted in the army in Washington, D.C. He was sent to Jefferson Barracks, Missouri, and on June 19, 1888, was assigned to Troop E of the 10th U.S. Cavalry at Fort Grant, Arizona Territory. The fort was in the heart of Apache country, the scene in earlier years of violent conflicts between U.S. troops and Native Americans. In 1886, the intrepid Apache leader Geronimo had been exiled to Florida, and by 1888, the Apache had been confined to the malarial San Carlos reservation. The army was charged with patrolling and keeping the peace in the region. At Fort Grant, Bivins demonstrated an aptitude for marksmanship, placing second in his first shooting competition.

Troop E was transferred to Fort Apache, Arizona Territory, in 1889. There, Bivins served as a clerk in the regiment adjutant's office from November 19, 1889, until June 15, 1890. He subsequently was stationed in the Dakotas and Montana, where his constant companion was his messenger dog, Booth, an Irish water spaniel that he trained as a pup. He continued to win shooting contests, and in 1894 won three gold medals when he represented the Department of the Dakotas in an army competition at Fort Sheridan, Illinois. Impressed by this display of prowess, Buffalo Bill Cody invited Bivins to tour with his Wild West Show, but Bivins declined the offer.

In April 1898, the 10th Cavalry received orders to report to Chickamauga, Tennessee, to train for service in the Spanish-American War. The explosion and sinking of the USS *Maine* in Havana Harbor on the night of February 15, 1898, had triggered this brief, popular war. The cause of the blast was never determined, but the United States, eager to liberate Cuba from Spanish control and end European colonization in North America, blamed Spain.

All four African-American regiments—the 9th and 10th Cavalry and the 24th and 25th Infantry—would take part in the Spanish-American

War. The U.S. fighting force would also include the Rough Riders, a band of adventurers under the command of Colonel Theodore Roosevelt.

On April 19, Sergeant Bivins's unit left Fort Assiniboine, Montana. Enthusiastic crowds greeted the soldiers' train as it traveled through the Midwest, and grateful civilians presented them with flags and flowers at various stops. Then, as the tracks turned south, the public welcomes diminished. Bivins, a southerner by birth, was taken aback by the Jim Crow segregation that had become entrenched in the former Confederate states during his years of western service. He called the racial separation that he witnessed in waiting rooms and restaurants and on trains "the curse of the South."

From Tennessee, the men of the 10th Cavalry went to Tampa, Florida, and on June 14, they sailed for Cuba. Upon his arrival, Bivins reflected in a letter to a friend on the irony of African Americans who were denied basic rights at home fighting to free the Cubans. "There is no people on earth more loyal and devoted to their country than the Negro," he wrote. "God grant the time will soon come when this country will have the power to enforce the teaching of this heavenly doctrine that all men are created free and equal."

The 10th Cavalry first encountered the enemy on June 24, at a gap in the Cuban hills known as Las Guasimas, which had been the site of a skirmish between Spanish troops and Cuban insurgents. Although casualties were high, the Americans drove the Spanish from their positions.

Both the 10th Cavalry and the Rough Riders were part of the force that won a decisive battle of the war, fought July 1 at San Juan Hill. Battle conditions were intense. "It was a hot day and we had no water. Some of us had canteens but they had been pierced by bullets. All of this time we were under a terrific fire," Bivins recalled. As Bivins fired a Hotchkiss gun, a small, breech-loading cannon, a Spanish bullet bounced from the cannon's wheel and glanced off his temple. "It stunned me for about two minutes," he said. "I recovered, resighted my gun, pulled the lanyard, then watched with my glasses the result of the shot."

With the victory at San Juan Hill, the United States penetrated the outer defense of the city of Santiago de Cuba. American losses were high, however, especially among the black units. One-fifth of the black soldiers who fought at San Juan Hill and more than half of the 10th Cavalry's white officers were killed. (One unsung hero of San Juan Hill was Bivins's dog, Booth. The spaniel guarded the body of a Buffalo Soldier killed in the charge, Private Staughter, until the Americans found and retrieved it.)

On July 3, the United States defeated a Spanish naval squadron in the harbor at Santiago de Cuba, and on July 18, Spain asked for a settlement. Bivins suffered through an attack of dysentery before he and the surviving Buffalo Soldiers returned home, arriving at Montauk Point, Long Island, New York, in August 1898. Later in the year, President William McKinley acknowledged the black soldiers' contribution in the recent war. "They vindicated their own liberty on the field," the president said, "and with other brave soldiers gave the priceless gift of liberty to another suffering race."

Following the Spanish-American War, Bivins served at Fort Clark and Fort Brown in Texas. He was married on November 7, 1900; he and his wife, Claudia, would have three children. From 1901 until his retirement in 1913, Bivins was stationed at army posts in the Philippines, Montana, Arizona, Wyoming, New York, and Vermont. He qualified as an expert marksman in 1908, 1909, and 1910. In retirement Bivins lived with his family in Billings, Montana, where Claudia Bivins was active in the Colored Women's Club. Horace Bivins died in 1937.

Further Reading

Astor, Gerald. *The Right to Fight.* Novato, Calif.: Presidio Press, 1998, pp. 59–60, 70.

Buckley, Gail. *American Patriots.* New York: Random House, 2001, pp. 144–146, 148–149.

Cashin, Herschel V. *Under Fire with the Tenth U.S. Cavalry.* Niwot, Colo.: University Press of Colorado, 1993.

Smith, Jessie Carney, ed. *Notable Black American Men. Book II.* Detroit, Mich.: Thomson Gale, 2007, pp. 46–47.

Black, Barry C.

(1948–   ) *rear admiral, first African-American chief of navy chaplains, first African American and first military chaplain to be chaplain of the U.S. Senate*

On June 12, 2007, the U.S. Senate passed a resolution honoring its 62nd chaplain, Barry C. Black, a retired U.S. Navy rear admiral. Black was the first African American and the first military chaplain to minister to the Senate. In the resolution, the Senate's Black Legislative Staff Caucus recognized his "exemplary achievements; his leadership and personal integrity in service to the United States Senate and the larger community; and his altruism and commitment to public service, touching the lives of many who bear witness to his spiritual leadership."

Black had come a long way. He was born to poor parents in Baltimore's inner city and grew up in a public housing project. His father, an alcoholic, was often absent, leaving Black's mother to raise their eight children. "In spite of unpromising beginnings, my siblings and I bucked the statistics and turned out fine," Black has written. Pearline Black gave the children a strong foundation in religion. Barry Black attended primary and secondary schools affiliated with the Seventh-day Adventist Church and Oakwood College (now Oakwood University), a historically black Seventh-day Adventist school in Huntsville, Alabama. He earned a bachelor's degree and began a career in the ministry in South Carolina and North Carolina. When five African-American sailors stationed at Norfolk, Virginia, began making regular trips to his church to hear him preach,

Black decided to become a navy chaplain. "It was the fact that there were people who looked like me and were from my religious tradition whose worship needs were not being met that motivated me to come into the Navy," he said.

In 1976, he was commissioned as a navy chaplain and assigned to Fleet Religious Support Activity in Norfolk. Subsequent assignments took him to the U.S. Naval Academy in Annapolis, Maryland; the First Marine Aircraft Wing in Okinawa, Japan; the Naval Training Center in San Diego, California; the USS *Belleau Wood*, an amphibious assault ship; and Marine Aircraft Group 31 in Beaufort, South Carolina. He served as assistant staff chaplain, Naval Education and Training, in Pensacola, Florida, and fleet chaplain, U.S. Atlantic Fleet, in Norfolk.

Black continued his education, completing the advanced course at the Naval Chaplains School in Newport, Rhode Island, and studying as well at Andrews University in Berrian Springs, Michigan; North Carolina Central University in Durham; Eastern Baptist Theological Seminary (now Palmer Theological Seminary) in Wynnewood, Pennsylvania; Salve Regina University in Newport; and United States International University (now Alliant International University) in San Diego. He earned master's degrees in divinity, counseling, and management and doctorates in ministry and psychology.

In 1997, Black became deputy chief of chaplains for the U.S. Navy, and in 2000 he was promoted to chief of navy chaplains, having attained the rank of rear admiral. His duties included advising the secretary of the navy, chief of naval operations, and commandants of the Marine Corps and Coast Guard on religious, ethical, and moral matters. He also oversaw the work of 1,350 chaplains of varied faiths ministering to 800,000 men and women, active and reserve, in the navy, Marine Corps, and Coast Guard. As both deputy chief and chief of navy chaplains, Black took part in events of national importance. He officiated at the burial at sea of John F. Kennedy, Jr., in 1999, and at the reburial of the Arctic explorer Matthew Henson at Arlington National Cemetery in 2000. In 2001 and 2002, he conducted memorial services at the Pentagon for the people killed there in the September 11, 2001, terrorist attack.

Black had been a guest chaplain in the U.S. Senate several times before June 27, 2003, when he was chosen to be the Senate's 62nd chaplain. He was the first African American and the first military chaplain to hold this position since the Senate elected its first chaplain in 1789. The Senate chaplain opens all legislative sessions with prayer and counsels the senators and their families and staff. The chaplain also performs weddings, conducts funerals, and officiates at other ceremonies. Black began his work in the Senate on July 7, 2003.

Barry C. Black remained in his Senate post after he retired from the navy on August 15, 2003. His military decorations include the Legion of Merit, the Defense Meritorious Service Medal, the Meritorious Service Medal (two awards), and the Navy and Marine Corps Commendation Medals. Among his civilian honors are the 1995 Renowned Service Award from the National Association for the Advancement of Colored People (NAACP), the 2002 Benjamin Elijah Mays Distinguished Leadership Award from the Morehouse School of Religion, and the 2004 Image Award from the Dominion University chapter of the NAACP. Black published a memoir, *From the Hood to the Hill*, in 2006.

Further Reading

Allen, Lahai. "In His Own Words: Barry Black." *Adventist Review.* Available online. URL: http://www.adventistreview.org/2003-1532/story3.html. Downloaded on June 27, 2008.

Black, Barry C. *From the Hood to the Hill: A Story of Overcoming.* Nashville, Tenn.: Nelson Books, 2006.

"Honoring Senate Chaplain Barry C. Black." GovTrack. us. Available online. URL: http://www.govtrack.

us/congress/record.xpd?id=110-s20070612-26. Downloaded on July 25, 2008.

"Profile: U.S. Senate Chaplain Barry Black." *Religion and Ethics Newsweekly.* Available online. URL: http://www.pbs.org/wnet/religionandethics/week1043/profile.html. Downloaded on July 25, 2008.

Rivera, John. "Admiral Serves God and Country." International Pentecostal Holiness Church. Available online. URL: http://chaplains.iphc.org/stories/black_prn.html. Downloaded on July 28, 2008.

Bluford, Guion S., Jr.

(1942–) *U.S. Air Force pilot, first African-American NASA astronaut*

Guion Bluford surprised high school teachers who dismissed him as a middling student by becoming an outstanding air force officer and aerospace engineer and, on the night of August 30, 1983, when the shuttle *Challenger* lifted off from Cape Canaveral, Florida, the first African American to represent the United States in space.

Born in Philadelphia on November 22, 1942, Guion Stewart Bluford, Jr., was the oldest of three brothers. His father, Guion Bluford, Sr., was a mechanical engineer who retired early due to epilepsy. His mother, Lolita Bluford, was a special-education teacher in the Philadelphia public schools. The Blufords lived in a racially mixed neighborhood where young Guion, who was nicknamed Bunny, delivered newspapers.

Bluford was a quiet, introspective child who enjoyed solving brainteasers and building model planes. He was fascinated with the dynamics of flight and, while in high school, with early achievements in space exploration. In 1957, the Soviet Union launched *Sputnik*, the first artificial satellite, and in 1958, President Dwight D. Eisenhower established the National Aeronautics and Space Administration (NASA). The following year, NASA officials selected the first seven astronauts from among the nation's military test pilots.

Bluford labored over his schoolwork and maintained a C-plus average in a rigorous science and mathematics curriculum at predominantly white Overbrook Senior High School. With persistence he mastered the challenging material, just as he worked his way up in the Boy Scouts of America to the highest level, Eagle Scout. Bunny "was always slugging it out," his brother Kenneth recalled. Knowing that his grades failed to reflect his capabilities, Bluford and his parents ignored advice from a guidance counselor who suggested that he pursue a course other than college. After graduating from Overbrook in 1960, Bluford entered Pennsylvania State University, where he was the only African American in the engineering school. He was enrolled as well in the Reserve Officers' Training Program, and once again he earned average grades.

During his senior year Bluford married fellow student Linda Tull, who was also from Philadelphia. He graduated from Penn State in 1964 with a bachelor of science degree and was commissioned a second lieutenant in the U.S. Air Force. Later in 1964, his son Guion III was born. Bluford completed tactical flight training at Williams Air Force Base in Arizona, and in 1965 earned his pilot's wings. A second son, James, was born the same year.

In 1966, after completing F-4C combat training, Bluford went to Vietnam, where he was assigned to the 577th Tactical Fighter Squadron and flew 144 combat missions, 65 of them over North Vietnam. His heroism earned him the Air Medal with nine Oak Leaf Clusters, an Air Force Commendation Medal, and three Air Force Outstanding Unit Awards. He returned to the United States in 1967, having been promoted to the rank of lieutenant colonel, and in 1968 became a test pilot and pilot trainer with the 3630th Flying Training Wing at Sheppard Air Force Base in Texas. In 1971, he qualified to become deputy commander of operations at Sheppard.

Bluford continued his education in the air force. In 1974, he received a master of science degree in aerospace engineering from the Air Force Institute of Technology in Dayton, Ohio. Also in 1974, he was made staff-development officer and chief of the Aerodynamics and Airframe Branch of the Flight Dynamics Laboratory at Wright-Patterson Air Force Base in Dayton. In 1978, he completed the requirements for a doctorate in aerospace engineering and laser physics from the Air Force Institute of Technology, having written his dissertation on the physics of airflow around delta wings at supersonic speeds. The one-time mediocre student had learned how to excel in school: Bluford consistently placed in the top 10 percent in his graduate courses.

The United States had made significant progress in space exploration in the decade that was coming to a close. In 1968, astronauts aboard the *Apollo 8* spacecraft had orbited the moon; in July 1969, *Apollo 11* had landed on the moon, and astronauts Neil Armstrong and Edwin "Buzz" Aldrin had become the first human beings to walk on the lunar surface. Unmanned spacecraft launched in the 1970s had explored Venus and Mars or had been designed to collect data on the outer planets and more distant regions of space. In 1976, NASA began recruiting astronauts to train for the Space Transportation System (STS), which would employ reusable spacecraft to shuttle cargo and personnel. Bluford was one of more than 8,000 applicants for the program. He also was among the 35 who were selected.

In 1978, he reported to the Johnson Space Center in Houston, Texas, to begin five years of intensive training. He would spend three months learning to operate the mechanical arm designed to move payloads such as satellites out of the shuttle's cargo bay. He enjoyed meeting the challenges that astronaut training presented. "The job is so fantastic, you don't need a hobby," he said. "The hobby is going to work."

Two other African Americans, FREDERICK DREW GREGORY and Ronald E. McNair, Ph.D., were among the trainees. Although Bluford liked to be seen simply as one member of the team, he understood that the three African Americans were breaking new ground. He said that he and the others had "had to be ready in 1977 and 1978, when the doors of opportunity were opened to us and the cloak of prejudice was raised. As black scientists and engineers and aviators, we had to prove that black people could excel." The training class also included Sally K. Ride, Ph.D., who would become the first woman in space.

There had been two previous African-American astronaut candidates. Captain Edward Dwight, who began training in 1962, left NASA in 1966, claiming that he had been pressured to quit. Major ROBERT H. LAWRENCE, JR., who was selected to be an astronaut candidate in June 1967, died just months later, on December 8, 1967, in the crash of a jet fighter at Edwards Air Force Base in California.

Space shuttle flights began in 1981, when the *Columbia* was launched from the Kennedy Space Center at Cape Canaveral. In 1982, Bluford and four other astronauts were selected as the crew of the third *Challenger* flight, which was to be the eighth shuttle mission. With the launch of the *Challenger* on August 30, 1983, he made history as the first African American in space. Reflecting on that accomplishment, he said, "I felt an awesome responsibility, and I took that responsibility very seriously, of being a role model and opening another door to black Americans." (The first black space traveler was Arnaldo Tamayo Mendez, a Cuban who flew on a Soviet mission in 1980.)

Bluford's 1983 shuttle flight was the first to include a nighttime launch and landing. As the craft completed 98 Earth orbits, Bluford performed experiments related to diabetes research. He and another mission specialist, Dale Gardner, launched a weather satellite for the government of India. The *Challenger* landed in California on September 5.

From October 30 to November 6, 1985, Bluford made his second shuttle flight as part of an

In 1983, Guion S. Bluford, Jr., became the first African American in space. *(National Aeronautics and Space Administration)*

eight-member crew on a mission that was a joint venture with West Germany. Then, on January 28, 1986, the *Challenger* exploded shortly after liftoff, killing all seven people aboard, including teacher Christa McAuliffe and astronaut Ronald McNair. NASA shut down the STS program until 1988. In the meantime Bluford earned an MBA degree from the University of Houston in 1987.

On April 28, 1991, he began his third mission in space, studying atmospheric conditions and phenomena such as the aurora borealis. His final space flight, in 1992, was a military mission on which five astronauts conducted experiments for the Defense Department. Bluford retired from NASA in 1993 to pursue employment in the private sector.

His many honors include the National Society of Black Engineers Award (1979), the NAACP Image Award (1983), the Distinguished Service Medal from the state of Pennsylvania (1984), the NASA Exceptional Service Medal (1992), and 13 honorary doctorates.

Further Reading

Bigelow, Barbara Carlisle, ed. *Contemporary Black Biography.* Vol. 2. Detroit: Gale Research, 1992, pp. 19–21.

Burns, Kephra, and William Mills. *Black Stars in Orbit.* San Diego, Calif.: Harcourt, Brace and Co., 1995, pp. 37, 49–51.

"Guion S. Bluford, Jr. (Colonel, USAF, Ret.) NASA Astronaut (Former)." Lyndon B. Johnson Space Center. Available online. URL: http://www.jsc.nasa.gov/Bios/htmlbios/bluford-gs.html. Downloaded on August 2, 2008.

Hawkins, Walter L. *African American Biographies: Profiles of 558 Current Men and Women.* Jefferson, N.C.: McFarland and Co., 1992, pp. 42–43.

Phelps, J. Alfred. *They Had a Dream: The Story of African-American Astronauts.* Novato, Calif.: Presidio Press, 1994, pp. 68–99.

Bolden, Charles F., Jr.

(1946–) *First African-American permanent head of NASA*

A decorated military pilot, Charles Bolden completed four scientific missions as an astronaut in NASA's STS program before returning to active duty in the Marine Corps. In 2002, Bolden rejoined NASA as deputy administrator, and seven years later he became the first African-American permanent head of the space agency.

Charles Frank Bolden, Jr., was born in Columbia, South Carolina, on August 19, 1946. His parents, Charles and Ethel Bolden, were teachers who encouraged study and learning. Charles graduated with honors from Columbia's C. A. Johnson High School in 1964, and entered the U.S. Naval Academy at Annapolis, Maryland, where he majored in electrical science. In 1968, he received a bachelor of science degree from the academy and accepted a commission in the Marine Corps. The same year, he married Alexis "Jackie" Walker, who was also from Columbia.

Second Lieutenant Charles Bolden underwent two years of flight training and was designated a naval aviator in 1970, when the United States was heavily involved in the military conflict in Vietnam. In 1972 and 1973, Bolden served as a fighter pilot, flying more than 100 sorties over North and South Vietnam, Laos, and Cambodia in an A-6A *Intruder.*

After completing his tour of duty, Bolden spent two years as a marine recruiting officer in Los Angeles and another three years at the Marine Corps Air Station at El Toro, California. By 1977, when he earned a master's degree in systems management from the University of Southern California, Charles and Jackie Bolden had two children: Anthony and Kelly.

Charles Bolden had considered applying for astronaut training in 1976, when NASA announced the start of the STS program, but believing he would be rejected, he decided against it. Although he had logged nearly 3,000 hours of flying time, he had no test-pilot experience, and most previous astronauts had been military test pilots. After obtaining his master's degree he therefore enrolled in the U.S. Naval Test Pilot School at Patuxent River, Maryland. He graduated in 1979 and was assigned to the Systems Engineering and Strike Aircraft Test Directorates of the Naval Air Test Center at Patuxent River. At last he felt sufficiently prepared to apply to NASA, and in 1980 he was admitted to the shuttle program.

Astronaut Charles Bolden first went into space on January 12, 1986, when the shuttle *Columbia* lifted off from the Kennedy Space Center. The crew launched a communications satellite and conducted experiments in astrophysics before the *Columbia* landed at Edwards Air Force Base in California on January 18. Ten days later, the shuttle *Challenger* exploded following liftoff; NASA postponed further shuttle missions indefinitely, while an investigative team headed by Bolden determined that faulty "O-ring" seals in a solid-rocket booster had caused the *Challenger* disaster.

Manned space flight resumed in 1988, and in April 1990, Bolden piloted the shuttle *Discovery* as a five-member crew launched the $1.5 billion *Hubble Space Telescope*. This powerful instrument provides information about the universe that would be impossible to acquire with ground-based equipment. Orbiting at a record-setting altitude, more than 400 miles above the surface of Earth, the crew conducted experiments and used a variety of cameras to photograph their home planet.

Bolden commanded the crew of the shuttle *Atlantis* on a nine-day mission beginning March 24, 1992. This flight was a multinational effort in which scientists representing NASA, the European Space Agency, Belgium, France, Germany, the Netherlands, Switzerland, and Japan conducted experiments designed to yield information about Earth's climates and atmosphere. In one experiment, the crew used a beam of electrons to trigger an auroral discharge similar to the northern lights. Although Bolden was a career military officer and a pilot, for him the surprises of scientific discovery were one of the greatest joys of space travel. He has said, "People always ask me, 'What are we going to discover?' I don't know. I don't have any idea. If I knew, we wouldn't have to go."

In 1992, as NASA dealt with budget cutbacks and a tarnished public image resulting from allegations of mismanagement and lingering memories of the *Challenger* explosion, the agency's new director, Daniel Goldin, appointed Bolden assistant deputy administrator of NASA. Based in Washington, D.C., Bolden evaluated efficiency within the agency and reported to Congress.

Bolden made his fourth and final shuttle flight in 1994, when he commanded a joint U.S. and Russian crew aboard the *Discovery*. Following this mission, he left NASA to return to active duty in the marines and completed a one-year tour as deputy commandant of the U.S. Naval Academy. In 1995, he was appointed assistant wing commander of the 3rd Marine Aircraft Wing, stationed at Miramar, California.

In July 1997, he was stationed in Japan as deputy commanding general, 1st Marine Expeditionary Force (1 MEF). From February through June 1998 he was commanding general of 1 MEF in support of Operation Desert Thunder, the Kuwait-based military effort to force the government of Iraq to permit United Nations inspectors free access to suspected weapons sites. Promotions came with regularity; in July 1998, Bolden was promoted to major general and returned to his post in Japan. Beginning in 2002, he was deputy administrator of NASA.

Bolden retired from the U.S. Marine Corps on January 1, 2003, and worked in private industry. Then, on May 23, 2009, President Barack Obama appointed Bolden to head NASA. The Senate confirmed the appointment on July 15, 2009, making Bolden the first African-American permanent administrator of the space agency. (FREDERICK DREW GREGORY served as acting administrator in 2005.) Bolden's awards include three NASA Exceptional Service Medals (1988, 1989, and 1991), the NASA Outstanding Leadership Medal (1992), Defense Superior Service Medal, Defense Meritorious Service Medal, Distinguished Flying Cross, Air Medal, Strike/Flight Medal, and University of Southern California Alumni Award of Merit (1989). He has received honorary degrees from the University of Southern California, Winthrop College, and Johnson C. Smith University.

Further Reading

Bigelow, Barbara Carlisle, ed. *Contemporary Black Biography*. Vol. 7. Detroit: Gale Research, 1994, pp. 16–18.

Burns, Kephra, and William Miles. *Black Stars in Orbit: NASA's African-American Astronauts*. San Diego, Calif.: Gulliver Books, 1995, pp. 58–69.

"Charles F. Bolden Jr." Marathon. Available online. URL: http://www.marathon.com/About_Marathon/Corporate_Profile/Board_of_Directors/Charles_F_Bolden_Jr/. Downloaded on August 2, 2008.

Phelps, J. Alfred. *They Had a Dream: The Story of African-American Astronauts*. Novato, Calif.: Presidio Press, 1994, pp. 145–162.

Bowser, Mary Elizabeth

(ca. 1839–unknown) *former slave who spied in the home of Jefferson Davis during the Civil War*

When one of his generals complained to Confederate president Jefferson Davis that the "enemy not only knows everything going on within our lines, but seems absolutely to know what we intend doing in the future as if the most secret counsels of our cabinet were divulged," he had no idea that decisions made in those confidential meetings had been revealed to Union leaders by an African-American servant in Davis's household.

The future spy, a slave named Mary Elizabeth, was born on the plantation of John Van Lew near Richmond, Virginia, around 1839. Upon Van Lew's death, Mary Elizabeth and the other plantation slaves became the property of Van Lew's wife and his daughter, Elizabeth Van Lew. According to some reports, Van Lew died in 1843; other accounts state that he died in 1851. It is known, however, that around 1851 the women of the Van Lew family freed their slaves. Elizabeth Van Lew had been educated in Philadelphia by Quakers and had returned to Richmond a zealous abolitionist who believed that any government permitting slavery "is arrogant, is jealous and intrusive, is cruel, is despotic."

Mary Elizabeth remained in the Van Lew family's employ as a servant, as did another former slave named Minton, who is thought to have been her father. Elizabeth Van Lew recognized that Mary Elizabeth was intelligent and sent her to Philadelphia for schooling. Mary Elizabeth remained in the North until the start of the Civil War, when she returned to Richmond to work for the Van Lews. In Richmond she married a free African American named William or Wilson Bowser.

As an active but covert Union sympathizer, Elizabeth Van Lew nursed imprisoned Union soldiers and helped many to escape, often hiding them in her mansion, Church Hill. The escapees gave Van Lew valuable information on Confederate troop movements and strategies; she then encoded the information and conveyed it to Generals Ulysses S. Grant and Benjamin Butler and other Union military leaders. She feigned mental illness to cover the secrecy of her work and acquired the nickname Crazy Bet.

Van Lew's next tactic was to spy directly on Jefferson Davis, president of the Confederacy, and she did so by securing employment for Bowser in Davis's Richmond home. There, by pretending to be dull-witted "Ellen Bone," Bowser was allowed access to conversations among Davis and his advisers as she served their meals. Assumed to be illiterate, she studied letters and dispatches as she straightened and dusted. Bowser was able to remember accurately large amounts of detailed information, which she passed along to Van Lew on regular visits to Church Hill. At times she conveyed what she had learned to Thomas McNiven, a Richmond baker who spied for the Union, when he made deliveries to the Davis home.

Bowser recorded much of her espionage activity in a diary that has since been lost. After Richmond fell to the advancing Union forces in 1865, she went north, and history lost track of her; the place and date of her death are unknown. The U.S. government destroyed its records on Van Lew and her agents after the war in order to protect its spies from retaliation by Confederate sympathizers.

On June 20, 1995, Bowser was inducted into the U.S. Army Military Intelligence Corps Hall of Fame at Fort Huachuca, Arizona. According to the written account prepared by army researchers for that occasion, "Ms. Bowser certainly succeeded in a highly dangerous mission to the great benefit of the Union effort. She was one of the highest-placed and most productive espionage agents of the Civil War."

Further Reading

Hine, Darlene Clark, ed. *Black Women in America: An Historical Encyclopedia.* Brooklyn, N.Y.: Carlson Publishing, 1993, pp. 157–158.

Ryan, David D., ed. *A Yankee Spy in Richmond: The Civil War Diary of "Crazy Bet" Van Lew*. Mechanicsburg, Pa.: Stackpole Books, 1996.

Sakany, Lois. *Women Civil War Spies of the Union*. New York: Rosen Publishing Group, 2004, pp. 36–46.

Williams, Jasmin K. "Mary Elizabeth Bowser—Tea and Secrets." *New York Post*. Available online. URL: http://www.nypost.com/seven/03272008/news/cextra/mary_elizabeth_bowser___tea_and_secrets_103665.htm. Downloaded on August 3, 2008.

Branch, Frederick C.

(1922–2005) *first African-American officer in the Marine Corps*

Although denied the opportunity to serve as an officer in World War II, Frederick Branch made history after the war's end, when he was commissioned a second lieutenant in the U.S. Marine Corps, and again, during the Korean War, when he commanded white marines.

Frederick Clinton Branch was born on June 24, 1922, in Hamlet, North Carolina. He was the fourth of seven sons born to an American Methodist Episcopal Zion minister and his wife. He enrolled in historically black Johnson C. Smith University, in Charlotte, North Carolina, after graduating from high school, but transferred to Temple University in Philadelphia.

In 1943, with the United States engaged in World War II and thousands of young men joining the armed forces, Branch took a test to qualify for training as an army officer. Before learning that he had passed, however, he was drafted into the Marine Corps and sent to the Montford Point Training Center, a camp for African Americans located on swampy, forested land five miles from Camp Lejeune, North Carolina, where white marines trained.

In 1943, the Marine Corps was permitting some outstanding black recruits to act as drill instructors; nevertheless, Branch completed his training at Montford Point under white commissioned and noncommissioned officers. "I felt it wasn't right," he said, but when he expressed a renewed desire to secure an officer's rank, his superiors offered no encouragement. "They told me to shut that blankety-blank stuff up about being an officer," Branch recalled.

Most of the recruits at Montford Point were trained for noncombat duty, to be stewards or messmen or to guard and deliver ammunition, although two units—the 51st and 52nd Defense Battalions—were being trained for combat. Branch volunteered for duty with the 51st, which spent 19 months in the Pacific but never saw action, and in 1945 he was selected for the navy's V-12 program, a college-level preparatory course for future officers, which he completed at Purdue University. Branch, the only African American in a class of 250, made the dean's list. He was then

Frederick C. Branch smiles as his wife, Camilla Robinson Branch, pins a second lieutenant's bars to his uniform. *(National Archives)*

sent to Quantico, Virginia, as the sole African American in the 16th Platoon Commander's Class, Marine Corps Officer Candidate School.

Previously, three African-American marines had entered officer candidate school, but none had graduated. Branch stayed the course, and on November 10, 1945, the 170th anniversary of the founding of the Marine Corps, was commissioned a second lieutenant. With the war over, he was placed on inactive duty although he remained active in the reserves. In 1949, he commanded an African-American volunteer unit in Philadelphia.

The following year, Branch returned to active duty in the Korean War. As a first lieutenant, he was assigned to Quantico and later to Camp Pendleton, California, where he served with the 1st Anti-Aircraft Artillery Automatic Weapons Battalion, as a platoon commander and then as battery executive officer and battery commander. With the armed forces moving steadily toward integration, Branch was placed in command of an all-white platoon. He has said that racism in no way impeded his ability to carry out his duties, stating, "I went by the book and trained and led them; they responded like Marines do to their superiors."

Branch was not the only African-American marine to gain greater opportunities to serve during the Korean War. In 1950, when the conflict began, half of the 1,075 African Americans in the Marine Corps were mess stewards. By 1953, when the warring nations were negotiating the terms of armistice, there were more than 15,000 African-American marines, most of them serving in combat units.

Branch remained in the reserves after the war, was promoted to captain in 1954, and resigned his commission in 1955. Having decided that he wanted to teach, he had returned to Temple University, where he earned a degree in physics and completed graduate courses in physics, chemistry, mathematics, and science education. Thus prepared, he taught science in the public schools of

Philadelphia for 35 years and developed the science program at Murrell Dobbins High School.

On July 9, 1997, Branch was guest of honor as the Marine Corps dedicated its remodeled academics building, which had been named in his honor in consideration of his distinguished work in education. In July 1999, he was inducted into the Montford Point Hall of Fame. He died of an infection in 2005, at age 82, and was buried with full military honors at Marine Corps Base Quantico. On April 25, 2005, Senators Elizabeth Dole and Richard Burr of North Carolina introduced a resolution in the U.S. Senate honoring Frederick C. Branch.

Further Reading

Culp, Ronald K. *The First Black United States Marines: The Men of Montford Point, 1942–1946.* Jefferson, N.C.: McFarland and Co., 2007.

"First Black Marine Officer Frederick C. Branch Has Base Building Named in His Honor." *Jet* 92, no. 11 (August 4, 1997), p. 18.

Schudel, Matt. "Frederick C. Branch: Was 1st Black Officer in U.S. Marine Corps." *Washington Post,* April 13, 2005, p. B6.

"Senators Dole, Burr Sponsor Resolution Honoring Frederick C. Branch." U.S. Senator Richard Burr. Available online. URL: http://burr.senate.gov/public/index.cfm?FuseAction=PressReleases. Detail&PressReleas e_id=7a2a7888-80d7-460d-bbf3-01dace91799b&Month=4&Year=2005. Downloaded on August 3, 2008.

Shaw, Henry I., Jr., and Ralph W. Donnelly. *Blacks in the Marine Corps.* Washington, D.C.: History and Museums Division, U.S. Marine Corps, 1975.

Brashear, Carl Maxie

(1931–2006) *first amputee to be certified as a U.S. Navy diver, first African-American U.S. Navy master diver*

Carl Brashear put himself through a rigorous course of rehabilitation after his leg was severed in

1966 and became the first amputee to be certified as a navy diver in 1968. Two years later, he was the first African American to be certified as a U.S. Navy master diver.

Brashear was born in Tonieville, Kentucky, to parents who were sharecroppers, and he attended school through the eighth grade. Explaining why he enlisted in the navy on February 25, 1948, he said, "I always dreamed of doing something challenging."

He quickly learned that in the military he would have to seek his own challenges. After he completed basic training, the navy assigned him to Key West, Florida, as a steward. President Harry Truman had recently signed Executive Order 9981, ending segregation in the U.S. armed forces, but African Americans in the navy had traditionally been limited to steward service.

Brashear requested and received a transfer to a beachmasters' unit after observing navy crews swimming into the Gulf of Mexico to beach seaplanes. He developed into a strong swimmer and learned to love the sea, and then one day he saw a navy deep-sea diver suiting up. Immediately, he knew what he wanted to do. He applied several times to the Naval Diving and Salvage School in Bayonne, New Jersey, and was finally accepted in 1954.

The next challenge he had to face was racism. Brashear regularly received anonymous threats, but he stayed with the program, and in 1955 he became the first African American to graduate from the school. He was not the first black navy diver, though; during World War II there were three. Historically, navy divers have conducted underwater surveys and performed search and rescue missions, ship and submarine maintenance, and demolition or salvage operations. Today their duties also include antiterrorism activities and spacecraft retrieval. Brashear completed a high school equivalency course to qualify for further diver training, and in 1964 he graduated from the Deep-Sea Diving School in Washington, D.C., as a first-class diver.

On March 23, 1966, Brashear took part in the recovery of a hydrogen bomb that had fallen into the Mediterranean Sea near the fishing village of Palomares, Spain, after the collision of a B52-G bomber of the U.S. Air Force Strategic Air Command and a KC-135 tanker during an attempted midair refueling. The operation was well underway when a towing line broke loose, sending a heavy pipe smashing into Brashear's left leg and nearly severing it.

He was flown to the Naval Regional Medical Center in Portsmouth, Virginia, where doctors battled to save his leg. Eventually, unable to halt persistent infection and tissue death, they amputated the leg below the knee. Believing that "It's not a sin to get knocked down. It's a sin to stay down," Brashear spent 10 long months of recovery and rehabilitation before returning to active duty; in March 1967 Senior Chief Brashear was assigned to Harbor Clearance Unit TWO, a mobile salvage unit, and in April 1968 he was recertified, thus becoming the first amputee to be a certified navy diver. In 1970 he was the first African American to attain the designation U.S. Navy Master Diver.

In 1979, Brashear retired from the navy as a master chief boatswain's mate and master diver after more than 30 years of service. He went to work as a civilian at Naval Station Norfolk, Virginia. He retired from the federal payroll in 1993 and in 2000 saw his heroism portrayed by Cuba Gooding, Jr., in the film *Men of Honor.*

After Brashear's death from respiratory failure at Portsmouth Naval Medical Center in 2006, his sons Dawayne and Phillip Brashear began the Carl Brashear Foundation to raise public awareness of their father's inspiring achievements. On October 24, 2007, the Newport News, Virginia, Fire Department dedicated a 30-foot (9.1-meter) high-speed fireboat named the *Carl Brashear* to be used by its dive and marine incident response teams. The U.S. Navy scheduled the christening and launch of the USNS *Carl Brashear* (T-AKE 7), a cargo ship, for September 18, 2008.

Brashear's military decorations included the Good Conduct Medal (eight awards), Navy Commendation Medal, Navy Achievement Medal, National Defense Service Medal, China Service Medal, Korean Service Medal, United Nations Medal, Navy and Marine Corps Medal, Armed Forces Expeditionary Medal, Presidential Unit Citation, and Navy Occupation Service Medal.

Further Reading

"Carl Brashear, Navy Diver, Dies at 75." MSNBC.com. Available online. URL: http://www.msnbc.com/id/14031320/. Downloaded on May 29, 2008.

"Master Chief Boatswain's Mate Carl Maxie Brashear, UNS (Ret.)." Naval Historical Center. Available online. URL: http://www.history,navy.mil/faqs/faq105-1.htm. Downloaded on May 29, 2008.

The Reminiscences of Master Chief Boatswain's Mate Carl M. Brashear, U.S. Navy (Retired). Annapolis, Md.: U.S. Naval Institute, 1998.

Thomas, Joseph J., ed. *Leadership Embodied: The Secrets to Success of the Most Effective Navy and Marine Corps Leaders.* Annapolis: Naval Institute Press, 2005, pp. 165–167.

"USNS *Carl Brashear* (T-AKE-7)." Carl Brashear: The Legacy of Courage Lives On. Available online. URL: http://www.carlbrashear.org/usns_brashear.html. Downloaded on May 29, 2008.

Brooks, Vincent K.

(Vincent Keith Brooks)
(1958–) *brigadier general, commander of the 1st Infantry Division, Fort Riley*

As a deputy operations director with Forward Headquarters Staff of U.S. Central Command (CENTCOM), Brigadier General Vincent K. Brooks served as the chief spokesperson for the U.S. military during the war in Iraq in 2003 and 2004.

Vincent Keith Brooks was born in Anchorage, Alaska, on October 24, 1958, the son of Leo A. Brooks, Sr., an army officer, and Naomi Brooks, a teacher. Like most military families, the Brookses moved frequently, making their home wherever Leo Brooks, Sr., was stationed. Over the course of his childhood, Vincent lived not only in Alaska but also in Texas, West Germany, Kansas, Virginia, and California.

Throughout his school years, Vincent was a straight-A student who looked forward to a career in medicine. His plans changed during his junior year at Jesuit High School in Carmichael, California, the same year his brother, Leo Brooks, Jr., was a plebe, or freshman, at the U.S. Military Academy. When Vincent observed his brother in uniform during the Christmas break, he decided that he, too, would attend the academy.

At West Point, Vincent Brooks was a diligent cadet who excelled physically, militarily, and academically. In 1979, as he began his fourth and final year at West Point, he became the first African American in the academy's history to serve as first captain. Although an African-American cadet was no longer a rarity at West Point, the selection of Brooks for the highest student post pushed him into the media spotlight and generated controversy and hate mail. Brooks strove, he said, "To make it clear that the corps of cadets was in good hands, that I had been chosen for a good reason ... that there was trust and confidence."

Brooks achieved his goals as first captain and graduated from the military academy on May 27, 1980, first in his class in military discipline. Second Lieutenant Vincent K. Brooks then embarked on an army career that took him to Panama, Europe, and the Middle East. He rose in rank, and in the early 1990s served as a major in the 1st Cavalry Division under General Wesley Clark. Clark, who has since retired, called Brooks "a no-nonsense leader who has studied his profession carefully, works hard and delivers."

Brooks continued his education as an army officer, earning a master of military art and science degree in 1999 from the School of Advanced Military Studies at the U.S. Army Command and

General Staff College, Fort Leavenworth, Kansas. He was also a National Security Fellow at the John F. Kennedy School of Government at Harvard University.

Subsequently, Brooks led a force of 3,000 on a peacekeeping mission with the 101st Airborne Division in Kosovo. In 1999, NATO had intervened militarily in this province of the former Yugoslavia to halt atrocities against ethnic Albanians being carried out by forces under Serbian president Slobodan Milošević. Upon completion of that assignment, Brooks was placed in command of the 1st Brigade, 3rd Infantry Division, at Fort Stewart, Georgia.

President George W. Bush nominated Brooks for promotion to brigadier general on June 6, 2002, making Brooks the youngest officer ever nominated for general. When the Senate confirmed the promotion later that year, Brooks held the same rank as his father, who retired from active duty in 1984, and his brother, who in 2002 became commandant of cadets at West Point and has since retired from active duty. The Brookses were the first African-American family to produce three generals and one of the few families of any race with three generals in two generations. To Vincent Brooks, his family set an example for youth from all walks of life. "[W]e are role models to a lot of young people, not just African Americans and soldiers," he said. "People can see the achievement and how hard work leads to it." Brooks was also the first general in his class at West Point.

Brooks was working at the Pentagon and living in northern Virginia with his wife, Carol, a physical therapist, in February 2003, when he was called to MacDill Air Force Base in Tampa, Florida, to join CENTCOM. His duties as a deputy operations director with CENTCOM Forward Headquarters Staff soon took him to the troubled Middle East.

Because Iraqi leader Saddam Hussein had repeatedly denied United Nations weapons inspectors access to critical sites within his coun-

try, President Bush had given him until 8 P.M. Eastern Standard Time on March 19, 2003, to leave Iraq and enter exile. When Hussein ignored the deadline, the United States and its coalition allies initiated military action. In the days that followed, as U.S. missiles struck Baghdad and U.S. and British ground troops marched into southern Iraq, Brooks acted as chief spokesperson for the military, giving daily press briefings that were broadcast around the world. Each morning he outlined the progress of the war, presented still and video images of coalition bombs hitting their targets, and responded to tough questions from journalists.

On April 24, 2004, Brooks reported to the Pentagon to assume the duties of deputy director for the war on terrorism, J-5, Joint Staff. In this position, he helped develop policies and procedures for controlling the global proliferation of nuclear weapons. In December 2004, he was appointed chief of Army Public Affairs.

On February 23, 2007, the army honored the Brooks family during a Black History Month event at the Library of Congress in Washington, D.C. Although his parents and brother attended, Brigadier General Vincent Brooks, who was then deputy commanding general of the 1st Cavalry Division, was on active duty in Iraq. On March 25, 2008, the army chief of staff announced Brooks's assignment as special assistant to the commanding general of III Corps and Fort Hood. Fort Hood, in central Texas, is one of the largest military posts in the world. Approximately 55,800 soldiers were assigned to the fort in March 2008. In April 2009, Brooks took command of the 1st Infantry Division at Fort Riley, Kansas.

General Brooks's military decorations include the Defense Superior Service Medal, Legion of Merit (with Oak Leaf Cluster), Defense Meritorious Service Medal, Meritorious Service Medal (with seven Oak Leaf Clusters), Joint Service Commendation Medal, Army Commendation Medal (with Oak Leaf Cluster), and Army Achievement Medal (with Two Oak Leaf Clusters).

Further Reading

Harris, Hamil R. "Black History Event Pays Tribute to Veterans' Service." *Washington Post,* March 1, 2007, p. A6.

Latty, Yvonne. *We Were There: Voices of African American Veterans, from World War II to the War in Iraq.* New York: Amistad, 2004, pp. 177–181.

Neill, Alex. "Chief Briefer Says West Point Prepared Him for Spotlight." Gannett News Service. Available online. URL: http://wtsp.gannettonline.com/gns/iraq/20030421-21460.shtml. Downloaded on August 3, 2008.

"Vincent Brooks." *Current Biography.* Available online. URL: http://www.hwwilson.com/currentbio/cover_bios/cover_bio_6_03.htm. Downloaded on August 3, 2008.

Brown, Erroll M.

(ca. 1950–   ) *rear admiral, first African-American flag officer in the Coast Guard*

Erroll Brown was born in Oklawaha, in central Florida. His family moved to the city of St. Petersburg, on Florida's west coast, when he finished the second grade. As a student at Dixie Hollins High School in St. Petersburg, Brown looked forward to attending Florida Agricultural and Mechanical University—until he received a recruiting postcard from the U.S. Coast Guard Academy at New London, Connecticut. The engineering programs offered at the academy looked appealing, so he applied for admission and was accepted.

Ensign Brown graduated from the Coast Guard Academy in 1972 with a degree in marine engineering. Individuals working in this specialized field apply the principles of engineering to improve the design, manufacture, and use of seagoing vessels and to lessen the impact of ships on the marine environment. By 1972, the Coast Guard had begun to reduce its presence in Southeast Asia; therefore, at a time when many men and women in other branches of the armed forces were

fighting in Vietnam, Brown first served aboard the Coast Guard icebreaker *Burton Island* as damage control assistant and assistant engineering officer.

Brown quickly learned that "[m]ilitary service, and the Coast Guard in particular, offers a whole bunch of opportunities and challenges that are unique." For him, the educational opportunities open to a Coast Guard officer were among the choicest. He earned two master's degrees from the University of Michigan, one in naval architecture and marine engineering and the other in industrial operations and engineering. In 1986, he received a master of business administration (MBA) degree from Rensselaer Polytechnic Institute in Troy, New York, and in 1994 he graduated from the Naval War College with a master's degree in national security and strategic studies.

Brown's career highlights include service as engineering officer aboard the Coast Guard cutter *Jarvis* and as executive officer aboard the cutter *Rush.* He was an instructor of marine engineering at the Coast Guard Academy. He also was military assistant to the secretary of transportation and chief of the Budget Division in the Office of the Chief of Staff, U.S. Coast Guard Headquarters, Washington, D.C. More recently he was commanding officer of U.S. Coast Guard Integrated Support Command in Portsmouth, Virginia, and commander of Maintenance and Logistics Command Atlantic in Norfolk, Virginia.

On July 1, 1994, Brown was promoted to captain, and in July 1998, he became the first African-American admiral in Coast Guard history. Upon being promoted to rear admiral, Brown was "shocked, humbled and honored," he said. "Less than 1 percent of officers make it to flag rank, so it's a significant accomplishment."

In June 2000, along with his wife, the former Monica Hayes of Groton, Connecticut, and their two children, Aaron and Elise-Estee, Brown relocated to Bellingham, Washington. On June 2, he took command of the Coast Guard's 13th District, neering and logistics. He was the Coast Guard's highest-ranking engineer and was responsible for 2,000 military and civilian personnel and naval, civil, and aeronautical engineering projects. His many awards include the Legion of Merit, the Meritorious Service Medal, the Secretary's Award for Meritorious Achievement, two Coast Guard Commendation Medals, and the National Defense Service Medal. He is a member of the American Society of Naval Engineers, the Society of Naval Architects and Marine Engineers, and the American Society of Engineering Educators.

Further Reading

Bates, Bryna L. "Coast Guard's First Black Admiral: Erroll M. Brown Breaks 207-Year Barrier." *Ebony* (August 1998). Available online. URL: http://findarticles.com/p/articles/mi_m1077/is_n10_v53/ai20971223. Downloaded on August 5, 2008.

"Erroll M. Brown Coast Guard's First African-American Admiral." U.S. Department of Defense. Available online. URL: http://www.defenselink.mil/news/newsarticle.aspx?id=27387. Downloaded on August 5, 2008.

Hawkins, Walter L. *Black American Military Leaders.* Jefferson, N.C.: McFarland and Co., 2007, pp. 64–65.

Rear Admiral Erroll M. Brown was the Coast Guard's first African-American flag officer. *(Courtesy of the Department of Defense)*

which encompasses the states of Washington, Oregon, Idaho, and Montana. This was a high-profile assignment, one of only nine such positions in the Coast Guard. Stationed in Seattle, Brown was responsible for 1,827 active-duty military and civilian personnel, 600 reservists, and 1,600 uniformed Coast Guard Auxiliary volunteers. The staff under his command rescued boaters in distress, interrupted international drug traffic, and safeguarded the environment. Brown also oversaw the operation of the only three icebreakers then in use in the U.S. military. These ships were deployed primarily for research in the Arctic Circle and the Antarctic.

Rear Admiral Brown retired from the Coast Guard in 2005 as assistant commandant for engi-

Brown, Jesse

(1944–2002) *decorated Vietnam veteran, secretary of veterans affairs under President Bill Clinton*

A battlefield wound that left him disabled for life profoundly influenced the course of Jesse Brown's career. For more than 30 years, as secretary of veterans affairs and in the private sector, he dedicated himself to the welfare of those who fought in America's wars.

Jesse Brown was born on March 27, 1944, to a single mother, Lucille Brown of Detroit, Michigan. Lucille Brown moved briefly to Alabama with Jesse and his sister, Dorothy, 21 months his junior, but in 1958, the Browns settled in Chicago, where

Jesse attended Hyde Park High School. After graduating in 1963, he enlisted in the Marine Corps.

Brown's unit was sent to Vietnam to take part in the escalating military conflict in that divided nation. In 1965, while he was on patrol near the coastal city of Da Nang in South Vietnam, a sniper's bullet shattered his right arm, leaving it permanently paralyzed. Although he was awarded the Purple Heart, the Presidential Unit Citation, and the Vietnam Service Medal, Brown has insisted that he was no battlefield hero. "I was just one of the 300,000 people that got wounded [in Vietnam]," he stated matter-of-factly in 1992.

Brown was flown to the United States for treatment and underwent a year of physical therapy at Great Lakes Naval Hospital, near Chicago. As he learned to use his left hand for writing and other tasks, he worried about his future. "[T]here were not very many jobs for black people that were productive, and most of those that were involved manual labor," he explained. At the time, he asked himself, "What can I do now?"

His question was answered when he came into contact with the Disabled American Veterans (DAV). This congressionally chartered nonprofit organization helps veterans with disabilities related to their military service get benefits to which they are entitled. DAV offered Brown a job, and from 1967 to 1973 he was national service officer for the organization's Chicago bureau. In that position, he interviewed veterans, determined their disability status and requirements, and helped them apply for benefits. He also earned an associate's degree from Kennedy-King Junior College, which is part of the Chicago City College System, graduating with honors in 1972. Additionally, Brown completed courses at Roosevelt University in Chicago and Catholic University in Washington, D.C.

In 1973, Brown moved to the nation's capital to become supervisor of appeals at DAV headquarters. He joined the organization's legislative staff in 1982, and was named its first African-American director in 1988. In that role he oversaw a staff of 320 serving approximately 2 million disabled veterans nationwide. As director, he lobbied Congress to protect veterans' interests, and he secured benefits for Vietnam-era veterans affected by post-traumatic stress disorder and health problems resulting from exposure to Agent Orange.

In December 1992, the newly elected Clinton nominated Brown to be secretary of veterans affairs. (On March 15, 1989, according to a bill signed into law by President Ronald Reagan in 1988, the Veterans Administration had become the Department of Veterans Affairs, the 14th cabinet department.) Veterans' groups praised the nomination. Said Joseph Guido of the DAV's Chicago office, "He knows what it's like to go through the VA rehabilitative system, to face vets one on one, to talk about problems and to do something about problems." At his January 9, 1993, confirmation hearing before the Senate Veterans' Affairs Committee, Brown stressed his commitment and his competence, saying that he had "an intimacy with veterans' issues that can only come from hard work, every day, year in, year out. . . ." The Senate easily confirmed the nomination on January 21, 1993.

Calling himself "secretary *for* veterans affairs," Brown had responsibility for a government department employing 260,000 people and with a budget of $34.3 billion. He was in charge of the government's effort to provide health care, disability pensions, and social services to the nation's 27 million veterans.

Brown assumed the cabinet post at a time when the reputation of the VA hospital system had been sullied by reports of poor management and substandard service. Also, constituents were angry over looming budget cuts and a Bush-administration proposal to open some VA hospitals to nonveterans. Brown dedicated himself to improving the system's efficiency, extending benefits to more veterans, and developing programs for homeless and drug-dependent veterans; he secured a $1.2 billion increase in the VA budget in fiscal year 1994. In 1993, he was named to First

Lady Hillary Rodham Clinton's unsuccessful Health Care Reform Committee.

Brown left the VA in 1997 to form Brown and Associates, a consulting firm. In addition, he became executive director of the foundation sponsoring an American Veterans Disabled for Life Memorial in Washington, D.C., after President Clinton signed a bill authorizing the memorial on October 24, 2000.

Jesse Brown died on August 15, 2002, of amyotrophic lateral sclerosis, also known as Lou Gehrig's disease. At the time of his death, Brown and his wife, Sylvia, made their home in Warrenton, Virginia. They had two grown children, Scott and Carmen, and a granddaughter. In 2006, DAV began awarding the Jesse Brown Memorial Youth Scholarships. To be eligible, applicants must volunteer for at least 100 hours at a VA medical center in the calendar year of application.

Further Reading

Barringer, Felicity. "Clinton Selects Ex-Mayor for H.U.D. and an Ex-Marine for Veterans Affairs." *New York Times,* December 18, 1992, p. 32.

Clare, D. "Jesse Brown Scholarships Encourage Youth Volunteerism." *DAV Magazine* 48, no. 4 (July/August 2006), p. 21.

Locin, Mitchell. "'I Was Just One of the 300,000.'" *Chicago Tribune,* December 18, 1992, p. 22.

Scott, Matthew S. "The New Powers That Be." *Black Enterprise* 23, no. 8 (March 1993), pp. 76–79.

Stein, Sharman. "Insiders Predict New Boss Will Be a Hard-Driving Head of Veterans Affairs." *Chicago Tribune,* December 26, 1992, p. 10.

Brown, Jesse Leroy

(1926–1950) *first African American to fly for the navy, Korean War hero, first African-American naval officer to have a ship named for him*

Jesse L. Brown accomplished much in his brief life. Not only did he demonstrate to the U.S. Navy that African Americans were capable of flying its planes, thus opening the door to pilot training for others of his race, but he also distinguished himself in battle. He touched the hearts of his fellow citizens when he became a casualty of war.

Jesse Leroy Brown was born on October 13, 1926, in Hattiesburg, Mississippi, a racially divided farming community that had witnessed nine lynchings since 1890. The Browns were poor sharecroppers, and as a boy Jesse worked alongside his family picking cotton when he was not in school. His relatives remembered him pausing in his work whenever a plane flew overhead to gaze into the sky and predict, "Some day I'm going to fly one of those."

Jesse excelled in athletics at all-black Eureka High School, where he was on the track, basketball, and football teams. He was also a diligent student who put in extra time studying with the principal, Nathaniel R. Burger, to prepare for college. He was salutatorian of the 1944 graduating class and then spent three years at Ohio State University. In 1946, while in college, Brown joined the U.S. Naval Reserve, and in 1947 he became an aviation cadet and began flight training at Pensacola, Florida. Although blacks had flown for the Army Air Corps in World War II, navy pilots had always been white. Breaking the navy's color barrier, he endured insults and harassment from the white pilot candidates, but his determination kept him going, as did encouragement from his wife, the former Daisy Pearl Nix of Hattiesburg, whom he married secretly in October 1947, while still in flight training.

On October 21, 1948, Brown received his "Wings of Gold," becoming the first African American to fly for the navy. December 23, 1948, was another memorable date in his life: His daughter, Pamela, was born on that day.

Brown had been commissioned an ensign and assigned to an aircraft carrier, the USS *Leyte,* when the North Korean army invaded South Korea on June 25, 1950. Almost immediately, President Harry S. Truman ordered U.S. military

Jesse L. Brown stands with other recent graduates of the navy's pilot-training program at Pensacola, Florida, 1947. *(Library of Congress)*

forces into action against North Korea, and on September 6, the *Leyte* left Norfolk, Virginia, to join Task Force 77, whose mission was to provide tactical air support to ground forces. The *Leyte* reached Sasebo, Japan, on October 8, and the crew made final preparations for combat operations.

Jesse L. Brown flew his first mission over Korea on his 24th birthday, October 13, 1950, and by December he had completed 20 successful missions and had earned the Korean Service Medal and the Air Medal. His Air Medal citation stated,

in part: "Leading his section in the face of hostile antiaircraft fire, he vigorously pressed home his attacks, thereby materially contributing to the success of his division in inflicting serious losses upon the enemy and providing effective support for friendly ground forces." He had also gained the friendship and respect of his white fellow pilots and the admiration of the black mess attendants and seamen aboard ship.

On December 4, 1950, Brown was one of four pilots ordered to help the 1st Marine Division, which was surrounded by communist troops near the Chosin Reservoir, in mountainous country about 40 miles inland. He had completed a series of attacks on hostile positions when he radioed the other pilots that he had been hit by enemy gunfire, and that he was losing oil pressure. Unable to maintain altitude and miles from the nearest landing field, he crash-landed in a snow-covered forest clearing. His plane broke apart upon impact, but the other pilots could see from the air that he was still alive.

As the strike leader called for a marine rescue helicopter, Lieutenant Thomas J. Hudner crash-landed his own plane and attempted to free Brown, who was trapped in the smoldering wreckage of his F4U Corsair. Despite the heroics of Lieutenant Hudner, Brown died of injuries sustained in the crash before rescuers were able to free him. He was posthumously awarded the Purple Heart and the Distinguished Flying Cross for his courage and competence, and he had the unfortunate distinction of being the first black naval officer to die in the Korean War.

The African-American community keenly felt the loss of the first black naval pilot, especially when the press reported that, after learning of his death, Daisy Brown received a letter written by her husband on the night before his final mission. This warm, intimate letter contained words of love and loneliness, but in it Brown also described his devotion to duty. "Knowing that he's helping those poor guys on the ground," he wrote, "I think every pilot here would fly until he dropped in his tracks."

In March 1972, the navy honored Brown by launching the destroyer escort USS *Jesse L. Brown* at Avondale Shipyards, Westwege, Louisiana. This was the first navy ship named for an African American. In 1994, the navy decommissioned the *Jesse L. Brown*, took it out of active service, and sold it to Egypt.

Further Reading

Hardesty, Von, and Dominick Paisano. *Black Wings: The American Black in Aviation.* New York: HarperCollins, 2008, pp. 120, 130.

"The Last Days of a Navy Pilot." *Ebony* 6, no. 6 (April 1951), pp. 15–17.
Taylor, Theodore. *The Flight of Jesse Leroy Brown.* Annapolis, Md.: Naval Institute Press, 2007.
Weems, John E. "Black Wings of Gold." *Proceedings of the U.S. Naval Institute* 109, no. 7 (July 1983): 35–39.

Brown, Roscoe Conkling, Jr.

(1922–   ) *Tuskegee Airman, one of the first African Americans in World War II to shoot down a German jet, president of Bronx Community College*

As a fighter pilot who reacted quickly to the presence of German jets during a World War II bomber-escort mission and became the first member of the Fifteenth Air Force to shoot down an enemy plane, Roscoe Brown viewed himself as a leader. He applied lessons learned in the skies over Europe to become a national leader in the field of education.

Roscoe Conkling Brown, Jr., was born in Washington, D.C., on March 9, 1922, to parents with intellectual interests. His father, Dr. Roscoe C. Brown, Sr., held a degree in dentistry from Howard University. As director of the National Negro Health Movement of the U.S. Public Health Service, he served in President Franklin D. Roosevelt's unofficial "black cabinet" of advisers on issues related to African Americans. Brown's mother, Vivian Kemp Brown, was a teacher who had graduated from Virginia Union University. Through their parents, young Roscoe and his sister, Portia, met W. E. B. DuBois, Mary McLeod Bethune, and other prominent African Americans. The Browns took their children to the Smithsonian Institution, where Roscoe saw the *Spirit of St. Louis,* in which Charles Lindbergh crossed the Atlantic in 1927, and other historic planes.

Roscoe Brown, Jr., attended Washington's Paul Laurence Dunbar High School, which he called "the best segregated school in history." Among

Dunbar's outstanding teachers were men and women with doctorates who had been turned down for jobs in universities because of their race. Dunbar's faculty encouraged the students to achieve, and a high percentage of the school's graduates went on to college. Military training was part of Brown's high school experience as well. Not only did he take part in a junior ROTC program, but he also spent summers in a Citizens' Military Training Camp, earning a commission as a lieutenant in the Army Reserve after four years of participation.

Brown was a premed major at Springfield College in Massachusetts and graduated in March 1943 with high honors. Three days later, with the nation at war, he was called to active duty in the army. He had heard about the 322nd Fighter Group, consisting of three squadrons of African-American pilots, which was training for assignment overseas. Knowing that prior to this war African Americans had been barred from flying military planes and wanting to be part of aviation history, he resigned his Army Reserve commission and enlisted in the Army Air Force.

He was sent to Tuskegee Army Air Field, a facility constructed in Alabama specifically for the training of African-American pilots, where he learned to fly the P-47. After earning his wings in March 1944, he proceeded to Walterboro Air Base in South Carolina for advanced training. Even for a young man who had grown up in the segregated city of Washington, racial inequality in the armed forces was difficult to stomach. As officers, Brown and his fellow pilots strived for the rights and privileges that whites of equal rank enjoyed. They achieved a small measure of equality by repeatedly refusing to sit apart from white officers in Walterboro's movie theater. Rather than create an incident and generate negative publicity, the army suspended the separate-seating rule.

His training complete, Brown was placed in command of the 100th Fighter Squadron of the 322nd Fighter Group, Fifteenth Air Force. Sent to Ramitelli Air Base in Italy, these Tuskegee Airmen had two days to learn to pilot the P-51 Mustang, the plane they would be using to support troops on the ground and provide escort during bombing and photo-reconnaissance missions.

On March 25, 1945, Colonel BENJAMIN O. DAVIS, JR., commanding officer of the 322nd, led Brown and others on the longest escort mission ever flown by the Fifteenth Air Force. The mission entailed flying 1,600 miles round trip to Berlin, where bombers would attack the Daimler-Benz tank works. Brown, who had completed about 60 previous missions, was flying at the rear of his squadron's formation and breaking in a new flight leader when enemy planes came in from the left. He radioed to the others that he was taking the lead, ordered them to drop back, and went after the German fighters. He managed to get one in his gun sight, fired, and scored a hit. The enemy pilot ejected just moments before his damaged plane exploded.

Other pilots scored hits that day, but Brown was the first member of the Fifteenth Air Force to shoot down an enemy plane. He celebrated upon returning to Ramitelli by taking up his refueled P-51, buzzing the field, and flying upside down and under telephone lines. For successfully carrying out this mission, the 322nd was awarded the Distinguished Unit Citation. Brown's service in World War II earned him the Distinguished Flying Cross and the Air Medal with eight Oak Leaf Clusters.

Speaking of the 322nd Fighter Group, Brown said: "Every person in that unit wanted to fly. But we also wanted to improve the quality of life for our people. We knew we were different, and everyone was watching us." Their wartime experience, he continued, "helped to make us the men we needed to be, to come back and do the many, many things that had to be done."

Brown was discharged from the army at war's end, having reached the rank of captain. Confident that doors had been opened for blacks in postwar America, he applied for a job as a pilot with Eastern Airlines—only to have a white clerk throw his application in the trash and explain, "We don't hire colored." Brown then decided to pursue education as a career, to create opportunities for himself and others. He taught physical education at West Virginia State College from 1946 until 1948. He then returned to school and earned a master of arts degree and a doctorate from New York University in 1949 and 1951, respectively, conducting research in exercise psychology.

Brown was director of the Institute of Afro-American Affairs and professor of education at New York University from 1950 through 1977. From 1977 until 1993, he was president of Bronx Community College of the City University of New York (CUNY). He subsequently became director of the Center for Urban Education Policy of CUNY's Graduate School and University Center. He and his wife, Josephine, had four children; they later divorced.

A man with varied interests, Brown has hosted New York–based television and radio programs, including *Black Arts* (WCBS-TV, 1972–73), *Soul of Reason* (WNBC-AM/FM, 1971–86), and the 26-part series *African-American Legends* (CUNY-TV, 1994). He has written extensively on education, exercise, and African-American issues. His books include *The Negro Almanac* (1967), written with Harry Ploski; *Classical Studies on Physical Activity* (1969), with Gerald S. Kenyon; and *The Black Experience* (1972), with Mae G. Henderson and Mathias A. Freese. A long-distance runner, Brown also has completed nine New York City Marathons.

Roscoe C. Brown, Jr., has won numerous awards, most notably the Distinguished Community Service Award from the National Urban Coalition (1985), the Humanitarian Award from the Boys and Girls Clubs of America (1987), and the Congressional Award for Service to the African-American Community (1991). In 1998, the Museum of the City of New York honored him as a "New York City Treasure." He has given of his time to a great many professional, civic, and charitable organizations that are as varied as the Boys and Girls Clubs of America, the American Council on Education, the Greater Harlem Nursing Home, and the Arthur Ashe Athletic Association.

On March 29, 2007, Brown was one of 300 people—airmen and widows or relatives of airmen—who gathered in the Capitol Rotunda as President George W. Bush presented the Congressional Gold Medal to the Tuskegee Airmen. The medal is the highest honor that Congress can give to civilians. "Because of our great record and our persistence, we inspired revolutionary reform in the armed forces," Brown said on this occasion, "and provided a symbol to America that all people can contribute to this country and be treated fairly."

Further Reading

Astor, Gerald. *The Right to Fight: A History of African Americans in the Military.* Novato, Calif.: Presidio Press, 1998, pp. 191–192, 236–237, 305, 513.

Douglas, William. "WWII Black Pilots, Tuskegee Airmen, Get Top Civilian Honor." Post-Gazette Now. Available online. URL: http://www.post-gazette.com/pg/07089/773747-84.stm. Downloaded on August 5, 2008.

Kifner, John. "A Pioneer in the Cockpit, Still at the Controls." *New York Times,* August 30, 2001, p. B2.

Leuthner, Stuart, and Oliver Jensen. *High Honor: Recollections by Men and Women of World War II Aviation.* Washington, D.C.: Smithsonian Institution Press, 1989, pp. 238–247.

Brown, Wesley Anthony

(1927–   ) *first African-American graduate of the U.S. Naval Academy*

Throughout a 20-year military career, Lieutenant Commander Wesley A. Brown preferred to be recognized as "a darn good officer" rather than as someone unique, the first African American to graduate from the Naval Academy. In military and civilian life, this self-described "regular Joe" was a highly successful civil engineer.

Wesley Anthony Brown was born on April 3, 1927, in Baltimore, Maryland, and raised in Washington, D.C. His father, William Brown, was a truck driver who delivered meat and produce to city hotels. William Brown worked steadily through the Great Depression, and he was often able to bring home surplus food for his appreciative relatives and friends. Wesley's mother, Rosetta Brown, was a presser in a laundry, so Brown spent much of his childhood under his grandmother's watchful eye. As a child, Wesley sold magazines and sorted clothes for a dry cleaner to supplement the family income.

During World War II, while his mother worked days as a clerk for the burgeoning War Department in Washington, the teenage Wesley Brown held a night job sorting mail for the navy. He got to know several naval officers, and when he learned that the navy undertook numerous engineering projects, he decided to attend the U.S. Naval Academy at Annapolis, Maryland, and study engineering. On his bedroom wall he hung a picture of the USS *Lexington*, the World War II aircraft carrier nicknamed the "Blue Ghost" by Tokyo Rose because it was never covered with camouflage. Enrolled at Dunbar High School, the same school that had graduated ROSCOE C. BROWN, JR., he took courses in advanced mathematics to prepare for the academy, and he joined the school's Cadet Corps, which was founded by Civil War hero CHRISTIAN A. FLEETWOOD. Twice a week, from 7:00 to 9:00 A.M., the cadets donned uniforms, marched, and drilled.

The next step in Brown's plan to ready himself for Annapolis was to enroll in a prep school, but none would accept him because of his race. He instead enlisted in the Army Reserve, which sent him to Howard University for a year to study electrical engineering. Brown then learned that Congressman Adam Clayton Powell, Jr., of New York wished to appoint an African American to the Naval Academy. A family friend, Congressman William Dawson of Illinois, recommended Brown to Powell, and using a false New York address,

Brown received the appointment in the spring of 1945. After obtaining a discharge from the army, he entered the navy.

Five African Americans had attended the Naval Academy before Brown arrived in the summer of 1945, but they had been subjected to intense hazing and isolation, and all had dropped out. Brown met with one of those former midshipmen, George Trivers, who warned him of some of the obstacles he might face. Brown buoyed his courage by telling himself, "If anybody's ever done it, then I can do it. If no one's ever done it, then I'm going to be the first one to do it."

Brown did experience a good deal of hazing as a plebe and accumulated a hefty toll of demerits (140 of the 150 allowed during his first semester) for such minor infractions as marching out of step or talking in ranks. He sometimes suspected that he had been targeted because of his race. He interacted socially with others in his class, however, although he chose to room alone rather than subject a roommate to possible harassment at his expense. Midshipman Brown enjoyed summer cruises aboard navy vessels to such ports as London, Lisbon, and Casablanca, but when asked to state his choice of duty as graduation approached, he selected the navy's Civil Engineering Corps rather than assignment to a ship.

After graduating on June 3, 1949, with a degree in mechanical engineering, Ensign Wesley A. Brown underwent further training at the Boston Naval Shipyard in Charleston, Massachusetts. In 1951, he earned a master of chemical engineering degree from Rensselaer Polytechnic Institute, and in September of that year he was assigned to the Naval Supply Center at Bayonne, New Jersey, where he supervised the engineering design division.

Brown's naval career took him to Europe, South America, Antarctica, and Africa. From 1959 through 1962, he was assistant public works officer at Barber's Point, Hawaii, one of the largest air stations in the Pacific. As a lieutenant commander, he was the highest-ranking African American in the navy. While on special assign-

Wesley A. Brown graduated from the U.S. Naval Academy in 1949. *(United States Naval Academy)*

ment with the State Department in the early 1960s, he planned road construction in Liberia, Upper Volta, and the Central African Republic. Brown and his first wife, Jean Brown, had four children: Willetta, Carol, Wesley, Jr., and Gary.

After retiring from the navy in 1969 and receiving the Secretary of the Navy's Commendation for Achievement Medal, Brown was an engineer with the State University of New York (SUNY). He supervised construction of academic buildings, libraries, laboratories, and other facilities on the SUNY campus at Stony Brook, New York, and at Nassau Community College in Garden City, New York. From 1976 until 1988, he helped to develop a master plan for Howard University and made sure that new construction was consistent with that plan. Between 1984 and 1988, he also worked as a consultant.

Brown and his second wife, Crystal M. Brown, reside in his hometown, Washington, D.C. In 1998, Brown was appointed to the District of Columbia Water and Sewer Authority Board of Directors. He is a member of the Secretary of the Navy's Advisory Board on Naval History, the Howard University Advisory Board on Black Civil War Sailors Project, and the Association for the Study of Negro Life and History. From 1988 through 1990, Brown chaired the Congressional Nominating Review Board, U.S. Service Academies, for D.C. congressional delegate Walter Fauntroy. Beginning in 1991, he was a member of the review board for Fauntroy's successor, Eleanor Holmes Norton.

On May 10, 2008, Brown returned to the U.S. Naval Academy campus for the dedication of the Wesley A. Brown Field House. Admiral Michael Mullen, chairman of the Joint Chiefs of Staff, told the crowd in attendance that it was Brown's "noble calling and it was his call to service and citizenship that led to lasting change in our Navy and in our nation."

Further Reading

Astor, Gerald. *The Right to Fight: A History of African Americans in the Military.* Novato, Calif.: Presidio Press, 1998, pp. 340–343, 432.

Brown, Wesley A. "The First Negro Graduate of Annapolis Tells His Story." *Saturday Evening Post* 221, no. 52 (June 25, 1949), pp. 26–27, 111–112.

"First Navy Grad Makes Good." *Ebony* 15, no. 6 (April 1960), pp. 71–75.

Rucker, Philip. "Facility Dedicated to Black Pioneer." *Washington Post,* May 11, 2008, p. C3.

Bryant, Cunningham C.

(Cunningham Campbell Bryant)

(1921–2003) *first African-American general in the National Guard*

A decorated veteran of World War II, Cunningham C. Bryant spent most of his army career with the Washington, D.C., National Guard. In 1971, he became the first African-American general to serve in any National Guard unit.

Cunningham Campbell Bryant was born in Clifton, Virginia, on August 8, 1921. He was a graduate of Cardozo High School in Washington, D.C. From 1940 until 1943, when he was called to active duty in the Second World War, he attended Howard University, where he was an Army ROTC cadet. The army sent him to Infantry Officer Candidate School at Fort Benning, Georgia, and in 1944 he was commissioned a second lieutenant.

Bryant was a company commander with the 317th Engineer Battalion of the 92nd Regiment, an African-American unit that fought in Italy. Following the Italian armistice of September 3, 1943, the Germans had established a defensive line in the Apennine Mountains of northern Italy, hoping to hold the rich agricultural and industrial resources of the Po River Valley. Bryant's battalion was in the forefront of the Allied assault on the German "Gothic Line."

After the war, having attained the rank of captain, Bryant served at Fort Benning, Georgia, and Fort Belvoir, Virginia. He was promoted to major in 1949 and released from active duty the same year. Bryant went to work for the Post Office Department and remained in the U.S. Army Reserve until 1954; he and his wife, the former Hyacinth F. Bowie, had three children, a son and two daughters.

In 1954, Bryant joined the Washington, D.C., Army National Guard as a training and battalion executive officer. The 50 states, the District of Columbia, Puerto Rico, and the Virgin Islands maintain trained and equipped Army and Air National Guard units that are available for mobilization in times of war or domestic emergency. Most members are civilians serving part-time.

Bryant was promoted to lieutenant colonel in 1962, and in 1964 he was placed in command of the D.C. National Guard Officer Candidate School. His promotion to colonel came on January 1, 1968.

On July 29, 1971, when he was awarded his general's stars in a ceremony at the Pentagon, Cunningham C. Bryant became the first African-American general in the National Guard. The D.C. National Guard was then a 3,250-member organization that included a 2,000-member army unit that was 65 percent African American.

In October 1974, President Gerald Ford announced that he had named Bryant to be the next commanding officer of the D.C. National Guard. Such news usually is released at the state or local level, but Ford chose to make the announcement himself because Bryant was African American and because the District of Columbia National Guard is known as the "President's Own." Bryant was the second African American to command a National Guard unit. The first was Colonel Gerard L. James, appointed by President Richard Nixon in July 1974 to head the Virgin Islands National Guard.

Upon taking command, Bryant said that his goal would be the same as his predecessor's: to recruit and develop a corps of junior officers that would be ready to handle any emergency. "We're the posse, the volunteer fire department, and the relief agency when we're needed," he said, "and we've got to be prepared."

Brigadier General Bryant retired in 1981. His military decorations include the Bronze Star, Army Commendation Medal, Purple Heart, Army of Occupation Medal, World War II Victory Medal, National Defense Service Medal, European-African-Middle Eastern Campaign Medal with two stars, Combat Infantry Badge, and American Campaign Medal. In 2001, he received the Image Award from the District of Columbia Emancipation Day Foundation.

Further Reading

"Black Armed Forces Brass." *Crisis* 80, no. 10 (December 1973): 341–346.

"Cunningham C. Bryant." Arlington National Cemetery Web site. Available online. URL: http://www.

arlingtoncemetery.net/ccbryant.htm. Downloaded on November 22, 2008.

Daniels, Lee. "Black Slated to Head Guard." *Washington Post*, October 8, 1974, p. C1.

Greene, Robert Ewell. *Black Defenders of America, 1775–1973.* Chicago: Johnson Publishing Co., 1974, p. 234.

"Maj. Gen. Cunningham Bryant, 81." *Washington Post*, August 1, 2003, p. B4.

Bullard, Eugene Jacques

(1894–1961) American expatriate who fought for France in World War I, the only black pilot to serve in World War I

The valiant Eugene Jacques Bullard, who fled the United States to escape prejudice, fought with distinction in World War I for his adopted homeland, France. He was the first black of any nation to serve as a combat pilot.

Born in Columbus, Georgia, in 1894, Bullard was descended from Africans who had been transported to the French colony of Martinique. After his mother died when he was six years old, he was raised by his father and grandfather, a former slave. As a child, Eugene Bullard received a harsh lesson in the brutality of southern racism when his older brother Hector died at the hands of a lynch mob. On that occasion and often, Eugene's father talked to the boy about France and nurtured in him a dream of living in that idealized nation where blacks and whites viewed one another as equals.

Later, in telling the story of his life, Bullard claimed that he left home when he was eight years old, determined to find his way to France. He said that he worked at odd jobs for several years before stowing away on a German freighter bound for Scotland, where he lived by his wits. Whether that account was accurate or embellished, Bullard was in France in 1914, at the start of World War I, and enlisted in the French foreign legion. This branch of the French armed forces accepts volunteers of all nationalities who desire to serve France. He was a machine gunner with a unit known as the Swallows of Death, a fighting force renowned for its swift and furious bayonet attacks.

Later in the war, Bullard was transferred to a regular infantry unit of the French army and took part in the Battle of Verdun, the longest battle of World War I, which was part of a failed German campaign to take the offensive on the Western Front. The Germans attacked the French city of Verdun on February 21, 1916; by the time the battle ended on December 19, with the Germans pushed back to their earlier positions, 760,000 soldiers—300,000 German and 460,000 French—were missing in action, killed, or wounded.

Despite a serious leg wound received early in the battle, Bullard requested a transfer to the French Flying Corps, allegedly to win a $2,000 bet. In October 1916, French military leaders approved his request based on his record of combat heroism, and on May 7, 1917, Bullard became the world's first black fighter pilot and the only one to serve in World War I. He was one of approximately 200 Americans in the French Flying Corps.

Many of those Americans were permitted to transfer to the U.S. Army Air Force after the United States entered the war in 1917. Bullard, too, sought a transfer, but his application was rejected because of his race. He continued to fly for France and distinguished himself in battle, completing more than 20 missions against the Germans and engaging in numerous dogfights, always accompanied by his pet spider monkey, Jimmy. Reports of the number of enemy aircraft he shot down range from one to five. Once he was forced to land behind enemy lines, twice he was wounded, but he continued to fly until American officers attached to his unit succeeded in having him grounded because of his 1916 leg wound. In January 1918, he was transferred to the 170th French Infantry and served with that regiment until the November 11 armistice. His wartime bravery earned him the French Croix de Guerre.

After the war, Bullard settled in Paris, where he played drums in a Dixieland band and owned a series of nightclubs and a gymnasium. He married Marcelle Straumann, the daughter of a countess, and had two children, Lolita and Jacqueline. Always one to relish the spotlight, he engaged in exhibition boxing matches while touring Egypt.

Early in World War II, Bullard worked as a spy for the French Underground. Nazis frequenting his nightclub never suspected that a black man might understand German and spoke unguardedly in his presence. As a result, Bullard easily overheard valuable information, which he passed along to a French espionage network. Then, in 1940, with his wife recently deceased and Nazi occupation of France imminent, Bullard returned to the United States. As a black, he had special cause to fear for his safety at the hands of the "master race." French friends ensured that his daughters soon joined him in New York.

Bullard lived out his life in a small Harlem apartment, surrounded by his mementos. In the 1950s, he was an elevator operator at New York's Rockefeller Center. He returned to Paris in 1954 at the invitation of the French government to assist in rekindling the everlasting flame that burns at the Tomb of the Unknown Soldier beneath the Arc de Triomphe. In 1959, he received the Legion of Honor, awarded by France for exemplary military or civilian service. He was buried in the French Veterans' Cemetery in Flushing, New York.

Further Reading

Carisella, P. J., and James W. Ryan. *The Black Swallow of Death: The Incredible Story of Eugene Jacques Bullard*. Boston: Marlborough House, 1972.

Lloyd, Craig. *Eugene Bullard: Black Expatriate in Jazz-Age Paris*. Athens: University of Georgia Press, 2006.

Smith, Mary H. "The Incredible Life of Monsieur Bullard." *Ebony* 23, no. 2 (December 1967), pp. 120–128.

C

Cadoria, Sherian Grace
(1940–) *brigadier general*

When Sherian Cadoria was promoted to brigadier general in 1985, she became the highest-ranking African-American woman in the armed forces and one of only four female generals in the army. She was also the first woman to achieve a general's rank by rising through the military police—traditionally a man's route—rather than through the nurse corps.

Sherian Grace Cadoria was born on January 26, 1940, in the small town of Marksville, Louisiana. Because her father, Joseph Cadoria, was chronically ill, her mother, Bernice McGlory Cadoria, supported the family and raised the couple's three children. Money was tight, and even as a young child, Sherian picked cotton alongside her mother and older brother and sister to help make ends meet.

Bernice Cadoria had a strict moral code, and she expected her children to follow it. As an adult Sherian Cadoria recalled a day when the three children were shopping and a salesclerk gave them a penny too much in change. When their mother learned about the clerk's mistake, she insisted that the youngsters immediately hike back into town—a distance of five miles—to return the extra cent. All three were at fault, she said, because not one of them had alerted the clerk to the error. The punishment taught Cadoria that one person can fight injustice by speaking up to say, "This is wrong."

The children walked those five miles daily to attend Holy Ghost Elementary School in Marksville, although a bus regularly passed their home. The family preferred to avoid the humiliation of segregated seating and insults from the white drivers.

After high school, Sherian entered Southern University in Baton Rouge, Louisiana, where she majored in business education. In the summer of 1960, she spent four weeks in a Women's Army Corps (WAC) training program at Fort McClellan, Alabama. The training was tough on a college junior, Cadoria admitted, "But it was also fascinating to see the jobs and responsibilities that these young lieutenants had." The experience persuaded her to enlist in the army following graduation in 1961.

As she began her military career at Fort McClellan, however, she learned that there were limits on what was possible for African Americans in the army in 1962. Under the Jim Crow laws of the South, for example, a black officer could not take white soldiers off base. Ku Klux Klan members regularly stood outside the gates of the base to protest integration in the military and harass the African-American soldiers inside. Venturing into town, a uniformed Cadoria was refused service at the back door of a restaurant because she was black. Yet she was not intimidated; throughout her years in uniform, she would overcome more formidable obstacles, facing up to discrimination based on her race and also on her sex.

Captain Sherian Cadoria was in Vietnam from 1967 until 1969, at the height of U.S. military involvement in Southeast Asia. In late 1967, she was considered for the job of protocol officer with Qui Nhon Support Command. The interviewing colonel, hesitant to place a woman in the position, warned her that she might find the job too strenuous, because she would be required to travel frequently and to lift heavy luggage. Cadoria responded, "Nobody said I couldn't carry those hundred-pound bags of cotton when I was just a little child," and she got the job.

Although she returned to the United States a major in October 1969, Cadoria was so exhausted from more than 33 months in Vietnam that she made up her mind to leave the army and enter a convent. She learned that she was the first African-American woman selected to attend the U.S. Army Command and General Staff College at Fort Leavenworth, Kansas, but she was prepared to pass up that opportunity—until her mother persuaded her to accept it. Bernice Cadoria reminded her daughter that all African Americans—women and men alike—benefited from her achievements. Sherian Cadoria graduated from the Command and General Staff College in 1971, and in 1978 she became the first African-American woman to study at the U.S. Army War College at Carlisle Barracks, Pennsylvania. In the meantime, in 1974 she earned a master's degree in human relations from the University of Oklahoma. In 1975 and 1976, she was a White House social aide to President Gerald Ford.

In 1978, with the dissolution of the Women's Army Corps, WAC personnel were integrated into the regular army. Cadoria, who was promoted to colonel on September 1, 1980, served at posts in Europe and the United States. In August 1985, she was the first African-American woman to be appointed director of manpower and personnel for the Joint Chiefs of Staff. In that position she oversaw the placement of personnel in all branches of the armed forces, active and reserve.

On October 1, 1985, Cadoria stood proudly at attention as her mother and General Robert Elton pinned a brigadier general's stars on her shoulders. In September 1987, she became deputy commanding general of Total Army Personnel Command at Alexandria, Virginia. In that key position, it would be up to her to provide replacements for commanders in battle if the United States were to go to war anywhere in the world.

Brigadier General Sherian Cadoria retired from the army in 1990, at age 50. Never married, she settled in Pineville, Louisiana, and established a consulting firm, Cadoria Speaker and Consultancy Service. In 1997, upon learning that Holy Ghost Elementary School was in danger of closing due to a lack of funds, she volunteered to serve as the principal of her old school for a year, drawing no salary. She took over a crumbling school building in which children learned from outdated textbooks and teachers who lacked certification. Holy Ghost needed so much help that Cadoria stayed on as principal after the initial year ended. Between 1998 and 2000, students and faculty members from Benedictine University in Lisle, Illinois, offered their assistance, traveling to Marksville to repair the building and serve as tutors and mentors to the 175 students in kindergarten through grade eight.

Cadoria's military decorations include the Legion of Merit, three Bronze Stars, two Meritorious Service Medals, the Air Medal, and four Army Commendation Medals. She has received the Distinguished Alumni Award from Southern University (1984) and the NAACP's Roy Wilkins Meritorious Service Award (1989), and she was named to the Louisiana Black History Hall of Fame in 1992. In addition, she holds honorary doctorates from Ohio Dominican College and Benedictine College. On August 1, 2008, she was inducted into the Louisiana Justice Hall of Fame.

Further Reading

African Americans: Voices of Triumph: Perseverance. Alexandria, Va.: Time-Life Books, 1993, pp. 172–173.

Dent, David. "Sherian Grace Cadoria: General at the Top." *Essence* 20, no. 12 (April 1990), p. 41.

Hawkins, Walter L. *Black American Military Leaders.* Jefferson, N.C.: McFarland and Co., 2007, p. 79.

Hine, Darlene Clark, ed. *Black Women in America.* Vol. 1. New York: Oxford University Press, 2005, p. 181.

Lanker, Brian. *I Dream a World: Portraits of Black Women Who Changed America.* New York: Stewart, Tabori and Chang, 1989, pp. 150–151.

"Museum Will Induct Nine into Hall." Theadvocate.com. Available online. URL: http://www.theadvocate.com/news/24842374.html. Downloaded on August 6, 2008.

Cailloux, Andre

(1825–1863) *captain of the 1st Louisiana Native Guards, first African-American hero of the Civil War*

In May 1863, at Port Hudson, Louisiana, Union army leaders sent African Americans into battle for the first time and wondered: Would these black soldiers have the courage to fight, or would they turn and run? Under the leadership of Captain Andre Cailloux, the two African-American regiments performed competently and bravely and silenced many critics. Cailloux, who was mortally wounded in the assault, is remembered as the first African-American hero of the Civil War.

Andre Cailloux was born into slavery on an unknown date in 1825, on a plantation owned by Joseph Duvernay near Pointe à la Hache, Plaquemines Parish, Louisiana. When Andre was five years old, his master died, leaving his slaves to his wife. Duvernay's widow moved with Andre and his parents to New Orleans, where the boy learned the cigar maker's trade. He also learned to read at this time, possibly because cigar factories commonly employed "readers" who informed and entertained the workers by reading to them from newspapers and novels.

Cailloux acquired his freedom at age 21, but the circumstances of his emancipation are unknown. Soon after becoming a free man, he married Felicie Coulon, another emancipated slave. He adopted her son and would have four more children with her in the years ahead. He acquired real estate in New Orleans during the 1850s and was prosperous although far from wealthy. He enjoyed an active social life among the free black Creoles of New Orleans, belonged to the Friends of Order, and was elected secretary of this fraternal organization in 1860. Cailloux had a reputation for fine manners, and he proudly called himself "the blackest man in New Orleans."

Conforming to societal expectations at the start of the Civil War, the free African Americans of New Orleans volunteered to serve the Confederacy. The Friends of Order formed a company in the Louisiana Native Guards, an African-American militia unit, and company captain Andre Cailloux recruited as soldiers 100 men who were free, enslaved, or fugitives from slavery. The Louisiana Native Guards marched in Confederate parades, but when the Union captured New Orleans in 1862, they offered their services to Union general Benjamin Butler, thus becoming the first African-American soldiers in the Union army during the Civil War. Butler commissioned 75 African-American officers for the guards, with the result that most of the line officers in the 1st Louisiana Native Guards were black. Similar regiments, such as the 3rd Louisiana Native Guards, were led mostly by white officers. Cailloux's company—Company E of the 1st Regiment—was designated the color company and given the task of carrying the regimental banner into battle.

On May 27, 1863, the 1st and 3rd Louisiana Native Guards became the first African-American troops to participate in a major Civil War engagement when they took part in the siege of

Port Hudson, Louisiana. Union general Nathaniel Banks was determined to occupy the Mississippi River town of Port Hudson in order to gain control of the river and divide and weaken the Confederacy. The Confederates, however, were just as determined to hold the town. They had fortified Port Hudson with earthen walls 20 feet thick that were surrounded by a water-filled ditch 15 feet deep and a ring of sharpened tree branches. By the time the Louisiana Native Guards were ordered into action, the siege had been underway for six days, and the Confederates had repelled repeated Union assaults.

At 10:00 A.M., Captain Andre Cailloux led the African-American regiments into battle. Making their advance on the far right of the Union line, the African Americans marched into the fire of Confederate cannon and sharpshooters. Forming battle lines, they raised their muskets and charged the Confederate positions, with Cailloux shouting words of encouragement in French and English: "*En avant, mes enfants!* Follow me!" Forced to retreat, the 1st and 3rd regiments charged five more times under heavy fire. Cailloux, his arm already shattered by a bullet, was killed during the final charge.

The siege ended on July 9, 1863, when the Confederates surrendered Port Hudson upon learning of the fall upriver of Vicksburg, Mississippi, to General Ulysses S. Grant. In all, 7,200 Confederate soldiers and 5,000 Union men—including 600 African Americans—had died in the encounter. The battle was a victory for the Union and for the African Americans who fought in it and proved that black soldiers were the equal of whites in courage. General Banks wrote: "The severe test to which they were subjected, and the determined manner in which they encountered the enemy, leaves upon my mind no doubt of their ultimate success."

Cailloux's body lay on the battlefield 41 days before being returned to New Orleans for an elaborate funeral. One hundred thirty-five years later, in November 1998, New Orleans honored Andre Cailloux and all African-American Civil War veterans with a jazz Mass and the placing of a plaque near Cailloux's grave in St. Louis Cemetery No. 2.

Further Reading

McPherson, James M. *The Negro's Civil War.* New York: Ballantine Books, 1991, pp. 188–189.

Mullener, Elizabeth. "Remembering Bravery." Reprinted from the *New Orleans Times-Picayune*, October 31, 1998. Netdoor. Available online. URL: http://www2.netdoor.com/~jgh/bravery.html. Downloaded on August 6, 2008.

Ochs, Stephen J. *A Black Patriot and a White Priest: Andre Cailloux and Claude Paschal Maistre in Civil War New Orleans.* Baton Rouge: Louisiana State University Press, 2000.

Smith, Jessie Carney, ed. *Notable Black American Men, Book II.* Detroit, Mich.: Thomson Gale, 2007, pp. 102–104.

Carney, William Harvey

(1840–1908) *Civil War sergeant, hero of the Battle of Fort Wagner, first African American to be awarded a Medal of Honor*

On July 18, 1863, with his regiment leading an attack on a heavily fortified Confederate position that was bound to result in many casualties, Sergeant William Carney spoke eloquently through his actions. By carrying the American flag to the battlefront, he turned a failed charge into a statement of patriotism on behalf of every African-American soldier and earned the Medal of Honor.

William Harvey Carney was born in Norfolk, Virginia, on February 29, 1840, to William Carney, Sr., a free African American, and Ann Dean Carney, who was enslaved. Little is known about William Carney's childhood, but he and his mother were freed in 1854, and he briefly attended a clandestine school run by a minister. The clergyman's influence on the boy was profound, and at age 15 William felt called to devote his life to God. In 1856, Carney's father removed his family from the South and settled them in New Bedford, Massachusetts, where William worked at a series of jobs and saved for his training in the ministry.

With the outbreak of the Civil War, however, Carney's religious vocation was permanently deferred. At first, blacks were denied the right to participate in this "white man's war," largely because many whites believed that they lacked the courage and intelligence to be effective soldiers. The Union army abandoned that policy in 1863, out of necessity, and began accepting African-American recruits; on February 17 of that year, William Carney enlisted in the Massachusetts 54th Colored Infantry, the first African-American regiment formed in a free state and one of the most celebrated units to fight in the Civil War. (The 54th Infantry was the subject of the 1990 film *Glory*, starring Denzel Washington.) As in all black units in the segregated Union army, every officer in the unit above the rank of lieutenant was white. Commanding the regiment was 25-year-old Robert Gould Shaw, who was from a prominent Massachusetts abolitionist family.

On May 28, 1863, after completing training at Camp Meigs, Massachusetts, and cheered by the largest crowd to date ever to assemble in Boston, the 54th Infantry departed for the coastal islands of South Carolina. Less than two months later, the men were ordered to participate in the assault on Fort Wagner, a Confederate installation located on sandy Morris Island at the entrance to the harbor at Charleston, in an effort that was part of the Union campaign to take control of that city. Protected by a waist-deep moat and double walls of sand and logs, defended by 16 to 20 cannon, and large enough to hold 1,700 Confederate soldiers, the fort was a formidable target. Yet Gould volunteered the 54th to lead the charge, recognizing an opportunity to demonstrate the valor of his regiment.

The first assault on Fort Wagner began at dusk on July 18. Approximately 600 men of the 54th

William H. Carney was awarded the Medal of Honor for valor displayed on July 18, 1863, during the Battle of Fort Wagner. *(Library of Congress)*

got within 60 feet of the fort, but intense enemy fire forced them to retreat. The second assault got underway after dark, and this time there was no turning back.

Carney saw Colonel Shaw reach the top of the earthen parapet protecting Fort Wagner only to be hit by a Confederate bullet and die. When he saw Sergeant John Wall, the regiment's color bearer, fall as well, he stepped forward to become a hero. Sergeant William Carney of Company C took the American flag from the hands of his stricken comrade and hurried into the thick of the fight. This battle was an especially brutal one in which half of the men in Carney's Massachusetts regiment would be killed or wounded by both enemy and friendly fire. In the darkness, some panicked soldiers were firing at anything that moved. Carney himself was wounded three times, but he managed to hold the flag high as he mounted the parapet. He planted the colors atop the thick wall, guiding the men toward their goal. The sight of the national flag bolstered the soldiers' courage and reminded them of the values for which they fought.

On that summer night, the Union forces attacking Fort Wagner were no match for the Confederates defending it. "They mowed us down like grass," was one discouraged participant's comment. When the order came to retreat, Carney again lifted the Stars and Stripes. A white soldier from a New York regiment saw him struggling and offered to help, but Carney declined any assistance, stating, "No one but a member of the 54th should carry the colors." Reaching the field hospital behind Union lines, he boasted to the survivors of his regiment, "Boys, the old flag never touched the ground."

In recognition of his bravery and patriotism, Carney became the first person of his race to be awarded the Medal of Honor, although he would not be issued his medal until May 23, 1900. His citation read, "For conspicuous gallantry and intrepidity at the risk of life, above and beyond the call of duty, in action involving actual conflict with an opposing armed force." Carney's wounds left him with some permanent disability, and he was honorably discharged from the army at Black Island, South Carolina, on June 30, 1864.

In October 1864, Carney married Susanna Williams of New Bedford, the first African-American woman to graduate from New Bedford's high school and one of the first African Americans to teach in the Massachusetts public schools. The couple had one daughter, Clara, who taught piano as an adult. In 1867, the Carneys moved to San Francisco, where William Carney was employed as a shipping clerk. The family returned to Massachusetts in 1869, and Carney delivered mail in New Bedford for 32 years. After retiring from the post office in 1901, he worked as a messenger at the State House in Boston.

A local celebrity, Carney spoke at Memorial Day gatherings, and in 1897 he participated in the dedication of a monument to the 54th Infantry sculpted by the American artist Augustus Saint-Gaudens, which stands on Boston Common. He took pleasure in pointing out to visitors the flag he had carried at Fort Wagner, which was—and continues to be—displayed at the State House.

William Carney died on December 9, 1908, of injuries received in an elevator accident. The governor of Massachusetts ordered the flag flying outside the State House lowered to half-mast in his honor.

Further Reading

Doherty, Kieran. *Congressional Medal of Honor Recipients.* Springfield, N.J.: Enslow Publishers, 1998, pp. 19–27.

Garraty, John A., and Mark C. Carnes, eds. *American National Biography.* Vol. 4. New York: Oxford University Press, 1999, pp. 421–422.

Lee, Irvin H. *Negro Medal of Honor Men.* New York: Dodd, Mead, 1969, pp. 24–26.

Palmer, Colin A., ed. *Encyclopedia of African American Culture and History.* Vol. 2. Detroit, Mich.: Thomson Gale, 2006, p. 414.

Carter, Edward Allen, Jr.

(1916–1963) *Medal of Honor recipient, California's most-decorated African-American World War II veteran*

In 1997, the U.S. government awarded the Medal of Honor to Edward A. Carter, Jr., for battlefield heroism in 1945. Not only did Carter die before his contribution was properly recognized, but he also died believing that his country considered him unworthy to serve.

Carter was born in Los Angeles, but his parents, Edward A. Carter, Sr., and Mary Carter, were missionaries who took their young son first to India and then to the busy port of Shanghai, China. Unlike his mother and father, young Edward longed for the glory of a soldier's life, and at 15 he ran away to join the Chinese Nationalist Army, which was responding to threats from imperialist Japan and a growing, militant communist movement. The military authorities soon discovered Edward's age, however, and sent him home to his parents. Back in Shanghai, Edward enrolled in a military school with a curriculum that emphasized foreign languages, including German, and combat training.

School was nothing like the real thing, though, and by 1937, Carter was in Spain, battling for the Loyalist cause. The democratically elected Spanish Republican government was fighting against an attempted military takeover led by General Francisco Franco, who was receiving support from Nazi Germany and Fascist Italy. Idealists and intellectuals from countries around the world had flocked to Spain in support of the Republicans, or Loyalists, and many fought with the all-volunteer International Brigades. Carter signed on with the Abraham Lincoln Brigade, an American unit, whose members also included OLIVER LAW. For African Americans such as Carter and Law, the struggle in Europe against the extreme nationalism represented by fascism paralleled the unceasing effort by blacks in their own country to achieve equality.

After Spanish prime minister Juan Negrín withdrew the International Brigades from battle in spring 1938, Carter went to Paris and then to the United States. Still yearning for a soldier's life, he enlisted in the U.S. Army on September 26, 1941. The United States entered World War II a little more than two months later, but Staff Sergeant Carter had stateside assignments until 1944, when he went to Europe as part of a supply unit.

At the time, the Allies were pushing their way into Germany. Losses were heavy, so in December 1944, the Allied supreme commander, General Dwight D. Eisenhower, instituted the Ground Force Replacement Command to draw volunteers from noncombat duty to take the place of battlefield casualties. The command welcomed black soldiers as well as whites, and by February 1945 more than 4,500 African Americans had been assigned to units attached to previously all-white infantry and armored divisions. Carter volunteered and was assigned to the Seventh Army Infantry, Company 1 (Provisional), attached to the 56th Armored Infantry Battalion, 12th Army Division, which was advancing with General George Patton's Third Army toward the German city of Speyer on the Rhine River with the objective of securing bridges.

On March 23, 1945, Carter was riding on a tank that came under enemy fire, which seemed to come from a warehouse in an outlying area. Carter offered to lead a patrol to the site and headed toward the warehouse with three soldiers. To approach the building, the men had to cover 150 yards of open space exposed to German guns. When one of the soldiers was killed, Carter sent the others back, ordering them to seek shelter and to cover him with their weapons while he advanced. He was soon on his own, though, because both soldiers were shot (one fatally).

Carter reached a protective ridge about 30 yards from the warehouse, wiped out two German machine-gun nests and a mortar crew, and then exchanged fire with the Germans inside. Bullets from machine guns tore into Carter and knocked him to the ground. He was badly wounded on the left side—in the arm, leg, and hand. He also sustained three shrapnel wounds that would cause him pain for the rest of his life.

Eight German soldiers emerged from the warehouse, intending to silence forever this troublesome American. Carter lay motionless, fooling the approaching party into assuming he was dead—until, without warning, he opened fire with his .45-caliber machine gun. He killed six of the Germans and captured the other two, using them to shield his body as he retreated to the tank. Although his wounds required treatment, he refused to be evacuated until he had given a full report and interrogated his prisoners about enemy positions.

Edward Carter had shown extraordinary bravery, and he was awarded the Distinguished Service Cross, the army's second-highest decoration and the highest military honor given to any African American serving in World War II. By October 1945, he had also received the Bronze Star, Purple Heart, American Defense Service Medal, and Combat Infantry Badge. After the war, he was stationed at Fort Lewis, Washington.

Carter tried to re-enlist in 1949, but to his amazement, the army turned down his request because of suspicions that he was a communist. Bitter and "disappointed in democracy," he mailed his Distinguished Service Cross to Herbert M. Levy, staff counsel for the American Civil Liberties Union, with the request that it be returned to President Harry Truman. "In my country's hour of need I was in the front lines with a submachine gun," he stated. "My reward? A stab in the back." Carter went to work in the automobile tire business, raised a family, and in 1962 was diagnosed with lung cancer. He died at UCLA medical center in Los Angeles on January 30, 1963, at age 47, still saddened and confused by the army's rejection of him.

Three decades later, hoping to right a larger wrong, the army commissioned a team of historians to determine why no African Americans had received the Medal of Honor during the war and recommend individuals who had deserved it. The investigators' report, titled *The Exclusion of Black Soldiers from the Medal of Honor in World War II*, was based on solid scholarship and placed the blame for this grievous oversight on the white commanders of the war years, who considered black personnel inferior. The historians identified 10 men whose actions were worthy of recognition with the Medal of Honor, and the army selected seven of these to be so honored, including Staff Sergeant Edward A. Carter, Jr. Only one of the soldiers, VERNON J. BAKER, was still living.

On January 13, 1997, President Bill Clinton presented the Medal of Honor to Baker and to surviving relatives of the other six recipients, including Carter's son, Edward A. Carter III. Soon afterward, Carter was reburied with full military honors at Arlington National Cemetery.

The fact that an acknowledged hero was denied the opportunity to re-enlist in the army continued to bother Carter's family. Under the provisions of the Freedom of Information Act, his daughter-in-law, Allene Carter, obtained copies of 57 pages of declassified documents pertaining to Carter's military service. These told her that army intelligence officers had kept Carter under surveillance since 1941, because of his past service with the Abraham Lincoln Brigade, which had attracted many communists, although in eight years the army had uncovered no evidence of his disloyalty.

On November 10, 1999, the government made amends for such mistreatment of a brave and loyal soldier to the extent that this was possible. In a ceremony at the Pentagon, Clinton, assisted by Army Vice Chief of Staff John Keane, offered a full apology to the Carters and the nation. Clinton presented to the Carter family a set of corrected military records and posthumous awards of the Army Good Conduct Medal, Army of Occupation Medal, and American Campaign Medal.

In February 2000, "An American Hero," an exhibit at the California Military Museum in Old Sacramento, surveyed the military career of Edward A. Carter, Jr., the state's most-decorated African-American World War II veteran.

Further Reading

"Army Issues Official Apology to Wronged World War II Medal of Honor Winner." *Jet* 96, no. 26 (November 20, 1999), pp. 46–47.

Carroll, Peter N., Michael Nash, and Melvin Small, eds. *The Good Fight Continues: World War II Letters from the Abraham Lincoln Brigade.* New York: New York University Press, 2006, pp. 253–254.

Carter, Allene G., and Robert L. Allen. *Honoring Sergeant Carter: A Family's Journey to Uncover the*

Truth about an American Hero. New York: Amistad, 2004.

"The Making of a Hero: Staff Sgt. Edward A. Carter, Jr." Military Sealift Command. Available online. URL: http://www.msc.navy.mil/N00p/pressrel/press01/press21.htm. Downloaded on August 15, 2008.

McPherson, Ernest. "Staff Sergeant Edward A. Carter: Medal of Honor Recipient." The California State Military Museum. Available online. URL: http://www.militarymuseum.org/Carter.htm. Downloaded on August 15, 2008.

Cartwright, Roscoe Conklin

(1919–1974) *first African-American brigadier general from the field artillery*

Roscoe Conklin Cartwright was born on May 27, 1919, in Kansas City, Kansas, and raised in Tulsa, Oklahoma. Growing up, he rarely saw African Americans in military uniform. His teachers were his role models, and after graduating from Booker T. Washington High School in 1936, he entered Kansas State Teachers College to prepare for a career in education. The United States was in the midst of the Great Depression, though, and Cartwright's family was experiencing financial hardship. Unable to afford to remain in school, Roscoe Cartwright went home and worked for the University of Tulsa and a soft-drink bottling company.

Cartwright was drafted into the army in 1941 and assigned to the 349th Field Artillery Regiment at Fort Sill, Oklahoma. He completed Officer Candidate School in November 1942 and was commissioned a second lieutenant in the 599th Field Artillery Battalion of the 92nd Infantry Division, the African-American unit that fought courageously in Italy during World War II and suffered heavy casualties. Cartwright was promoted to first lieutenant on August 24, 1944.

The 599th returned to the United States after the war ended and was stationed at Camp Robinson near Little Rock, Arkansas. While there, Cartwright met and married Gloria Lacefield of Hope, Arkansas. The Cartwrights would have two sons and two daughters.

Cartwright was promoted to captain on June 15, 1950, and served in Korea in the integrated army. From 1951 through 1955, he was an instructor in the ROTC program at West Virginia State College. During that period, on August 18, 1954, he was promoted to major. Cartwright also furthered his own education while in the army. He received a bachelor's degree in social sciences from San Francisco College in June 1960, and he later would earn a master's degree in business administration from the University of Missouri.

On November 28, 1961, Cartwright, who was known as the Rock, was promoted to lieutenant colonel. Two years later, he assumed the duties of comptroller at the army garrison at Fort Leavenworth, Kansas. He became a mentor to younger officers at Fort Leavenworth and offered them career guidance and advice. He also was a founder of the No Name Club, an organization of African-American commissioned officers that fostered professional and social interaction.

The Cartwrights moved to the Washington, D.C., metropolitan area in August 1966, when Lieutenant Colonel Cartwright first served in the office of the comptroller of the army. From August 1968 through June 1969, he attended the Industrial College of the Armed Forces at Fort McNair in Washington.

In August 1969, the army sent Cartwright, who was now a colonel, to Vietnam. He was assigned first as commander of the 108th Artillery Group and then as deputy commanding officer of the United States Army Support Command at Cam Ranh Bay, Vietnam. Always striving to offer opportunities for improvement to those under him, Cartwright created a library for military personnel in Vietnam and established college courses taught by accredited teachers in uniform.

Cartwright left Vietnam in July 1970 to join the office of the assistant chief of staff for force development in Washington. In July 1971, he was named a special assistant in that office.

On August 1, 1971, President Richard M. Nixon promoted Cartwright to brigadier general, making him the first African-American general in U.S. history to rise from the ranks of the field artillery. Soon afterward, Cartwright became director of management, review, and analysis in the office of the comptroller of the army in Washington.

General Cartwright spent his final years of active duty stationed in Heidelberg, Germany, from February 1972 through July 1973 as assistant division commander of the 3rd Infantry Division, Europe, and beginning in August 1973 as deputy chief of staff, Office of the Comptroller, U.S. Army, Europe, and Seventh Army. He retired on August 31, 1974.

Settling with his wife in Oxon Hill, Maryland, Cartwright joined the National Petroleum Council, a policy-making body of the oil industry, as a director. On December 1, 1974, Roscoe and Gloria Cartwright were flying home from Columbus, Ohio, where they had been visiting a daughter, when their jetliner crashed as it approached Dulles Airport in heavy rain. All 92 people aboard the plane died.

Soon afterward, the members of the No Name Club voted to call themselves The Rocks, Inc., in Cartwright's honor. They also established the Roscoe C. Cartwright Memorial Scholarship Fund. The organization now maintains 23 chapters, including one in Iraq. Members serve as mentors for junior African-American officers, raise funds for scholarships, and provide speakers to historically black colleges and universities.

Further Reading

Hawkins, Walter L. *Black American Military Leaders.* Jefferson, N.C.: McFarland and Co., 2007, pp. 86–87.

"Roscoe Conklin Cartwright, Brigadier General." Real African American History. Available online. URL: http://www.raahistory.com/military/army/cartwright.htm. Downloaded on August 8, 2008.

Shaffer, Ron. "Final Tribute Paid to Black General." *Washington Post* (December 7, 1974), pp. D1–D3.

Smith, J. Y., and Martha M. Hamilton. "General, Hill Aides Among 92 Victims." *Washington Post,* December 2, 1974, p. C1.

Cary, Mary Ann Shadd

(1823–1893) *Civil War recruiting officer, journalist, teacher, lawyer*

Mary Ann Shadd Cary left the peace and freedom of Canada during the Civil War to enlist black soldiers in the Union army. She is thought to have been the only woman commissioned as a recruiting officer in the Civil War.

Mary Ann Shadd was born in Wilmington, Delaware, on October 9, 1823, the oldest of 13 children. Her parents, Abraham Doras and Harriet Shadd, were free African Americans who frequently sheltered runaway slaves passing through Delaware, a state in which slavery was allowed. When Shadd was 10 years old, she entered Prince's Boarding School in West Chester, Pennsylvania, which had been established by Quakers in 1830. She returned to Wilmington after six years of study and briefly operated a school for African-American children.

She was teaching in Norristown, Pennsylvania, in 1850, when the federal government enacted a stringent fugitive slave law. Denying alleged fugitives the right to a trial by jury, this law made even free African Americans vulnerable to slave hunters. Twenty thousand black Americans responded to the passing of this law by fleeing to Canada, where their rights would be protected without regard for race. In 1850, Shadd and her brother Isaac left the United States for Canada West, as Ontario was then known administratively. Within few years, the rest of the family also had immigrated, and the Shadds settled near one another in Chatham, the terminus of the Underground Railroad.

In the British colony of Canada, where blacks had opportunities that had been denied to them in the United States, Shadd began to realize her potential. In 1854, she became the first black woman to publish and edit a newspaper when she founded the *Provincial Freeman*, the first anti-slavery journal in Canada West. The paper's motto reflected Shadd's own philosophy: "Self Reliance Is the True Road to Independence." Enthusiastic about her adopted homeland, she published in 1852 A *Plea for Emigration, or, Notes of Canada West*, a pamphlet designed to persuade African Americans to migrate north. In 1855, she embarked on a lecture tour of Michigan, Ohio, Pennsylvania, and Illinois, encouraging African-American audiences to settle in Canada.

In the summer of 1856, Shadd married Thomas F. Cary of Toronto. The marriage was an unconventional one, especially for the 19th century: Thomas continued to reside in Toronto while Mary Ann remained in Chatham. She carried on her newspaper work and assisted fugitives from slavery, sometimes snatching them from the reach of slave hunters who had pursued them across the border. Through her actions she gained the admiration of prominent African Americans, including Frederick Douglass, who said, "We do not know her equal among the colored ladies of the United States."

Thomas Cary died on November 29, 1860, leaving Mary Ann with a small daughter, Sarah, and pregnant with the couple's son, Linton. For a time Mary Ann Shadd Cary depended on her parents and siblings for support, but in 1861 she was again on the road, raising funds for a racially integrated school operated by her sister-in-law Amelia Shadd in Chatham. She was in Michigan when the American Civil War began.

Cary returned to Canada in 1862 and became a naturalized British subject. She and her fellow African Canadians closely watched events in the United States. Wanting to end slavery and fearing that their own freedom might be at risk if the South were to win the war, many African-Canadian men desired to fight for the Union. Like

This is the only known photograph of Mary Ann Shadd Cary. *(David Shadd Collection/National Archives of Canada/c-029977)*

blacks in the United States, however, they initially were denied the right to serve in the U.S. armed forces. In January 1863, Massachusetts governor John Andrew was authorized to form the first black regiments in the North. Cary's brother Abraham W. Shadd enlisted in the 55th Massachusetts Infantry, which was formed in the spring of 1863. By summer, Rhode Island, Ohio, Maryland, and other states were assembling black units as well.

Cary first aided the war effort in 1863, when physician and journalist MARTIN ROBISON DELANY asked her to help him recruit soldiers for an African-American unit being established in Connecticut. She was to receive $15 for every slave and $5 for every free black she persuaded to enlist in the 29th Regiment Connecticut Volunteers. Appointed a recruiting officer by special order, she worked primarily in the Midwest, possibly risking her own freedom by venturing into Kentucky to lure potential soldiers away from slavery. Canvassing in free states was dangerous as well: Whites in the Midwest were increasingly antiblack as large numbers of refugees from slaveholding states crossed their borders. The town of New Albany, Indiana, where Delany had his headquarters, had been the scene of an 1862 race riot lasting 30 hours.

In 1864, Cary was one of several recruiters hired by Governor Oliver P. Morton of Indiana to raise the 28th U.S. Colored Infantry, which was based in Indianapolis. Between 800 and 1,500 African Americans were recruited in Indiana for this and other regiments; Cary's work contributed significantly to that total.

Cary returned to Chatham in fall 1864. Her brother Isaac had published the *Provincial Freeman* in her absence and continued to produce issues until the Civil War was nearing its end. After the war, the Shadds and the Carys drifted back to the United States. Isaac and Amelia Shadd moved to Mississippi, where he served several terms in the state legislature and she taught in a school for freedmen. Mary Ann Shadd Cary went to Washington, D.C., and was a teacher and principal in the Lincoln Mission School, a school for African Americans. She also contributed articles to periodicals published by Frederick Douglass and others. In 1869, she enrolled in the first class at Howard University Law School. She attended evening classes and taught during the day, and in 1883, at age 60, she at last received a bachelor of laws (LL.B.) degree and was admitted to the bar. She then devoted her energy to the practice of law and the cause of woman suffrage. In 1887 she was one of two African Americans to attend the annual congress of the Association for the Advancement of Women in New York. The other was poet and abolitionist Frances Ellen Watkins Harper.

Cary died at home of stomach cancer in 1893, at age 70. Although she visited Canada infre-

quently in later life, Canadians continue to hold her in esteem. In 1987, the city of Toronto named a school in her honor; Canadian folksinger Faith Nolan wrote a tribute to her in song.

Further Reading

Bearden, Jim, and Linda Jean Butler. *Shadd: The Life and Times of Mary Ann Shadd Cary.* Toronto: NC Press, 1977.

Hancock, Harold B. "Mary Ann Shadd: Negro Editor, Educator, and Lawyer." *Delaware History* 15, no. 3 (April 1973): 187–194.

Hine, Darlene Clark, ed. *Black Women in America.* Vol. 1. New York: Oxford University Press, 2005, pp. 189–191.

McDonald, Cheryl. "Last Stop on the Underground Railroad: Mary Ann Shadd in Canada." *Beaver* 70, no. 1 (1990), pp. 32–38.

Rhodes, Jane. *Mary Ann Shadd Cary: The Black Press and Protest in the Nineteenth Century.* Bloomington: Indiana University Press, 1998.

Chambers, Lawrence Cleveland

(1929–   ) *rear admiral, second African American to graduate from the U.S. Naval Academy*

Lawrence Chambers, the second African American to graduate from the naval academy, was its first black graduate to rise to flag rank. In the course of a 32-year career, he piloted military aircraft, commanded ships, and held positions of responsibility on land.

Lawrence Cleveland Chambers was born in Bedford, Virginia, on June 10, 1929, and grew up in Washington, D.C., under what he called "low income circumstances." His father, a mortician, died when he was a boy, leaving his mother, Charlotte Chambers, to support five children on her salary as an office worker in the War Department. As a child, Lawrence played games of battle with his younger brother, Andrew, and looked forward to being an aviator or an engineer when he grew up. "I didn't know which I wanted to do more," he said.

Both Lawrence and Andrew enrolled in an ROTC program during high school. As his graduation approached, Lawrence heeded advice from Midshipman WESLEY A. BROWN, JR., who would be the first African-American graduate of the U.S. Naval Academy in 1949, to seek admission to the academy. There, he could be educated at no expense to his family. Lawrence Chambers passed the qualifying examination and on June 30, 1948, entered the naval academy in Annapolis, Maryland, as a midshipman. On June 6, 1952, he became the academy's second black graduate.

Ensign Lawrence Chambers realized one of his childhood ambitions in November 1952, when he reported to the Naval Air Station at Pensacola, Florida, to begin pilot training. On June 9, 1954, he received his wings, becoming a naval aviator. He was promoted to lieutenant on July 1, 1956, and in August 1959 he achieved the second part of his early goal when he received a degree in aeronautical engineering from the Naval Postgraduate School in Monterey, California.

Andrew Chambers, meanwhile, followed a different route to a military career. He attended Howard University and upon graduation had achieved a second lieutenant's rank in the army through the ROTC program.

Lawrence Chambers spent most of his long naval career at sea, serving with attack squadrons and aboard aircraft carriers. He was promoted to lieutenant commander on September 1, 1961; when he was promoted to commander, on July 1, 1966, he was stationed on land at the Naval Postgraduate School in an administrative position. He and his wife, Phyllis, had two daughters, Lori and Leila.

From 1968 through 1971, Chambers participated in the Vietnam War as a fighter pilot, flying missions from the aircraft carriers USS *Ranger* and USS *Oriskany*. He was promoted to captain on July 1, 1972, and placed in command of the USS *White Plains*. Nicknamed the "Orient Express," this combat replenishment vessel transported supplies, fuel, spare parts, and mail to aircraft carriers and their escorts.

From January 1975 through December 1976, Chambers was in command of the USS *Midway*, which evacuated more than 3,000 U.S. personnel and South Vietnamese citizens following the fall of Saigon in April 1975. When a single-seat Cessna airplane carrying fleeing South Vietnamese major Buong Ly and six members of his family had no place to land, Captain Chambers made a controversial decision and ordered helicopters valued at $10 million dumped into the South China Sea to create landing space on deck and save the lives of those aboard the plane.

On August 1, 1977, when Chambers attained the rank of rear admiral, he was stationed in St. Louis, Missouri, with the Bureau of Naval Personnel. In August 1979, he was made commander of Carrier Group 3, comprising six ships, 85 planes, and 6,000 personnel, stationed in the Indian Ocean. Next, as commander of the USS *Coral Sea*, he spent 102 days in Middle Eastern waters supervising air operations and maintaining a military presence near Iran, where more than 50 Americans had been taken hostage.

The senior African-American officer in the navy, Chambers enjoyed a friendly rivalry with his brother, Andrew, who reached the rank of lieutenant general in the army. "My brother and I have always had philosophical differences," Admiral Chambers said, adding that "all in all, I think both of us have done quite well."

In May 1981, Admiral Chambers began his final navy assignment, with Naval Air System Command in Arlington, Virginia. He retired on March 1, 1984. His military decorations include the Bronze Star, the Meritorious Service Medal, the China Service Medal, and the Vietnam Service Medal with three Bronze Stars.

Further Reading

"Admiral Chambers Heads Persian Gulf Naval Force." *Jet* 57, no. 26 (March 13, 1980), p. 57.

"Brothers-in-Arms." *Ebony* 37, no. 1 (November 1981), pp. 118–121.

Hawkins, Walter L. *Black American Military Leaders.* Jefferson, N.C.: McFarland and Co., 2007, pp. 88–89.

Charlton, Cornelius H.

(1929–1951) *Medal of Honor winner who died leading an attack on an enemy position during the Korean War*

In 1951, while fighting in Korea, Sergeant Cornelius Charlton demonstrated a rare courage when he disregarded his own safety in order to achieve his mission. The United States honored him posthumously with the Medal of Honor.

Cornelius Charlton was born in East Gulf, West Virginia, on July 24, 1929. He was the eighth of 17 children born to Van Charlton, a coal miner, and his wife, Esther. In 1944, the family moved to the Bronx, New York, where Van Charlton was superintendent of an apartment building, and Cornelius, who was called Connie, enrolled in James Madison High School. World War II was being fought in Europe and the Pacific, and Connie envied the young men going overseas in uniform. Eager to be part of the war, he begged his parents to let him drop out of school and join the army, but they refused to be part of that plan. When he graduated in 1946 as insistent as ever, although the war was over, they signed his enlistment papers, giving 17-year-old Connie permission to become a soldier.

Cornelius Charlton entered the army in November 1946, and after completing basic training was stationed in Germany as part of the postwar occupational force. He served out his enlistment in Germany and upon reenlisting was assigned to an engineering battalion at Aberdeen Proving Ground in Maryland.

In 1950, the army sent Sergeant Cornelius Charlton first to Okinawa and then to Korea, where he worked at a desk job while other U.S. military personnel fought the North Koreans and Chinese in the Korean War. Charlton had joined the army to do battle; not content to sit out another war, he requested a transfer to the front lines and was assigned to Company C of the 24th Infantry.

This once-proud Buffalo Soldier regiment, which had served with distinction on the frontier and in Cuba, was reeling from accusations of cowardice due to its disappointing performance in the early months of the Korean conflict. In September 1950, the division commander, Major General William B. Kean, had recommended that the 24th be disbanded because its members were "untrustworthy and incapable of carrying out missions expected of an infantry regiment."

A study undertaken in 1987 by the U.S. Army Center of Military History would conclude that the 24th Infantry in Korea was hampered by racial prejudice and inexperienced troops and that, all too often, the black soldiers were blamed for the failures of their white leaders. Vindication was 36 years away, however, when Charlton joined the 24th Infantry in 1951. The company commander looked with suspicion at this new squad leader who had exchanged a comfortable administrative job for service with a line regiment—until Charlton demonstrated his commitment and competence by building his squad into a model unit. By May the company commander had placed him in charge of a platoon and recommended him for a battlefield commission.

As June approached, the 24th Infantry prepared to take part in Operation Piledriver, an effort to push Chinese and North Korean forces back toward the north. On June 1, Charlton's battalion attempted to capture Hill 1147, a rocky elevation held by the Chinese. As the men proceeded under heavy mortar fire, the lieutenant leading them fell, gravely wounded. Tall, stocky Charlton immediately took command and roused the soldiers' courage. Leading the way up the slope, he single-handedly destroyed two hostile positions and killed six enemy soldiers with rifle fire and grenades.

Three times, as casualties mounted, Charlton attempted to lead a charge against the hill. Even when wounded in the chest, he refused medical attention and kept pushing forward. At last, perceiving that the enemy emplacement responsible for the barrage was on the far side of Hill 1147, he charged alone to the top of the hill and repeatedly fired his rifle to silence the Chinese guns. Hit by a grenade, he continued to shoot for as long as he was able. Charlton died that day, on June 1, 1951.

"The wounds received during his daring exploits resulted in his death but his indomitable courage, superb leadership, and gallant self-sacrifice reflect the highest credit upon himself, the infantry, and the military service," read his Medal of Honor citation. The medal was presented posthumously to Van and Esther Charlton on March 12, 1952. (The 24th Infantry had been disbanded in 1951.)

In 1952, the army named its ferryboat 84, used in New York Harbor, for Sergeant Cornelius Charlton. In September 1954, West Virginia honored this native son by dedicating the Charlton Memorial Bridge on the West Virginia Turnpike. And nearly half a century later, in 2000, the navy christened the USNS *Charlton*, a 950-foot strategic sealift vessel that carries army vehicles and supplies to points of conflict throughout the world.

Further Reading

Bowers, William T., William M. Hammond, and George L. MacGarrigle. *Black Soldier, White Army: The 24th Infantry Regiment in Korea*. Washington, D.C.: Center of Military History, U.S. Army, 1996, p. 256.

Ecker, Richard E. *Korean Battle Chronology: Unit-by-Unit United States Casualty Figures and Medal of Honor Citations*. Jefferson, N.C.: MacFarland and Co., 2005, pp. 103–104.

Murphy, Edward F. *Korean War Heroes*. Novato, Calif.: Presidio Press, 1992, pp. 175–177.

Cherry, Fred Vann

(1928–   ) *U.S. Air Force pilot imprisoned in North Vietnam*

Major Fred Cherry's scheduled departure from Southeast Asia was days away when his plane went down over North Vietnam. Instead of going home, he spent seven years in Viet Cong prisons, where he was subjected to physical and psychological torture. Ignoring the irony of his situation, Cherry managed to find its bright side. "I realized things about myself I never would have become aware of had I not had this experience," he said.

Fred Vann Cherry was born on March 24, 1928, in Suffolk, Virginia. Nicknamed Pepper as a child, he was the youngest of eight children in a family of farmers and laborers, people who kept their eyes to the ground. Pepper, in contrast, was always looking at the sky, at the navy planes from a nearby auxiliary field that frequently flew overhead.

Pepper was 11 when his father died. America was still coping with the poverty and unemployment of the Great Depression, and the boy's mother, unable to support her large family, sent him to live with his married sister, Beulah. A proponent of education, Beulah insisted that her young charge earn good grades in order to become a physician one day. Meanwhile, when he reached his teens, Fred read newspaper articles about the Tuskegee Airmen, African-American pilots training for duty with the Army Air Force in World War II.

Following high school, Fred Cherry enrolled in Virginia Union University in Richmond, where he majored in biology, although medical school was his sister's ambition for him and not his own. "What I really wanted to do was fly planes," he said. As graduation approached, he went to Langley Air Force Base in Norfolk, Virginia, and took the qualifying examinations for flight school. The only African American among 20 applicants, he received the highest score. Cherry entered the air force in October 1951, and upon completing flight

Fred Cherry contemplates a portrait of himself that hangs in the Pentagon. *(Defense Visual Information Center)*

training was sent to Korea, where he flew 52 combat missions.

In the early 1960s, when U.S. military involvement in Southeast Asia was increasing, Cherry was married with four children and was stationed in Japan. He left his family behind when he was ordered to Thailand with the 35th Tactical Fighter Squadron to fly missions over Laos in order to bomb North Vietnamese supply lines along the Ho Chi Minh Trail. As the only F-105 pilot in the squadron with previous combat experience, Cherry earned the nickname "Chief" and the esteem of his younger comrades.

On October 25, 1965, with one more week to serve in Thailand before going home, Major Fred Cherry was leading a mission over enemy territory when an ominous thump told him that his plane had been hit by gunfire from below. While he still had control of the aircraft, he flew to the target and dropped his bombs. It was then that the cockpit filled with smoke and the plane exploded.

Cherry ejected safely but managed to open his parachute only moments before hitting the ground. He landed hard, breaking his left shoulder, wrist, and ankle, and was immediately surrounded by the enemy, both military and civilian. He had become the 43rd American and the first African American captured in Vietnam. Soldiers and farmers alike marched the injured pilot through miles of rice paddies to Hoa Lo Prison, the infamous "Hanoi Hilton," where he endured three weeks of torture. Despite being beaten and having his limbs bound and stretched, Cherry revealed nothing to his captors beyond name, rank, date of birth, and service number.

On November 16, 1965, the Vietcong moved Cherry to Cu Loc Prison, which the American prisoners of war called "the Zoo." There, Cherry shared a cell with a captured navy flyer named Porter Halyburton, a white southerner with a deeply ingrained bias against blacks. As the two cellmates helped one another survive, they dropped preconceived notions and became friends.

Mistreatment was the way of life in the Zoo, but Cherry was subjected to tortures that went beyond the beatings with rubber straps and bamboo sticks and the long periods of solitary confinement that all of the inmates endured. Because his broken shoulder had failed to heal properly, North Vietnamese doctors operated in February 1966 and covered his upper body in a cast. They then proceeded to neglect his incision, and in the sultry climate of North Vietnam, under the heavy plaster, a serious infection set in. As Cherry's fever rose to dangerous levels, he hallucinated. Only Halyburton's efforts to feed him and clean the wound kept him alive. When the doctors returned a month later and removed the cast, his weight had dropped to 80 pounds.

Cherry underwent a subsequent surgical procedure lasting three hours—this time without anesthesia—for the purpose of debridement (the removal of dead or infected tissue). Experiencing the "worst straight pain" he had ever known, the African-American pilot confounded his physicians by smiling into their faces. Then, four days after Cherry was returned to his cell, the Vietcong moved Halyburton to another location. Cherry would not see his friend again until after the war.

His captors tried to destroy Cherry's loyalty to the United States through constant reminders of racial hatred at home. They talked to him about slavery, lynchings, and segregation, hoping to convince him to make videotaped statements against the nation of his birth and its goals in Vietnam.

Believing that he represented all African Americans and, indeed, all Americans, Cherry refused to be persuaded, although cooperation would have meant better treatment. "I'm just not going to denounce my government or shame my people," he said.

Cherry's more then seven years of imprisonment ended in January 1973, when the United States and North Vietnam reached an agreement on the release of prisoners of war. Cherry recovered his health after returning to the United States, but because his shoulder would never function normally again, the air force restricted him to training flights and intelligence work. His family life suffered from the long separation, however. He and his wife discovered that they had little in common after the long separation, and they divorced.

In 1981, Colonel Fred Cherry retired from the air force after 30 years of service. He settled in Silver Spring, Maryland, and was director of technical support services for E. H. White and Company and director of marketing and business development for Data Transmission Corporation and Scruples, Inc. He married and divorced again, and in 1992, he founded Cherry Engineering Support Services, Inc., a company that supervises the design and development of equipment for use in air traffic control and other flight-related fields.

Fred Cherry has received the Distinguished Flying Cross, the Silver Star, the Air Force Cross, two Bronze Stars, and two Purple Hearts. He was the 2001 recipient of the C. Alfred "Chief" Anderson Award, presented in recognition of his "shining example of courage, integrity, self-reliance, adventure and contribution to others."

Further Reading

Hirsch, James S. *Two Souls Indivisible: The Friendship That Saved Two POWs in Vietnam.* Boston: Houghton Mifflin, 2004.

Montgomery, Annette. *Suffolk.* Charleston, S.C.: Arcadia Publishing, 2005, p. 113.

Reef, Catherine. *Black Fighting Men: A Proud History.* New York: Twenty-First Century Books, 1994.

Terry, Wallace, ed. *Bloods: An Oral History of the Vietnam War by Black Veterans.* New York: Ballantine Books, 1984.

Cochran, Donnie L.

(1954–   ) *first African American to head the Blue Angels*

Donnie Cochran broke down a racial barrier in 1986 when he became the first African American to join the Blue Angels, the navy's famed flight-demonstration squadron. He made naval history again in 1994, when he was named the squadron's commander.

Donnie L. Cochran was born on July 6, 1954, and grew up on a farm near Pelham, Georgia. Like FRED VANN CHERRY, BENJAMIN O. DAVIS, JR., and many other military pilots, he learned to love flying in childhood. Military planes frequently flew over his home, sometimes so low that he could wave to the pilots. By the time he reached high school, he had decided that he, too, would fly planes and perform aerial acrobatics.

Donnie discovered a way to achieve his goal when an older brother came home to visit from Savannah State College dressed in his ROTC uniform. After finishing high school, Donnie Cochran also enrolled in Savannah State. (In fact, seven of the 12 children in the Cochran family attended this school.) Studying on a naval ROTC scholarship, he received a bachelor's degree in civil engineering in 1976.

In 1978, Ensign Cochran completed basic and advanced jet-pilot training at Naval Air Station Kingsville in Texas and was assigned to a light photographic squadron, which is trained to fly photo reconnaissance missions. He was subsequently stationed on two aircraft carriers, the USS *Nimitz* and the USS *Enterprise.* His dream, though, was to fly with the Blue Angels, and in 1984 he applied to join the navy's precision flying team, meeting all of the criteria for acceptance.

Membership in the elite Blue Angels squadron is open to navy or Marine Corps pilots who have amassed more than 1,500 flight hours in tactical jet aircraft. The application process is highly competitive, however, and Cochran was rejected. When he applied again in 1985, he had logged more than 2,000 hours flying navy jets, and this time he was accepted. At age 31, Lieutenant Commander Donnie Cochran became the first African-American member of the Blue Angels in the squadron's 40-year history. To Cochran, acceptance was "verification of the fact that you're one of the best—that you represent the expertise and professionalism that you have in the Naval fleet."

From January through March, at the Naval Air Facility at El Centro, California, where desert conditions provide many days of good flying weather, the Blue Angels prepare for their many air shows. For the rest of the year, the squadron's home base is Pensacola, Florida. Traveling with the Blue Angels often required Cochran to be apart from his wife, Donna, who worked for a mortgage company in San Diego, California, and their son, Donnie, Jr.

At speeds as great as 600 miles per hour and at altitudes ranging from 500 feet to 7,000 feet, the Blue Angels fly in tight formation, crossing one another's paths and thrilling audiences with their flips and loops. In 1986, his first year with the squadron, Cochran flew plane number three, one of the four A-4 Skyhawk jets in the group's trademark diamond formation. (The squadron leader flies in the lead jet, plane number one.) Maneuvering while their aircraft are separated by 36 inches of airspace demands extraordinary concentration and control.

Cochran made one of his most memorable flights with the Blue Angels on July 4, 1986, when the team took part in festivities honoring the restoration of the Statue of Liberty. On that occasion, he said, "What I am doing is not just a job, it's an opportunity. I would like to show young people the roads that are open to them in America." In 1987, Cochran moved to plane number four, in the rear of the formation, and was in charge of training the pilots in positions two and three. In that year, the Blue Angels began flying F-18 jets.

Navy and Marine Corps pilots serve with the Blue Angels for two years. After completing his tenure, Cochran was assigned to Naval Air Station Miramar in California and then aboard the carrier USS *Ranger*. Next, Cochran furthered his education at the Air War College in Montgomery, Alabama, and Troy State University in Troy, Alabama, where he earned a master's degree in human resource management. In March 1992, Cochran assumed the duties of executive officer with Fighter Squadron 1. He also commanded the squadron from July 1993 until it was disestablished in September 1993. He then commanded Fighter Squadron 111.

Cochran rejoined the Blue Angels in November 1994, this time as the unit's first black commander, flying plane number one in formation. He preferred to view the assignment not in terms of race but "as an opportunity to be the boss," he said. He understood, however, that his appointment was a milestone, adding, "I am perfectly aware that I am an African American."

Safety concerns led Cochran in September 1995 to ground the Blue Angels temporarily and cancel two exhibitions. "[F]or the Blue Angels safety is paramount," he said. "We simply cannot perform these demanding maneuvers unless the entire team is 100 percent ready in every respect." Commander Cochran painfully came to realize that the pilot less than 100 percent ready was himself. Disappointed with his own performance in training, he resigned from the Blue Angels on May 28, 1996.

Donnie Cochran retired from the navy in 2000 as a captain, having accumulated more than 4,600 flying hours and having made 888 successful carrier landings. He became a flight engineer for United Parcel Service in Atlanta and, later, professor of naval science at Florida A & M University in Tallahassee. His awards include the Meritorious Service Medal, Air Medal, and Navy Commendation Medal.

Further Reading

Blazar, Ernest. "Skipper Quits Blue Angels." *Navy Times* 45 (June 10, 1996): 22.

Collier, Aldore. "The First Black Blue Angel." *Ebony* 41, no. 8 (June 1986), pp. 27–34.

Phillips, Noelle. "Skills for War, Life One and the Same." Savannah Morning News on the Web. Available online. URL: http://www.savannahnow.com/stories/110201/LOCcochran.shtml. Downloaded on August 9, 2008.

Veronico, Nicholas A. *The Blue Angels: A Fly-By History, Sixty Years of Aerial Excellence*. St. Paul, Minn.: Zenith Press, 2005.

Cooper, J. Gary

(Jerome Gary Cooper)
(1936–) *major general, first African-American officer to lead a marine rifle company in combat*

"I left Mobile, Alabama, on the back car of the Hummingbird, a segregated train, to go to Quantico, Virginia, to become a Marine officer," J. Gary Cooper has said. Not only did he become a distinguished officer in the integrated Marine Corps, but as a captain in Vietnam he was also the first African American to lead marines into battle. In both military and civilian life, General Cooper has dedicated himself to serving his country, his community, and his race.

Jerome Gary Cooper was born on October 2, 1936, in Lafayette, Louisiana, but for most of his life he has considered Mobile his home. In 1958, he earned a degree in finance from Notre Dame

In 1966, Marine Corps general J. Gary Cooper led a rifle company into combat in Vietnam. *(J. Gary Cooper)*

University in Indiana and was commissioned a second lieutenant in the Marine Corps. He completed basic training at the Marine Corps Base at Quantico and was promoted to first lieutenant in 1959 and to captain in 1963. From the start of his military career, he impressed his superior officers with his intelligence and exemplary conduct.

On May 6, 1966, Cooper went to Vietnam as a company commander. He became the first African American to lead a marine rifle company into combat, participating with his men in patrols, ambushes, and search and destroy missions. Commented Lieutenant General V. H. Krulak, commanding general, Fleet Marine Force, Pacific, upon awarding Cooper the Bronze Star, "[H]is determination and courageous fighting spirit were an inspiration to all who observed him and contributed significantly to the success

of these operations." In addition, Cooper received the Republic of Vietnam Gallantry Cross with Palm, Silver and Bronze Stars, and, for wounds received in action on July 4, 1966, and April 28, 1967, two Purple Hearts.

While in Vietnam, Cooper also directed the Civil Action Program for the 9th Marines, 3rd Marine Division. He oversaw the construction of a school and a bridge in the South Vietnamese village of Bich Bac, and he helped to establish programs in nurses' training and medical assistance for the people of South Vietnam. In order to communicate with the people he served and to understand their needs, he learned to speak Vietnamese.

Cooper was released from active duty in July 1969. He served as director of the Christian Benevolent Insurance Company, a family-owned business in Mobile, Alabama, and in January 1970 he joined the Individual Ready Reserve, an organization made up primarily of people who have been on active duty in the armed forces. As the first African American to command a marine reserve unit, Cooper led the 13th Force Reconnaissance Company of Mobile, and the 4th Battalion, 14th Marines, 4th Marine Division.

In 1973, Cooper became one of the first African Americans elected to public office in the South since Reconstruction when he won a seat in the Alabama House of Representatives. He held office until 1978, when he resigned to serve as commissioner of the Alabama Department of Human Resources. In that cabinet position, he managed a staff of 4,000 and the largest agency budget in the state.

In 1981, Cooper became a vice president with David Volkert and Associates, an architectural and engineering firm with offices throughout the Southeast, and he continued to be active in the reserve. On May 18, 1984, he was promoted to brigadier general; on June 3, 1988, he was promoted to major general and returned to active duty as director of personnel at Marine Corps Headquarters in Washington, D.C. He transferred to standby reserve status in October 1988.

The following year, President George H. W. Bush appointed Cooper to be assistant secretary of the air force for manpower affairs, installation and environment. Cooper served in that role for the duration of the Bush administration and helped plan the January 1991 assault on Iraqi positions known as Operation Desert Storm.

Cooper retired from the Marine Corps in 1993 but remained an active public servant. In 1994, President Bill Clinton nominated him to be U.S. ambassador to Jamaica, and the Senate confirmed the appointment. Cooper represented the United States in Jamaica from November 1994 until December 1997.

General Cooper is currently chairman and chief executive officer of Commonwealth National Bank in Mobile, the only minority-owned national bank in Alabama. He is active in community organizations, especially those that assist youth, and he has served on the boards of Spring Hill College and Talladega College. He currently serves on the boards of United States Steel Corporation, GenCorp, Protective Life, and other business and civic organizations. In 2000 he was named Patriot of the Year by the Mobile Bay Area Veterans Day Commission, and in 2001 he was designated a Living Legend by the University of the District of Columbia. In addition to the military decorations previously mentioned, he was awarded the Distinguished Service Medal and the Legion of Merit.

Further Reading

Division of Public Affairs, United States Marine Corps. "Major General Jerome G. Cooper, USMCR." Washington, D.C.: Headquarters Marine Corps, August 10, 1989.

Hawkins, Walter L. *Black American Military Leaders.* Jefferson, N.C.: McFarland and Co., 2007, p. 107.

"Major General J. Gary Cooper, USMCR." National Veterans Day in Birmingham. Available online. URL: http://www.nationalveteransday.org/honorees/cooper.htm. Downloaded on August 9, 2008.

Cromwell, Oliver

(1752–1853) *free African American who fought in the Revolutionary War*

During the six years and nine months that he spent in the Continental Army under the direct command of General George Washington, Oliver Cromwell took part in several key battles of the American Revolution.

Oliver Cromwell was born on an unknown date in 1752 near Burlington, New Jersey, and was "brought up a farmer," he said. At the start of the American Revolution, he enlisted in an infantry company attached to the New Jersey Regiment. He joined an American army numbering less than 3,000 that was poorly equipped and fed. Under Washington's gifted leadership, however, the Americans scored important victories against superior British forces and ultimately won the war.

Cromwell was with Washington on Christmas night in 1776, when the general led his troops across the Delaware River from Pennsylvania to Trenton, New Jersey, to surprise and overpower 900 Hessian mercenaries fighting for the British. A few days later, on January 3, 1777, Cromwell fought at Princeton, New Jersey, where Washington's men "knocked the British about lively," he said, routing three regiments belonging to a force under General Charles Cornwallis.

Not every battle in which Cromwell participated was a win for the Americans, though. He was at Brandywine, Pennsylvania, in September 1777, when British soldiers under General William Howe defeated the Continental army. He fought as well in the inconclusive Battle of Monmouth in New Jersey, on June 28, 1778. After a long, hot day of combat, the forces under British general Sir Henry Clinton slipped away under cover of darkness rather than face the Americans again in the morning.

Cromwell claimed to have seen the last man fall at Yorktown, Virginia, in October 1781. Thanks to information received from African-American spy JAMES ARMISTEAD, Washington and his French allies were able to surround and defeat the British at Yorktown and bring about Cornwallis's surrender.

For the rest of his life, Oliver Cromwell treasured his honorable discharge with badge of merit, which was signed by George Washington on June 5, 1783. (This document is now in the collection of the National Archives.) Cromwell, who was illiterate, obtained a yearly veteran's pension of $96 with help from Burlington lawyers, judges, and politicians. He used his money to buy a 100-acre farm near Burlington, where he and his wife raised 14 children.

In the spring of 1852, the *Burlington Gazette* carried a story about the African-American centenarian who had fought in the War for Independence. Cromwell was then living in his final home, in Burlington City, where some of his descendants continue to live. The *Gazette* told its readers that Cromwell was "among the survivors of the gallant army that fought for the liberties of our country 'in the days which tried men's souls.'"

Cromwell's name was adopted by the Oliver Cromwell Black History Society, founded in 1983, which researches Burlington's African-American heritage and works to preserve historic sites. The society also sponsors an annual art and essay contest for students and enlists young men to portray African-American soldiers in Revolutionary War reenactments at the Old Barracks Museum in Trenton, New Jersey.

Further Reading

"Biographies of Three African American Soldiers at Monmouth." The African American Experience in Monmouth County, 1700–1865. Available online. URL: http://zorak.monmouth.edu/~afam/Military7.htm. Downloaded on August 9, 2008.

Kaplan, Sidney, and Emma Nogrady Kaplan. *The Black Presence in the Era of the American Revolution.* Amherst: University of Massachusetts Press, 1989, pp. 52–54.

Nell, William Cooper. *The Colored Patriots of the American Revolution, with Sketches of Several Distinguished Colored Persons: To Which Is Added a Brief Survey of the Condition and Prospects of Colored Americans.* Chapel Hill: University of North Carolina: Documenting the American South. Available online. URL: http://docsouth.unc.edu/neh/nell/nell.html. Accessed on November 24, 2009.

"Oliver Cromwell." Burlington City, N.J. Available online. URL: http://08016.com/cromwell.html. Downloaded on August 9, 2008.

Smith, Jessie Carney, ed. *Notable Black American Men. Book II.* Detroit, Mich.: Thomson Gale, 2007, p. 149–151.

D

Dabney, Austin

(unknown–unknown) *Georgia slave who fought in his master's place in the Revolutionary War*

In the American Revolution, some white men who preferred not to face the dangers of war sent blacks to fight in their place. For Austin Dabney and others, such army service offered an escape from slave status—along with the risk of battlefield injury and death.

Austin Dabney, the slave of a man named Aycock, was born in Virginia. His birthdate is unknown, but he was living in Wilkes County, Georgia, at the time of the Revolutionary War. When Aycock was drafted for the militia, he freed Dabney on condition that the servant enlist as his substitute. Georgia, like Virginia and other colonies, permitted only free African Americans to join its militia.

Most African-American Revolutionary War soldiers fought in the infantry, but Dabney was an artilleryman serving under Colonel Elijah Clark. Clark's artillery corps was part of a force of 340 Georgia soldiers who defeated British Loyalists in the Battle of Kettle Creek, which was fought near present-day Washington, Georgia, on February 14, 1779. On that morning, the Americans made a surprise attack on 600 or more Loyalists who had camped beside Kettle Creek en route to Augusta, Georgia, where the British army was headquartered.

In the three hours of fighting that ensued, 21 Loyalists were killed and 22 were captured before the rest broke ranks and fled. The American militia leader Colonel Andrew Pickens called the battle, one of the most important to be fought in Georgia, "the severest check and chastisement, the tories ever received in South Carolina or Georgia." The Americans counted only seven killed and 14 or 15 wounded, but among the latter group was Austin Dabney, who had been shot in the leg and left on the battlefield with a badly broken thigh.

Dabney's life was saved when a man named Harris carried him home and nursed him back to health. In return, a grateful Dabney devoted himself to serving the Harris family. Because of his war injury, Dabney received a pension from the federal government. He guarded this income and later paid for Harris's son to attend Franklin College near Athens, Georgia (now Franklin College of Arts and Sciences of the University of Georgia). The young man later found employment with Stephen Upson, a prominent upper Georgia attorney who was later elected to the state legislature.

This connection served Dabney well in 1819, when the state of Georgia distributed by lottery land that had been obtained by treaty with the Creek and Cherokee Indians to white males age

18 and older who were U.S. citizens and three-year residents of the state. Rather than see Dabney denied land because of his race, Stephen Upson persuaded the legislature to grant him a valuable plot in recognition of his service in the Revolution.

It was said that Austin Dabney enjoyed horse racing, and that he frequented a tavern in Danielsville, Georgia, where judges and lawyers gathered for discussion. He continued to serve the Harrises, but the date and place of his death are unknown.

Further Reading

"Austin Dabney (ca. 1765–1830)." *New Georgia Encyclopedia.* Available online. URL: http://www.georgiaencyclopedia.org/nge/Article.jsp?id=h-3298. Downloaded on August 9, 2008.

Gilmer, George R. *Sketches of Some of the First Settlers of Upper Georgia, of the Cherokees, and the Author.* Baltimore: Genealogical Publishing Co., 1965, pp. 164–167.

Hornsby, Alton, Jr. *Southerners, Too? Essays on the Black South, 1733–1990.* Dallas, Texas: University Press of America, 2004.

Lanning, Michael Lee. *Defenders of Liberty: African Americans in the Revolutionary War.* New York: Citadel Press, 2000.

Quarles, Benjamin. *The Negro in the American Revolution.* Chapel Hill: University of North Carolina Press, 1996.

Davis, Benjamin O., Jr.

(1912–2002) *U.S. Air Force general, commander of the 99th Pursuit Squadron (the first African-American flying unit) during World War II*

Benjamin O. Davis, Jr., is best known as the tall, steady colonel who commanded the Tuskegee Airmen, the African-American pilots of World War II, but his accomplishments were many. For example, in 1936, he was the first African American to graduate from the United States Military Academy in 43 years; in 1954, when he was promoted to brigadier general, he became the highest-ranking African American in the U.S. armed forces.

Benjamin Oliver Davis, Jr., was born on December 18, 1912, in Washington, D.C. He was the son of BENJAMIN O. DAVIS, SR., an army colonel, and Elnora Dickerson Davis, who died in 1916. In 1920, Colonel Davis and his second wife, the former Sadie Overton, moved with young Benjamin and his two sisters to the Tuskegee Institute in Alabama. Colonel Davis had been assigned to teach military science and tactics at this famous vocational school for African Americans that was founded by Booker T. Washington in 1881.

In 1926, during a summertime trip to Washington, D.C., 13-year-old Benjamin visited Bolling Field, where barnstormers performed airborne acrobatics. Colonel Davis paid for his son to ride in an open cockpit with one of the daredevil pilots and charted the course of the boy's life. "That one ride made me fall in love with airplanes and gave me the desire to be a pilot myself," Davis recalled.

In Tuskegee and in Cleveland, Ohio, where the Davises moved in 1926, "Mother Sadie" insisted that the children earn good grades, and they did. Benjamin was class valedictorian when he graduated from Central High School in 1929. Still yearning to fly but knowing that pilot-training programs were closed to African Americans, he enrolled in Western Reserve University (now Case Western Reserve University) in Cleveland. The career paths open to college-educated blacks were limited, though, and Davis had no desire to be a lawyer, teacher, doctor, or engineer. He felt that he was wasting his time at Western Reserve, and when Colonel Davis suggested that he apply to the U.S. Military Academy at West Point, New York, Benjamin followed his father's advice. Briefly attending the University of Chicago, he was appointed to the academy by Congressman Oscar

De Priest of Illinois. He passed the entrance examination in March 1932 and reported to West Point four months later.

Davis said that during his four years at the military academy, he felt like an "invisible man." Not only was he required to room alone because of his race, but also, in an effort to make him resign, no white cadet spoke to him outside the line of duty. Such treatment usually was reserved for cadets who had violated the school's honor code, but Davis had committed no transgressions. He survived the lonely ordeal by focusing on his studies and through his friendship with Agatha Scott of New Haven, Connecticut, whom he married in June 1936, two weeks after graduating 35th in a class of 276. Davis was the fourth African American to graduate from West Point, following HENRY OSSIAN FLIPPER (1877), JOHN HANKS ALEXANDER (1887), and CHARLES YOUNG (1889).

Second Lieutenant Benjamin Davis, Jr., was first stationed at Fort Benning, Georgia, where he was assigned to an African-American maintenance company, although a West Point graduate would have expected to be put in command of troops. After attending Infantry School at Fort Benning, he was ordered to Tuskegee, to teach the classes his father had taught in the 1920s. This was another disappointing career move for a young and capable officer.

In September 1940, Davis learned that his father had been promoted to brigadier general, becoming the first African-American general in U.S. history. General Davis requested that his son be assigned to serve as his aide at Fort Riley, Kansas, where he commanded the 9th and 10th Cavalry, two African-American regiments.

World War II had begun in Europe, and the United States was gearing up for its inevitable involvement. Until that time, African Americans had been barred from military flight training in the United States, but in early 1941, President Franklin Delano Roosevelt bowed to pressure from civil rights groups to sanction the formation of an African-American flying unit, the 99th Pur-

suit Squadron (later renamed the 99th Fighter Squadron). Captain Benjamin O. Davis, Jr., 28 years old, was to be its commander.

The squadron trained at the Tuskegee Army Air Field in Alabama, which had been established so that black and white pilots would train separately. At last, in August 1941, when the men completed their classroom work and began learning to fly, Davis's long-held dream came true. "[F]lying over the green trees, the streams, and the ordinary plots of farmland below," he wrote, "was more exhilarating than anything I could have imagined."

Davis and the other squadron members received their wings on March 7, 1942, three months after the United States entered the war, but they waited a year—until March 1943—to be ordered overseas. Stationed in North Africa, the "Tuskegee Airmen" flew strafing and bomber-escort missions as the Allies captured Pantelleria, an island off Tunisia. The 99th disrupted enemy shipping lanes and provided cover during the Allied invasion of Sicily, which began on July 10,

Benjamin O. Davis, Jr., climbs into an advanced trainer at Tuskegee Army Air Base in 1942. *(Library of Congress)*

1943. On July 19, they moved their air base to that Italian island.

In September 1943, Davis returned to the United States to take command of the 332nd Fighter Group, which consisted of three squadrons of African-American pilots-in-training, and to counter reports of poor performance by the 99th. Understanding that the allegations were based on prejudice rather than fact, he persuaded the government to conduct a study of the 99th. That investigation found "no significant general difference between this squadron and the balance of the P-40 squadrons in the Mediterranean."

In March 1944, the 332nd was assigned to escort duty, and in June 1944, it moved to Ramitelli, Italy, its base for missions over Germany and France. The group flew approximately 200 escort missions and never lost a bomber to enemy fire. Davis himself flew 60 missions and logged 224 combat hours.

After the war in Europe ended, on June 8, 1945, Colonel Davis commanded the 477th Bombardment Group, which was preparing for combat in the Pacific. The Japanese surrendered on August 14, 1945, and the group was then stationed at Lockbourne Army Air Base in Ohio, making Lockbourne the first air base controlled by a black officer.

The air force became a separate branch of the U.S. military in September 1947; in May 1949, the air force abolished segregation, which made it possible for Davis to be, in 1950, chief of the Air Defense Branch of Air Force Operations, supervising all air force fighter units during the Korean War. He saw action in that war when in 1953 he commanded the 51st Fighter Interceptor Wing at Suwon Air Base, South Korea.

Davis was promoted to brigadier general in 1954 and held positions of responsibility in Japan and Taiwan before being named deputy chief of staff of the U.S. Air Force in Europe in 1957, the same year he was promoted to major general. He was director of manpower and organization for the air force in 1961; in 1965, he served as chief of

staff of the United Nations Command and U.S. Forces in Korea and attained the rank of lieutenant general. He commanded the 13th Air Force in the Philippines in 1967 and retired from the air force in 1970.

Davis briefly served as director of public safety for the city of Cleveland, Ohio, before helping the Department of Transportation solve the problem of commercial airline hijacking. There had been more than 100 skyjackings in the United States in the 1960s, but once Davis placed armed sky marshals aboard commercial flights and increased airport security, the problem diminished. Davis next aided American travelers by lobbying for a highway speed limit of 55 miles per hour. The nation adopted that limit in 1973, and a year later the death toll from traffic accidents had dropped by 9,100.

On December 9, 1998, President Bill Clinton awarded Davis a fourth star, raising his rank to full general. Speaking at the award ceremony that day, Secretary of Defense William S. Cohen said, "Throughout a lifetime of service in the Air Force, few did more than General Davis to prove that black and white Americans could not only serve together—indeed, that white soldiers would serve under a black superior—but that they could succeed together."

General Davis died in Washington, D.C., on July 4, 2002. His numerous military decorations included three Distinguished Service Medals, two Silver Stars, a Distinguished Flying Cross, three Legions of Merit, and an Air Medal with five Oak Leaf Clusters.

Further Reading

Davis, Benjamin O., Jr. *Benjamin O. Davis, Jr., American: An Autobiography.* Washington, D.C.: Smithsonian Institution Press, 1991.

Gropman, Alan L. "Benjamin Davis, American—USA." *Air Force Magazine* 80, no. 8 (August 1997): 70–74.

Hardesty, Von, and Dominick Paisano. *Black Wings: The American Black in Aviation.* New York: HarperCollins, 2008.

Sprekelmeyer, Linda, comp. and ed. *These We Honor: The International Aerospace Hall of Fame.* San Diego: San Diego Air and Space Museum, 2006, p. 62.

Weinraub, Judith. "The Long, Lonely Flight of General Benjamin Davis." *Washington Post,* February 4, 1991, p. B1.

Davis, Benjamin O., Sr.

(1880–1970) *first African-American general in the U.S. armed forces*

Through patience, perseverance, and exemplary service, Benjamin O. Davis, Sr., rose slowly through the ranks. In 1905, he became one of only two African-American officers on active duty in the U.S. Army; 35 years later, nearing the end of a long career, he was the first African American to wear a general's stars.

Benjamin Oliver Davis, Sr., was born on May 28, 1880, in Washington, D.C. He lied about his age in 1898, when he joined the army to fight in the Spanish-American War, according to biographer Marvin Fletcher, because he did not have his parents' permission to enlist. That lie remained alive beyond his death, and his birthdate is still listed as July 1, 1877, in official military records and other sources.

His father, Louis Davis, was a government messenger, and his mother, Henrietta Stewart Davis, was a nurse. Having two incomes permitted the Davises to be one of the few African-American families in Washington to own a house. Benjamin, the youngest of the three Davis children, discovered his vocation in boyhood, while watching a troop of the African-American 9th Cavalry parade at Fort Myer, Virginia.

During his senior year at all-black M Street High School, he took courses at Howard University. As a member of his high school cadet corps, he practiced military drills, learned to shoot a Springfield rifle, and rose to the rank of captain of Cadet Company B. He talked about becoming a soldier, but his father steered him toward a job in government, and his mother urged him to be a minister.

With the outbreak of the Spanish-American War in 1898, Benjamin Davis enlisted as a temporary first lieutenant in the 8th United States Volunteer Infantry, an ad hoc black army unit being formed to meet wartime needs. The war with Spain ended before he could be sent to Cuba, and no longer needed by the army, he was discharged.

Determined to live a soldier's life, Davis sought an appointment to the United States Military Academy at West Point, New York. The color barrier at the academy had been broken by HENRY OSSIAN FLIPPER, who graduated in 1877; nevertheless, President William McKinley was unwilling to appoint an African-American cadet. Therefore, on June 18, 1899, Davis enlisted in the army as a private and was stationed at Fort Duschene, Utah, with Troop 1 of the 9th Cavalry.

All of the officers assigned to the regiment were white, with the exception of Major CHARLES YOUNG, the third African American to graduate from West Point (in 1889), who was the only black officer in the army at that time. Young took Davis under his wing and for two years coached him in academics, surveying, and drill regulations, preparing him to take an examination to qualify as an officer. Davis passed the test and was commissioned a second lieutenant on February 2, 1901.

The United States had acquired the Philippine Islands from Spain following the Spanish-American War. Davis served with the 9th and 10th Cavalry in the Philippines in 1901, before being sent to Fort Washakie, Wyoming, as adjutant with the 10th Cavalry. He married Elnora Dickerson, a Washington seamstress, in 1902.

Army brass took great pains in choosing Davis's assignments to avoid the "indignity" of a black officer commanding white troops. Davis was professor of military science and tactics at historically black Wilberforce University in Ohio

England, 1942: General Benjamin O. Davis, Sr., inspects a soldier's rifle. *(Library of Congress)*

from September 1905 through September 1909, and again from February 1915 until the summer of 1917. Between those assignments, from late 1909 to January 1912, he was military attaché to the African nation of Liberia. Davis spent the period of U.S. involvement in World War I in the Philippines, as supply officer with the 9th Cavalry. He had been promoted to first lieutenant on March 30, 1905, and to captain on December 24, 1915.

Elnora Dickerson Davis died in 1916, following the birth of the couple's third child; in 1919, Benjamin Davis, Sr., married Sadie Overton, a professor of English at Wilberforce. On July 1, 1920, Davis was promoted to lieutenant colonel; in that year the Davis family moved to Tuskegee,

Alabama, site of the famed vocational school for African Americans, the Tuskegee Institute, where Davis once more taught military science and tactics. In July 1924, he was placed in command of the 372nd Infantry, an African-American unit of the Ohio National Guard, stationed at Cleveland.

The army failed to make the best use of this capable officer, giving him disappointing and unchallenging assignments because of his race. Davis served uncomplainingly and to the best of his ability, however, and attained the rank of colonel on February 18, 1930. From 1930 to 1933, he escorted widows and mothers of U.S. soldiers killed in World War I to Europe to visit their loved ones' graves. The secretary of war and the quartermaster general commended him for the sensitivity and tact with which he carried out this duty.

Davis taught at Tuskegee until August 1937, when he was sent back to Wilberforce for a year. He next served as instructor and commanding officer of the 369th Infantry, New York National Guard, and, beginning in January 1941, as a brigade commander with the 2nd Cavalry Division at Fort Riley, Kansas.

On October 25, 1940, Davis was promoted to brigadier general, becoming the first African-American general in U.S. history. He retired less than a year later, officially having reached the mandatory retirement age of 64. Then, as the United States readied itself militarily for its eventual entry into World War II, General Davis was called back to active duty and stationed in Washington, D.C., in the office of the inspector general. The army anticipated the induction of 100,000 African-American soldiers, and Davis was to report on morale and discipline in black units.

In October 1942, with the United States involved in the war in Europe and in the Pacific, General Davis was ordered to Great Britain to advise the army on racial problems within units stationed there. After interviewing white and black enlisted personnel, Davis determined that white soldiers resented the fact that most British people lacked prejudice based on skin color and treated all Americans in uniform equally. In a statement that might have applied to his own career as much as to the problem at hand, Davis reported to his superiors, "I fear overmuch emphasis is being placed on color in our Army."

In 1944, at Ramitelli, Italy, Davis pinned a Distinguished Flying Cross on his son, Colonel BENJAMIN O. DAVIS, JR., who commanded the Tuskegee Airmen, the first African-American pilots in the U.S. armed forces. In November 1944, General Davis was stationed in Paris as special assistant to the commanding general of the Communications Zone for the European Theater of Operations.

In 1947, General Benjamin O. Davis, Sr., represented the United States in Liberia at a ceremony marking the 100th anniversary of that nation's independence. He retired from the army in 1948, the year President Harry S. Truman signed Executive Order 9981, ending segregation in the military. Following his retirement, he inspected American cemeteries at Anzio, Italy, and other World War II battle sites for the Battle Monuments Commission.

Declining health forced General Davis to retire from public life in 1960. He died of leukemia on November 26, 1970, and was buried at Arlington National Cemetery. Toward the end of his life, he summed up his career by saying, "I did my duty. That's what I set out to do—to show that I could make my way if I knew my job."

General Davis's decorations included the Bronze Star and the Distinguished Service Medal. He received the Croix de Guerre with Palm from France and the Grade of Commander of the Order of the Star of Africa from Liberia.

Further Reading

Bankston, Carl L., III. *African American History*. Vol. 3. Pasadena, Calif.: Salem Press, 2006, p. 1,103.

"Benjamin Oliver Davis, Sr." U.S. Army Center of Military History. Available online. URL: http://www.history.army.mil/topics/afam/davis.htm. Downloaded on August 10, 2008.

Fletcher, Marvin. *America's First Black General: Benjamin O. Davis, Sr.: 1880–1970*. Lawrence: University Press of Kansas, 1989.

Davison, Frederic Ellis

(1917–1999) *third African-American general in U.S. history, first African American to command an army division*

In 1941, Frederic E. Davison joined an army in which blacks and whites served separately and positions of authority went to whites. He rose quickly through the ranks once the barrier of segregation was removed, becoming in 1968 the third African-American general in the U.S. armed forces.

Frederic Ellis Davison was born in Washington, D.C., on September 28, 1917. His father, Albert Charles Davison, died when he was a baby, and Frederic was left in his grandmother's care while his mother, Sue Bright Davison, worked. His grandmother instilled strong values in the boy, counseling him to "Be something worthwhile."

Frederic was a member of the National Honor Society while a student at all-black Dunbar High School. For a time, he viewed medicine as a possible career. He studied zoology and chemistry at Howard University, graduating cum laude in 1938 and earning a master's degree in 1940.

Davison completed ROTC training in college and in 1939 was commissioned a lieutenant in the Army Reserve. On April 6, 1941, he married Jean E. Brown, a teacher, and just months before the United States entered World War II, he was called to active duty.

During the war, Captain Frederic Davison led an African-American unit, Company B of the 371st Infantry, 92nd Division, which fought from Sicily into mainland Italy. The white officers assigned to the 92nd were of low caliber, the men were poorly trained, and equipment issued to the division was old. To Davison, segregation in the military was a double-edged sword, a hated impediment as well as a challenge. "We didn't feel we were given the true opportunity to show our capabilities," he said. "On the other hand, we tried to prove that even under these handicaps the job could be done." The soldiers of the division took 3,000 casualties and received 12,000 decorations. For his service in World War II, Davison earned the Distinguished Service Medal, the Legion of Merit, the Bronze Star, and the Army Commendation Medal.

Davison enrolled in Howard University Medical School after the war but left after a year to accept a commission in the regular army. In 1947,

he was assigned to train an ROTC unit at South Carolina Agricultural and Mechanical College (now South Carolina State University) in Orangeburg. In the early 1950s, he was a battalion operations officer in Germany, serving in the newly integrated armed forces.

Through the 1950s and 1960s, as he and his wife raised four daughters, Davison moved steadily up the army career ladder. In 1954, he attended the Command and General Staff College at Fort Leavenworth, Kansas. In 1957 he was promoted to lieutenant colonel, and in 1959 he went to Korea as chief of personnel services with the Eighth Army. In 1962, Davison was the first African American to enter the Army War College at Carlisle Barracks, Pennsylvania. A year later he graduated from George Washington University with a master's degree in international affairs and was placed in charge of manpower and reserve matters at the Pentagon. Beginning in 1965, he commanded the 3rd Training Brigade at Fort Bliss, Texas.

In 1967, Davison requested duty in Vietnam and was made deputy commander of the 199th Light Infantry brigade, which was stationed in the defense perimeter of Saigon. The brigade commander was absent in February 1968, when the North Vietnamese launched the series of attacks known as the Tet Offensive, and it was left to Davison to direct the defense of the base at Long Binh. The courage and dedication that Davison displayed earned him profound respect from the soldiers under his command. In August 1968, he became brigade commander.

As commander, Davison was often in the field with the soldiers. "[I]f you want to get to the grass roots and know exactly what the problems and the attitudes of the men are, you've got to talk to them," he explained. On Sundays, he visited the wounded in hospitals, to "let them know I appreciate what they've done, that they've not been forgotten." Davison's decorations earned in Vietnam include the Gallantry Cross with Palm and the Distinguished Service Order, First Class.

In September 1968, in a promotion ceremony at Binh Chanh, General Creighton W. Abrams, U.S. commander in Vietnam, pinned a general's stars on Davison's uniform, making him the third African-American general in U.S. history. Davison followed army general BENJAMIN O. DAVIS, SR., who was retired, and his son, air force general BENJAMIN O. DAVIS, JR., who would retire in 1970.

While Davison and thousands of other African-American soldiers fought a continuing battle for equality within the armed forces, some young African Americans in the United States were joining militant groups such as the Black Panthers and advocating racial separation. Davison was an outspoken critic of this trend, saying, "I envision one America, an integrated America." To the general, contributing to society entitled any citizen to enjoy the full rights of that society.

For nine months—from September 1971 to May 1972—Davison was deputy chief of staff for U.S. Army personnel in Europe. In April 1971, he was promoted to major general. In May 1972, he assumed command of the 8th Infantry Division in Germany, becoming the first African American to lead an army division. He quickly proved himself to be a tough leader who tolerated nothing less than excellence: He relieved from duty three post commanders who failed to enforce regulations designed to further racial tolerance, and he took decisive measures against drug use and drunk driving by soldiers.

On November 12, 1973, Davison was made commander of the Military District of Washington, D.C. He oversaw a force of 3,600 that performed ceremonial functions and remained ready to carry out security and rescue operations at the White House and to aid civil authorities in case of domestic disorder. At the time he was the highest ranking of 12 African-American generals in the army.

General Davison retired from active duty in 1974 and became an executive assistant to the president of Howard University. Before retiring from Howard in 1985, he helped to streamline the university's computer system. In retirement, Davis volunteered on behalf of the homeless, and a homeless shelter in the District of Columbia was named in his honor.

Jean Brown Davison died in 1996; General Frederic E. Davison died on January 24, 1999, following surgery for a kidney ailment. He was buried at Arlington National Cemetery.

Further Reading

"Colonel Recalls D.C. Days." *Washington Evening Star* (July 14, 1968), p. A18.

"Frederic Ellis Davison." Arlington National Cemetery Web site. Available online. URL: http://www.arlingtoncemetery.com/fdavison.htm. Downloaded on August 10, 2008.

Moritz, Charles, ed. *Current Biography 1974.* New York: H. W. Wilson Co., 1974, pp. 100–102.

"A Star for Davison." *Ebony* 24, no. 1 (November 1968), pp. 128–132.

Westheider, James E. *The African American Experience in Vietnam: Brothers in Arms.* Lanham, Md.: Rowman and Littlefield, 2008, pp. 50–51, 156.

Delany, Martin Robison

(1812–1885) *army major, highest-ranking African-American officer to lead troops in the Civil War*

Martin Delany dedicated his life to securing freedom and equality for African Americans. This commitment led him both to seek a homeland for African Americans outside the United States and to further the Union cause in the Civil War as a recruiter and as an army major leading a regiment.

Martin Robison Delany was born on May 6, 1812, in Charles Town, Virginia (now West Virginia). His mother, Pati Delany, was a free African American who helped her husband, Samuel, purchase his freedom.

Martin and his siblings learned to read covertly from an itinerant bookseller and teacher because it was against the law to teach African Americans to read and write in the antebellum South. In 1822 Samuel and Pati Delany moved their family to Chambersburg, Pennsylvania, where the children could be educated at school. Martin was an outstanding student, and in 1831 he moved to Pittsburgh to study medicine with a local physician, Dr. Andrew N. McDowell, and to enroll in a private academy for African Americans.

Delany left Pittsburgh before completing his studies and went to the Sea Islands of South Carolina, where he practiced dentistry. In 1843, he returned to Pittsburgh and began publishing the *Mystery*, the first weekly newspaper for African Americans in the United States. Also in 1843, he

Martin R. Delany was commissioned a major in the Union army in 1865. *(Schomburg Center for Research in Black Culture, New York Public Library)*

married Catherine Richards of Pittsburgh. The couple's seven surviving children would all be named for distinguished blacks.

Having shut down the *Mystery* because of dwindling financial support, in 1847 Delany joined Frederick Douglass in Rochester, New York, to publish the *North Star*, an abolitionist newspaper. He also spoke at abolitionist rallies.

Delany left the *North Star* in 1848 to continue his medical education, but despite his fine academic record he was denied admission to several Pennsylvania medical schools because of his race. In 1850, he was admitted to the medical school at Harvard College, but white students protested so strongly against his presence that the school dismissed him after he had completed just one term of study. Delany believed that he had acquired enough knowledge to practice medicine, but the dismissal convinced him that African Americans would never enjoy equality in the United States.

In 1852, Delany published *The Condition, Elevation, Emigration, and Destiny of the Colored People of the United States*, a book that called for African Americans to find a new home in Africa or South America. He took his resettlement plans a step further in 1854, when he organized the National Emigration Convention in Cleveland, bringing together more than 100 participants to discuss colonization.

In 1856, the Delanys moved from the United States to Chatham, Canada West (present-day Ontario), where Martin Delany established a medical practice and befriended MARY ANN SHADD CARY. Three years later, he journeyed to Africa to explore the Niger Valley as a possible site for African-American immigration and negotiated for land with the Yoruba people.

He returned to Canada to announce, "My duty and destiny are in Africa, the great and glorious," but with the United States on the brink of the Civil War, he soon renewed his commitment to life in America and the abolition of slavery. In 1863, George L. Stearns, a wealthy abolitionist, engaged

Delany to help recruit soldiers for an African-American regiment being formed in Massachusetts. The War Department had authorized Massachusetts governor John Andrew to raise such a regiment, but the state's African-American population was small, and men needed to be enlisted elsewhere. As Delany recruited soldiers for regiments taking shape in Massachusetts as well as in Rhode Island and Connecticut, his son Toussaint L'Ouverture Delany signed on and fought with the first African-American regiment formed in the North, the 54th Massachusetts Infantry.

In early 1865, the Delanys moved to Wilberforce, Ohio. As soon as they were settled, President Abraham Lincoln commissioned Delany as a major with the 104th U.S. Colored Troops in South Carolina, making him the highest-ranking African-American officer to lead troops in the Civil War. Delany recruited two regiments of former slaves, but the war ended in April 1865, before he could see combat. His plan to create a "Corps d'Afrique," an army of African-American officers and enlisted men, remained a dream.

After the war, Delany worked with the Freedmen's Bureau, the government agency that helped former slaves adjust to life as free Americans. In 1869, he was mustered out of the army, and his family joined him in South Carolina. He became active in state politics, and in 1874 he ran unsuccessfully for lieutenant governor as an Independent Republican. In 1875, he was appointed to a judicial position.

Around 1877, at the end of the period of Reconstruction, the Delany family left South Carolina for Xenia, Ohio. In 1879, Martin Delany published *Principia of Ethnology: The Origin of Races and Color,* his book on the contributions of blacks to world civilization. He died on January 24, 1885.

Further Reading

Foner, Eric, and John A. Garraty, eds. *The Reader's Companion to American History.* Boston: Houghton Mifflin, 1991, pp. 274–275.

Levine, Robert S., ed. *Martin R. Delany: A Documentary Reader.* Chapel Hill: University of North Carolina Press, 2003.

McGuire, William, and Leslie Wheeler. *American Social Leaders.* Santa Barbara, Calif.: ABC-CLIO, 1993, p. 126.

Palmer, Colin A., ed. *Encyclopedia of African American Culture and History.* Vol. 2. Detroit, Mich.: Thomson Gale, 2006, pp. 596–597.

Smith, Jessie Carney, and Joseph M. Palmisano, eds. *The African American Almanac.* 8th ed. Detroit: Gale Group, 2000, pp. 386–387.

"To Be More Than Equal: The Many Lives of Martin Robison Delany, 1812–1885." University Libraries, West Virginia University. Available online. URL: http://www.libraries.wvu.edu/delany/home.htm. Downloaded on August 10, 2008.

Ullman, Victor. *Martin R. Delany: The Beginnings of Black Nationalism.* Boston: Beacon Press, 1971.

Denison, Franklin A.

(1862–1932) *first African American to command a U.S. regiment in wartime*

Franklin Denison ably commanded the men of his Illinois National Guard regiment in Cuba during the Spanish-American War, thus becoming the first African-American officer to lead a regiment into combat, but when it was time for the regiment to fight overseas in World War I, the army replaced him with a white officer.

Franklin A. Denison was born in San Antonio, Texas, in 1862. He was educated at Lincoln University, a Pennsylvania school founded for African-American men, and in 1879 was admitted to the Illinois bar. After settling in Chicago, he began a long and successful legal career.

In 1898, Denison helped to organize the 8th Regiment of the Illinois National Guard. All the regiment's personnel, including its officers, were African American. The 8th Illinois, led by Major Franklin A. Denison, served in Cuba both during and after the Spanish-American War, from August

Major Franklin A. Denison led the 8th Illinois National Guard, which was mobilized during the Spanish-American War. *(Courtesy of the New York Public Library)*

1898 until May 1899. Denison therefore became the first African-American officer to lead a U.S. regiment into war.

In June 1916, Denison was part of the Illinois delegation to the Republican National Convention, held at the Chicago Coliseum, which resulted in the nomination of Charles Evans Hughes of New York for president. The same year, the 8th Illinois was again made part of the U.S. Army and sent to the Mexican border to help hunt down Pancho Villa, the Mexican revolutionary leader whose forces had attacked Columbus, New Mexico, on March 9, 1916, killing several citizens and destroying part of the town. Colonel Denison and his troops were part of a 5,000-man force under Brigadier General John J. Pershing that also included two regiments of Buffalo Soldiers, the 24th Infantry and 10th Cavalry.

Not only was searching for Pancho Villa like "trying to find a rat in a cornfield," as Pershing said, but also the Mexican terrain was harsh, the weather was severe, and supplies were low. Soldiers endured cold nights without adequate clothing or shelter, and the cavalry's horses weakened and died. After a year of fruitless searching, army leaders abandoned the campaign and focused their attention on World War I.

Denison and the 8th Illinois—the only national guard unit with a full complement of African-American officers—received mobilization orders in March 1917. In October they were ordered to Camp Logan in Houston, Texas, the regular training station for the Illinois National Guard. On August 23, Houston had been the scene of the nation's first race riot, a clash between white citizens and soldiers of the 24th Infantry that left 16 whites and four blacks dead. The incident resulted in a hastily staged court-martial, the execution of 19 African-American soldiers, and the imprisonment of many others. Chicago's African-American leaders voiced concern about the regiment entering such a racial climate, but the order had to be obeyed.

The segregation of the South stunned the black Chicagoans as they traveled by train to Camp Logan, and some reacted angrily at stops along the way, tearing down signs designating separate seating for blacks and whites in waiting rooms and looting a store that had denied them service. In Houston, however, there was only minor trouble. A few members of the 8th Illinois were placed in the guardhouse for fighting with local residents, and the entire regiment was barred from the city's buses for refusing to obey the rules of Jim Crow seating.

On December 1, 1917, the 8th Illinois was renamed the 370th Regiment of the 93rd Division. In March 1918, the regiment went to Newport News, Virginia, a town the regimental chaplain called "a place of a thousand prejudices." Both townspeople and white military personnel stationed at Newport News had heard rumors that the 370th was going to start trouble and were primed for confrontation. Denison instituted strict discipline within the ranks and avoided further incidents, but when the regiment sailed for France, a white inspecting officer predicted that it never would be ready for combat with blacks in command.

His words echoed the prejudice of the army's top brass. The 370th marched ashore in Brest on April 16, 1918; on July 12, Denison was relieved of his command ostensibly because of ill health. (In a more widely publicized case, the army denied Colonel CHARLES YOUNG the opportunity to lead troops in World War I for a similar reason.) All six of the regiment's black field officers, including Denison, were replaced by whites and sent home. Although bitter over the change in command, the soldiers of the 370th served with distinction alongside the French. The regiment was decorated for its participation in the Battles of Lorraine and Oise-Aisne.

Denison retired from the army in 1922 at his own request. He returned to the practice of law and with his wife, Edna, raised five children. He served as an assistant corporation counsel in the Chicago municipal government and for six years was an assistant city prosecuting attorney. He died on April 14, 1932, after a long illness.

Further Reading

Barbeau, Arthur E., and Florette Henri. *The Unknown Soldiers: African-American Troops in World War I.* New York: Da Capo Press, 1996, pp. 75–77, 122–124.

Buckley, Gail. *American Patriots: The Story of Blacks in the Military from the Revolution to Desert Storm.* New York: Random House, 2001, pp. 187–188.

Field, Ron. *Buffalo Soldiers 1892–1918.* Oxford, U.K.: Osprey Publishing, 2005, pp. 47–48.

Kletzing, H. F., and W. H. Crogman. *Progress of a Race, or The Remarkable Advancement of the Afro-American.* New York: Negro Universities Press, 1969, p. 533.

Dorman, Isaiah

(ca. 1821–1876) *War Department courier, army scout who died at Little Bighorn*

A black man on the western frontier, Isaiah Dorman found a home among the Lakota but earned his livelihood among whites. For reasons that will remain forever unclear, he fought with the U.S. forces in the Battle of Little Bighorn and in so doing lost his life.

Isaiah Dorman's early life is obscure. Although his date of birth is unknown, he is thought to have been born in 1821. Also, there is evidence that he escaped from slavery: One of several slaves reported missing in the 1840s by the d'Orman family of Louisiana was named Isaiah. How or why he traveled to the Dakota Territory is unknown.

Dorman's name first appeared in the written historical record on November 11, 1865, when the War Department hired him as a courier. Once a month, he carried mail between Fort Wadsworth, near present-day Lake City, South Dakota, and Fort Rice, on the west bank of the Missouri River, in present-day North Dakota. The government paid him a generous $100 per month, because while making the 200-mile round-trip journey on foot he risked being attacked by wolves or Indians or succumbing to severe weather.

In 1867, Dorman worked as a "woodhawk" for the firm of Durfee and Peck, which operated trading posts along the Missouri River. The traders paid him $1.50 per cord to cut and stack wood that would stoke fires at western army forts. Dorman married a Santee Lakota woman and in 1867 went to live with her people. The Lakota gave him the name On Azinpi, meaning Teat, possibly because it sounded vaguely like Isaiah. They also called him the "Black White Man."

Dorman gained a reputation as a knowledgeable guide and interpreter, and in 1871 the army hired him to accompany a team of surveyors for the Northern Pacific Railroad. By the spring of 1876, he was working as an interpreter at Fort Rice, earning $75 a month. Lieutenant Colonel George Armstrong Custer of the 7th Cavalry Regiment learned of Dorman's facility in the Lakota language and on May 14, 1876, requested his services. The U.S. Army had begun a campaign to crush the Sioux (Lakota, Dakota, Nakota), and Custer's regiment of 655 constituted the advance guard of the forces under General Alfred Howe Terry.

The 7th Cavalry located an Indian encampment beside the Little Bighorn River in what is now Montana. Custer grossly underestimated its size and on June 25, despite instructions to reconnect with Terry, he ordered an immediate attack. While Custer led a center column of 264 men, Dorman followed Major Marcus Reno, who headed a contingent assaulting the south end of the camp. As Reno's soldiers dismounted and prepared to fight on foot, an estimated 2,500 to 4,000 armed men streamed from the Indian village and made short work of the U.S. troops. The entire center column, including Custer, was destroyed.

Private Roman Rutten, a survivor, recalled riding past Dorman, who was on his knees beside his dead horse, firing a rifle. Perhaps prophetically, Dorman shouted, "Good-bye, Rutten!" He was soon badly wounded in the chest. Many Indians recognized the big African American they had once considered a friend, and although the great Lakota leader Sitting Bull offered him water, others viewed him as a traitor and took revenge. George Herendeen, a white scout who escaped death by hiding in a thicket, reported seeing Indians shoot Dorman and pound him with stone hammers. According to Lakota accounts, Indian warriors sliced Dorman's lifeless body with knives and pierced it with arrows. As a final insult, they mutilated his genitals.

Further Reading

Burton, Art T. *Black, Buckskin, and Blue.* Austin, Texas: Eakin Press, 1999, pp. 41–43.

Connell, Evan S. *Son of the Morning Star: Custer and the Little Bighorn.* New York: Perennial Library, 1984, pp. 25–28, 254, 347.

"Isaiah Dorman: 'Black White Man' at the Little Bighorn." National Park Service. Available online. URL: http://wwwnps.gov/untold/banners_and_backgrounds/militarybanner/militarystories/dorman. htm. Downloaded on August 10, 2008.

Utley, Robert M. *The Lance and the Shield: The Life and Times of Sitting Bull.* New York: Henry Holt and Co., 1993, p. 153.

Doughty, Gene

(1924–   ) Marine Corps sergeant who participated in the invasion of Iwo Jima during World War II

"I spent my twenty-first birthday on the sands of Iwo Jima," Gene Doughty has recalled. Although sent to the small Pacific island in a noncombat role, Doughty joined the fight to capture heavily fortified Iwo Jima from the Japanese.

Doughty was born in Stamford, Connecticut, as one of eight children. His parents had immigrated to the United States from Barbados, and his father was a plumber. When Gene was six years old, the Doughtys moved to New York City. Gene Doughty graduated from the High School of Commerce in Manhattan, and he enrolled at the City College of New York (CCNY) to study physical and health education.

He had completed one year of study in spring 1943 when he was approached by a Marine Corps recruiter. The marines were opening their ranks to African Americans for the first time and soliciting bright, educated recruits. Doughty welcomed the opportunity to join the marines, which was something he had never expected to do. He enlisted and was sent to Montford Point, the newly established Marine Corps training camp for African Americans in North Carolina. Making this trip, he was venturing beyond the New York metropolitan area for the first time.

Doughty was assigned to the 48th Platoon, one of the first 50 platoons formed at Montford Point. Among his fellow recruits was FREDERICK C.

BRANCH, who in 1945 became the first African-American officer in the Marine Corps. Most of the drill instructors assigned to Montford Point were white officers from the South, and it seemed to Doughty that many had no interest in seeing the blacks succeed. His motto became "grin and bear it," and he maintained a positive attitude and did his best.

After basic training, Doughty began learning the duties of a company clerk. With the United States involved in fighting World War II, though, he was soon transferred to an infantry unit, where men were needed. The Marine Corps assigned him to the 36th Depot Company, an African-American unit, as a squad leader. Depot companies delivered supplies to combat troops and performed occasional guard duty. In November 1944, the 36th Depot Company went for further training to Camp Catlin, Hawaii, closer to the Pacific Theater of Operations. Although their main duty would be to unload and distribute provisions, the men learned to fire the M-1 rifles they would be issued.

The 36th was one of three African-American depot companies that supported the marines' landing on Iwo Jima, which began on February 19, 1945. Allied military leaders believed that control of the volcanic island and its airfields would be useful for a planned invasion of the Japanese mainland, but the extensive system of heavily defended tunnels and bunkers that the Japanese had created there took the Allies by surprise. They made the battle for Iwo Jima long, fierce, and costly in human life.

Combat and supply forces, white and black, came under fire equally on Iwo Jima. Doughty went ashore with the first wave of marines, on February 19, and he and his squad struggled to establish a supply depot amid exploding artillery shells, thick smoke, flying sand, and fallen comrades.

Slowly, the marines pushed inland. On the fifth day of battle, five marines and a navy corpsman raised the U.S. flag atop Mount Suribachi, the island's volcanic peak, in an event that was seen around the world, thanks to a picture taken by the photojournalist Joe Rosenthal. The battle for Iwo Jima had yet to be won, but Doughty felt joy upon witnessing the flag-raising from a distant airfield. "I guess it's gonna be the end of the war. We'll be home pretty soon. That was the attitude," he said.

On March 26, with the battle nearly won, the 36th Depot Company was providing security for U.S. airmen when the Japanese launched a desperate early-morning attack, descending on the marines and airmen with machine guns, grenades, swords, and knives. The African-American marines picked up guns and joined the three-hour fight that left 53 Americans dead and 92 wounded. In addition, 262 Japanese soldiers were killed, and 18 were taken prisoner.

The surviving members of Doughty's company returned to Hawaii after the Allied victory at Iwo Jima to train for the invasion of Japan, but the atomic bombs dropped on the Japanese cities of Hiroshima and Nagasaki ended the war and thus made the invasion unnecessary. Doughty was discharged from the Marine Corps in 1946 and returned to CCNY, where he completed his coursework and earned a degree in health and physical education. He married a teacher and worked briefly as a youth recreation leader for the Police Athletic League before becoming an investigator for the New York City Department of Social Services. He entered the sales field in 1954, and he retired in 1985.

In retirement Doughty served as president of the Montford Point Marine Association, a veterans' group, and he was on the board of the Marine Corps Scholarship Foundation. In November 2005, he was one of five veterans honored as role models and leaders in a ceremony at the Intrepid Sea, Air and Space Museum in New York City.

Further Reading

Culp, Ronald E. *The First Black United States Marines: The Men of Montford Point, 1942–1946.* Jefferson,

N.C.: McFarland and Co., 2007, pp. 198–199, 202.

"Montford Point Marines: Loyalty and Service in the Face of Prejudice and Discrimination; Gene Doughty, June 29th, 2005." Library, University of North Carolina at Wilmington. Available online. URL: http://library.uncw.edu/web/montford/transcripts/Doughty_Gene.html. Downloaded on June 27, 2008.

Smith, Larry. *The Few and the Proud: Marine Corps Drill Instructors in Their Own Words.* New York: W.W. Norton and Co., 2006, pp. 181–189.

"Thompson Honors Five City Leaders at Veterans' Recognition Event." The New York City Office of the Comptroller. Available online. URL: http://www.comptroller.nyc.gov/press/2005_releases/PR05-11-122.shtm. Downloaded on August 10, 2008.

E

Earley, Charity Adams

(1918–2002) *commander of the only unit of African-American women to serve overseas in World War II*

As commander of the 6888th Central Postal Battalion, Charity Adams Earley made an important contribution to the morale of U.S. personnel in Europe in World War II. She also combated racism in the armed forces at home and abroad.

The oldest of four children, Charity Edna Adams was born in Kittrell, North Carolina, on December 5, 1918. Her parents, Eugene Adams, a minister, and Charity A. Adams, a teacher, expected their children to be models of good behavior for the African-American youth of their community, and young Charity did not disappoint them. She was valedictorian of her high school graduating class and won a scholarship to historically black Wilberforce University in Ohio. As she prepared to leave home for college, her father let her know that she must continue to meet her parents' high expectations. Charity Adams Earley recalled him saying, "We have tried to teach you right from wrong. Just do right!" She commented, "What a burden that advice put on my shoulders!"

Adams retained her good study habits at Wilberforce and earned a bachelor of arts degree in 1938, with majors in mathematics, physics, and Latin. She had also completed the necessary courses for teacher certification, and from 1938 to 1942 she taught mathematics and science to African-American public school students in segregated Columbia, South Carolina. In 1942, she was planning to begin graduate study in psychology at Ohio State University when the dean of women at Wilberforce recommended her as a candidate for officer training in the new Women's Army Auxiliary Corps (WAAC; renamed the Women's Army Corps [WAC] in 1943). With the United States involved in World War II, Adams decided to postpone any further education and serve her country. She reported to the WAAC training center at Fort Des Moines, Iowa, a converted cavalry post.

The corps of women captured the public's interest and received extensive press coverage. *Liberty* magazine reported that the women would be going "through the army mill just as their brothers do." Black and white recruits had traveled to Fort Des Moines together and, upon arrival, had eaten a meal together. It therefore came as a surprise when the officers in command assembled the new arrivals in the base's reception center to announce that the "colored girls" would be assigned to separate quarters. "There was a moment of stunned silence," Earley said, "for even in the United States of the forties it did not occur to us that this could happen."

Charity Adams nevertheless approached army life with her usual drive to excel, and on August 29, 1942, she was one of 440 women—40 of them African American—to graduate from WAAC officer candidate school. She was assigned to train incoming black female soldiers.

Before long, Adams was made a supervisor of basic training and was the only African American on the supervisory staff. In the summer of 1943 she was promoted to major, and in November 1944 she was one of the first WAC officers to enter the U.S. Army Command and General Staff School at Fort Leavenworth, Kansas. She had barely begun her studies, though, when she was ordered to prepare for duty overseas.

In January 1945, 500 African-American WAC personnel, including Charity Adams, underwent an intensive course of training at Fort Oglethorpe, Georgia, to ready them for overseas service. After demonstrating her ability to hike five miles in full combat gear under simulated battle conditions, climb up and down a cargo net, and survive a simulated poison-gas attack, Adams sailed for Great Britain, where she was to command the 6888th Central Postal Directory Battalion, which directed all V-Mail addressed to any of the 7 million Americans serving in Europe: the men and women of the armed forces, civilian employees of the military, American Red Cross workers, and traveling dignitaries. Headquartered in Birmingham, England, and later in France, this unit of 800 African-American female soldiers—the only battalion of African-American women to serve overseas in World War II—worked around the

Major Charity Adams, followed by Captain Abbie N. Campbell, inspects the first African-American members of the Women's Army Corps to report for duty overseas. *(National Archives)*

clock, with members putting in eight-hour shifts, seven days a week.

Adams's responsibilities and achievements offered no insulation from racism in the army, but they put her in a position to combat it. The most telling incident occurred in England, after a white general intentionally found fault with Adams's unit during a troop review. When the general offered to have a white junior officer show her how to do her job, Adams replied, "Over my dead body, Sir."

That remark prompted the general to order court-martial papers drawn up against Adams. Not easily intimidated, Adams had court-martial papers drawn up against the general for allegedly disobeying a directive from Supreme Headquarters that warned commanders against using language that emphasized racial segregation. (The U.S. government hoped to present its Allies with an image of harmony within the ranks.) Three days after Adams filed her case, she learned that the charges against her had been dropped. She, too, dropped charges and later dealt politely with the general when working alongside him in France.

On other occasions, Adams organized boycotts of segregated recreational facilities and military housing in Europe. As the ranking American officer in Birmingham, she represented the United States at approximately 30 memorial services held in that city following the death of President Franklin D. Roosevelt on April 12, 1945.

The 6888th Central Postal Directory Battalion was disbanded in December 1945. Charity Adams left the army in 1946 as a lieutenant colonel, holding the highest possible rank in the WAC with the exception of its director. She immediately pursued her education at Ohio State University, and before the year was over had fulfilled the requirements for a master's degree in vocational psychology. From 1946 through 1949, she held administrative posts at Tennessee Agricultural and Industrial State College (now Tennessee State University) in Nashville and Georgia State College (now Savannah State College).

On August 24, 1949, Adams married Stanley A. Earley, Jr., who was studying medicine at the University of Zurich. The Earleys began their married life in Switzerland, where Charity Adams Earley pursued studies at the University of Zurich and the Jungian Institute of Analytical Psychology. The Earleys' two children, Stanley III and Judith, were born after the couple returned to the United States and settled in Dayton, Ohio.

Charity Adams Earley then devoted herself to charitable and educational causes, serving organizations such as the United Way, the American Red Cross, and the Black Leadership Development Program. She was also on the board of directors of the Dayton Power and Light Company. In 1982, the Smithsonian Institution included her in its list of outstanding black women in U.S. history, "Black Women Against the Odds." Also in 1982, the Atlanta chapter of the NAACP presented her with the Walter White Award for her groundbreaking work in the military. In 1989, Earley published her autobiography, *One Woman's Army: A Black Officer Remembers the WAC.* "Because historical material included slight mention of women who served in World War II and nothing about black women, I wrote to record my knowledge of that period and my personal experiences," she said.

In 1991, Earley received honorary doctorates from Wilberforce University and the University of Dayton. The same year, upon her retirement, the Dayton Power and Light Company established a scholarship at Wilberforce in her name.

One of the closing sentences of Earley's autobiography effectively sums up a lifetime's contributions: "I have opened a few doors, broken a few barriers, and, I hope, smoothed the way to some degree for the next generation." Charity Adams Earley died in Dayton on January 13, 2002.

Further Reading

Commire, Anne, ed. *Dictionary of Women Worldwide: 25,000 Women through the Ages.* Vol. 1: A–L. Detroit, Mich.: Thomson Gale, 2002, p. 9.

Earley, Charity Adams. *One Woman's Army: A Black Officer Remembers the WAC.* College Station, Tex.: Texas A & M University, 1989.

Haskins, Jim. *African American Military Heroes.* New York: John Wiley and Sons, 1998, pp. 110–114.

Hine, Darlene Clark. *Black Women in America: An Historical Encyclopedia.* Vol. 1, A–G. New York: Oxford University Press, 2005, pp. 379–380.

Trotsky, Susan M., ed. *Contemporary Authors.* Vol. 132. Detroit: Gale Research, 1991, p. 109.

Europe, James Reese

(1881–1919) *leader of the regimental band of the 369th Infantry*

A successful entertainer in civilian life, James Reese Europe went to France with the 369th Infantry during World War I as a line officer whose duties as bandleader were secondary. Yet he is remembered as a cultural ambassador, the man who brought American jazz to France.

James Reese Europe was born on February 22, 1881, in Mobile, Alabama. His father, Henry J. Europe, was a Baptist minister who had worked for the federal government during Reconstruction. James's mother, Lorraine Saxon Europe, was a teacher and church musician. She introduced her five children to music, inspiring three of them—including James—to pursue musical careers.

Around 1890, the family moved to Washington, D.C., where Henry Europe had accepted a job with the post office. James studied the violin and piano with several accomplished musicians living in the nation's capital, and after his father died in 1899, he helped to support his family as a musician.

In 1905, Europe joined the Memphis Students, a troupe of black musicians, dancers, and singers that performed for white audiences in New York theaters. Between late 1905 and 1910, he was musical director for popular African-American revues, including *The Shoo-Fly Regiment*, *The Red Moon*, and *Mr. Lode of Kole*.

Because New York's musicians' union was for whites only, on April 11, 1910, Europe and several other black instrumentalists and composers founded the Clef Club, which served as a union and booking agency for black musicians. He also brought the organization's members together to form the Clef Club Orchestra, which showcased the talents of black artists. With more than 100 instrumentalists taking part, the orchestra gave its first performance on May 27, 1911, at the Manhattan Casino in Harlem. The Clef Club Orchestra had its Carnegie Hall debut on May 12, 1912, and returned to Carnegie Hall in 1913 and 1914.

Commenting on Europe's influence, composer and performer Eubie Blake said, "Before Europe, Negro musicians were just like wandering minstrels. Play in a saloon and pass the hat and that's it. Before Jim, they weren't even supposed to be human beings. Jim Europe changed all that. He made a profession for us out of music."

In 1913, Europe married Willie Angrom Starke. (His only child, James Reese Europe, Jr., would be born to entertainer Bessie Simms in 1917.) In 1914, Europe resigned from the Clef Club and joined the musicians' union when it dropped its exclusionary rule, and he urged other African Americans to do the same. He formed a new band, the Tempo Club. He soon began to play for the dance team of Vernon and Irene Castle, who popularized dances such as the fox trot and the one-step.

On September 18, 1916, Europe enlisted in the 15th Infantry Regiment of the New York National Guard, an African-American unit. By April 1917, when the United States entered World War I, he had passed the officer's examination. Hoping to boost enrollment, the regiment's white commander, Colonel William Hayward, asked Europe to do what he did best: organize a band. Europe signed up some of the nation's finest African-American performers, including NOBLE SISSLE as tenor soloist and tap dancer Bill "Bojangles" Robinson as drum major. He even secured permission to recruit clarinetists in Puerto Rico.

On October 8, 1917, the 15th New York departed for training at Camp Wadsworth in Spartanburg, South Carolina, where civic leaders openly opposed the presence of African-American soldiers from the North. Although the regiment refused to respond to provocation, reports of several minor racial clashes persuaded army leaders to relocate the regiment to France for further training.

The 15th New York, renamed the 369th Infantry, reached Brest on New Year's Day, 1918. Almost immediately, the regimental band was ordered to entertain Allied troops and civilians in cities throughout France. Its music electrified audiences and generated interest in France and at home. On March 14, First Lieutenant Europe and his musicians rejoined their regiment, which went into combat on April 23. Fighting alongside French soldiers, the 369th was the first African-American unit to fight in Europe. Its members spent 191 days in the trenches, more than any other Americans, and earned the nickname "Hellfighters" for their bravery. Privates HENRY JOHNSON and Needham Roberts of the 369th were awarded the French Croix de Guerre.

An August 1918 directive that the officers in black units be of a single race, either black or white, removed Europe from duty with the 369th before it became the first American regiment to reach the Rhine. He and his band went to Paris, where they performed for eight weeks before enthusiastic audiences. Europe commented, "Everywhere we gave a concert, it was a riot." The French called the music jazz, although musicologists say that it resembled traditional band music more than fully developed jazz. It did, however, contain some elements of jazz, such as improvisation, blue notes, slurs, and changes in rhythm and dynamics.

Europe and the regimental band rejoined the 369th after the November 11, 1918, armistice and gave their final performance in France on January 31, 1919. Seventeen days later, the ship carrying

First Lieutenant James Reese Europe (left) leads the 369th Infantry Regiment Band in a performance for patients at the American Red Cross Hospital No. 9, Paris. *(National Archives)*

the Hellfighters sailed into New York Harbor. New Yorkers turned out to cheer the regiment as it marched from lower Manhattan to Harlem with the famous band leading the way.

Soon after Europe returned to civilian life, the Clef Club hired him as its president, and he took the club's orchestra on tour. The group was performing in Boston on May 9, 1919, when drummer Herbert Wright, who had an imagined grievance against Europe, stabbed the bandleader in the neck. His jugular vein severed, Europe died that night.

New York City held its first public funeral for Europe. The body of the musician who had marched triumphantly up Fifth Avenue was carried from a Harlem funeral home to St. Mark's Episcopal Church, located then on West 53rd Street. Europe was buried at Arlington National Cemetery.

Further Reading

Badger, Reid. "The Conquests of Europe: The Remarkable Career of James Reese Europe." *Alabama Heritage* 1, no. 1 (summer 1986): pp. 34–49.

———. *A Life in Ragtime: A Biography of James Reese Europe.* New York: Oxford University Press, 1995.

"James Reese Europe, 1881–1919 [biography]." Library of Congress, Performing Arts Encyclopedia. Available online. URL: http://memory.loc.gov/diglib/ihas/loc.natlib.ihas.200038842/default.html. Downloaded on August 13, 2008.

Schuller, Gunther. *Musings: The Musical Worlds of Gunther Schuller.* New York: Da Capo Press, 1999, pp. 37–41.

Smith, Jessie Carney, ed. *Notable Black American Men.* Detroit, Mich.: Gale Research, 1999, pp. 382–386.

F

Fields, Arnold

(1946–) *major general, deputy commander of U.S. Marine Corps Forces Europe*

Arnold Fields joined the Marine Corps after receiving his draft notice in 1969, never intending to have a military career. Because the opportunities offered to him as an African American in the armed forces were greater than those available in civilian life, he remained in the marines and rose to the rank of major general.

Arnold Fields was born on October 9, 1946, and grew up in Varnville, South Carolina. Money was tight in the Fields household, so while their father drove a truck for a living, Arnold and his older brother and sister often helped their mother pick cotton. By the time he was 14 years old, Arnold could pick 100 pounds of cotton in a day, adding a welcome $3 to $4 to the family's income.

Gifted with a rich bass-baritone voice, Fields stood out in the choir at all-black North District High School. A teacher encouraged him to apply for a music scholarship to South Carolina State University and drove him to the audition in Orangeburg, 65 miles away. Fields was accepted and financed his education with his $150-per-semester scholarship, loans, and summer jobs picking crops. He earned a degree in agriculture in 1968.

He had just embarked on a career as a high school teacher when, in the spring of 1969, he received notice that he was being drafted into the army. From a Marine Corps recruiter he learned that by joining the marines with a deferred induction he could finish the school year and attend officer candidate school. He followed this course and was commissioned a Marine Corps second lieutenant on November 1, 1969, having no idea that he would spend 34 years in the military.

Those years he served in Asia, Africa, the Middle East, and Europe. He also received regular promotions, attaining the rank of major general on August 6, 1999.

In February 1971, Fields was assigned to the 3rd Marine Division in Okinawa, Japan, where he was an 81mm mortar platoon commander and company executive officer with the 2nd Battalion, 4th Marines. In 1985, he went to North Africa to command Company B of the Marine Security Guard Battalion, serving embassies and consulates throughout North Africa, the Middle East, and southwest Asia. In 1990 and 1991, when the United States launched Operations Desert Shield and Desert Storm to remove Iraqi forces from Kuwait and prevent an invasion of Saudi Arabia, Fields commanded the 3rd Battalion, 6th Marines, 2nd Marine Division. He was awarded a Bronze Star with Combat V after his battalion cleared six paths through a minefield with no casualties during Operation Desert Storm.

Between overseas assignments, Fields was stationed in the United States at locations that included the Marine Corps Recruit Depot at Parris Island, South Carolina; the Marine Corps Development and Education Command at Quantico, Virginia; MacDill Air Force Base, Florida; and Kaneohe, Marine Corps Base Hawaii, at which he was base commander.

In 2002, when he spoke at a Black History Month forum in Munich, Germany, Fields was deputy commander of the U.S. Marine Corps Forces Europe. He said that the Marine Corps has fostered racial harmony in the ranks by focusing on "intellect, human understanding and moral character." He also noted that the devastating terrorist attacks of September 11, 2001, had helped to equalize Americans of all races and ethnic backgrounds. "I'm not saying that we are all entirely equal," he explained. "But we were all affected equally; it was a common denominator."

Major General Fields retired from active duty in early 2004. On June 25, 2004, five months after his retirement, he was awarded the Distinguished Service Medal in a ceremony in his hometown, Varnville, South Carolina. He continued to serve his government in retirement, first as chief of staff of the Iraq Reconstruction Management Office, a temporary organization that coordinated U.S. spending to rebuild infrastructure in Iraq despite ongoing hostility. Next, beginning in January 2007, he was deputy director of the Africa Center for Strategic Studies at the National Defense University in Washington, D.C. On May 29, 2008, President George W. Bush selected Fields to head a new office investigating reconstruction spending in Afghanistan for evidence of corruption, bribery, and favoritism.

Fields's many military decorations include the Defense Superior Service Medal with Oak Leaf Cluster, the Meritorious Service Medal, the Joint Service Commendation Medal, the Navy and Marine Corps Achievement Medal, the Combat Action Ribbon, the Joint Meritorious Unit Award, the Southwest Asia Service Medal, and the Kuwait Liberation Medal.

Further Reading

De Young, Karen. "IG Is Named to Scrutinize Afghan Efforts." *Washington Post,* May 30, 2008, p. A11.

Kester, Brian. "Retired Major General Awarded for Service." Headquarters Marine Corps. Available online. URL: http://www.marines.mil/units/hqmc/tecom/mcrdparrisisland/Pages/2004/Retired%20major%20general%20awarded%20for%20service.aspx. Downloaded on August 17, 2008.

Smyser, A. A. "Marine Brig. Gen. Arnold Fields' Success Story." *Honolulu Star Bulletin.* Available online. URL: http://starbulletin.com/1999/05/13/editorial/smyser.html. Downloaded on August 18, 2008.

Fields, Evelyn J.

(Evelyn Juanita Fields)
(1949–   ) *rear admiral, director of the National Oceanic and Atmospheric Administration (NOAA)*

In May 1999, when the Senate confirmed the appointment of Admiral Evelyn Fields as director of the Office of Marine Operations and the NOAA Commissioned Corps, she became the first African American and the first woman to hold the position.

The oldest of five children, Evelyn Juanita Fields was born in Norfolk, Virginia, on January 29, 1949. Although she grew up in an important seaport and military center, she never considered a seagoing career. She studied mathematics at Norfolk State College, graduating in 1971. In 1972, she took a job in Norfolk as a cartographer with NOAA's Atlantic Marine Center.

NOAA, an agency within the U.S. Department of Commerce, collects data on the oceans, the atmosphere, the Sun, and space. The NOAA Commissioned Corps, consisting of military officers who are also scientists, engineers, or mathematicians, is the smallest of the nation's uniformed services. The NOAA Corps conducts research, but the president can assimilate its members into the armed forces in the event of a national emergency.

Fields joined the NOAA Commissioned Corps in 1973, when the uniformed service began recruiting female officers, and was the first African-American woman to join the corps. She served on NOAA research vessels, as operations officer on the *Mt. Mitchell* and *Peirce,* and as executive officer on the *Rainier.* Sailing the Atlantic and Pacific Oceans, the Gulf of Mexico, the Caribbean, and the waters of Alaska, the scientists aboard these ships conducted hydrographic surveys and fisheries and oceanographic research. Fields gained expert knowledge of hydrography—the scientific study of surface waters—and participated in a hydrographer exchange program with Canada.

In 1989, when she was placed in command of the NOAA ship *McArthur,* Fields became the first woman to command a federal ship. The 32 men of the *McArthur*'s crew quickly discovered that a woman could be as competent as a man in command. "They were standing back a little to see what was going to happen," she said, "but after a month they realized it was business as usual." Fields learned everything she could about her ship, including its engine systems, and sometimes surprised her subordinates. "[O]nce the engineers began to explain things to me, I could just see the amazement in their eyes when I was able to ask [intelligent] questions," she remarked.

In July 1990, Fields was selected to take part in the U.S. Department of Commerce Science and Technology Fellowship Program. Participants in this program spend 10 months in a policy-making office of the executive or legislative branch of the federal government, where they study national and international issues involving science and technology. The experience that she gained qualified Fields to hold high-level positions, including that of administrative officer with the National Geodetic Survey. She also served as director of NOAA's Commissioned Personnel Center and as assignment coordinator for the Office of NOAA Corps Operations. Next, as assistant administrator of the National Ocean Service, a division of NOAA, she significantly improved NOAA's nautical charting capabilities. In 1996, the National Technical Association named Fields one of the top 50 minority women in science and engineering.

On January 19, 1999, President Bill Clinton nominated Captain Evelyn Fields to be director of NOAA's Office of Marine and Aviation Operations, which manages the agency's research ships and survey aircraft, and the NOAA Commissioned Corps. The Senate confirmed the appointment in

Rear Admiral Evelyn J. Fields directed the NOAA Commissioned Corps from 1999 through 2003. *(National Oceanic and Atmospheric Administration)*

May 1999, and Fields was immediately promoted from captain to rear admiral. She has insisted that neither her race nor her sex inhibited her ability to excel in the NOAA Corps. "I came up through the chain of command and was given the opportunity to prove myself," she said. On another occasion she noted, "The fact that I'm female is nice; the fact that I'm black is nice, but I don't think those were the reasons I was selected."

Admiral Fields's awards include the Congressional Black Caucus's Ralph M. Metcalfe Health, Education and Science Award (1999); the Maryland Federation of Business and Professional Women's Clubs' Woman of the Year (1999); and the Department of Commerce's Gold Medal for leadership (2000). Also in 2000, the Virginia legislature passed a joint memorial resolution honoring her contributions to her home city of Norfolk. Fields retired on December 1, 2003, after 30 years of active service.

Further Reading

"First Woman Ship Captain." *Ebony* 45, no. 8 (June 1990), pp. 88–90.

Henderson, Ashyia N., ed. *Contemporary Black Biography.* Vol. 27. Detroit: Gale Group, 2001, pp. 60–62.

Lei, Cecelia. "Journey to Empowerment: Rear Admiral Evelyn Fields Recounts Her Journey." University of California at San Diego. Available online. URL: http://www.diversity.ucsd.edu/articles/evelynfields.asp. Downloaded on August 18, 2008.

Sarasohn, Judy. "New Admiral Pilots Smallest U.S. Corps." *Washington Post*, May 24, 1999, p. A23.

Fishburne, Lillian Elaine

(1949–   ) *first African-American woman promoted to flag rank in the U.S. Navy*

In 1998, Secretary of Defense William Cohen called Rear Admiral Lillian Fishburne "a woman whose story helps us to understand the truth that women are an indispensable part of today's military." In her nearly 25 years as a naval officer, Fishburne held positions of responsibility in Washington, D.C., and elsewhere as she rose to become the navy's first African-American woman admiral.

Lillian Elaine Fishburne was born in Patuxent River, Maryland, the site of a naval air station, on March 25, 1949, and raised in Rockville, Maryland, a suburb of Washington, D.C. Her father, who was on active duty in the navy, encouraged her in her ambition to pursue a naval career. After graduating in 1971 from Lincoln University in Oxford, Pennsylvania, with a degree in sociology, she attended the Women Officers School at Newport, Rhode Island. She was commissioned an ensign in February 1973.

Fishburne's first duty as a naval officer was as personnel and legal officer at the Naval Air Test Facility, Lakehurst, New Jersey. From there she went in August 1974 to Miami, Florida, where she was an officer programs recruiter. Beginning in November 1977, she was the officer in charge of the Naval Communications Center at Great Lakes, Illinois.

She continued her education while in the navy, earning in 1980 a master of arts in management from Webster College in St. Louis and in 1982 a master of science in telecommunications systems management from the Naval Postgraduate School in Monterey, California. She was regularly promoted as well, reaching the rank of lieutenant commander in June 1982.

Married to Albert J. Sullivan, a native of Daytona Beach, Florida, and the mother of one daughter, Cherese, Fishburne took on her next assignment, as assistant head of the Joint Allied Command and Control Matters Branch of the Command, Control, and Communications Directorate in the Office of the Chief of Naval Operations in Washington, D.C. Beginning in December 1984, she served for more than two years as executive officer of the Naval Command Station at Yokosuka, Japan. Then in February 1987 she returned to the Command, Control, and Communications Directorate in the Office of the Chief of Naval Operations as a special projects officer. She was promoted to commander on September 1, 1988, and placed in command of the Naval Computer and Telecommunications Station at Key West, Florida, in July 1990.

Like most career military officers, Fishburne moved frequently to new jobs and new locations. She viewed each move as an opportunity for growth. "Every promotion or job assignment I get makes me more confident and draws upon my strengths and wisdom to do it correctly," she said. She attributed her steady rise in rank to her commitment to doing each job well, and her success as a manager to her belief in asking no more of subordinates that she was willing to do herself.

In June 1993, Fishburne graduated from the Industrial College of the Armed Forces at Fort McNair in Washington, D.C. She was promoted to captain on March 1, 1994, and in August 1995 reported to Honolulu, Hawaii, to command the Naval Computer and Telecommunications Area Master Station Eastern Pacific.

On February 1, 1998, Lillian Fishburne became the first African-American woman to hold the rank of rear admiral in the United States Navy. She was assigned to Information Space Warfare Command and Control at the Pentagon before retiring in February 2001.

Rear Admiral Fishburne's awards and decorations include the Defense Superior Service Medal, the Legion of Merit, the Meritorious Service Medal (two awards), the Navy Commendation Medal (two awards), and the Navy Achievement Medal.

Further Reading

Boyd, Charles E. "African-American Military Women: Soaring Beyond the Glass Ceiling." Black Collegian Online. Available online. URL: http://www.black-collegian.com/issues/1998-04/womenmil.shtml. Downloaded on August 18, 2008.

Hawkins, Walter L. *Black American Military Leaders.* Jefferson, N.C.: McFarland and Co., 2007, pp. 159–160.

"Rear Admiral Lillian Fishburne." Real African American History. Available online. URL: http://www.raahistory.com/military/navy/fishburne.htm. Downloaded on August 18, 2008.

Fleetwood, Christian Abraham

(1840–1914) *sergeant major in the Civil War, awarded the Medal of Honor for his actions at Chaffin's Farm, Virginia*

Christian A. Fleetwood discovered in the 19th century that even a Medal of Honor winner had no future in the U.S. Army if he was African American. He resigned from the army rather than remain in an organization that discriminated on the basis of race, became active in the National Guard, and established a military cadet program for African-American youth.

Christian Abraham Fleetwood was born on July 21, 1840, in Baltimore, Maryland, to Charles and Anna Maria Fleetwood, free people of color. Charles Fleetwood was head steward in the home of a wealthy Baltimore sugar merchant, John C. Brunes. Brunes and his wife provided young Christian with an education, and at age 16, the boy journeyed to Africa, visiting Liberia and Sierra Leone.

Upon returning to the United States, Christian Fleetwood attended the Ashmun Institute (later Lincoln University), a college for African-American men. The school was named for Jehudi Ashmun, a white agent of the American Colonization Society, the organization that founded Liberia. Fleetwood graduated in 1860 and went to work for a Baltimore shipping company. He also helped to launch the *Lyceum Observer*, which is thought to be the first African-American newspaper published in the South.

Fleetwood hoped to return to Liberia in 1863, but with the North and South involved in the

Civil War, very few ships were carrying passengers to Africa. He decided instead to remain in the United States, "to assist in abolishing slavery and to save the country from ruin," by joining the Union army. On August 17, 1863, he enlisted as a sergeant in Company G of the 4th Regiment, U.S. Colored Infantry. Two days later, he was promoted to sergeant major.

The 4th Regiment served in campaigns in North Carolina and Virginia, including the bloody encounter at Chaffin's Farm, near New Market Heights, Virginia, on September 29 and 30, 1864. Both the 4th and the 6th U.S. Colored Troops lost half their men in this brutal fight that ended in victory for the Union. Fleetwood earned the Medal of Honor when he lifted the regimental

Christian Fleetwood displays his Medal of Honor. *(Library of Congress)*

colors after two flag bearers had been shot down and "bore them nobly through the fight." Of the 16 African Americans who won Medals of Honor for their actions in the Civil War, 14 were so honored because of their bravery at New Market Heights and Chaffin's Farm.

The 4th Regiment's officers petitioned the War Department to give an officer's commission to Fleetwood, who was considering an army career. Secretary of War Edwin Stanton declined to recommend the appointment, however, and Fleetwood decided to leave the army at the end of his period of enlistment. "I see no good that will result to our people by continuing to serve," he wrote, "on the contrary it seems to me that our continuing to act in a subordinate capacity, with no hope of advancement or promotion is an absolute injury to our cause. It is a tacit but telling acknowledgement on our part that we are not fit for promotion, & that we are satisfied to remain in a state of marked and acknowledged subserviency."

Fleetwood was honorably discharged on May 4, 1866, and worked as a bookkeeper in Columbus, Ohio, until 1867. He then settled in Washington, D.C., and held jobs with the Freedmen's Bank and the War Department. On November 16, 1869, he married Sara Iredell. He was active in community life, serving as a choirmaster at several Washington churches and calling for equitable treatment for African-American servicemen in speeches to community and National Guard groups.

In an effort to expand opportunities for African Americans in the armed forces, he organized the 6th Battalion of the District of Columbia National Guard. On July 18, 1887, he was appointed major and commanding officer of this all-black unit. In 1888, he was a principal founder of the Colored High School Cadet Corps of the District of Columbia, which instructed young men in military science and drilling. Graduates of the program in later years included BENJAMIN O. DAVIS, SR., the nation's first African-American general, and WESLEY A. BROWN, the first African-

American graduate of the U.S. Naval Academy. Fleetwood served as the first instructor of the cadet corps until 1897.

In 1891, the D.C. National Guard consolidated several African-American battalions into one, the First Separate Battalion. After being passed over as commander of this unit, Fleetwood resigned from the National Guard in 1892. In 1898, prominent African Americans in Washington worked to establish an African-American army regiment under his command to take part in the Spanish-American War, but without support from the army's white leadership, the project failed.

Christian A. Fleetwood died suddenly of heart failure on September 28, 1914. His Medal of Honor is in the collection of the Smithsonian Institution.

Further Reading

"Biography: Christian Fleetwood." Library of Congress. Available online. URL: http://memory.loc.gov/ammem/aap/fleetw.html. Downloaded on August 18, 2008.

Claxton, Melvin, and Mark Puls. *Uncommon Valor: A Story of Race, Patriotism, and Glory in the Final Battles of the Civil War.* Hoboken, N.J.: John Wiley and Sons, 2006.

"Diary of Sergeant Major Christian A. Fleetwood, U.S. Colored Infantry, 4th Regiment, Company G, 1864: Excerpts." National Humanities Center. Available online. URL: http://nationalhumanities center.org/pds/maai/identity/text7/fleetwooddiary. pdf. Downloaded on August 18, 2008.

Greene, Robert Ewell. *Black Defenders of America, 1775–1973.* Chicago: Johnson Publishing Co., 1974, pp. 66–67, 351, 376, 388–389.

Johnson, Charles, Jr. "Fleetwood Biography." National Park Service. Available online. URL: http://nps. gov/rich/flee~172.htm. Downloaded on August 18, 2008.

Lang, George, Raymond L. Collins, and Gerard F. White, comps. *Medal of Honor Recipients, 1863–1994.* Vol. 1. *Civil War to 2nd Nicaraguan Campaign.* New York: Facts On File, 1995, p. 71.

"Medal of Honor, Christian A. Fleetwood." Smithsonian Institution. Available online. URL: http://www.civilwar.si.edu/soldiering_medal_of_honor.html. Downloaded on August 18, 2008.

". . . to benefit my race." *Civil War Times Illustrated* 16, no. 4 (July 1977): pp. 18–19.

Flipper, Henry Ossian

(1856–1940) *first African American to graduate from the U.S. Military Academy*

Since 1977, the United States Military Academy has presented the Henry O. Flipper Award to the graduating cadet who has best displayed leadership, discipline, and perseverance "in the face of unusual difficulties," qualities associated with Flipper himself. The first African-American graduate of the academy persevered through four years of racially motivated harassment to become a second lieutenant in the army in 1877. Even as an officer he remained a target for racists, however, and he was forced out of the army on a bogus charge in 1882. His honor ultimately was restored—36 years after his death.

Henry Ossian Flipper was born on March 21, 1856, in Thomasville, Georgia, to Festus and Isabella Buckhalter Flipper, both slaves. Festus Flipper was a shoemaker and carriage trimmer, one of the minority of slaves who were skilled artisans. After the Civil War, he opened a cobbler's shop in Atlanta and earned enough to educate his five sons. Henry, the oldest, had a year of instruction with a private tutor before enrolling in 1866 in a school for blacks operated by the American Missionary Association.

In 1873, while a student at Atlanta University, Flipper secured an appointment to the U.S. Military Academy at West Point, New York. Four African Americans had been admitted to the academy before him, but all left before graduating. He arrived at West Point in July 1873 to begin four years of study that would prepare him for a career as an army officer. These turned out to be four

Lieutenant Henry O. Flipper endured insults to become the first African-American graduate of the U.S. Military Academy. *(National Archives)*

lonely years of ostracism and hounding by the white cadets. It was especially painful to Flipper when cadets who were friendly to him in private ridiculed him in public. He bore the insults stoically, however, believing, "We must force others to treat us as we wish, by giving them such an example of meekness and of good conduct as will at least shame them into a like treatment of us."

On June 14, 1877, he accepted his diploma, becoming the first African American to graduate from the military academy and a second lieutenant in the U.S. Army—the lone African American among 2,100 army officers. He was assigned to Troop A of the 10th Cavalry, an African-American unit formed after the Civil War.

Flipper arrived at his first post, Fort Sill in Indian Territory (present-day Oklahoma), on January 1, 1878. As the fort's signal officer, he instructed the troops in military signaling. He also went on scouting expeditions, surveying the plains for signs of Indian unrest. In 1879, Troop A moved to Fort Elliott, Texas, where Flipper served as adjutant to the post commander, Captain Nicholas Nolan. He mapped and surveyed the fort and helped erect a telegraph line from Fort Elliott to Fort Supply, Indian Territory. While at Fort Elliott, he formed a friendship with Captain Nolan's sister-in-law, Molly Dwyer, who lived with Nolan and his wife. Flipper and Dwyer often went riding together.

Flipper next returned to Fort Sill, where in March 1880 he supervised construction of a road connecting the fort to the railroad station at Gainesville, Texas. The next month, he designed and built a drainage ditch to draw pools of stagnant water—breeding places for malaria-carrying mosquitoes—away from the fort. Today that drainage system, known as "Flipper's Ditch," is a national landmark.

These engineering projects completed, Flipper was transferred in May 1880 to Fort Concho, Texas, where the 9th and 10th Cavalries were hunting Victorio, a chief of the Warm Springs Apache. Victorio had fled the San Carlos Reservation in Arizona and with a band of followers was attacking southwestern ranchers, killing and plundering. On one occasion, Flipper was ordered to carry a message about Victorio's location to General Benjamin F. Grierson, commander of the 10th Cavalry, who was stationed at Eagle Springs, Texas. Traveling on horseback, Flipper covered 98 miles in 22 hours. The American soldiers eventually chased Victorio into Mexico, where he was killed by Mexican cavalry on October 14, 1880.

Soon afterward, Colonel William R. Shafter, commander of Fort Davis, Texas, named Flipper acting commissary of subsistence. In that job, Flipper was responsible for housing, supplies, and equipment for the fort, and for handling the commissary funds. Although Flipper strived to be a model officer, he discovered in July 1881 that a significant portion of the commissary's money was missing from his trunk. Knowing that Shafter had long resented his friendship with Molly Dwyer, Flipper suspected that he had been the victim of foul play. Nevertheless, he endeavored to make up the shortfall from his own money, which included earnings from his book, *The Colored Cadet at West Point* (1878).

On August 31, 1881, however, Shafter accused Flipper of embezzling government funds. Although the African-American lieutenant's friends repaid the amount that was missing, Shafter moved to have Flipper court-martialed. At the trial Flipper's lawyer stated that the case was about a larger issue than missing commissary funds, telling the court, "The question before you is whether it is possible for a colored man to secure and hold a position as an officer in the Army." The verdict confirmed the attorney's assertion: Flipper was found not guilty of embezzlement but guilty of "conduct unbecoming an officer," and was dishonorably discharged from the army on June 30, 1882.

Flipper maintained his innocence for the rest of his life, insisting that his arrest and conviction had been racially motivated. Nine times he would appeal his conviction and petition the army to reinstate him, but he never would be successful. He remained in the Southwest, where he had a productive career as a mining engineer. In fact, some historians consider him to have been among the vanguard more as an African-American engineer than as an army officer. In 1886, he became chief engineer with the Sonora Land Company, which was based in Chicago. In 1887, he opened his own civil and mining engineering office in Nogales, Arizona, and in 1889 he became the editor of the *Nogales Sunday Herald*. From 1890 to 1892, he was chief engineer of the Altar Land and Colonization Company, and from 1902 to 1919 he was stationed in Chihuahua, Mexico, as resident engineer with the Balverna Mining Company. In 1923, Flipper went to Caracas, Venezuela, as chief engineer with the Pantapec Oil Company.

Between mining jobs, he was employed by the federal government. He worked as a special agent for the U.S. Justice Department Court of Private Land Claims from 1893 to 1901, as a translator and interpreter for the Senate Committee on Foreign Relations from 1919 to 1923, and as assistant to the secretary of the interior for the construction and operation of Alaskan railroads in 1921.

Henry Flipper never married. After retiring in 1930, he went to live with his brother Joseph in Atlanta. He died of a heart attack on April 26, 1940, "unwept, unhonored, unsung," as one of his friends said. On the death certificate, Joseph Flipper listed his brother's name and occupation as "Lieutenant Henry O. Flipper . . . Retired Army Officer."

Henry Flipper received his honorable discharge posthumously in 1976, after Ray MacColl, a Georgia schoolteacher, and Irsle King, Flipper's niece, persuaded the Army Board for Correction of Military Records to reexamine the details of his case. MacColl and King argued that because the charge of improper conduct was dependent on the charge of embezzlement, Flipper had been wrongly convicted of the first since he had been found not guilty of the second. The board lacked authority to overturn Flipper's court-martial, but it concluded that his conviction and discharge were "unduly harsh and unjust." In 1978, Flipper's remains were exhumed from an unmarked grave in Atlanta and reburied in Thomasville, Georgia, next to those of his parents.

On February 19, 1999, President Bill Clinton pardoned Lieutenant Henry O. Flipper.

Further Reading

Bigelow, Barbara Carlisle, ed. *Contemporary Black Biography*. Vol. 3. Detroit, Mich.: Gale Research, 1993, pp. 66–68.

Dinges, Bruce J. "The Court-Martial of Lieutenant Henry O. Flipper." *American West* 9, no. 1 (January 1972): 12–17, 59–61.

Eppinga, Jane. *Henry Ossian Flipper: West Point's First Black Graduate*. Plano, Texas: Republic of Texas Press, 1996.

Katz, William Loren. *The Black West*. Rev. ed. New York: Harlem Moon, 2005, pp. 212–213.

"Lieutenant Henry Ossian Flipper, U.S. Army 1856–1940." U.S. Army Center of Military History. Available online. URL: http://www.army.mil/cmh-pg/topics/afam/flipper.htm. Downloaded on August 18, 2008.

Maraniss, David. "Due Recognition and Reward." *Washington Post Magazine,* January 20, 1991, pp. 15–36.

Wilson, Steve. "A Black Lieutenant in the Ranks." *American History* 18, no. 8 (December 1983): 31–39.

Wooster, Robert. *Frontier Crossroads: Fort Davis and the West.* College Station: Texas A&M University Press, 2006, pp. 86–87.

Forten, James

(James Fortune)

(1766–1842) *powder boy and prisoner in the American Revolution, abolitionist*

James Forten was a patriot who dedicated himself to defending his nation in war and improving it from within in times of peace. A boy at the time of the American Revolution, he served aboard a ship and spent seven months as a prisoner of war. He also helped to defend Philadelphia, his lifelong home, during the War of 1812. Throughout his adult life, he used his influence, his pen, and his purse to combat slavery and racial injustice.

James Forten was born James Fortune on September 2, 1766, to Thomas and Sarah Fortune, free African Americans. Thomas Fortune was a sailmaker employed by Robert Bridges of Philadelphia. James attended the African School, which had been established by Quakers for free black children, until 1773, when his father died of an unknown illness. Needing to support his mother and his sister, Abigail, James worked as a chimney sweep and a grocery-store clerk.

Such tedious jobs could hardly satisfy a boy's yearning for adventure, especially during the American Revolution, when the city where he lived was an important center for privateering. Merchant vessels that had been made over into warships at the port of Philadelphia roamed the Atlantic Ocean along the East Coast, as their crews searched for British ships to commandeer. James repeatedly begged his mother to allow him to go to sea, and in 1781, she reluctantly granted him permission.

Three months before his 15th birthday, Fortune sailed out of the Chesapeake Bay aboard the *Royal Louis,* a privateer outfitted with 22 guns and carrying a crew of 200, 20 of whom were African American. By order of Congress, one-third of the crew aboard all privateers consisted of inexperienced landsmen in order to make seasoned sailors available to serve on navy ships. The captain of the *Royal Louis,* Stephen Decatur, was a veteran commander, however, although only 29 years old. On its first cruise, the *Royal Louis* seized four ships, including the *Active,* which was carrying an important dispatch on the position of England's fleet to British military leaders in New York.

At home between voyages, Fortune watched George Washington's army march through Philadelphia on its way to Yorktown, Virginia, where Lord Cornwallis was headquartered. In 1831, he recalled that the marchers had included several companies of African Americans, "as brave men as ever fought," men whose exploits "[appear] to be forgotten now. . . ."

The first sailing of the *Royal Louis* was a great success, but the second one was a disaster. In October 1781, the privateer engaged a larger British warship, the *Amphion,* and was forced to surrender. Being taken prisoner was especially frightening for Fortune and the other African Americans, because the British usually brought black captives to the West Indies and sold them into slavery. Fortune was lucky, though, because the sons of John Bazely, the captain of the *Amphion,* were aboard ship, and Bazely selected Fortune to be the companion of his younger son, 12-year-old Henry. As the ship sailed toward New York, Bazely offered to send Fortune to England with Henry and to provide for his education. The opportunity was tempting, but Fortune refused it, saying, "I have been taken prisoner for the liberties of my country, and never will prove a traitor to her interest."

James Fortune therefore became prisoner 4102 aboard the British prison hulk *Jersey*, which was anchored in New York's East River, off Long Island. Conditions aboard the rotting, leaking prison ship were dreadful, with thousands of men living crowded together in the filthy space below deck. The prisoners fought over meager rations of spoiled food and counted themselves lucky if they survived outbreaks of influenza, yellow fever, and smallpox. Fortune had a chance to escape by hiding in the trunk of an officer of the Continental Navy who was being exchanged for a British officer, but he allowed an ailing white companion, Daniel Brewton, to go in his place. Brewton never forgot that act of generosity and became Fortune's lifelong friend. Fortune regained his freedom after seven months aboard the *Jersey* when he was released in a general prisoner exchange. He made his way on foot to Philadelphia, where his family had given him up for dead.

The Revolution over, Fortune's brother-in-law secured a job for him aboard a ship bound for Liverpool. Fortune reached the British port in March 1785; during a year in England he met several prominent British abolitionists who encouraged him to be active in the nascent antislavery movement in the United States.

By fall 1786 he had returned to the United States. Now calling himself James Forten, he worked in the sail loft of Robert Bridges, his father's former employer. By 1788 he knew how to design, cut, and sew sails and had been made foreman. He bought the business in 1798, when Bridges retired. Forten also rose in stature in Philadelphia's African-American community, becoming in 1796 a member of the vestry of St. Thomas's African Episcopal Church and a friend of its pastor, the Reverend Absolom Jones.

A prosperous businessman, Forten purchased a three-story house at 92 Lombard Street in Philadelphia. In 1803, he married Martha Beatte. Little is known about Martha Beatte Forten, who died

This watercolor portrait by an unknown artist is thought to be of James Forten. *(The Historical Society of Pennsylvania, Portrait of James Forten from the Leon Gardiner Collection)*

in 1804, and the marriage produced no children. In December 1805, Forten married Charlotte Vandine, with whom he would have four daughters and four sons.

In January 1800, Forten began the abolitionist activities for which history would remember him when he became one of the first black Philadelphians to sign a petition to the House of Representatives protesting the Fugitive Slave Act of 1793 and the continuing slave trade. The petition also urged Congress to adopt "such measures as shall in due course emancipate the whole of their brethren from their present situation." Only one member of Congress, Representative George Thatcher of Massachusetts, supported the petition; the remainder adopted a resolution against acknowledging such appeals.

In 1813, Forten wrote the pamphlet *Letters from a Man of Colour* to protest a bill before the Pennsylvania legislature that would bar out-of-state African Americans from moving to Pennsylvania. Forten wrote, "Has the God who made the white man and the black left any record declaring us a different species? . . . [S]hould we not then enjoy the same liberty, and be protected by the same laws?" The bill was never passed. In 1817, Forten and Bishop Richard Allen of the African Methodist Episcopal Church organized 3,000 black Philadelphians to speak out against the activities of the American Colonization Society, which was working to establish a colony outside the United States for African Americans. (This protest was less effective: The society's colony, Liberia, would be founded in 1822.)

Forten remained ready to serve his country, and during the War of 1812, together with Jones and Allen he enlisted 2,500 African Americans to build fortifications that would protect Philadelphia from British occupation.

With $100,000 amassed from his sail-making business and investments, Forten by 1832 was one of the wealthiest African Americans. He had used some of his money to fund William Lloyd Garrison's abolitionist newspaper, the *Liberator*, which was first published on January 1, 1831. He also financed the American Anti-Slavery Society, which he founded with Garrison and other abolitionists in 1833.

Forten's health began to decline in 1841, and on March 4, 1842, he died. His funeral was one of the largest to be held in Philadelphia, attracting thousands of mourners, both black and white.

Further Reading

Bankston, Carl L., III, ed. *African American History.* Vol. 3. Pasadena, Calif.: Salem Press, 2006, pp. 1,105–1,106.

Billington, Ray Allen. "James Forten: Forgotten Abolitionist." *Negro History Bulletin* 13, no. 2 (November 1949): pp. 31–36.

Kranz, Rachel, and Philip J. Koslow. *The Biographical Dictionary of African Americans.* New York: Facts On File, 1999, pp. 81–82.

Winch, Julie. *A Gentleman of Color: The Life of James Forten.* New York: Oxford University Press, 2002.

G

Gaskin, Walter E., Sr.

(1951–) *major general, highest-ranking African American in the Marine Corps*

Walter E. Gaskin, Sr., began opening doors for African Americans as a teenager in the 1960s, when he helped to integrate Savannah High School. Through hard work and perseverance, he became the first African American to command one of the premier units in the Marine Corps.

Walter Gaskin was born in Savannah, Georgia, on May 8, 1951. In 1959, he moved with his parents and two brothers to Liberty City, a new community outside Savannah's city limits that offered affordable housing to African Americans. Liberty City was a typical suburb of the baby-boom era, a close-knit, middle-class, child-centered neighborhood.

Gaskin ventured out of Liberty City when he became one of the first African Americans to attend Savannah High School. His mother worried about his safety as one of 20 to 30 African Americans in a student body of 2,500, remembering the threats and hostility directed toward the students who integrated Central High School in Little Rock, Arkansas, in 1957. Gaskin soon found his niche, however, and proceeded through high school without incident. He excelled academically, earning high grades in mathematics, history, and English, and he joined the school's junior

ROTC program. He also worked part time at Peggy's, his family's barbecue restaurant.

After high school, Gaskin went to Savannah State University on a naval ROTC scholarship. In 1974, he was in the first graduating class of the university's naval ROTC program, and on June 2 of that year he was commissioned a second lieutenant in the Marine Corps and assigned to the 2nd Marine Division.

In May 1977, military service took Gaskin to Okinawa, Japan, where he was senior watch officer in the 3rd Marine Division Command Center. A year later, he reported to the Marine Corps Recruit Depot at Parris Island, South Carolina, where he served as series commander and executive officer of Company F, 2nd Recruit Training Battalion. In 1980, he returned to his alma mater as marine officer instructor in the naval ROTC unit.

Gaskin, his wife (the former Dora Hall of New Orleans), and their four children moved frequently over the course of Gaskin's Marine Corps career. In 1990, Gaskin was stationed in Seoul, South Korea, where he headed the Ground Forces Branch, Operations Division, of the Combined Forces Command (CFC). CFC is a defense team established in 1978 by the United States and the Republic of Korea to deter or defeat outside aggression against the Republic of Korea. CFC's peacetime force includes 600,000 active-duty military personnel in both countries. In July 1992, Gaskin served in Norway as operations officer during the planning and execution of Battle Griffin, a program of joint allied field exercises conducted every three years in conjunction with NATO to strengthen the Norwegian National Forces.

In 1992, Gaskin received a master's degree in public administration from the University of Oklahoma, and in June 1994 he graduated from the Army War College at Carlisle Barracks, Pennsylvania. He then became executive officer of the 6th Marine Regiment, 2nd Marine Division. In April 1995, he took command of the 2nd Battalion, 2nd Marines. The battalion was deployed to the Mediterranean Sea in January 1996 and participated in Operations Assured Response and Quick Response. In Operation Assured Response, conducted from April 9 through June 18, 1996, the U.S. Navy, Air Force, and Marine Corps evacuated from Liberia 2,444 people—Americans and citizens of other countries—following intensification of Liberia's civil war. Operation Quick Response was a cooperative effort between the navy and Marine Corps that was conducted from May through August 1996 to evacuate Americans from Bangui, the capital of the Central African Republic, and secure the embassy there during a period of civil unrest and rebellion.

In January 1999, after assignments at Marine Corps Headquarters in Washington, D.C., and at Camp Lejeune, North Carolina, Gaskin was selected to command the 22nd Marine Expeditionary Unit, a large-scale operational unit with land, sea, and air capabilities. The 22nd is one of seven marine expeditionary units that can be deployed all over the world. Colonel Gaskin was the first African American to command a marine expeditionary unit, but he insisted that his selection was based on his capabilities. "The idea that I'm black is coincidental to the fact that I worked hard to be a MEU commander," he said, adding, "But I'm not naive, and I know that represents a lot to people of color. . . ."

In 1999, the 22nd took part in Exercise Bright Star, a combined joint exercise involving more than 73,000 military personnel from 12 countries in North America, Europe, and the Middle East. Activities included an amphibious landing on the Egyptian coast, air operations, surface engagements, and information sharing. From Egypt the unit went to Jordan for Exercise Infinite Moonlight, another cooperative endeavor.

The 22nd returned to Camp Lejeune in March 2000, and Gaskin was transferred to Training Command at Marine Corps Base Quantico in Virginia. In September 2001, he was promoted to brigadier general, becoming the fifth African-American general in the history of the Marine Corps. Gaskin subsequently served in Naples, Italy, as deputy commanding general of Fleet Marine Forces Europe. In September 2004, he headed Marine Corps Recruiting Command, based in Quantico. His promotion to major general, in October 2005, made him the highest-ranking African American in the Marine Corps.

Beginning in June 2006, as commander of the 2nd Marine Division, Gaskin supervised the training of more than 22,000 marines and sailors for duty in Iraq, Afghanistan, and the Horn of Africa in what the government has labeled the Global War on Terrorism. He was also deployed overseas alongside the forces under his command.

Between February 2007 and February 2008, Gaskin was stationed in Iraq, as commander first of the Second Marine Expeditionary Force (Forward) and then of Multi-National Force West (MNF-W). More than 35,000 strong, MNF-W patrolled the Iraqi province of al Anbar, a region disrupted by al-Qaeda and insurgent activity. Under Gaskin's leadership, MNF-W brought stability and security to the province and left it ready to be placed under Iraqi control. On July 27, 2008, Gaskin was appointed to the Pentagon as vice director of the Joint Staff.

Major General Gaskin's military decorations include the Defense Superior Service Medal,

Legion of Merit with Gold Star, Bronze Star with Combat V, Defense Meritorious Service Medal, Meritorious Service Medal, Navy and Marine Corps Commendation Medal with two Gold Stars, and Navy and Marine Corps Achievement Medal.

Further Reading

Fishman, Jane. "The Military Is a Good Mesh for Savannah Native." *Savannah Now.* Available online. URL: http://www.savannahmorningnews. com/stories/012999/ACCfishman.html. Downloaded on August 18, 2008.

"An Interview with Major General Walter E. Gaskin." *Diversity Spectrum Corporation.* Available online. URL: http://diversityspectrum.com/index2.php?option=com_content&do_pdf=1&id=771. Downloaded on August 18, 2008.

Jones, Brian D. "Major General Gaskin Relinquishes Command of 2nd Marine Division." *2nd Marine Division.* Available online. URL: http://www.iimefpublic.usmc.mil/__852571150047CCBC.nsf/rssNews/A13CA121F325B8148 5257474006BBA9 4?OpenDocument. Downloaded on August 19, 2008.

Phillips, Noelle. "Savannah Native Nominated to Be Brigadier General." *Savannah Now.* Available online. URL: http://www.savannahnow.com/stories/042300/LOCsavannahgeneral.shtml. Downloaded on August 18, 2002.

Gaston, Mack Charles

(1940–   ) *rear admiral, first African American to command the Great Lakes Naval Training Center*

Naval officer Mack C. Gaston modeled himself on the Reverend Martin Luther King, Jr., whom he called "the gentle warrior who believed in his country. . . ." Before retiring in 1995, Gaston reached the rank of rear admiral and commanded a major installation, the Naval Training Center at Great Lakes, Illinois.

Mack Charles Gaston was born in Dalton, Georgia, on July 17, 1940. He graduated from the Tuskegee Institute in Alabama with a degree in engineering in 1964; on August 20 of that year he entered the navy.

Gaston was first assigned to a destroyer, the USS *Buck,* in 1965. He attended the Naval Destroyer School at Newport, Rhode Island, from March to September 1967 before serving aboard another destroyer, the USS *O'Brien.* Subsequently, from May 1969 until May 1971, he was on the staff of Destroyer Squadron 5. His years at sea included duty in Vietnam. Gaston next became the personal aide of the director of Research, Development, Test and Evaluation in the Office of the Chief of Naval Operations in Washington, D.C.

In the years that followed, Gaston held a broad range of naval assignments and moved up in rank. He and his wife, the former Lillian Bonds of Dalton, had a daughter, Sonja. In 1984, Gaston earned a master's degree in business administration from Marymount College in Virginia, and in December 1985 he was assigned to the Surface Warfare Officers School Command, a Newport, Rhode Island, training facility that prepares naval officers for duty at sea.

In February 1986, Gaston was placed in command of the USS *Josephus Daniels,* a guided missile frigate. Captain Bernard T. Jackson, who served under him on the *Josephus Daniels,* said in 2002, "His mentoring and leadership were inspirational." Wherever he was stationed, Gaston acted as a role model, guiding and encouraging younger African-American officers.

Gaston returned to the Office of the Chief of Naval Operations in July 1988, first as director of Surface Warfare Manpower and Training Requirements and then as director of Manpower and Training Requirements of Surface Ships. In the latter position he managed a budget of $1 billion. In 1990, Gaston was made chief of the Nuclear Test Organization, the largest program in the Defense Nuclear Agency. He did much as the organization's chief to streamline management of the nation's nuclear stockpile. Also in 1990, he was selected for promotion to rear admiral.

Gaston left the Defense Nuclear Agency in 1990 to become the first African American to command the Naval Training Center at Great Lakes, Illinois. Staffed by 30,000 military and civilian personnel, the center provides academic, technical, and physical training to 40,000 naval recruits annually. The center had a student success rate below 50 percent when Gaston arrived, but he introduced instructional methods that raised the success rate to 85 percent.

As someone who came of age during the Civil Rights movement, Gaston remained an admirer of the Reverend Martin Luther King, Jr. In 1994, he reflected on King's example, saying, "Dr. King never lost faith in the American promise. He never lost faith in the inherent decency of the American people, and the great promise of the American system, even when many people were discouraged. That is why he fought—to help the United States attain its own high promise."

Gaston retired in 1995, ending a 30-year military career that had enabled him to fulfill his own high promise. He became vice president of leadership development with Waste Management, Inc., a national provider of waste-removal services, which is headquartered in Houston, Texas. In 1998, he joined Electronic Data Systems (EDS), a firm that advises businesses on ways to improve efficiency and better use technology, and in 2008, he accepted a position with the SPECTRUM Group, a consulting firm based in Alexandria, Virginia.

Rear Admiral Gaston's military decorations include the Meritorious Service Medal with one Gold Star, the Navy E Ribbon, the Vietnam Campaign Medal, the Vietnam Service Medal with one Bronze Star, and the Navy Commendation Medal with Combat "V."

Further Reading

Hawkins, Walter L. *Black American Military Leaders.* Jefferson, N.C.: McFarland and Co., 2007, pp. 177–178.

"RADM Mack C. Gaston, USN-Ret." Military Officers Association of America. Available online. URL: http://www.moaa.org/about/about_leadership/about_bod_list/about_bod_2008_gaston.htm. Downloaded on August 20, 2008.

"Rear Admiral Mack Gaston, USN (ret)." The Spectrum Group. Available online. URL: http://www.spectrumgrp.com/our-people/members/mack-gaston. Downloaded on August 20, 2008.

Gooding, James Henry

(ca. 1837–1864) *sergeant with the 54th Massachusetts Infantry, reporter for the* New Bedford [Massachusetts] Mercury

As a sergeant with the 54th Massachusetts Infantry, James Henry Gooding fought for his country in the Civil War. As a correspondent for his hometown newspaper, he created an important historical record of his unit's experiences.

James Henry Gooding was born in Troy, New York, around 1837. Nothing is known about his parents, James and Sarah Gooding, and almost nothing is known about his life prior to 1856. He was educated, but when and where he went to school remain unexplained.

In the summer of 1856, Gooding arrived in New Bedford, Massachusetts, where he was hired by the firm of J. & W. R. Wing to sail aboard the *Sunbeam*, a three-masted ship about to embark on a whaling expedition. There were more than 650 ships in the U.S. whaling fleet in 1856, and African Americans were common among their sailors. The crews of several ships were mostly or even entirely African American, and a few whaling vessels had African-American officers. There was only one other African American aboard the *Sunbeam*, however.

The ship left New Bedford on July 21, 1856, to hunt sperm whales in the Indian and Pacific Oceans. Gooding wrote poetry while at sea, and six of his poems were later published. The *Sunbeam* returned to New Bedford on April 13, 1860;

a month later, Gooding sailed as steward aboard the *Black Eagle,* which made a whaling voyage to the Arctic. In early 1862, three months after the *Black Eagle* returned to port, he left New Bedford on the *Richard Mitchell,* a merchant ship bound for Montevideo. As the ship's cook and steward he earned $20 a month. Gooding was home at the end of the summer, and on September 28, 1862, he married Ellen Louisa Allen of New Bedford.

Gooding traded the life of a seaman for that of a soldier when he enlisted in the 54th Massachusetts Infantry on February 14, 1863. The unit was the first African-American regiment formed in the North to fight in the Civil War.

There are no surviving documents to explain how Gooding became associated with the *New Bedford Mercury,* but the newspaper began publishing his accounts of the 54th's activities on March 3, 1863. Gooding signed his early missives with the initials J. H. G., but in September 1863, he adopted the pseudonym "Monitor."

Gooding described for the *Mercury*'s readers the attitude of the men as they trained at Camp Meigs in Readville, Massachusetts, aware that white America was watching to see if blacks had the courage to be soldiers. "[T]heir position is a very delicate one," he wrote; "the least false step, at a moment like the present, may tell a dismal tale at some future day." At times his reports contained humor. On June 30, 1863, when the regiment had reached St. Simon's Island, Georgia, he summed up the southern scenery by writing, "If a person were to ask me what I saw South, I should tell him stink weed, sand, rattlesnakes, and alligators."

The same day, the men of the 54th learned that white and black soldiers were to be paid at different rates. Whereas a white soldier received $13 per month and $3.50 to buy a uniform, a black soldier was to be given $10 per month and have $3 deducted for his clothing. Gooding wrote a letter of protest to President Abraham Lincoln, stating, "We have done a soldier's duty. Why can't we have a soldier's pay?" The men of the 54th refused to accept their money, preferring to serve without

Corporal James Henry Gooding is buried in Andersonville National Cemetery. *(Andersonville National Historic Site)*

compensation rather than be paid less than they were due. (Their protest eventually persuaded Congress to take a step toward acknowledging the equality of black and white soldiers. Beginning in August 1864, blacks in the Union army were paid at the same rate as whites.)

Sergeant Gooding reported on the July 18, 1863, attack on Fort Wagner, the Confederate installation near the entrance to the harbor at Charleston, South Carolina. The battle immortalized the 54th Infantry, which led the disastrous assault, and made heroes of men such as Sergeant WILLIAM H. CARNEY. Gooding wrote, "We met the foe on the parapet of Wagner with bayonet— we were exposed to a murderous fire from the batteries of the fort. . . . Mortal men could not stand such a fire, and the attack on Wagner was a failure." The unit's 25-year-old white commander, Colonel Robert Gould Shaw, numbered among the dead. "When the men saw their gallant leader fall," Gooding wrote, "they made a desperate effort to get him out, but they were either shot down, or reeled in the ditch below."

On December 5, 1863, Gooding was promoted to corporal. In January 1864, he was wounded in battle at Olustee, Florida, and taken prisoner. He died at Andersonville, the infamous Confederate prison camp in Georgia, on July 19, 1864.

Further Reading

Adams, Virginia M., ed. *On the Altar of Freedom: A Black Soldier's Civil War Letters from the Front.* Amherst: University of Massachusetts Press, 1991.

Berlin, Ira, ed. *Freedom's Soldiers: The Black Military Experience in the Civil War.* Cambridge, U.K.: Cambridge University Press, 1998, pp. 114–116.

"We Feel as Though Our Country Spurned Us": Soldier James Henry Gooding Protests Unequal Pay for Black Soldiers, 1863." History Matters. Available online. URL: http://historymatters.gmu.edu/d/65/19/. Downloaded on August 21, 2008.

Goodman, Robert Oliver, Jr.

(1956–   ) *navy flier imprisoned in Syria in 1983*

His capture by the Syrians after being shot down over Lebanon and his subsequent release made a national hero of Lieutenant Robert O. Goodman, Jr. Once out of the limelight, this soft-spoken family man resumed his career as a naval officer.

Robert Oliver Goodman, Jr., was born on November 30, 1956, near Ramsey Air Force Base in Puerto Rico, where his father, air force officer Robert O. Goodman, Sr., was stationed. Young Robert, called Goodie, was the oldest of three brothers who would all pursue military careers.

Following a series of moves, Robert Goodman, Sr., was stationed at Pease Air Force Base in Newington, New Hampshire. He and his wife, Marilyn Dykers Goodman, settled with their boys in the nearby town of Portsmouth. Goodie thought seriously about his future while a student at Portsmouth High School, and during his senior year he secured appointments to the Merchant Marine Academy, the U.S. Military Academy, and the U.S. Naval Academy. He chose the naval academy and reported to Annapolis, Maryland, in 1975. In January 1976, while a midshipman, he married his high school sweetheart, Terry Lynn

Bryant. The couple's first daughter, Tina, was born the following year.

Goodman earned a degree in operations analysis from the naval academy in 1978, and was assigned to the Naval Recruiting District, Boston. After just seven months, he went to Pensacola, Florida, to begin flight training at Naval Aviation Schools Command. He received his pilot's wings in August 1981, and reported for duty with Attack Squadron 85 at Oceana Naval Air Station in Virginia Beach, Virginia. There, the Goodmans' second daughter, Morgan, was born.

In October 1983, Goodman's unit was ordered to war-torn Lebanon, where the United States was maintaining a military presence until foreign forces could be withdrawn. As part of its peacekeeping mission, the U.S. military routinely flew reconnaissance flights over the region. Then, on December 3, from locations within Lebanon, Syrian forces attacked unarmed U.S. reconnaissance planes with antiaircraft guns and surface-to-air missiles. The United States responded by ordering a naval air strike against terrorist-related targets in the Beka'a Valley of Lebanon.

Among the planes that took off into the sunrise on December 4 was an A-6E Intruder with Lieutenant Mark O. Lange as pilot and Lieutenant Robert O. Goodman, Jr., as navigator-bombardier. The jet was flying low over mountains in Syrian-held territory when it was hit by fire from enemy antiaircraft guns. Lange and Goodman ejected and parachuted to the ground, but Lange was shot and killed. Goodman landed hard, dislocating his shoulder, injuring his knee, and briefly losing consciousness.

When he came to, he was stripped to his underwear, his hands were bound, and his head was covered. His captors locked him in a basement cell and subjected him to periodic interrogations and beatings. After a December 8 visit from a Red Cross worker, however, the beatings stopped.

Goodman might have remained a prisoner of the Syrians indefinitely if not for the intercession of the Reverend Jesse Jackson. In late December, Jackson traveled to Damascus with a delegation of ministers and Louis Farrakhan of the Nation of Islam. Jackson conferred with Syrian foreign minister Abdel Halim Khaddam and President Hafez al-Assad and secured Goodman's release.

On January 2, 1984, a C-141 cargo plane carried Goodman, Jackson, and the other Americans to West Germany. Two days later, Goodman stepped from a plane onto American soil at Andrews Air Force Base in Maryland and was reunited with his family. To the 200 people—mostly strangers—who had gathered to welcome him home, he said simply, "God bless America." Later that day, the Goodmans and Jackson met with President Ronald Reagan at the White House.

Goodman's knee injury required surgery and kept him grounded for several months. In May 1985, he entered the Naval Postgraduate School in Monterey, California, where he earned a master's degree in systems technology. In 1987, he was promoted to lieutenant commander and assigned to the USS *America*, an aircraft carrier. In July 1992, he reported to U.S. Space Command Headquarters at Peterson Air Force Base in Colorado. His promotion to commander came in 1994.

Goodman retired from the navy in 1995 and settled in Colorado Springs, Colorado. In 2008, he was a senior consultant with Booz Allen Hamilton, a strategy and technology consulting firm.

Further Reading

Cheers, D. Michael. "Lt. Robert Goodman: The Story Behind His Rescue." *Ebony* 39, no. 5 (March 1984), pp. 155–162.

Haskins, Jim. *African American Military Heroes*. New York: John Wiley and Sons, 1998, pp. 157–162.

Milloy, Marilyn. "White House Welcome for Airman." *Newsday*, January 5, 1984, pp. 4, 15.

Rabil, Robert G. *Syria, the United States, and the War on Terror in the Middle East*. Westport, Conn.: Praeger Security International, 2006, p. 75.

Gorden, Fred Augustus

(1940–   ) *army general, first African-American commandant of West Point*

The 41st African American to graduate from the United States Military Academy and the only one in his class of 601, Fred A. Gorden pursued an army career that emphasized his expertise in two areas: field artillery operations and command, and Spanish language and culture. He returned to West Point twice, in 1969 as a faculty member and in 1987 as the first African-American commandant of cadets.

Fred Augustus Gorden, the youngest of his parents' four children, was born in Anniston, Alabama, but was raised from infancy by his mother's oldest sister, a childless aunt who lived in Atlanta. Gorden attended elementary school in Atlanta until 1950, when he moved to Michigan with his aunt at the time of her second marriage. He graduated from Central High School in Battle Creek, Michigan, in 1957, and entered Battle Creek Community College (now Kellogg Community College) as the first recipient of a scholarship from the Post Cereal Company, for which his uncle was employed.

He intended to transfer to Wayne State University in Detroit to study architectural engineering, but in 1958 he successfully competed for a congressional appointment to the U.S. Military Academy. "I accepted the appointment," Gorden said. "West Point, after all, was and is more than a military academy: It also offers one of the most prestigious undergraduate educations of any college or university in America; and the price was right—it would cost me nothing." In college as in high school, he particularly enjoyed studying Spanish.

Gorden graduated from the academy in June 1962 with a bachelor of science degree and a commission as a second lieutenant of artillery; shortly afterward, on July 26, 1962, he married Marcia Ann Stewart, whom he had met in his "plebe," or freshman, year, and who came from a military family. Not only was her father a career soldier, but her maternal grandfather had served in Mexico with the 25th Infantry Regiment during the 1916 Punitive Expedition under General John J. "Black Jack" Pershing.

Gorden's military career got underway in August 1962, when he reported to the U.S. Army Artillery and Missile School at Fort Sill, Oklahoma, to attend the Field Artillery Officer Orientation Course. He then earned his Ranger tab and parachutist badge at Fort Benning, Georgia, before reporting in March 1963 to the 22nd Artillery, 193rd Infantry Brigade at Fort Kobbe in Panama. Marcia Gorden, who was expecting the couple's first child, remained with her parents at Fort Ord in California. In August, she and daughter Shawn Nicole joined Fred in Panama.

Fred Gorden was promoted to captain on November 9, 1965. In 1966, after fulfilling the

General Fred A. Gorden was commandant of West Point from 1987 until 1990. *(United States Military Academy)*

four-year service obligation then required of all West Point graduates, he elected to remain in the army. Over the course of his career he held a series of command positions in the Field Artillery branch, always in support of infantry units. For example, during six months of his 1967 tour of duty in Vietnam, he commanded a six-gun howitzer battery that was part of the 320th Field Artillery, 1st Brigade of the 101st Airborne Division. From May 1975 through July 1976, he was executive officer of the 1st Battalion, 15th Field Artillery of the 2nd Infantry Division in Korea. From March 1977 through September 1978, he was commander of the 1st Battalion, 8th Field Artillery of the 25th Infantry Division in Hawaii. "I found each and every one of my Army assignments interesting and challenging," Gorden said. "I did not think of them as jobs but as successive career progression assignments within my chosen profession. . . ."

Beginning in May 1968, Gorden completed the requirements for a master's degree in Spanish language, literature, and civilization from Middlebury College in Vermont. Because his course of study included graduate work in Madrid, the Gordens spent a year in Spain. A second daughter, Michelle Elizabeth, was born at Torrejon Air Force Base, near Madrid, in 1969.

Marriage has been a close partnership for Marcia and Fred Gorden. "Although she attended college, Marcia never pursued a career outside the home after we were married. However, as my partner in army career endeavors spanning more than thirty-four years, her contribution and role have been central," General Gorden explained in 2002, "with her role and achievements frequently exceeding my own."

His successful army experience and Middlebury education qualified Gorden, who had been promoted to major, to join the Department of Foreign Languages and Literature at West Point in August 1969, first as an instructor of Spanish and later as an assistant professor. He left the military academy in 1972 for studies at the Armed Forces

Staff College in Norfolk, Virginia. Several years later, from August 1979 through June 1980, he was a student at the National War College at Fort McNair in Washington, D.C.

Gorden was promoted to lieutenant colonel on June 7, 1976, and to colonel on August 7, 1980. At the time of the latter promotion, he was assigned to the army's Office of the Chief of Legislative Liaison in Washington. He next was commander of Division Artillery, 7th Infantry Division (Light) at Fort Ord before returning to Washington to be director of the Inter-American Region in the office of the assistant secretary of defense. In this position, his knowledge of the Spanish language and Hispanic cultures proved invaluable. On October 1, 1985, Gorden was promoted to brigadier general, and a year later he was made assistant division commander of the 7th Infantry Division at Fort Ord.

General Gorden received what he called "a singularly distinct assignment within the Army" when he was named the 61st commandant of cadets at West Point in August 1987. He was the first African American to hold that prestigious position. In January 1990, Gorden, who was now a major general, assumed command of the 25th Infantry Division (Light) at Schofield Barracks in Hawaii.

As commander of the army Military District of Washington, from May 20, 1993, until August 29, 1995, General Gorden was often in the public eye. He was responsible for the conduct of numerous military ceremonies and events in the nation's capital, including many at the White House. He frequently escorted President Clinton and other foreign heads of state, including President Nelson Mandela of South Africa and Emperor Akihito of Japan. He also helped to conduct the funeral of President Richard M. Nixon, held in Yorba Linda, California, on April 27, 1994, and attended by all five living presidents and dignitaries from around the globe.

In August 1995, Gorden began his final army assignment, as chief of public affairs in the office of the secretary of the army in the Pentagon. He retired from active duty effective October 1, 1996, aiming to spend five years employed in the private sector before retiring fully. He first became a vice president with ICF Kaiser Engineers, Inc., of Fairfax, Virginia. In May 1999, he became a senior vice president with United Services Automobile Association, based in San Antonio, Texas. This Fortune 500 company is a leading provider of insurance and financial services to military personnel and their families.

In October 2001, Gorden settled in Georgia, where in addition to pursuing civic and church interests, he studied African-American military history. "I am proud to have served my country as a member of The Long Gray Line and the Army," he has said, "and to have followed in the footsteps of the Buffalo Soldiers, whose history I continue to research."

General Gorden's military decorations include the Defense Distinguished Service Medal, Army Distinguished Service Medal, Legion of Merit, Bronze Star with "V" Device and Oak Leaf Cluster, Meritorious Service Medal with Oak Leaf Cluster, Air Medal, and Army Commendation Medal with Oak Leaf Cluster.

Further Reading

"Biography of Major General Fred A. Gorden." West Point, N.Y.: Public Affairs Office, United States Military Academy, n.d.

Hawkins, Walter L. *Black American Military Leaders.* Jefferson, N.C.: McFarland and Co., 2007, pp. 185–186.

Goyens, William

(William Goings)
(1794–1856) *free African American who negotiated with the Indians in the Texas War for Independence*

William Goyens's success in business fed rumors of buried treasure on his land. Goyens was a man of varied talents; not only did he have a knack for making money, but also his fluency in the Cherokee language made him an asset to Texas military and government leaders. As a trusted interpreter, he helped to maintain peaceful relations with Native Americans during the Texas Revolution.

William Goyens was born in 1794 in Moore County, North Carolina. His father, William Goings, was a former slave who had fought in the American Revolution in exchange for his freedom. (It is not known when the younger William changed the spelling of the family name to Goyens.) Goyens grew up near lands inhabited by the Eastern Band of the Cherokee people, and he learned the Cherokee language and customs.

In 1820, William Goyens was among the first easterners to migrate to Texas, which was then under Spanish control. He settled in the East Texas town of Nacogdoches, which would be his lifelong home, and he set up shop as a blacksmith, plying a trade that was common among free African Americans in the South. He also worked as a gunsmith, made and repaired wagons, hauled freight, and speculated in land. Before long, he was employing slaves and paid white laborers in his blacksmith's shop. In 1832, he married Mary Sibley, a widow from Georgia, who was white. Her son, Henry Sibley, became his ward.

In 1822, when Mexico gained its independence from Spain, Texas came under Mexican control. By the 1830s, though, American colonists greatly outnumbered Mexicans living in Texas. There was also a large Indian population in Texas that included part of the Western Band of the Cherokee, a group that had been forced to leave the Southeast. In 1832, President Andrew Jackson commissioned Sam Houston, who had spent time among the Cherokee in Tennessee before serving in the War of 1812, to negotiate a treaty with the Native Americans of Texas. With his knowledge of the Cherokee language and ways, Goyens helped Houston conduct business with the native people.

Many Americans had brought enslaved workers into Texas to farm cotton; by 1835, Texas had a population of 24,000 that included 4,000 slaves. Efforts by Mexican dictator Antonio López de Santa Anna to discourage American settlement through such steps as abolishing slavery and enforcing customs duties led to the Texas Revolution of 1835–36.

Armed conflict began on October 2, 1835. As the Americans battled the Mexicans at Gonzales and elsewhere, they worried that the Indians living in Texas might remain loyal to the Mexican government or take advantage of the upheaval created by war to raid American settlements. (The U.S. Senate was still debating the treaty negotiated by Houston and Goyens.) Goyens now served the provisional government of Texas as an interpreter and helped the government remain at peace with the Indians. In a letter to Cherokee leaders dated September 24, 1835, Texas general Thomas Jefferson Rusk praised Goyens, stating, "We believe him to be a man that will not tell a lie either for the White man or the Red man."

By the end of 1835, the Americans had pushed the Mexican army south of the Rio Grande; but in spring 1836, Santa Anna led a large force into southern Texas and won strategic battles. A convention of Texans meanwhile adopted a declaration of independence and wrote a constitution for the Republic of Texas.

The war ended quickly with an unexpected turn of events. On April 12, 1836, the army of Texas defeated the Mexicans in the Battle of San Jacinto, captured Santa Anna, and won the revolution. Goyens continued to negotiate with the Indians after Sam Houston became the first president of Texas.

Goyens's career in government service came to a close in 1839, when Mirabeau Lamar, the second president of Texas, removed the Cherokee and other Native American groups from the nation by force. Goyens continued to operate his blacksmith shop and to speculate in land, and he made frequent court appearances. Most of his court cases pertained to his business dealings, but he called upon the judiciary several times to affirm his status as a free African American.

A census conducted in 1840 by the Congress of the Republic of Texas listed William Goyens as the owner of 5,067 acres, a town lot in Nacogdoches, livestock, a silver watch, and a clock. By the early 1840s, he also owned a sawmill, a gristmill, and a large two-story house that served as his family's home and as an inn for travelers. By all measures, he was a wealthy man. When he died on June 20, 1856, he left an estate worth nearly $12,000 that included 12,423 acres.

Further Reading

Barr, Alwyn, and Robert A. Calvert, eds. *Black Leaders: Texans for Their Times.* N.p.: Texas State Historical Association, 1981, pp. 19–47.

"Goyens, William." Handbook of Texas Online. Available online. URL: www.tshaonline.org/handbook/online/articles/GG/fgo24.html. Downloaded on August 21, 2008.

McDonald, Archie P. "William Goyens." Texas Escapes.com. Available online. URL: http://www.texasescapes.com/DEPARTMENTS/Guest Columnists/East_Texas_all_things_historical/WilliamGoyensamd102.htm. Downloaded on August 21, 2008.

Gravely, Samuel Lee, Jr.
(1922–2004) *first African-American admiral in the navy*

"Success in life is the result of several factors," observed Admiral Samuel L. Gravely, Jr., in 2002. "My formula is simply education plus motivation plus perseverance." Gravely's willingness to add continually to his knowledge, his strong desire to excel, and his determination to pursue his goals despite racism carried him to a position high in the naval chain of command. In 1971, he became the first African-American admiral in the history of the U.S. Navy.

June 2, 1971: Samuel L. Gravely, Jr., speaks at the ceremony marking his promotion to rear admiral, aboard the USS *Jouett,* San Diego, California. *(U.S. Naval Historical Center)*

Samuel Lee Gravely, Jr., was born in Richmond, Virginia, on June 4, 1922. He was the son of Mary George Gravely and Samuel L. Gravely, Sr., a postal worker. The oldest of five children, young Samuel raised pigeons for fun and worked at odd jobs to earn money for college.

After high school, Gravely entered Virginia Union University in Richmond, but in 1942 he left, before graduating, to join the U.S. Naval Reserve and serve his country in World War II. From Great Lakes, Illinois, where he completed basic training, he went to the V-12 officer training camp attached to the University of California at Los Angeles and then to the midshipman's school at Columbia University. He became an officer on November 14, 1944, eight months after the first African-American naval officers—the "Golden Thirteen"—were commissioned.

On May 2, 1945, Ensign Gravely reported for duty aboard PC-1264, a submarine chaser. PC-1264 and the USS *Mason*, a destroyer escort, were the only two ships in the navy with predominantly African-American crews. Prior to June 1, 1942, the navy assigned all African Americans to the messman branch. After that date, African Americans could enlist in the navy for general service. Gravely, the lone black officer aboard PC-1264, called the ship's staffing an experiment that "was designed to test the ability of a group of African Americans to live, fight, and survive under wartime conditions on a small U.S. Navy subchaser." This was an ability that many white Americans doubted.

African Americans were still permitted to serve on ships in combat only as mess attendants, however. PC-1264 therefore patrolled for German U-boats off the East Coast of the United States and escorted convoys from New York to Guantanamo, Cuba, and Key West, Florida. Although he was opening doors for African Americans through his service aboard ship, Gravely experienced racial discrimination ashore, especially at the Key West naval base. Barred from entering the officers' club, he used his free time to take naval correspondence courses. "Knowledge is the most important weapon in our arsenal," he said.

Gravely returned to civilian life after the war, in 1946, but remained in the Navy Reserve. Later that year, he married Alma Bernice Clark and went back to college. He earned a degree in history from Virginia Union University in 1948, only to be recalled to active duty in 1949. He was a recruiting officer in Washington, D.C., when the Korean War began, but he would serve at sea and on shore during that conflict.

Gravely remained on active duty in the military when this war ended in July 1953. In 1955, he transferred from the reserve to the regular navy. As he and Alma Gravely raised three children— Robert (deceased), David, and Tracey—Samuel Gravely worked to gain expertise in naval communications. He also assumed greater responsibil-

ity and again broke ground. In 1961, when he temporarily served as skipper of the USS *Theodore E. Chandler*, he became the first African American to command a U.S. naval ship since ROBERT SMALLS did so briefly in the Civil War.

Gravely's naval career was distinguished by "firsts": In January 1962, when as a lieutenant commander he was assigned to the USS *Falgout*, a destroyer escort based at Pearl Harbor, Hawaii, he was the first African American to command a fighting ship. In 1966, having been promoted to commander, he became the first African American to lead a ship into direct offensive action. His ship was a destroyer, the USS *Taussig*, which provided gunfire support and aerial guard duty in Vietnam. In 1967, Gravely had the distinction of being the first African-American captain in naval history.

Captain Gravely easily earned the loyalty of the young officers under his command, because he believed in sharing responsibility. "If junior officers never get a chance to run the ship," he reasoned, "pretty soon they are senior officers and they still don't know how." He also demanded his subordinates' respect, emphasizing "smartness, appearance, seamanship, and most importantly, pride. Pride in ourselves! Pride in our ships! And pride in our Navy!"

In April 1971, when Secretary of Defense Melvin R. Laird announced that an African American would be promoted to the rank of admiral for the first time in U.S. history, the press quickly and correctly identified Gravely as the candidate. At the time Gravely was 48 years old and in command of the USS *Jouett*, a guided missile frigate based at Pearl Harbor. After he was promoted to rear admiral, he was named director of naval communications.

In 1976, Gravely was placed in command of the navy's Third Fleet, based in Hawaii. He was in charge of more than 100 ships that protected western sea approaches to the United States, guarded merchant vessels, and remained ready to provide emergency and rescue assistance. In 1978 he settled in his home state, Virginia, when he became director of the Defense Communication Agency, an organization with a budget of $120 million that employed more than 3,500 people.

His distinguished career earned him numerous honors. In 1974, for example, Savannah State College paid tribute to him with the Major Richard J. Wright Award of Excellence. In 1977, the city of Richmond renamed the street on which he grew up Admiral Gravely Boulevard, and in 1979, the Virginia Press Association named him Virginian of the Year.

Admiral Gravely retired from the navy in 1980. At his home in rural Haymarket, Virginia, he resumed his childhood hobby of raising pigeons, and he grew and canned vegetables. He also acted as a consultant to the military and private corporations. From 1984 to 1987, he was executive director of education and training for the Armed Forces Communications and Electronics Association, an international nonprofit organization of communications professionals. In 1988, he was named senior corporate adviser to Potomac Systems Engineering, a black-owned business supporting Department of Defense computer systems.

Gravely's many military decorations include the World War II Victory Medal, the Korean President's Unit Citation, the Korean Service Medal with two Bronze Stars, and the United Nations Service Medal. Gravely died in 2004, after a stroke.

Further Reading

Estrada, Louie. "Samuel Gravely Jr. Dies; Navy's First Black Admiral." *Washington Post,* October 24, 2004, p. C11.

Halloran, Richard. "Trail Blazer in the Navy: Samuel Lee Gravely Jr." *New York Times,* April 28, 1971, p. 29.

Haywood, Richard. "Ebony Update: Adm. Samuel L. Gravely, Jr." *Ebony* 46, no. 2 (December 1990), pp. 92–94.

Latty, Yvonne. *We Were There: Voices of African American Veterans, from World War II to the War in Iraq.* New York: Amistead, 2004, pp. 175–178.

Purdon, Eric. *Black Company: The Story of Subchaser 1264.* Annapolis, Md.: Naval Institute Press, 2000.

Thomas, Joseph J., ed. *Leadership Embodied: The Secrets to Success of the Most Effective Navy and Marine Corps Leaders.* Annapolis, Md.: Naval Institute Press, 2005, pp. 175–178.

Gregory, Frederick Drew

(1941–) *U.S. Air Force colonel, astronaut, NASA official*

A willingness to learn has characterized Frederick Gregory's career. Seeking new experiences, this seasoned U.S. Air Force pilot became an astronaut and the first African American to command a space-shuttle mission. In 2002, he was nominated to be deputy administrator of NASA.

Frederick Drew Gregory was born on January 7, 1941, in Washington, D.C. His mother, Nora Drew Gregory, was the sister of Charles R. Drew, the pioneering blood plasma researcher. His father, Francis A. Gregory, was a teacher. From childhood, Frederick Gregory had a dream: "I always wanted to fly," he said. Specifically, he wanted to fly military aircraft.

Gregory graduated from Anacostia High School in Washington in 1958 and secured an appointment to the U.S. Air Force Academy in Colorado Springs under the sponsorship of Representative Adam Clayton Powell, Jr., of New York. Gregory earned a degree in military engineering from the academy in 1964, and on June 3, 1964, he married Barbara Archer of Washington, D.C. He then went to Stead Air Force Base in Nevada, where he trained as a helicopter pilot. He received his wings in 1965 and was assigned to Vance Air Force Base in Oklahoma, where he flew the H-43 rescue helicopter.

In June 1966, Gregory went to Vietnam as an H-43 combat rescue pilot. Stationed at Danang Air Base, he flew 550 combat missions. He won the Distinguished Flying Cross in 1967 for exposing himself to small arms fire in order to rescue four marines from a downed helicopter.

After returning to the United States in 1967, Gregory underwent further training. He learned to pilot fixed-wing aircraft at Randolph Air Force Base in Texas before attending the U.S. Naval Test Pilot School at Patuxent River Naval Air Station, Maryland, from September 1970 to June 1971. He was subsequently assigned to Wright-Patterson Air Force Base in Ohio as an operational test pilot flying fighter jets and helicopters. In June 1974, he was temporarily attached to NASA's Langley Research Center in Hampton, Virginia, as a test pilot. This assignment allowed him to fulfill the requirements for a master's degree in information systems from George Washington University.

In January 1978, Gregory was accepted into NASA's astronaut program. His training group included two other African Americans, GUION S. BLUFORD, JR., and Ronald E. McNair, Ph.D. Although most candidates make their first space flights after about four years of preparation, Gregory spent more than seven years working behind the scenes on space-shuttle flights, managing flight data, and communicating with spacecraft from the Johnson Space Center in Houston, Texas. Barbara Gregory pursued a career as a clinical social worker, and the couple raised two children.

Astronaut Frederick D. Gregory first left Earth's atmosphere on April 29, 1985, when the space shuttle Challenger lifted off from the Kennedy Space Center in Florida. In the course of this seven-day mission, the crew deployed a satellite and conducted a variety of scientific experiments, observing the effect of weightlessness on monkeys and collecting data on solar particles attracted by Earth's gravity.

On this flight, Gregory was the first African American to pilot a space shuttle. (The pilot is the person second in command.) "The commander and the pilot have ultimate mission success as their goal," Gregory noted. "They make

sure everything assigned can be done in an efficient way, and they are also responsible for the maintenance of the orbiter once it is in orbit."

Gregory was lead capsule communicator at Mission Control in Houston on January 28, 1986, when the Challenger exploded 73 seconds after liftoff, killing all seven members of its crew, including teacher Christa McAuliffe. The accident was especially distressing to Gregory because among the crew were some of his closest friends. He and Ronald McNair had trained together; flight commander F. R. "Dick" Scobee had been his next-door neighbor. "They were family to me," Gregory said. NASA halted the shuttle program until the cause of the disaster—faulty "O-ring" seals in a solid-rocket booster—was identified and corrected.

On his second space flight, Gregory became the first African-American shuttle commander. This time he flew aboard Discovery on a mission beginning November 22, 1989. The nature of this mission was secret, involving Defense Department payloads.

Gregory commanded the shuttle Atlantis for his third and final space flight, lifting off on November 24, 1991. The primary task of this mission was to launch a Defense Department satellite used to detect rocket launches and nuclear tests by foreign powers. The astronauts aboard Atlantis also conducted an experiment to determine how much information an observer in space could gather about an opposing country's ground forces and military equipment and facilities. In addition, they evaluated medical efforts to counteract the physical effects of long space flights.

Frederick D. Gregory continued his career with NASA at the agency's headquarters in Greenbelt, Maryland. Beginning in June 1992, as associate administrator in the Office of Safety and Mission Assurance, he was responsible for maintaining standards of safety and quality in all NASA programs. He retired from the air force in December 1993 with the rank of colonel, having logged 7,000 hours of flight time in more than 50 types of aircraft.

In December 2001, Gregory was named associate administrator of NASA's Office of Space Flight; the position became permanent in February 2002. Then on May 8, 2002, President George W. Bush nominated him to be deputy administrator of NASA. Said NASA administrator Sean O'Keefe, "Fred's legacy of mission safety and his experience as a Space Shuttle commander, aviator and senior agency manager make him an excellent selection." Gregory assumed the position of deputy administrator in August 2002. He served briefly as acting administrator, from February 20 through April 14, 2005, and he submitted his resignation to NASA on September 9, 2005. In 2006, he joined the Lohfeld Consulting Group as managing director for aerospace and defense strategies.

Gregory has received the Defense Superior Service Medal, a second Distinguished Flying Cross, the Defense Meritorious Service Medal, the Meritorious Service Medal, 16 Air Medals, the Air Force Commendation Medal, three NASA Space Flight Medals, and the NASA Distinguished Service Medal. He has been honored as well with the NASA Outstanding Leadership Award, the National Society of Black Engineers Distinguished National Scientist Award, and the George Washington University Distinguished Alumni Award. He was the 2003 recipient of the Presidential Rank Award for Distinguished Executives. In addition, he was named an Ira Eaker Fellow by the Air Force Association in recognition of his contribution to aerospace history.

Fred and Barbara Gregory reside in Annapolis, Maryland, and take pride in their adult children, who followed their parents' career paths. Frederick Gregory, Jr., became an air force officer, and Heather Lynn Gregory Skeens trained to be a social worker.

Further Reading

Contemporary Black Biography. Vol. 51. Detroit, Mich.: Thomson Gale, 2005, pp. 42–44.

Narine, Dalton. "First Black Space Commander." *Ebony* 45, no. 7 (May 1990), pp. 78–82.

"NASA Acting Administrator Frederick D. Gregory." NASA. Available online. URL: http://www.nasa.gov/about/highlights/AN_Feature_Deputy.html. Downloaded on August 22, 2008.

Tobias, Russell, ed. *USA in Space.* Pasadena, Calif.: Salem Press, 2006, pp. 1,384, 1,389, 1,444, 1,460, 1,463, 1,939.

H

Hacker, Benjamin Thurman

(1935–2003) *rear admiral, first naval flight officer to become an admiral*

Naval aviation depends for success on the skill of pilots as well as the competence of naval flight officers, the men and women responsible for flight plans and navigation. In 1980, Benjamin T. Hacker, an African American, became the first flight officer in the U.S. Navy to be promoted to flag rank.

Hacker was born in Washington, D.C., on September 19, 1935, the oldest of three children. His father, Coleman Leroy Hacker, was a Baptist pastor, writer, and army chaplain, and his mother, Alzeda Hacker, was a musician. Hacker attended the University of Dayton and Wittenberg University, both in Ohio, and earned a bachelor's degree in science on June 1, 1957. Soon afterward, he entered the navy and attended Aviation Officer Candidate School in Pensacola, Florida. He married Jeanne House of Springfield, Ohio, in 1958, and was commissioned an ensign in September 1958. Hacker was designated a naval flight officer on June 7, 1960; he was promoted to lieutenant junior grade on March 19, 1960, and to lieutenant on October 1, 1962. His early naval assignments gave him practical experience aboard the P2V Neptune and P-3C Orion patrol aircraft over the Atlantic and Pacific Oceans and the Mediterranean Sea.

In 1963, Hacker reported to the Naval Postgraduate School in Monterey, California, to study engineering science. In 1964, he was assigned to patrol Squadron 31 at Moffett Field, California, as personnel officer and a flight and ground instructor in P-3A maritime patrol aircraft. He attended the Fleet Sonar School in Key West, Florida, beginning in June 1966, and in August 1966, he took on the duties of operations officer at the U.S. naval base at Argentia, Newfoundland. In 1967, he reported to Barbados to be executive officer and, later, commanding officer of the naval facility there. Beginning in 1970, while stationed at Moffett Field with Patrol Squadron 47, he frequently deployed P-3C aircraft to Adak, Alaska, and the western Pacific.

Promotions came with regularity, and in 1972, Commander Hacker established a naval ROTC program at Florida A & M University in Tallahassee. In that year, four schools, including Florida A & M, became the first historically black colleges and universities to offer naval ROTC. Hacker also was the first commanding officer and professor of naval science at Florida A & M, and he considered this assignment one of the most rewarding of his career.

He next commanded Patrol Squadron 24 as it carried out deployments in Keflavik, Iceland, and completed exercises in the north and central Atlantic. In 1975, he directed the Equal

Opportunity Division and served as special assistant for minority affairs in the Bureau of Naval Personnel in Washington, D.C. While stationed in the nation's capital, he also studied national security policy at the Industrial College of the Armed Forces and earned a master's degree in business administration from George Washington University.

Hacker commanded the Naval Air Station at New Brunswick, Maine, beginning in August 1978, and the U.S. Military Enlistment Processing Command, headquartered at Fort Sheridan, Illinois, beginning in August 1980. He was stationed at Fort Sheridan on September 1, 1980, when he was designated a rear admiral. He was the first flight officer of any race to attain an admiral's rank.

In 1982, the navy placed Hacker in command of Fleet Air Mediterranean; Maritime Surveillance and Reconnaissance Forces, U.S. 6th Fleet; and Maritime Air Forces, Mediterranean, headquartered in Naples, Italy. In October 1984, he was named director of the Total Force Training and Education Division (OP-11), on the staff of the chief of naval operations. In May 1986, George Washington University presented him with an honorary doctorate in education. Then, beginning in August 1986, he was commander of the Naval Training Center and the naval base at San Diego, California.

Rear Admiral Hacker retired from the U.S. Navy in 1988. He went on to direct the California Department of Veterans Affairs and to be regional senior vice president and general manager of the United Services Automobile Association (USAA), Western Region, headquartered in Sacramento, and Mid-Atlantic Region, headquartered in Norfolk, Virginia. USAA provides banking and investment services and insurance to current and past military personnel and their families. He retired from USAA in 1998, and died in 2003, after a long struggle with leukemia.

Hacker received the Defense Superior Service Medal, Legion of Merit with three Gold Stars, Meritorious Service Medal, Navy Unit Commendation, National Defense Service Medal, and Armed Forces Expeditionary Medal (Cuba). On November 3, 2005, the navy dedicated in his honor a new headquarters building for Commander Task Force 67 in Sigonella, Sicily.

Further Reading

"Center Commanders: Rear Adm. Benjamin T. Hacker, August, 1986–May, 1988." San Diego Navy Historical Association. Available online. URL: http://www.quarterdeck.org/book/cencoms/hacker.html. Downloaded on June 2, 2008.

Hawkins. Walter L. *Black American Military Leaders.* Jefferson, N.C.: McFarland and Co., 2007, p. 200.

"U.S. Navy Dedicates Building in Honor of RADM B. T. Hacker." Hampton Roads 200+ Men. Available online. URL: http://www.200plusmen.org/MServer/NewsArticles.aspx?articleID=283. Downloaded on June 2, 2008.

Hall, Charles B.
(1920–1971) *first African American to shoot down a German plane in World War II*

Charles Hall joined the Army Air Corps during World War II because he "thought it would be an opportunity for Negroes to win more freedom and recognition." As the first African American to shoot down an enemy plane, he gained recognition for himself and his race. Greater freedom, he discovered, would be more difficult to win.

Charles B. Hall was born in Brazil, Indiana, on August 25, 1920. He was a premed student at Illinois State Teachers College in December 1941, when the United States entered World War II. He had read about an "experiment" underway at the Tuskegee Army Air Field in Alabama, whereby the Army Air Corps was training pilots for the 99th Pursuit Squadron, the first unit of African-American military fliers. Because he "considered it a fine future for Negroes and a chance to show that we could do the same things white men were doing in the war," he left school to join the air corps.

Hall completed his training at Tuskegee and was one of the first pilots deployed to North Africa with the 99th Pursuit Squadron. The Germans and Italians had surrendered their holdings in North Africa on May 13, 1943; the black pilots arrived just days later to assist in the invasion of Italy. On July 2, while flying his eighth mission, escorting B-25s over enemy-held Castelvetrano Air Field, Captain Charles B. Hall spied two German Focke-Wulf 190s approaching the American bombers. He maneuvered his P-40 between the bombers and the German fighters and shot one of the German planes out of the sky, thus becoming the first African American officially credited with destroying an enemy plane in World War II.

Hall's feat earned him the Distinguished Flying Cross, and his squadron mates rewarded him with an ice-cold bottle of Coca-Cola, a rare treat in the Mediterranean theater of war. Louis R. Parnell of the 99th had acquired the soft drink during an overnight stop in Tunisia and had been storing it in the squadron safe for a special occasion. He and his fellow pilots chilled the bottle on ice obtained from a village 15 miles away. The celebration was clouded by sorrow, however, because two of the squadron's fliers—Sherman White and James McCullin—had been killed in the day's fighting.

During offensive action on January 27 and 28, 1944, Allied bombers destroyed 50 enemy planes, and Allied fighters shot down 85. The 99th Pursuit Squadron was responsible for 12 of those kills, with Hall taking credit for two. While overseas, Hall completed 108 combat missions over targets in Africa, Sicily, and mainland Italy. His own plane was shot eight times, but on each occasion he made it back to base.

Hall served as an instructor at the Tuskegee Army Air Field upon completion of his overseas duty and was discharged at war's end with the rank of major. He believed that their wartime contributions had earned blacks respect from the white population, but not enough. Like ROSCOE C. BROWN, JR., and other Tuskegee Airmen, he was denied employment as a civilian pilot because of his race. In 1947, he noted with disappointment, "There isn't a single Negro pilot employed by a major airline in the country."

Charles B. Hall instead became a restaurant manager at the Du Sable Hotel in Chicago. After moving to Oklahoma City, he spent 18 years as a civilian employee of the Oklahoma Air Logistics Center at Tinker Air Force Base. The center manages and maintains air force and navy aircraft and engines and performs sophisticated technical repairs. Hall died on November 22, 1971.

In 2002, the air force renamed the airpark at Tinker Air Force Base, which attracts many visitors, the Maj. Charles B. Hall Memorial Airpark.

Further Reading

Buckley, Gail. *American Patriots.* New York: Random House, 2001, pp. 283, 288–291, 294.

Hardesty, Von, and Dominick Paisano. *Black Wings: The American Black in Aviation.* New York: HarperCollins, 2008, pp. 74, 86, 88–91.

"Where Are the Heroes?" *Ebony* 2, no. 3 (January 1947), pp. 5–10.

Hall, William Edward

(1827–1904) *first black to receive the Victoria Cross, hero of the Crimean War and the Indian Mutiny*

African Canadians have distinguished themselves in military service since the years prior to their nation's independence, when Canada was under British rule. An outstanding military figure from that period is William Edward Hall of the Royal Marines, who was awarded Britain's Victoria Cross for heroism during the Indian Mutiny of 1857–58.

William Edward Hall was born on April 18, 1827, in Horton's Bluff, Nova Scotia. His parents,

Jacob and Lucinda Hall, had begun life as enslaved workers in the United States. During the War of 1812, they traveled on ships of the British navy to Halifax, Nova Scotia, where they married and began a new life in freedom. At the time of William's birth, Jacob Hall was a farmer.

It is thought that William Hall had little or no schooling. He joined the merchant marine in his teen years and worked as a deckhand on trading ships. When he reached age 20, he joined the Royal Navy and first was assigned to the naval vessel *Rodney.*

By the time the Crimean War began, in March 1854, Hall was a marine serving as a gunner aboard a recently commissioned warship, the *Shannon.* Great Britain and France had declared war against Russia, hoping to foil Russian efforts to seize from the Turks control of the straits linking the Black and Mediterranean Seas. The British and French also wanted to protect their own interests in the Middle East from Russian influence.

The crew of the *Shannon* served with valor in the campaign against Sebastopol, headquarters of Russia's Black Sea fleet. It took a year of fighting, including several bloody battles, before Sebastopol fell on September 9, 1855. Hall earned two British Medals with Sebastopol and Inkerman clasps as well as the Turkish Medal for his participation in the campaign. The Crimean War ended in a victory for Great Britain and France, but the loss of life on both sides was high.

In 1857, Hall was captain of the foretop aboard the *Shannon,* which was escorting troops to Hong Kong in preparation for an anticipated Chinese insurrection. On May 10, however, trouble broke out in a different part of the British Empire, and the *Shannon* and another warship, the *Pearl,* were diverted to Calcutta to help quash the Indian, or Sepoy, Mutiny.

The British East India Company, a trading company chartered by the British government that carried out administrative duties in India, employed Indian soldiers known as sepoys in the Bengal army. On May 10, 1857, resentful of social and cultural changes imposed by their British rulers, sepoys at Meerut revolted, killing most of their white officers and releasing native prisoners from jail. The mutineers then took possession of the walled capital of Delhi, 60 miles to the south, and continued the massacre. Regiments at Cawnpore (now Kanpur) and Lucknow were the next to revolt, and with sepoys outnumbering British soldiers, rebellion spread across north and central India.

Carrying 450 Royal Marines, two 24-pound howitzers, and other pieces of artillery, the *Shannon* reached Calcutta in mid-August and navigated 800 miles up the Ganges River, reaching Allahabad on September 2. From there, the marines dragged their weapons overland, although two heavy 18-inch guns had to be left behind.

By this time, the British had recaptured Cawnpore and Delhi, but Lucknow remained in rebel hands. On November 16, Hall and the other members of the "*Shannon* Brigade" took part in the assault on Shah Nuliff Fort, where 30,000 rebels defended the entrance to the city. The marines positioned their guns, and Hall joined the crew of a howitzer that was short one man.

The sepoys responded to the British artillery bombardment with rifle fire, causing many casualties. In fact, the mutineers picked off the members of Hall's crew until only he and a severely wounded gunner were left alive. Despite the danger, the pair kept on firing until they broke through the wall of the fort, causing the sepoys to panic and flee and permitting the British to move in. The long siege of Lucknow continued until March 1858, though, and it was not until April 1859 that the British completely quelled the widespread revolt.

Hall was awarded the Victoria Cross for his actions at Lucknow. The citation read, in part, "[I]n one of the most supreme moments in all the age long story of human courage, Hall fired the charge which opened up the walls and enabled the British to push through to the relief of the garrison and ultimately to the quelling of the mutiny and the restoration of peace and order in India."

The first black to receive Britain's highest award for valor, Hall retired from the Royal Navy on June 10, 1876, having reached the rank of petty officer first class. He purchased a farm in Hantsport, Nova Scotia, and raised cattle and poultry. In 1901, he rode in the royal procession when the Duke of York (later King George V) unveiled a memorial in Halifax to soldiers killed in the South African War (1899–1902).

William Edward Hall died on August 25, 1904. His Victoria Cross is in the collection of the Nova Scotia Museum in Halifax.

Further Reading

Bishop, Arthur. *Our Bravest and Our Best: The Stories of Canada's Victoria Cross Winners*. Toronto: McGraw-Hill Ryerson, 1995, pp. 8–12, 200.

Ruck, Calvin W. *The Black Battalion, 1916–1920: Canada's Best Kept Military Secret*. Halifax, Nova Scotia: Nimbus Publishing, 1987, pp. 4, 45, 65.

Soucy, Robert. "Black History Month." *Canadian Forces Personnel Newsletter* (February 22, 2006). Available online. URL: http://www.forces.gc.ca/hr/cfpn/engraph/2_06/2_06_dhrd_bhm_e.asp. Downloaded on November 22, 2008.

Harris, Marcelite Jordan

(1943–) *first African-American woman general in the U.S. Air Force*

Marcelite Jordan Harris excelled in the air force by gaining expertise in a male-dominated specialty, aircraft maintenance. The first African-American woman to reach a general's rank in the air force, Harris has attributed her own success to dedication and the achievements of women in all fields of endeavor. In 2000, she told female students at Texas College, a predominantly African-American school in Tyler, Texas, "Education has been our key to success in the past and it will be your key to success in the future."

Marcelite Jordan was born in Houston, Texas, on January 16, 1943. She was one of three children born to Cecil O'Neal Jordan, a postal supervisor, and Marcelite Terrell Jordan, a high school librarian. She graduated from Kashmere Gardens Junior-Senior High School in 1960 and enrolled in Spelman College, a traditionally black school in Atlanta, where she majored in speech and drama, intending to become an actor.

Jordan's student acting career took her to Germany and France as part of a USO tour and introduced her to military life, but at the time the armed forces held little interest for her. She earned a bachelor of arts degree in 1964 and looked for work on the stage. "If someone had told me when I graduated from Spelman that I would be in the Air Force a year and a half later, I would have laughed at them," she said in 1989. After acting jobs proved to be elusive, and after he spent several months working with a YMCA Head Start program by day and taking courses toward a law degree at night, Jordan found the air force appealing. In 1965, she entered the U.S. Air Force Officer Training School at Lackland Air Force Base in Texas. She was commissioned a second lieutenant on December 21, 1965.

Lieutenant Jordan's first air force assignment was as assistant director for administration with the 60th Military Airlift Wing at Travis Air Force Base, Texas. In January 1967, she was promoted to first lieutenant and named administrative officer for the 71st Tactical Missile Squadron at Bitburg Air Base, Germany.

While Jordan was stationed in Europe, a superior officer suggested that she change her career path from administration to aircraft maintenance, traditionally a man's domain in the air force. It would be a groundbreaking move at a time when the women's movement was in its infancy. Jordan accepted the challenge and in May 1969 became maintenance analysis officer with the 36th Tactical Fighter Wing at Bitburg. She also applied for the air force's aircraft maintenance officer course but was rejected. Marcelite Jordan persisted, and in May 1971 she completed the eight-month course at Chanute Air Force Base, Illinois, becoming the first woman aircraft maintenance officer in the air force.

The air force made use of her expertise in August 1971, by stationing her at Korat Air Base in Thailand as maintenance officer for the 469th Tactical Fighter Squadron, which flew combat missions over Vietnam. Unaccustomed to taking orders from a female officer, the maintenance crew initially resisted Jordan's authority. With effort, though, she developed a good working relationship with her subordinates, which resulted in an outstanding performance record.

Jordan next served as control officer for the 916th Air Refueling Squadron at Travis Air Force Base, California; in September 1973, she became field maintenance officer for the 916th.

Although her career was to focus on aircraft maintenance, Jordan held a variety of positions in the air force. From 1975 through 1978, as a personnel staff officer at Air Force Headquarters in Washington, D.C., she served as a social aide to Presidents Gerald Ford and Jimmy Carter. In May 1978, she was reassigned to the U.S. Air Force Academy in Colorado Springs to command Cadet Squadron 39. She was thus one of the first two women to be "air officer commanding," or to have charge of a cadet squadron.

Jordan returned to maintenance in July 1980, when she was posted at McConnell Air Force Base in Kansas, as maintenance control officer for the 384th Air Refueling Wing. On November 29, 1980, she married Maurice Anthony Harris, a fellow air force officer.

In 1981, Marcelite Jordan Harris became the first woman maintenance squadron commander in the Strategic Air Command when she was given responsibility for the 384th Avionics Maintenance Squadron at McConnell Air Force Base. Eight months later, she took command of the 384th Field Maintenance Squadron. Air force duty took her back to Asia in November 1982, when she joined the Pacific Air Forces

Marcelite Jordan Harris, who retired from active duty on February 22, 1997, was the first African-American woman to become a general in the air force. *(U.S. Air Force)*

Logistic Support Center at Kadena Air Base, Japan. While overseas, she completed the requirements for a bachelor of science in business management from the University of Maryland, Asia Division. The degree was awarded in 1986.

Marcelite and Maurice Harris became the parents of two children, Steven and Tenecia, and balanced the demands of their family and careers. "Being a mother, being a wife, being an officer in the Air Force are not roles that pull in opposite directions. They identify me," said Marcelite Jordan Harris. She continued to receive challenging assignments, and she steadily moved up in rank. On September 1, 1986, she was promoted to colonel. On December 3, 1988, she assumed command of the 3300th Technical Training Wing at the Keesler Technical Training Center at Keesler

Air Force Base, Mississippi. She was the third woman to attain that level of responsibility in the air force.

Harris passed another milestone on September 8, 1990, when she was promoted to brigadier general and became the first African-American woman general in the air force. In her next assignment, as vice commander of the Oklahoma City Air Logistics Center at Tinker Air Force Base, General Harris was one of the officers responsible for a staff of 26,000 maintaining a broad range of military aircraft and missiles.

On May 25, 1995, Harris was promoted to major general. Not only was she the highest-ranking woman in the air force, but also she was the highest-ranking African-American woman in the Defense Department. The air force stationed her at the Pentagon, where as director of maintenance and deputy chief of staff she supervised a workforce of more than 125,000 carrying out maintenance operations at all air force bases in the United States and abroad.

In 1997, Harris helped to establish a permanent office for the Committee on Women in NATO. This committee concerns itself with policies affecting women in uniform in the armed forces of all nations in the alliance and encourages the use of women's full capabilities in the military.

Harris retired from the air force in 1997. Her military awards include the Legion of Merit with Oak Leaf Cluster, Bronze Star, Meritorious Service Medal with three Oak Leaf Clusters, Air Force Commendation Medal with one Oak Leaf Cluster, Presidential Unit Citation, Air Force Outstanding Unit Award with "V" device and eight Oak Leaf Clusters, and the Republic of Vietnam Campaign Medal. She was named a Black Woman of Courage by the National Federation of Black Women Business Owners (1995) and has won the Ellis Island Medal of Honor (1996) and the Living Legacy Patriot Award from the Women's International Center (1998). In retirement, General Harris served on the board of supervisors of the Florida Space Authority.

Further Reading

Hawkins, Walter L. *Black American Military Leaders.* Jefferson, N.C.: McFarland and Co., 2007, pp. 212–213.

Phelps, Shirelle, ed. *Contemporary Black Biography.* Volume 16. Detroit: Gale Research, 1998, pp. 79–82.

Smith, Jessie Carney, ed. *Epic Lives: One Hundred Black Women Who Made a Difference.* Detroit: Visible Ink, 1993, pp. 259–261.

Hastie, William Henry

(1904–1976) *civilian adviser to the secretary of war*

As a lawyer and activist, William H. Hastie worked tirelessly to chip away at the Jim Crow racial discrimination laws of the South. In 1940, he joined the U.S. War Department with the intent of improving opportunities for African Americans in the military, but less than three years later he resigned in frustration.

William Henry Hastie was born in Knoxville, Tennessee, on November 17, 1904. As a child he moved with his family to Washington, D.C., where his father, who was also named William Henry Hastie, was a government clerk, and his mother, Roberta Child Hastie, taught school. Young William was an outstanding student, and after graduating from Washington's Dunbar High School he enrolled in Amherst College in Massachusetts. He graduated from Amherst in 1925, first in his class and president of Phi Beta Kappa.

Hastie also distinguished himself at Harvard Law School, which he entered in 1927. He edited the *Harvard Law Review,* a student-run journal, and earned a bachelor of laws degree (LL.B.) in 1930. After being admitted to the bar in 1930, he went into practice with his cousin Charles H. Houston, who was vice dean of Howard University's School of Law. Hastie also continued his studies at Harvard and in 1932 was awarded a doctor of judicial science degree.

William H. Hastie left private practice and entered public service in 1933, following the election of Franklin Delano Roosevelt as president. As an assistant solicitor for the U.S. Department of the Interior, he frequently advised the president on racial matters. In 1937, he became the first African-American federal magistrate when Roosevelt appointed him judge for the federal district of the Virgin Islands. In 1939, Hastie joined the faculty of Howard University Law School as dean and professor of law and assumed chairmanship of the National Legal Committee of the NAACP. Along with special counsel Thurgood Marshall, he was to argue successfully several landmark civil rights cases. Two of the most notable were *Smith v. Allwright* (1941), in which Marshall and Hastie persuaded the U.S. Supreme Court that a Texas law limiting voting in primary elections to whites violated the Fifteenth Amendment, and *Morgan v. Virginia* (1946), in which they demonstrated to the Court that a Virginia law requiring segregated seating in passenger motor vehicles imposed an undue burden on interstate commerce.

In 1940, Roosevelt appointed Hastie to be a civilian aide to Secretary of War Henry L. Stimson. Hastie was to direct his attention to the racial situation in the armed forces, but he quickly discovered that white flag officers intended to ignore his directives and deny opportunities to black military personnel. On December 18, 1940, at Hastie's insistence, Stimson ordered that all "matters of policy which pertain to Negroes, or important questions arising thereunder" be referred to Hastie "for comment or concurrence before final action." The order elicited a backlash of complaints that Hastie was furthering the cause of racial equality at the expense of military efficiency.

Hastie spent 10 months surveying conditions for African Americans in the peacetime army and on September 22, 1941, issued a report suggesting that the army employ more African Americans in a greater variety of ways and that African Americans be organized more effectively for military service. He pointed out that the army assigned the majority of African Americans to "nonmilitary duties of unskilled and menial character" in the Corps of Engineers, Quartermaster Corps, and overhead installations (in which they were employed as cooks, orderlies, supply clerks, and the like) and that such assignments did not represent the best use of manpower and harmed military efficiency. In addition, he wrote, "The isolation of Negro combat troops, the failure to make many of them parts of large combat teams, the refusal to mingle Negro officers . . . with experienced officers of the Regular Army, are all retarding the training of Negro soldiers." Condemning the prevailing mindset within the army, he observed, "The traditional mores of the South have been widely accepted and adopted by the Army as the basis of policy and practice affecting the Negro soldier."

In the spring of 1941, the Army Air Force had begun training African-American combat pilots at the Tuskegee Army Airfield in Alabama. Although a segregated facility, Tuskegee was to be staffed eventually by black officers, thus opening opportunities in the army for African Americans. However, army leadership procrastinated in replacing white administrative officers at Tuskegee with blacks, gave black officers subordinate assignments, or gave them no work. Defending such actions, army brass insisted that African-American officers lacked the necessary technical background to be administrators and said, "The purpose and function of this command is military training and it has no interest in the racial question. . . ."

That fall, Hastie learned indirectly that the Army Air Force had plans for a segregated officer candidate school at Jefferson Barracks, Missouri. Not only was such a school contrary to policy in the rest of the army, but also Hastie had never been consulted in the matter. The situations at Tuskegee and Jefferson Barracks influenced Hastie's decision to leave the War Department effective January 31, 1943. "[R]etrogression is now so apparent and recent occurrences are so objectionable and inexcusable that I have no alternative but to resign in protest and to give public expression to my views," he stated. Following his resignation, Hastie published a series of articles that were highly critical of Army Air Force practices.

No African American had ever resigned from such a high-level government position, and many Americans praised Hastie's integrity. In 1943, the NAACP awarded him the Spingarn Medal, recognizing him as an "uncompromising champion of equal justice." The same year, he married Beryl Lockhart, with whom he would have two children, William, Jr., and Karen.

Many Americans also feared that by resigning Hastie had destroyed his career, but in 1946 President Harry S. Truman appointed him to be the first African-American governor of the Virgin Islands. In 1949, Hastie became the first African American nominated to the federal appeals court when Truman named him to the court of appeals for the Third U.S. Circuit, which encompassed the Virgin Islands, New Jersey, Delaware, and Pennsylvania. Hastie held the position for 21 years. He died on April 14, 1976.

Further Reading

Bennett, Lerone, Jr. "William H. Hastie Set New Standard by Resigning Top-Level Post." *Ebony* 49, no. 11 (September 1994), pp. 72–78.

Mabunda, L. Mpho, ed. *Contemporary Black Biography.* Vol. 8. Detroit, Mich.: Gale Research, 1995, pp. 107–109.

Martin, Waldo E., Jr., and Patricia Sullivan, eds. *Civil Rights and the United States.* Vol. 1. New York: Macmillan Reference USA, 2000, pp. 332–333.

"Oral History Interview with Judge William H. Hastie." Harry S. Truman Library and Museum. Available online. URL: http://www.trumanlibrary. org/oralhist/hastie.htm. Downloaded on September 3, 2008.

Ware, Gilbert. *William Hastie: Grace Under Pressure.* New York: Oxford University Press, 1984.

Haynes, Lemuel

(1753–1833) *Green Mountain Boy who participated in the attack on Fort Ticonderoga, first African American to serve as pastor to a white congregation*

A farmer with a passion for learning, Lemuel Haynes enlisted in the American revolutionary forces and fought at Lexington and Fort Ticonderoga. In peacetime he became a prominent cleric whose antislavery arguments preceded the abolitionist movement.

Lemuel Haynes was born on July 18, 1753, in West Hartford, Connecticut, to a white mother and an African father. Abandoned at birth, he was given the surname of the family in whose house he was born. At five months of age, he was taken to Middle Granville, Massachusetts. There, under an article of indenture, he grew up among

As a Green Mountain Boy, Lemuel Haynes was a part of the force that captured Fort Ticonderoga from the British on May 10, 1775. *(Collections of the Bennington Museum, Bennington, Vermont)*

the family of Deacon David Rose. The deacon instilled strong religious principles in the young Lemuel, while his wife nurtured the growing boy. "I remember it was a saying among the neighbors, that she loved Lemuel more than her own children," Haynes later remarked.

Haynes worked on the Rose farm, and he attended the local district school. Although he put in long workdays, he studied each night by the light of the hearth. "I made it my rule to know something more every night than I knew in the morning," he said.

The indenture ended in 1774, when Haynes turned 21. Upon achieving independence, he joined the minutemen, those patriotic New Englanders who enlisted to fight the British at a minute's notice in the event of hostilities. On April 19, 1775, he was among about 70 minutemen who took part in the skirmish that is remembered as the Battle of Lexington. Haynes was one of several African Americans to fight at Lexington; another was PETER SALEM. In this first military clash of the Revolutionary War, the Americans exchanged gunfire with a force of 700 British soldiers headed for the town of Concord, Massachusetts. Eight Americans died in the encounter before the minutemen retreated.

On May 10, 1775, while serving as a Green Mountain Boy under Ethan Allen of Vermont, Haynes was part of an expeditionary force that seized Fort Ticonderoga from the British. Possession of this fort, located in upstate New York near the border with Vermont, was key to securing passage between Canada and Lakes George and Champlain.

In 1776, while still a soldier, Haynes advocated the freeing of enslaved African Americans following the Revolution. In the essay "Liberty Further Extended," he asserted *that a Negro . . . has an undeniable right to his Liberty.*

At war's end, Haynes returned to Massachusetts and resumed farming. He also furthered his education, pursuing knowledge of Latin and Greek as well as a course of theological studies.

In late 1780, he was named pastor of a new Congregational church in Granville, becoming the first black clergyman to minister to a white flock in the United States. Nearly three years later, on September 22, 1783, he married Elizabeth Babbitt, a white schoolteacher who belonged to the church.

Haynes subsequently served as pastor at churches in Torrington, Connecticut (1786–88); West Rutland, Vermont (1788–1818); Manchester, Vermont (1818–21); and Granville, New York (1822–33). During his 53 years in the pulpit, he was recognized for his intelligence and wit. On July 4, 1801, he gave an antislavery speech in Rutland, Vermont, saying, "[B]y the cruel hands of oppressors [the enslaved] have been forced to view themselves as a rank of beings far below others. . . . This shows the effects of despotism, and should fill us with the utmost detestation against every attack on the rights of men." In 1804, he was awarded a master's degree from Middlebury College in Vermont, becoming the first African American to achieve that level of education.

Many of Haynes's 5,500 sermons were published during his lifetime. His last piece of writing was a letter to one of his 10 children, in which he advised, "Let not the fashions of the world divert your minds from eternity." Following his death on September 28, 1833, the *Colored American* called him, "The only man of *known* African descent who has ever succeeded in overpowering the system of American caste."

Further Reading

Kazin, Michael, and Joseph A. McCartin. *Americanism: New Perspectives on the History of an Ideal.* Chapel Hill: University of North Carolina Press, 2006, pp. 25, 27, 30, 31, 45 (n1).

"Lemuel Haynes." *The Crisis* 82, no. 10 (December 1975): 430.

Newman, Richard. *Lemuel Haynes: A Bio-Bibliography.* New York: Lambeth Press, 1984.

Newman, Richard, ed. *Black Preacher to White America: The Collected Writings of Lemuel Haynes,*

1774–1833. Brooklyn, N.Y.: Carlson Publishing, 1990.

Roberts, Rita. "Patriotism and Political Criticism: The Evolution of Political Consciousness in the Mind of a Black Revolutionary Soldier." *Eighteenth-Century Studies* 27, no. 4 (summer 1994), pp. 569–588.

Saillant, John. *Black Puritan, Black Republican: The Life and Thought of Lemuel Haynes, 1753–1833.* New York: Oxford University Press, 2003.

Healy, Michael A.

(1839–1904) *officer of the U.S. Revenue Cutter Service*

Serving the United States has taken Americans of African descent to many distant parts of the globe, including the waters of the Arctic. As a captain with the U.S. Revenue Cutter Service, the agency that preceded the Coast Guard, Michael Healy spent nearly 30 years on Alaska's waterways. A controversial figure, he nevertheless sought to improve living conditions for the native population and brought law and order to a remote region.

Michael Healy was born in Georgia on September 22, 1839. His father, Michael Morris Healy, was an Irish immigrant who had acquired, through lotteries, parcels of land that had been seized from the Native Americans of the Southeast. Healy's mother, Eliza Clark Healy, was an enslaved woman whom Michael Morris Healy had taken as his common-law wife. Michael was the fifth of 10 children born to this couple; eight of those children lived to adulthood.

In 1850, following the deaths of his parents, Michael Healy entered Holy Cross College in Massachusetts, where his older brothers had studied. In 1854, his brother James arranged for him to attend a seminary in France, but Michael preferred an active life. The following year, he signed on as a mate aboard a vessel bound for the Far East and spent the next 10 years sailing on merchant ships.

Michael Healy applied in 1864 for an appointment to the U.S. Revenue Cutter Service, a civilian agency under the jurisdiction of the Treasury Department that was formed on August 4, 1790, to enforce customs laws. The forerunner of the U.S. Coast Guard, which was founded in 1915, the Revenue Cutter Service employed the small, swift, single-masted sailing ships known as cutters to pursue and arrest smugglers, enforce regulations on international fishing, and provide emergency aid at sea.

In 1865, the same year he married Mary Jane Roach of Boston, who was the daughter of Irish immigrants, Healy was commissioned a third lieutenant in the Revenue Cutter Service by President Abraham Lincoln. For the next nine years, he served along the East Coast aboard the cutters *Reliance, Vigilant, Moccasin,* and *Active.* He was promoted to second lieutenant in 1866 and to first lieutenant in 1870. Because his service record contains no mention of his race, historians think that the people with whom he associated from this time forward had no idea that he was African American.

Healy was then posted to California for service with the Arctic fleet. Revenue Cutter Service ships regularly set sail from San Francisco and Oakland and, after cruising north along the coasts of Oregon and Washington, veered west toward the Aleutians. From a base on Unalaska Island, they patrolled the Bering Sea and Bering Strait. In 1874, Healy was second officer aboard the cutter *Rush;* in 1877, he was given command of the cutter *Chandler,* and in 1880 he took command of the *Thomas Corwin.* His promotion to captain came on March 3, 1883.

Captain Mike Healy gained a reputation as a skilled seaman and was admired by seafarers throughout the region. The *New York Sun* reported on January 28, 1884, that he "is a good deal more distinguished in the waters of the far Northwest than any president of the United States or any potentate of Europe has yet become. . . ." Most of Healy's siblings had gained some prominence as

Captain Michael Healy (seated, second from the left) and the crew of the *Bear* patrolled Alaskan waters in the late 19th century. *(National Archives)*

members of the Catholic clergy, with James Healy serving as the first black bishop in the United States. Another brother, Patrick Healy, was president of Georgetown University, and a third brother, Sherwood Healy, was an expert in canon law. Three of Healy's sisters had become nuns.

Michael Healy's competence impressed higher-ups in the Revenue Cutter Service, and in February 1886, they placed him in command of the *Bear*. Recently outfitted for service in the Bering Sea, this former whaler was to be the flagship of the Arctic fleet. Two hundred feet in length and armored with steel plating that enabled it to break through thick ice, the *Bear* had a crew of nine officers and 40 sailors. Captain and crew transported agents of the Treasury Department who came to observe the Revenue Cutter Service at work in the Arctic, and they brought suspects

accused of crimes as diverse as smuggling liquor and murder to California for trial. In 1888, they rescued 160 sailors from whaling ships that had become icebound near Point Barrow, Alaska.

By 1890, however, it came to the attention of Healy's superiors that his leadership was sometimes less than exemplary. Not only had bouts of heavy drinking earned him the nickname Hell Roaring Mike, but also there were charges of cruelty. Healy allegedly had used the painful practice called tricing to punish sailors under his command; in other words, men who had had their hands tied behind their backs were hoisted off the floor and left to hang for 15 minutes. The accusers claimed that Healy had ordered the tricings while drunk.

An investigating board cleared Healy of all charges, and he resumed his responsibilities aboard the *Bear*. Between 1892 and 1895, he carried supplies to King Island, Alaska, to aid the starving native people. Miners and adventurers who had come to Alaska armed with rifles in the late 19th century had drastically reduced the population of seals, on which the native Alaskans had depended for food. Knowing that the Chukchi people of Siberia ate reindeer meat, Healy transported 1,100 Siberian reindeer to Alaska. The U.S. Bureau of Education distributed the animals and trained the Alaskans to care for them, and by 1940, domesticated reindeer in Alaska would number 500,000.

Despite Healy's humanitarian efforts, claims of abusiveness persisted, and in 1896 he was court-martialed. Healy spoke out in his own behalf at the trial, saying, "When I am in charge of a vessel, I always command; nobody commands but me. I take all the responsibility, all the risks, all the hardships that my office would call upon me to take. I do not steer by any man's compass but my own." The court was not impressed, and on June 8, 1896, he was found guilty of seven charges. The secretary of the treasury ordered him dropped to the bottom of the captains' list and removed from active duty for four years without pay.

Healy returned to the service in 1900 and was given temporary command of the cutter *McCulloch*. He also commanded the *Golden Gate* and the *Hartley* before being restored to his previous position on the captains' list in January 1902 and assuming command of another cutter, the *Thetis*. Twenty months later, on September 22, 1903, Healy reached the mandatory retirement age of 64 and left the Revenue Cutter Service. He died of a heart attack in San Francisco in 1904.

The U.S. Coast Guard honored Michael Healy on November 15, 1997, by launching the 420-foot, 16,300-ton polar-class icebreaker *Healy*, which was named in his honor. Designed as a research vessel, the *Healy* is one of four icebreakers in the Coast Guard fleet.

Further Reading

"Captain 'Hell Roaring' Michael A. Healy." *Voyager* 29 (May 2006), p. 8.

"CGC Healy History." United States Coast Guard. Available online. URL: http://www.uscg.mil/pacarea/cgcHealy/history.asp. Downloaded on August 25, 2008.

Grunther, Ian, and Greg Johnson. "A Ship for the New Millennium: USCGC *Healy* to Be Launched 15 November at Avondale." *Sea Power* 40, no. 10 (October 1997), pp. 45–46.

"The History of Blacks in the Coast Guard from 1790." Washington, D.C.: U.S. Department of Transportation and U.S. Coast Guard, 1977, pp. 7–8.

O'Toole, James M. "Racial Identity and the Case of Captain Michael Healy, USRCS." NARA/Prologue. Available online. URL: http://www.archives.gov/publications/prologue/1997/fall/michael-a-healy-1.html. Downloaded on August 25, 2008.

Howard, Michelle J.

(1960–   ) *first female graduate of the U.S. Naval Academy to be selected for admiral, first African-American woman to command a ship in the U.S. Navy*

Even in childhood, Michelle Howard understood that barriers against people of her sex and race existed to be surmounted. Her self-confidence and ability propelled her to increasing levels of responsibility in the navy and enabled her to make history, both in 1999, when she became the first woman commander of a U.S. Navy vessel, and again seven years later, when she was selected for the rank of rear admiral, lower half.

Michelle Howard's family moved often when she was a child, making their home in Massachusetts, California, Guam, Alaska, and Colorado—wherever her father, an air force enlisted man, was stationed. Military life appealed to Michelle, and when she was 12 years old, she told her older brother, who had enlisted in the navy, that she would attend the U.S. Naval Academy in Annapolis, Maryland, one day. To Michelle, the fact that the academy accepted only men was merely a detail. Sure enough, the academy began admitting women in 1976, and she was able to pursue her dream after graduating from Gateway High School in Aurora, Colorado, in 1978.

Howard earned a bachelor of science degree from the naval academy in 1982 and reported for the first of a series of shipboard assignments. In May 1987, while serving aboard the USS *Lexington*, the historic aircraft carrier known as the Blue Ghost, she received the Captain Winifred Collins Award from the secretary of the navy and the Navy League. The award is given annually to one female officer in recognition of inspirational leadership.

From 1987 through 1990, Howard taught and coordinated the Steam Engineering Officer of the Watch course at the Naval Amphibious School, Coronado, California. (In 1994, the school became part of Expeditionary Warfare Training Group Pacific [EWTGPAC] San Francisco.) Beginning in 1990, she was chief engineer aboard the USS *Mount Hood*, an ammunition ship that was deployed to the Persian Gulf for Operations Desert Shield and Desert Storm. After service aboard the USS *Flint*, Howard was transferred to the Bureau of Personnel in Washington, D.C., as navy liaison to the Defense Advisory Committee on Women in the Military Services.

In January 1996, she became executive officer of the USS *Tartuga*, which was deployed to the Adriatic Sea in support of Operation Joint Endeavor, a peacekeeping effort in Bosnia. The *Tartuga* next participated in a cooperative training cruise with U.S. Marines and Coast Guard personnel, as well as with the navies of seven African nations, in the waters off West Africa.

After earning a master's degree in military arts and sciences from the U.S. Army Command and General Staff College, at Fort Leavenworth, Kansas, in June 1998, Howard considered leaving the military, but after hearing from professional women in civilian life that higher salaries and choicer promotions tended to go to men, she opted to stay in uniform, even though she experienced resentment from some naval personnel because she was a woman and an African American. These were "individuals who didn't want me at the command, or didn't want me in a particular position," she said.

Her decision proved to be a wise one, because on March 12, 1999, Howard was placed in command of the USS *Rushmore*, one of the navy's "smart ships," or one that integrates new technologies and evaluates them for possible use in the fleet. Upon assuming the duties of this new post, she became the first African-American woman to command a ship of the U.S. Navy. She still encountered prejudice and skepticism but concluded that "you just have to go out and do the best job you can, and you take care of your sailors and Marines and they'll come to appreciate that more than who you are in their eyes."

In November 2000, Howard was assigned to J-3 (Global Operations), Readiness on the Joint Staff in the Pentagon. This office provides expertise on the preparedness and war-fighting capabilities of the joint forces. Beginning in February 2003, she was executive assistant to the director of operations, Joint Staff.

Captain Howard was back at sea in May 2004, commanding Amphibious Squadron 7, which in 2005 supported humanitarian relief for tsunami survivors in Indonesia and guarded oil terminals in the Persian Gulf. Beginning in July 2006, she was a deputy director on the staff of the senior officer in the navy, the chief of naval operations.

When she was selected for elevation to the rank of rear admiral, lower half, in 2006, Howard became the first admiral who was a female graduate of the naval academy and the first from the academy's class of 1982. She served as a senior military assistant to the secretary of the navy from January 2007 through January 2009, when she assumed command of Expeditionary Strike Group 2.

Further Reading

Dylewski, Robert. "Amphibious Squadron 7 Commander Meets with Coalition Partners to Discuss

Humanitarian Relief Efforts." Navy.mil. Available online: URL: http://www.news.navy.mil/Search/display.asp?story_id=16584. Downloaded on June 14, 2008.

Hawkins, Walter L. *Black American Military Leaders.* Jefferson, N.C.: McFarland and Co., 2007, pp. 233–234.

Olson, Bradley. "Rear Admiral-to-Be Always a Trailblazer." *Baltimore Sun,* August 22, 2006, pp. 1A, 4A.

Huff, Edgar R., Jr.

(1919–1994) *first African-American sergeant major in the Marine Corps*

Edgar R. Huff joined a Marine Corps that had just begun to admit blacks but was unready to welcome them. Determined to do his best despite obstacles, he achieved small but important victories, becoming the first African-American noncommissioned officer, and later the first African-American sergeant major, in the marines.

Edgar R. Huff, Jr., who was born in 1919 in rural Gadsden, Alabama, used to say that he grew up in a log cabin in the middle of a cornfield. Exposure to poison gas while a soldier in France during World War I had left Edgar's father disabled, and when the boy was six years old, Edgar R. Huff, Sr., died. Young Edgar and his mother barely survived on the $3 she earned each week as a domestic servant and the extra 50 cents she was paid for taking in laundry. Edgar Huff, Sr., had wanted his son to enter the military, and the child especially longed to join the Marine Corps, which he viewed as the most elite branch of the armed forces. Throughout his childhood and adolescence, though, the marines enlisted only whites.

When Edgar was in the 10th grade, his mother was fired after her employers learned that she needed major surgery. The boy was forced to drop out of school and take a job at a Republic Steel plant. He was an overhead-crane operator in June 1942 when he learned that the Marine Corps was

to begin admitting African Americans. He presented himself at a recruiting station only to have an officer ask if he knew what he was doing. Huff replied, "I am more sure that I want to join the Marines than about anything else in my life."

Edgar R. Huff, Jr., entered the Marine Corps on September 24, 1942, at the Montford Point Camp in North Carolina, which was the receiving point for all African Americans coming into the corps. The camp had been established on swampy land adjacent to Camp Lejeune, the East Coast amphibious training facility for white recruits that was established in 1941.

Huff trained with the 51st Composite Defense Battalion, one of two African-American marine combat units. Most of the initial 17,000 African Americans admitted to the Marine Corps trained for noncombat duty, to be mess attendants, stewards, or members of the depot and ammunition companies that supported white combat units in World War II. Boot camp was rigorous, but at Montford Point for the first time Huff lived with electricity and indoor plumbing and enjoyed regular, nutritious meals. He also completed the requirements for a high school equivalency diploma.

Private Huff quickly learned that a marine's uniform did not necessarily command respect—even from his fellow leathernecks. While en route to Alabama to visit his sick mother in December 1942, he was arrested at the Atlanta railroad depot by white Marine Corps military police who insisted that there were no black marines. Huff spent five days in jail before he persuaded a local marine major to telephone Montford Point and verify his status.

His training complete, Huff served as gun commander with the 155mm gun battery of the 51st Battalion until early 1943, when Marine Corps leaders decided to train some of the outstanding African-American recruits to be drill instructors at Montford Point. Huff was among those selected. In March 1943, after completing drill instructor school, Sergeant Edgar R. Huff, Jr., became the first African-American noncommissioned officer in the Marine Corps. By May 1943, African-American sergeants and drill instructors were overseeing all training at Montford Point.

In November 1944, Huff was promoted to first sergeant and assigned to the 5th Depot Company, which provided logistic support to white combat troops stationed on Saipan and Okinawa and in northern China. He returned to Montford Point following the war to serve as noncommissioned officer in charge of recruit training. In May 1949, he was transferred to the marine barracks at the Earle, New Jersey, Naval Ammunition Depot, where he performed the duties of guard and infantry chief.

In May 1951, Huff was assigned to the 1st Marine Division, becoming one of the first African Americans sent into combat in Korea. On July 26, 1948, President Harry S. Truman had ordered an end to segregation in the armed forces, and the six-foot, five-inch Huff was the only African American in his company. As a gunnery sergeant with the 2nd Battalion, 1st Marines, he fought in the basin known as the Punch Bowl, a strategic location that was the site of several fierce battles of the Korean War. He saw action as well on the eastern and west-central fronts.

Huff returned to the United States in August 1952 and was assigned to the 2nd Marine Division. In March 1955, he went to French Morocco as guard chief of the marine barracks at the naval air station at Fort Lyautey. On December 31, 1955, he became the first African-American sergeant major in the Marine Corps, but his promotion was not uniformly welcomed by his fellow NCOs. One white master sergeant who resented being passed over for promotion resigned from the Marine Corps rather than take orders from an African American.

Edgar R. Huff subsequently served at marine bases in the United States and overseas. He completed two tours of duty in Vietnam with the III Marine Amphibious Force, from May 1967 through June 1968, and from October 1970 through October 1971. He was injured in a grenade attack during the Tet Offensive of January 1968 while rescuing a radio operator pinned down by enemy fire. Upon returning to the United States, Huff was assigned to Marine Corps Air Station New River at Jacksonville, North Carolina.

On September 30, 1972, Huff retired from active duty, stating, "The Marine Corps has been good to me and I feel I have been good to the Marine Corps." Three weeks later, vandals attacked his home and car with white phosphorus grenades, which are used by the military primarily to create smoke and screen troop movement. The four white marines who were arrested received only mild punishments, either transfer or dismissal.

Edgar R. Huff, Jr., died on May 2, 1994, at Camp Lejeune Naval Hospital. His military awards included three Purple Hearts, two awards of the Bronze Star with Combat "V," three Navy Commendation Medals, the Navy Achievement Medal, and the Combat Action Ribbon.

Further Reading

Astor, Gerald. *The Right to Fight: A History of African Americans in the Military.* Novato, Calif.: Presidio Press, 1998, pp. 226, 385, 400, 429–430, 467–468.

Buckley, Gail. *American Patriots.* New York: Random House, 2001, pp. 313–315.

Culp, Ronald K. *The First Black United States Marines: The Men of Montford Point, 1942–1946.* Jefferson, N.C.: McFarland and Co., 2007, pp. 34, 52, 88, 103, 228.

Johnson, Jesse J. *Roots of Two Black Marine Sergeants Major: Sergeants Major Edgar R. Huff and Gilbert H. "Hashmark" Johnson.* Hampton, Va.: Ebony, 1978.

Nalty, Bernard C. "The Right to Fight: African-American Marines in World War II." National Park Service. Available online. URL: http://www.nps.gov/archive/wapa/indepth/extcontent/usmc/pcn-190-003132-00/sec4.htm. Downloaded on August 26, 2008.

"Sergeant Major Edgar C. Huff, USMC." Marine Corps Legacy Museum. Available online. URL: http://

www.mclm.com/tohonor/erhuff.html. Downloaded on August 26, 2008.

Terry, Wallace. *Bloods: An Oral History of the Vietnam War by Black Veterans.* New York: Ballantine Books, 1992.

Hull, Agrippa

(1759–1838) *private in the Continental army, aide to General Thaddeus Kósciusko*

Like many African Americans in the army from the American Revolution through the Civil War, Agrippa Hull was a servant to white officers. More is known about his life, however, than about the lives of most who served in the same capacity.

Agrippa Hull was born free in Northampton, Massachusetts, in 1759. According to his life story as it has been passed down, at age six he was taken to live in Stockbridge, Massachusetts, by an African-American man named Joab, who had been a servant of the noted clergyman Jonathan Edwards.

On May 1, 1777, when he was 18 years old and the Revolutionary War had begun, Hull enlisted in the Continental army as a private in the brigade of General John Paterson and served as Paterson's orderly. He was with the brigade on July 5, 1777, when it was part of the American force that evacuated Fort Ticonderoga in New York to escape the advancing army of British general John Burgoyne. He was on hand as well on September 19, 1777, when Paterson's troops were held in reserve at the indecisive battle fought at Freeman's Farm, New York. This confrontation between Americans under the command of General Benedict Arnold and Burgoyne's army was a prelude to the Battle of Saratoga, which led to Burgoyne's surrender on October 17, 1777.

After two years with Paterson, Hull served for four years as orderly to General Thaddeus Kósciusko, the Polish military leader who fought in the American Revolution. Hull was present during the Battle of Eutaw Springs, the last major

Agrippa Hull served in the Continental army during the American revolution. *(Stockbridge Library Association Historical Collection)*

Revolutionary War battle fought in South Carolina, which began on September 8, 1781, when an American force numbering 2,092 surprised 2,300 British soldiers who were preparing their breakfast. Casualties resulting from the four-hour battle were extremely high, with 1,188 killed. Hull was ordered to assist the surgeons treating the many wounded and never forgot the brutal amputations that he witnessed. The Battle of Eutaw Springs had no clear winner, but it substantially weakened the British hold on the South. A little more than a month later, on October 19, 1781, British general Charles Cornwallis surrendered to George Washington, ending the war's hostilities.

Hull received his discharge from the army, signed by George Washington, at West Point, New York, in July 1783. Kósciusko reportedly invited him to settle in Poland, but Hull preferred to remain in the United States. He returned to

Stockbridge, where he farmed and did odd jobs. He adopted a girl named Mary Gunn, who was the daughter of a fugitive slave from New York, and he married twice. Hull's first wife, Jane Darby, was enslaved, and Hull went to court to secure her freedom. After her death, he married a woman named Margaret Timbroke.

In 1797, Kósciusko returned to the United States for a visit, and Agrippa Hull traveled to New York for a fond reunion with his former commander. In a show of gratitude for his wartime service, the U.S. government awarded Kósciusko $15,000 and a grant of land in Ohio. The Polish military leader in turn gave some land to Hull, who asked that it be sold and the proceeds used to establish a school for African Americans.

Agrippa Hull gained a reputation as a village storyteller and wise man in later life. The novelist Catharine Maria Sedgwick, a lifelong resident of Stockbridge, observed that Hull "had a fund of humor and mother-wit, and was a sort of Sancho Panza in the village, always trimming other men's follies with a keen perception, and the biting wit of wisdom." On one occasion, when asked by a white man to comment on a sermon by the Reverend LEMUEL HAYNES, who was of mixed racial heritage, Hull replied, "Sir, he was half black and half white; I like my half, how did you like *yours?*"

In 1828, when Hull endeavored to have his soldier's pension mailed to his home, it was with great misgiving that he submitted his written discharge to government officials. According to his friend Charles Sedgwick, Hull "had rather forego the pension than lose the discharge." Ten years later, in 1838, Agrippa Hull died following a long illness.

Further Reading

"Agrippa Hull: 1759–1838." Africans in America. Available online. URL: http://www.pbs.org/wgbh/aia/part2/2p13.html. Downloaded on August 27, 2008.

Davis, Burke. *Black Heroes of the American Revolution.* San Diego: Harcourt Brace Jovanovich, 1991, pp. 17–19.

Kaplan, Sidney, and Emma Nogrady Kaplan. *The Black Presence in the Era of the American Revolution.* Amherst: University of Massachusetts Press, 1989, pp. 40–44.

"May 1, 1777: Agrippa Hull Enlists." Mass Moments. Available online. URL: http://massmoments.org/moment.cfm?mid=30. Downloaded on August 27, 2008.

J

James, Chappie
(Daniel James, Jr.)
(1920–1978) *U.S. Air Force general, first African-American four-star general*

The long military career of General Daniel "Chappie" James began in the segregated Army Air Corps of World War II. James never let racial discrimination prevent him from achieving his goals, and he succeeded based on his skill both as a pilot and as a commander. He became the first African American to achieve the highest rank in the peacetime armed forces, that of four-star general.

Daniel James, Jr., was born on February 11, 1920, in Pensacola, Florida. He was the youngest of 17 children born to Daniel and Lillie Anna James, although only six of his siblings were alive at the time of his birth. Daniel James, Sr., was employed as a lamplighter by the city of Pensacola. Lillie James operated a school for the children of her African-American neighborhood, and young Daniel was one of her students. The boy greatly admired his brother Charles, a college athlete nicknamed Chappie, and called himself Little Chappie.

In 1933, Little Chappie entered Washington High School, where, like Charles, he played football. He looked forward to college, but in 1937, as graduation day approached, Daniel James, Sr., died, and it appeared that the family would be unable to afford his higher education. With financial help from his sister Lil and his earnings from part-time jobs, however, Little Chappie entered the Tuskegee Normal and Industrial Institute in Alabama, the vocational school for African Americans founded by Booker T. Washington. There, calling himself simply Chappie, he majored in physical education.

During his senior year, he enrolled in the Civilian Pilot Training Program, a government project to prepare nonmilitary personnel for combat flight duty in the event of war. James excelled as a pilot; in fact, one of his instructors recalled that, "He had more guts than anyone I had ever seen."

James's bravado also led to his expulsion from Tuskegee—for fighting—two months before he would have graduated in 1941. He took a job as a civilian flight instructor, and in November 1942 he married Dorothy Watkins, a Tuskegee resident. He also tried to enlist in the Army Air Corps Aviation Cadet Program.

On January 16, 1941, the War Department had formed the 99th Pursuit Squadron, the first unit of African-American military pilots, to be trained at the Tuskegee Army Air Field. It was not until January 1943, however, when the United States had been involved in World War II for more than a year, that the cadet program had a vacancy for James.

In July 1943, James graduated first in his cadet class and was commissioned a second lieutenant in the Army Air Corps. He was assigned to the 477th Bombardment Group, an African-American unit stationed at Selfridge Field in Michigan, to learn to fly the B-25 bomber. Yet instead of flying missions in Europe or the Pacific, he was to fight a war against racism.

Not only did the African-American officers at Selfridge Field fail to get promotions for which they were qualified, but also seating in the base's movie theater was segregated and the officers' club served whites only. At Selfridge and later at Freeman Field, Indiana, James was among the officers who staged nonviolent protests against the separatist policies. He also was one of more than 100 officers at Freeman who were arrested and restricted to their quarters on base. The army bowed to public pressure and dropped charges against the officers, but the protests prompted an official policy review in which Secretary of War Henry Stimson determined that officers' clubs and similar facilities were not to be segregated.

Despite the obstacles he faced as an officer, James elected to remain in the army at war's end. He told his friends, "I am staying in and I expect to make general."

By September 18, 1947, when the U.S. Air Force was established as a separate branch of the armed services, Chappie and Dorothy James had two children, Danice and Daniel III. In 1949, James reported for duty as a fighter pilot with the newly integrated 18th Fighter Group at Clark Air Force Base in the Philippines and quickly gained a reputation as an outstanding pilot and gunner. He showed courage and quick thinking in the spring of 1950, when he and another pilot crashed their T-33 training jet in a dry Philippine rice paddy. James suffered burns and hurt his back in the crash, but he pulled his unconscious copilot from the wrecked plane just before it burst into flame. He was awarded the Distinguished Service Medal for his actions.

James had recovered from his injuries by mid-August, when he joined the 18th Fighter Group to participate in the Korean War. Leading a flight

Daniel "Chappie" James of the U.S. Air Force was America's first black four-star general. *(National Archives)*

team known as the "Ferocious Four," he flew as many as eight combat missions a day in the P-51 Mustang. On October 15, 1950, James, who had been promoted to captain, earned the Distinguished Flying Cross for leading a mission in support of United Nations ground forces near Namchonjom, Korea. The haze and smoke of battle, combined with antiaircraft and automatic-weapons fire, made this mission especially treacherous, but the team kept up their attacks until they had expended all of their ammunition. With casualties high, the enemy was forced to retreat.

Following his service in Asia, James was assigned to Otis Air Force Base in Massachusetts. He was promoted to major in 1952. In 1953, when he was placed in command of a squadron, he became the first African American to command an integrated combat unit. The Jameses' third child, a son named Claude, was born while Chappie was stationed at Otis.

Chappie James was promoted to lieutenant colonel in 1956 and to colonel in 1964. In 1966, he was stationed in Ubon, Thailand, with the "Wolf Pack," the 8th Tactical Fighter Wing, which flew combat missions over Vietnam in the new F-4 Phantom jet. On January 2, 1967, James took part in Operation Bolo, which targeted the 15 MiG-21s serving the North Vietnamese. In 10 short minutes, the Wolf Pack fliers downed seven of the Soviet-made fighters in a key air battle of the war. James received the Legion of Merit in recognition of his contributions in Vietnam.

While James was in Vietnam, the nonviolent Civil Rights movement of the 1950s and early 1960s gave way to militancy, as groups such as the Black Panthers advocated racial separation and violent social change. At the same time, young Americans of all races were demonstrating against the war in Southeast Asia. James was motivated to write an essay, "Freedom—My Heritage, My Responsibility," in which he affirmed his commitment to racial harmony and to his country's mission in Vietnam. "Our greatest weapon is one we have always possessed—our heritage of freedom, our unity as a nation," he wrote. For this essay the Freedom Foundation awarded James its George Washington Medal.

On September 22, 1969, James arrived at Wheelus Air Force Base in Tripoli, Libya, to assume command. He found a base surrounded by the forces of Libya's new military leader, Muammar Qaddafi, who was demanding that the United States withdraw from his nation. James demonstrated a willingness to stand up to Qaddafi that led to the Libyans' retreat; nevertheless, the United States agreed to abandon the facility by June 30, 1970. James therefore had the duty of dismantling the base and overseeing the U.S. departure from Libya.

After returning to the United States in 1970, James was promoted to brigadier general, becoming the fourth African-American general in U.S. history and the second in the air force. He was assigned to the Office of Public Affairs at the Pentagon to inform the American people on military matters. He earned a second star and a third, and on September 1, 1975, he became the first African-American four-star general. On that occasion, he remarked that the value of his promotion was to be found in its inspiration to others. He said, "If my making an advancement can serve as some kind of spark to some young black or other minority, it will be worth all the years, all the blood and sweat it took getting here."

General James was subsequently named commander of the North American Air Defense Command (NORAD), a cooperative program between the United States and Canada to monitor human-made objects in space and detect and warn against attack from the air or space.

James retired from the air force on January 26, 1978, after 35 years of service. Less than a month later, on February 24, 1978, while in Colorado to deliver a speech, he suffered a major heart attack and died. He was buried in Arlington National Cemetery.

Further Reading

"General Daniel 'Chappie' James Jr." Air Force Link. Available online. URL: http://www.af.mil/history/person.asp?dec=&pid=123006480. Downloaded on August 27, 2008.

Hawkins, Walter L. *Black American Military Leaders.* Jefferson, N.C.: McFarland and Co., 2007, pp. 246–247.

McGovern, James R. *Black Eagle: General Daniel "Chappie" James, Jr.* University, Ala.: University of Alabama Press, 1985.

Phelps, J. Alfred. *Chappie: America's First Black Four Star General; The Life and Times of Daniel James, Jr.* Novato, Calif.: Presidio Press, 1991.

Time-Life Books, editors of. *African-Americans: Voices of Triumph: Perseverance.* Alexandria, Va.: Time-Life Books, 1993, pp. 170–171.

Joel, Lawrence

(1928–1984) *army medic awarded the Medal of Honor for heroism in Vietnam*

Trained by the army to provide lifesaving care to soldiers wounded in battle, Lawrence Joel earned the Medal of Honor in 1965 when he put his own life in danger to treat at least 15 wounded men in the jungles of Vietnam. According to the citation that accompanied his medal, "Joel's profound concern for his fellow soldiers, at the risk of his life above and beyond the call of duty are in the highest traditions of the U.S. Army and reflect great credit upon himself and the Armed Forces of his country."

Lawrence Joel was born on February 22, 1928, in Winston-Salem, North Carolina, the third of Trenton and Mary Ellen Joel's 16 children. The family was poor, and at age eight Lawrence moved three blocks away, into the home of Mr. and Mrs. Clayton Samuel, who were better able than his parents to support him. Because many of Winston-Salem's African Americans still burned wood for cooking and heating, as a teenager Lawrence earned money selling firewood door to door. At 17, he left high school to join the merchant marine; in 1946, he enlisted in the army in New York City.

Military service took Joel to Italy, Germany, Lebanon, and the Japanese island of Okinawa. In 1965, Specialist Fifth Class Lawrence Joel was in Vietnam, serving as a medic with the 1st Battalion, 503rd Airborne Infantry, 173rd Airborne Brigade.

On November 8, 1965, the battalion was taking part in Operation Hump, a search and destroy

President Lyndon Baines Johnson presented the Medal of Honor to Specialist Lawrence Joel on March 9, 1967. *(Lyndon B. Johnson Library Photo by Yoichi Okamoto)*

mission in the Iron Triangle, a 60-square-mile area adjacent to the Saigon River. The 36 soldiers of Joel's platoon entered the region by helicopter and divided into four squads before proceeding through the jungle, but they did not go far before they came under attack from a Viet Cong force that was well concealed in the dense foliage. Every member of the foremost squad was quickly killed or wounded.

Joel treated the wounded from his own platoon and then, despite continued gunfire from the numerically superior enemy force, he moved forward to treat other wounded soldiers of the battalion. When a machine-gun bullet ripped into Joel's right leg, he paused to bandage the gash and inject himself with morphine before resuming his mission to aid others.

Supporting himself on a makeshift crutch, Joel moved through the stifling heat from one wounded soldier to the next, binding bleeding limbs, dispensing plasma, and offering words of encouragement. Another bullet hit him, causing a deep thigh wound, but he continued to do his duty.

Administering emergency medical aid in the field often means making do with whatever is at hand, and Joel saved the life of one paratrooper by spreading a plastic bag over his sucking chest wound. When another platoon arrived and its medic was disabled by enemy fire, Joel helped the wounded soldiers of that unit and continued to dispense care until his superiors ordered him evacuated. In 24 hours of fighting, 410 Viet Cong had been killed; the Americans counted 12 killed and 15 wounded.

Lawrence Joel spent three months recuperating at army hospitals in Saigon and Tokyo before returning to the United States. On March 9, 1967, in a ceremony at the White House, President Lyndon Johnson presented him with the Medal of Honor. Placing the blue ribbon that held the medal around Joel's neck, Johnson called him not just "a very brave soldier," but also one who possessed "a special kind of courage." Johnson said, "As we salute the valor of this soldier, we salute the best in the American tradition." With Joel on that day were his wife, Dorothy, a beautician; the Joel children, Tremaine, 16, and Deborah, 14; Joel's parents and foster parents; and 14 of his siblings and foster siblings. Joel was the 47th African American and the first medical aid specialist to win the Medal of Honor.

Winston-Salem honored its hometown hero on April 8, 1967, with a military parade in which Joel received the salutes of 2,000 uniformed Americans. "I don't consider myself a hero," he insisted. "I just consider myself a soldier doing his job."

Joel retired from the army in 1973 as a specialist sixth class and settled in Hartford, Connecticut, where he worked for the Veterans Administration. The last years of his life were difficult ones: His marriage ended, and he suffered from diabetes and clinical depression. He returned to Winston-Salem in 1982, and died there on February 4, 1984, from complications of diabetes. He was buried in Arlington National Cemetery.

Lawrence Joel has been honored posthumously. In 1989, the city of Winston-Salem named its new Lawrence Joel Veterans Memorial Coliseum for him; in 1991, the army dedicated the main auditorium of the Walter Reed Army Medical Center in Washington, D.C., to his memory.

Further Reading

Greenwood, John T., and F. Clifton Berry, Jr. *Medics at War: Military Medicine from Colonial Times to the 21st Century.* Annapolis, Md.: Naval Institute Press, 2005, p. 140.

Lang, George, Raymond L. Collins, and Gerard F. White, comps. *Medal of Honor Recipients: 1863–1994.* Vol. II, *World War II to Somalia.* New York: Facts On File, 1995, p. 700.

Lantz, Ragni. "Dixie Town Fetes War Hero." *Ebony* 22, no. 8 (June 1967), pp. 27–36.

Murphy, Edward F. *Vietnam Medal of Honor Heroes.* New York: Ballantine Books, 1987, pp. 38–39.

Powell, William S. *Dictionary of North Carolina Biography.* Vol. 3, *H-K.* Chapel Hill: University of North Carolina Press, 1988, p. 282.

Johnson, Gilbert H.

(1905–1972) *Marine Corps drill instructor, one of the first African-American marines*

Thousands of African Americans who joined the marines in 1943 and 1944 never forgot the face and voice of Sergeant Gilbert "Hashmark" Johnson. This demanding drill instructor—one of the first black noncommissioned officers in the Marine Corps—pushed them to excel, to be a credit to the marines and the nation.

Gilbert H. Johnson was born in the small town of Hebron, Alabama, in 1905. In 1922, he enrolled in Stillman College, a training school for African-American ministers in Tuscaloosa, Alabama, which was founded in 1876 by the Presbyterian Church. He abandoned his plan to be a clergyman in 1923, when he left school to join the army. He was assigned to the 25th Infantry, an African-American regiment, and held the rank of corporal when he was discharged in October 1929.

Johnson spent four years as a civilian before returning to military life. In 1933, he enlisted in the navy and was assigned to the steward's branch, the only division of naval service open to African Americans. When the United States entered World War II, he was stationed aboard the battleship USS *Wyoming,* which was being used for gunnery training in the waters off New England and in Chesapeake Bay.

In 1942, the Marine Corps became the last armed service to accept African Americans, and Johnson transferred to the marines. When he reported to the Montford Point, North Carolina, training facility for African-American marines, he wore the uniform of a naval officer's steward, first class, and had spent 16 years in the army and navy. His long experience and the stripes on his sleeves earned him the nickname Hashmark.

There would be no African-American commissioned officers in the marines until November 10, 1945, when FREDERICK C. BRANCH was promoted to second lieutenant, but the Marine Corps began training African-American drill instructors in early 1943. EDGAR R. HUFF, JR., became the first African-American noncommissioned officer in the Marine Corps in March 1943, and a month later he recommended Johnson for training and promotion. By May, when African-American sergeants and drill instructors were training all recruits at Montford Point, Sergeant Gilbert Johnson was the camp's chief drill instructor.

Hashmark Johnson gained a reputation as a tough taskmaster, performing what he called the "nearly impossible" job of shaping, in a few short weeks, "a type of Marine fully qualified in every respect to wear that much cherished Globe and Anchor [the Marine Corps emblem]."

Before the war ended, Johnson served on Guam with the 52nd Defense Battalion, one of the first two African-American marine combat units. He was again stationed overseas during the Korean War, initially with the 1st Shore Party Battalion and subsequently with the 2nd Battalion, 1st Marines, and as an administrative adviser at the headquarters of the Korean Marine Corps. He insisted that he encountered no difficulty carrying out his duties as a black senior NCO in predominantly white units in the newly desegregated Marine Corps, saying, "I accepted each individual for what he was and apparently they accepted me for what I was."

In 1957, Johnson, who had been promoted to sergeant major, transferred to Fleet Marine Force Reserve, and in 1959 he retired. He died in August 1972, in Jacksonville, North Carolina, while addressing the annual meeting of the Montford Point Marine Association. More than half the members of this veterans organization completed basic training at Montford Point during World War II. In April 1974, the Marine Corps renamed its Montford Point facility Camp Johnson in tribute to the legendary drill instructor.

Further Reading

Astor, Gerald. *The Right to Fight: A History of African Americans in the Military.* Novato, Calif.: Presidio Press, 1998, pp. 225, 321.

Buckley, Gail. *American Patriots*. New York: Random House, 2001, p. 314.

Culp, Ronald K. *The First Black United States Marines: The Men of Montford Point, 1942–1946.* Jefferson, N.C.: McFarland and Co., 2007.

Johnson, Jesse J. *Roots of Two Black Marine Sergeants Major: Sergeants Major Edgar R. Huff and Gilbert H. "Hashmark" Johnson.* Hampton, Va.: Ebony, 1978.

Nalty, Bernard C. "The Right to Fight: African-American Marines in World War II." National Park Service. Available online. URL: http://www.nps.gov/archive/wapa/indepth/extcontent/usmc/pcn-190-003132-00/secs.htm. Downloaded on August 26, 2008.

Johnson, Henry

(1897–1929) *private with the 369th Infantry, one of the first Americans to receive the Croix de Guerre for actions in World War I*

On a dark battlefield in France in 1918, two American privates took on 24 German soldiers who had launched a surprise raid. It was a fight they should not have been able to win, but Henry Johnson and fellow infantryman Needham Roberts defeated the attackers and protected the men of two regiments, one American and one French. Their bravery earned them France's highest military decoration.

History recalls few details of Henry Johnson's early life. He was born in Albany, New York, in 1897. In 1917, when the United States entered World War I, he was married and working as a railroad porter at Albany's Union Station.

Johnson enlisted in the 15th New York National Guard, an African-American regiment, and in October 1917 traveled with the unit to Camp Wadsworth in Spartanburg, South Carolina, for training. The black soldiers from the North were unaccustomed to the legalized segregation of the South and encountered antagonism in the local population. For example, one unsus-pecting African-American guardsman, NOBLE LEE SISSLE, sparked hostility by buying a newspaper in a hotel lobby. Hoping to prevent a violent confrontation, the army shipped the regiment, renamed the 369th Infantry, to France at the end of December.

By that time the French had been fighting Germany, Austria-Hungary, and their allied nations since 1914 and were struggling to hold off the enemy with depleted units. General John J. Pershing, commander in chief of the American Expeditionary Force in France, loaned the hastily trained and untested 369th to the French in response to their urgent requests for more men. The regiment was attached to the French 161st Division, issued French uniforms, weapons, and rations, and taught enough French to understand orders.

Prejudice based on skin color, so deeply embedded in the United States, was largely absent in France. As the African Americans prepared to take their places on the battlefield, French families welcomed them into their homes.

All too soon, however, home for the soldiers was a muddy hole in the ground. On the night of May 14, 1918, Privates Henry Johnson and Needham Roberts of the 369th were on guard duty near the Argonne Forest. Behind them were trenches where French and American soldiers tried hard to sleep; before them was "no-man's land," a stretch of earth that separated the allies from an opposing line of German trenches. It was well past midnight when Johnson and Roberts heard a stirring in the darkness. Then, all at once, they were under attack by a German raiding party numbering at least 24 that had cut through the barbed-wire entanglement protecting the French and American line.

Both Johnson and Roberts were severely wounded by exploding grenades. They managed to fight back with rifle fire and grenades of their own, but the Germans still approached. Johnson ran out of grenades, and with the enemy upon him, he shot one man dead and clubbed another

New York City honors the returning heroes of the 369th Infantry. Private Henry Johnson stands in an open automobile holding flowers presented to him by an appreciative citizen. *(National Archives)*

to death with the butt of his rifle. Turning, he saw three Germans with their hands on Roberts, attempting to take him prisoner. Johnson drew from his belt a bolo knife—short, heavy, and razor sharp—and brought it down onto the head of one of Roberts's attackers. With his comrade free, Johnson snatched a grenade from the lifeless body of a German soldier and threw it at the enemy, and the conflict was over. He later commented that the Germans had to be sent home wrapped in newspaper.

The French commanding general investigated the incident, which quickly became known as the Battle of Henry Johnson. In a letter to General Pershing, he wrote, "This little combat does honor to all Americans!" Johnson and Roberts became the first Americans of any race to be awarded the Croix de Guerre, France's highest decoration for bravery.

Johnson spent months in a European hospital waiting for his wounds to heal. In February 1919, he and the other soldiers of the 369th—the "Harlem Hellfighters"—returned to the city of New York, which welcomed them as heroes. Johnson rode in an open car and waved to thousands of grateful, cheering New Yorkers as his regiment paraded up Fifth Avenue from lower Manhattan to Harlem. Former president Theodore Roosevelt praised him as one of the bravest people in the nation.

It was the high point of Henry Johnson's life. He was left permanently disabled by his war injuries and could no longer do the work of a railroad porter. He became dependent on alcohol, and his wife left him. Having never received government benefits, he died destitute and alone in 1929, at age 32.

In the 1990s, Americans again paid tribute to this heroic African-American soldier. In 1991, the city of Albany named a street after Private Henry Johnson and unveiled a memorial to him. A bronze bust of Johnson was added to the memorial in 1996. In June 1997, President Bill Clinton directed that he be awarded posthumously the Purple Heart for his battlefield wounds. Although the army denied a move to award Johnson the Medal of Honor, he was given the Distinguished Service Cross posthumously in 2002. Johnson's son, Herman Johnson, a Tuskegee Airman, accepted the medal in a ceremony at the Pentagon.

For years, Johnson's family and the military believed that he had been buried in an unmarked grave near Albany. In 2002, however, researchers discovered his grave at Arlington National Cemetery. Cemetery workers replaced his grave marker with one designating him a recipient of the Purple Heart and Distinguished Service Cross.

Further Reading

Barbeau, Arthur E., and Florette Henri. *The Unknown Soldiers: African-American Troops in World War I.* New York: Da Capo Press, 1996, pp. 116–117.

Dowling, Timothy C. *Personal Perspectives: World War I.* Santa Barbara, Calif.: ABC-CLIO, 2006, pp. 23–26.

Hagedorn, Ann. *Savage Peace: Hope and Fear in America, 1919.* New York: Simon and Schuster, 2008, pp. 91–103.

Johnson, Shoshana Nyree

(1973–   ) *army specialist, first African-American female prisoner of war in U.S. history*

Although she has insisted she was "a survivor, not a hero," Army Specialist Shoshana Johnson acted heroically when she fought to defend herself and her fellow soldiers after the convoy in which they were traveling was ambushed in Iraq in 2003. She was indeed a survivor, enduring wounding and capture, but she claimed that the heroes were the marines who rescued her, saying, "They took a chance, and because they did, I'm here."

Shoshana Johnson was born in Panama, the daughter of Claude Johnson, an army veteran, and Eunice Johnson. The Johnsons later settled in El Paso, Texas, where Shoshana served in the Army Junior ROTC, which stresses fitness, leadership, and teamwork as it teaches the history, purpose, and structure of the U.S. military. After graduating, she took classes at the University of Texas at El Paso, and in 1998 she joined the army, hoping the money she earned would cover the cost of culinary school.

The army assigned Johnson to Fort Bliss, Texas, as a food-service specialist with the quartermaster corps of the 507th Maintenance Company, which repaired equipment that was stored at the post for infantry divisions. In 2003, when the members of the 507th learned that they were being attached to the 3rd Infantry Division and posted to Iraq, Johnson was a single mother. She left her two-year-old daughter, Janelle, in her parents' care and in March 2003 landed in Kuwait and moved into Iraq with the rest of her company.

The war in Iraq was less than a week old on March 23, when Johnson rode in a convoy toward Baghdad along Highway 1, the principal route running north and south in Iraq. The convoy made a wrong turn and headed toward the city of Nasiriya, southeast of Baghdad, where, without warning, Iraqi forces surrounded and attacked the Americans.

The truck in which Johnson rode rolled over, but she and another specialist scrambled for cover behind it and began returning fire. She shot one round before sand jammed her weapon and before she felt a burning sensation in her legs. Looking down, she discovered that she had been shot in both ankles. Around her, 11 of her fellow soldiers lay dead. When the ranking officer surrendered, the surviving Americans were taken prisoner by the Iraqis, and Shoshana Johnson became the first black American woman in the U.S. military to be a prisoner of war. Captured as well was Private First Class Jessica Lynch, a white soldier who was badly wounded and held at a separate location from the other Americans.

Blood poured from Johnson's boots. She was wounded too severely to walk, so her captors carried her. The Iraqis beat the Americans with rifle butts and only when Johnson's helmet fell off did they realize she was a woman. They made sure that she received treatment from an Iraqi doctor and, later, that she had surgery on one of her feet. In defiance of international law, the Iraqis released to a middle eastern television network videotapes of interviews with the prisoners, which were soon picked up and broadcast throughout the world. As a result, Claude Johnson thought he recognized his daughter in a news report that he happened to see, and an official at Fort Bliss confirmed for him that she indeed had been taken prisoner.

U.S. military leaders knew that American soldiers were being held captive but had no idea where to find them. The Iraqis kept the prisoners on the move, transferring them from one hiding place to another within Baghdad and to the city of Samarra. The terrified prisoners never knew if they might be executed or, with bombs exploding nearby, killed by friendly fire. As a woman prisoner, Johnson feared rape, but her male captors never assaulted her sexually. Rescue occurred almost by chance, when U.S. marines heading toward Tikrit, north of Samarra, happened to learn that Americans were being held prisoner nearby. The marines fought their way into the building where the captives were being kept and delivered them to safety. Still unable to walk or run, Johnson had to be carried.

Within days, the former captives were flown home and reunited with their families. Johnson received the Bronze Star, Purple Heart, and Prisoner of War Medal for her service in Iraq and was discharged from the army in December 2003, after serving five years. Upon learning that she was receiving smaller disability payments than Jessica Lynch, who was rescued from an Iraqi hospital on April 1, 2003, Johnson appealed to the military and was granted a pension equaling 50 percent of her army salary from the time she served. In civilian life, Johnson embarked on a career speaking to corporate and school groups.

Further Reading

"Spc. Shoshana Johnson: Former POW Gets Hero's Welcome." *Ebony* 58, no. 10 (August 2003), pp. 46–50.

"Then & Now: Shoshana Johnson." CNN.com. Available online: http://www.cnn.com/2005/US/05/23/cnn25.tan.johnson/. Downloaded on May 29, 2008.

Wilgoren, Jodi. "A New War Brings a New Role for Women." *New York Times*, March 28, 2003, p. B1.

Johnson-Brown, Hazel Winifred
(1927–   ) *first African-American woman general*

Becoming the highest-ranking African-American woman in the U.S. military with her promotion to colonel in 1977 was just a stepping stone in the career of Hazel W. Johnson-Brown. She went on to be the first African-American woman to head the Army Nurse Corps and to hold the rank of general.

Hazel Winifred Johnson was born on October 10, 1927, in West Chester, Pennsylvania. She was raised on a farm in Chester County, Pennsylvania, near the town of Malvern, and attended high school in Berwyn, several miles away. Following graduation, she traveled to New York to continue her education and completed training as a registered nurse at Harlem Hospital in Manhattan in 1950.

Johnson joined the army in 1955, hoping that a career as a military nurse would broaden her experience and take her to distant parts of the world. She soon discovered that in the army she could also expand her horizons through education. In 1959, she earned a bachelor's degree in nursing from Villanova University in Pennsylvania, and on May 11, 1960, she received a direct commission as a second lieutenant in the U.S. Army Nurse Corps.

Hazel W. Johnson continued to improve her skills and expertise. In 1960, she was awarded a master's degree in nursing education by Columbia University. In 1967, she joined the staff of the U.S. Army Medical Research and Development Command (now the Army Medical Research and Materiel Command) in the Washington, D.C., region. This agency conducts scientific and technological research for the army and the Defense Department and provides the army with medical equipment and supplies. Nine years later, in 1976, she was named dean of the Walter Reed Army Institute of Nursing at Walter Reed Army Medical Center in Washington.

Johnson became the highest-ranking African-American woman in the U.S. armed forces in 1977, when she was promoted to the rank of colonel. At the time she was working toward a Ph.D. in education administration at Catholic University in Washington; she was granted her doctorate in 1978. She then served briefly as chief nurse with the U.S. Army Medical Command in South Korea.

There were further honors and accomplishments in the career of Hazel W. Johnson. On September 1, 1979, at age 52, she was promoted to brigadier general, becoming the first African-American woman general in U.S. history. At the time, she was also the first African-American chief of the Army Nurse Corps.

General Johnson retired from active duty on August 31, 1983, but remained active in nursing and nursing education. She directed the Government Affairs Division of the American Nursing Association and was adjunct professor at Georgetown University School of Nursing. In 1984, she married David Brown and settled with him in Clifton, Virginia. She also joined the nursing faculty at George Mason University in Fairfax, Virginia. After retiring from teaching, General Johnson-Brown chaired the Board of Advisors of the College of Nursing and Health Sciences at George Mason and advised doctoral candidates.

Her military awards include the Distinguished Service Medal, Legion of Merit, Meritorious Service Medal, and Army Commendation Medal with Oak Leaf Cluster.

Further Reading

"Brigadier General Hazel W. Johnson (USA Retired)." *Academy Women Focus* 1 (September 2006), p. 14.

Haskins, Jim. *African American Military Heroes.* New York: John Wiley and Sons, 1998, pp. 135–138.

"Hazel Johnson-Brown." National Visionary Leadership Project. Available online. URL: http://www.visionaryproject.org/johnsonbrownhazel/. Downloaded on September 3, 2008.

Hine, Darlene Clark, ed. *Black Women in America: An Historical Encyclopedia.* Volume I, A-L. Brooklyn, N.Y.: Carlson Publishing, 1993, p. 644.

Smith, Jessie Carney, and Joseph M. Palmisano, eds. *The African American Almanac.* 8th ed. Detroit: Gale Group, 2000, p. 1,237.

Jordan, George

(1847–1904) *sergeant with the 9th Cavalry, Medal of Honor winner*

Sergeant George Jordan was five feet, four inches tall, but what he lacked in height he made up for in valor. His first duty as a participant in the

In this group photograph of Company K of the 9th Cavalry, George Jordan is seated third from the left. *(Nebraska State Historical Society Photograph Collections)*

Indian Wars was to ensure the safety of settlers. The skill and bravery that he exhibited while carrying out this task earned him the Medal of Honor.

George Jordan was born into slavery in Williamson County, Tennessee, in 1847. He gained his freedom after the Civil War and was a farm laborer before enlisting in the army at Nashville on Christmas Day, 1866.

The army assigned Jordan to the 9th Cavalry, one of four regiments of Buffalo Soldiers—African-American units formed after the Civil War. Military service took Jordan first to Texas, to Fort Davis and Fort Griffin. Like many of the other Buffalo Soldiers, Jordan preferred army routine to the limited opportunities available to African Americans in civilian life, and he regularly reenlisted at the end of each tour of duty.

On January 3, 1880, when he enlisted for the fourth time, he was a sergeant stationed in Farmington, New Mexico, and was known as an expert rifleman. The 9th and 10th Cavalry, the two regiments of African-American soldiers on horseback, were in the Southwest to help contain the Apache. In 1876, the U.S. government had attempted to

confine the Apache people to the arid, inhospitable San Carlos Reservation in Arizona, but some, such as Chief Victorio, had resisted. Since fleeing San Carlos with 300 followers on September 2, 1877, Victorio had been moving between Mexico and the United States, attacking ranchers and stealing their livestock.

On the night of May 13, 1880, the army learned that Victorio was headed for Tularosa, a small New Mexico settlement. Colonel Edward Hatch, the white commander of the 9th Cavalry, ordered Jordan and a detachment of 25 soldiers to Tularosa. After the troop built a stockade to shelter the citizens, Jordan stationed his men around the town to fight off any attackers. It was an effective defense: Twice Victorio's army of 100 approached Tularosa, but each time the soldiers' bullets drove them back. At last, seeing that he could not break through the defense mounted by Sergeant Jordan and the 9th Cavalry, Victorio took his followers to Mexico, where he was killed by the Mexican army on October 14, 1880. Jordan's actions at Tularosa earned him the Medal of Honor, the presentation of which was published in Order 23 of the 9th Cavalry on January 4, 1890.

On August 12, 1881, Sergeant Jordan was one of 19 soldiers under Lieutenant Charles Parker who defended themselves against a band of Apache led by Nana, an aged and vengeful chief who had been one of Victorio's right-hand men. In the previous month, Nana's followers had murdered ranchers in the United States and Mexico, wounded one soldier, and stolen three army mules. Outnumbered two to one, the cavalrymen stood their ground against the Apache for an hour and a half until, with two troopers dead and another wounded, they were forced to retreat. Nana and his men escaped into New Mexico's Carrizo Canyon.

By January 1885, most Native Americans were living on reservations and Jordan was a first sergeant stationed at Fort Supply, Indian Territory (present-day Oklahoma). Two years later, he moved to Fort Robinson, Nebraska, where on January 24, 1887, the post commander commended him for his role in capturing an escaped prisoner.

Sergeant Jordan retired from active duty on March 30, 1897, and made his home in Crawford, Nebraska. In October 1904, his physician sought treatment for him at the base hospital at Fort Robinson. An army surgeon denied Jordan admission and advised him to go to an old soldiers' home, but the retired sergeant said that he was unable to travel. He died on October 24, 1904, "for the want of proper attention," said Dr. J. H. Hartwell of Crawford. "He lived alone and had no one to attend to his wants." Jordan's friends sought the opinion of Dr. Robert M. O'Reilly, surgeon general of the army, who said that military hospitals had no obligation to admit retired personnel. "[A]t the same time," O'Reilly added, "surgeons should be careful to show all practicable consideration towards retired soldiers, especially when their records and services were as excellent as those of 1st Sergeant George Jordan, Retired."

The entire command attended Jordan's funeral, which was held at Fort Robinson on October 26. Jordan was buried with full military honors. Ninety-five years later, the army's 6th Recruiting Brigade, Las Vegas, dedicated its new headquarters for the western region to Sergeant George Jordan.

Further Reading

Billington, Monroe Lee. *New Mexico's Buffalo Soldiers.* Niwot, Colo.: University Press of Colorado, 1991, pp. 95–96, 105.

Glasrud, Bruce A., and Michael N. Searles, eds. *Buffalo Soldiers in the West: A Black Soldiers Anthology.* College Station: Texas A & M University Press, 2007, p. 93.

Leckie, William H. *The Buffalo Soldiers: A Narrative of the Negro Cavalry in the West.* Norman: University of Oklahoma Press, 1967, pp. 221, 251.

O'Neal, Bill. *Fighting Men of the Indian Wars.* Stillwater, Okla.: Barbed Wire Press, 1991, pp. 33, 149.

Schubert, Irene, and Frank Schubert, comp. and ed. *On the Trail of the Buffalo Soldier II: New and Revised Biographies of African Americans in the U.S. Army, 1866–1917.* Lanham, Md.: Scarecrow Press, 2004, pp. 166–167.

L

Law, Oliver

(1899–1937) *commander of the Abraham Lincoln Brigade in the Spanish civil war, the first African American to command an integrated American combat unit*

Oliver Law joined the Loyalist cause in the Spanish civil war because he hated inequality and intolerance and viewed the conflict as a fight against fascism. He rose quickly through the ranks of the integrated Abraham Lincoln Brigade to serve for the last few months of his life as its commander, and in so doing became the first black American to lead white troops in time of war.

Oliver Law was born in 1899 and grew up on a Texas ranch. He served in World War I and reenlisted at the war's end, thus spending six years in uniform but reaching the rank only of private first class. Returning to civilian life, he worked for a short period in a cement factory before moving north to Chicago. It was the time of the Great Migration, the years between 1910 and 1940 when nearly 1.5 million African Americans left the rural South for jobs and better living conditions in the industrial North. In Chicago, Law drove a taxicab, loaded cargo onto ships at the waterfront, and opened a restaurant that eventually failed.

Law developed a strong political conscience at the start of the Great Depression, when he saw the hardship that had befallen large numbers of unemployed workers. Disillusioned with an economic system that left so many people vulnerable, he joined the Communist Party and soon chaired the Southside (Chicago) chapter of the International Labor Defense, the party's legal arm. On March 6, 1930, he was one of 14 activists arrested and beaten by Chicago police during a Communist-sponsored International Unemployment Day rally that was one of numerous protests held throughout the country involving more than a million participants.

In August 1935, Law was the opening speaker at a "Hands Off Ethiopia" demonstration in Chicago, held to protest Italian dictator Benito Mussolini's plan to invade the East African nation. Law's speech was cut short when police arrested him and carried him off to jail.

The protests became larger and more frequent after Italy carried out its invasion in October 1935, but leftists soon transferred their attention to another international situation. On July 19, 1936, Spanish general Francisco Franco and three other right-wing officers led an attack against their nation's legally elected government. With military assistance from Italy and Germany, their attempted coup developed into the Spanish civil war.

Approximately 35,000 opponents of fascism from 52 countries fought voluntarily in support of the Spanish government in the war. In January 1937, the same month in which Oliver Law sailed for Spain, the U.S. State Department prohibited travel in that war-torn country. In Spain, Law fought with the Abraham Lincoln Brigade, one of three American battalions composed of civilian volunteers from all walks of life and from every part of the United States. The Lincoln Brigade was not an official U.S. military unit; in fact, most of the "Lincolns" had communist leanings.

Law was one of three group leaders in a machine-gun company, and soon he saw action. On February 27, the Lincoln Brigade attacked Pingarron Hill in the Jarama River Valley of Spain. Casualties were high: Of 500 men who went over the hill, 300 were killed or wounded. Law's fellow Lincolns remarked on the courage he displayed in the Battle of Jarama, and Law himself told a reporter, "We came to wipe out the fascists; some of us may die doing that job. But we'll do it here in Spain. . . ."

The heavy losses left room for advancement in the brigade, and shortly after the battle Law was made a section leader. Two weeks later, the commander of the machine-gun company died in a minor conflict, and Law was promoted to take his place. The battalion commander, Martin Hourihan, recommended that Law be trained as an officer, noting that he had a "Good record as officer at [the] front. Showed good morale and discipline under fire." When Hourihan fell ill two months later, Law replaced him temporarily. Hourihan was then reassigned, and Law became the permanent commander of the brigade. For the first time, an African American would command an integrated U.S. fighting force.

Law had had only limited military experience before entering combat in Spain, but because most volunteers had none, his was considered an asset. Nevertheless, some white brigade members resented being passed over for promotion and saw Law's rise as the result of reverse discrimination. Adopting the slogan "Restore the whites to equality with the Negro," they blamed Communist Party leadership for using the war to showcase African Americans at the expense of victory.

Indeed, Law was poorly prepared for a command position, and his leadership was uneven. On July 6, 1937, when the Abraham Lincoln Brigade was ordered to attack and take Villanueva de la Canada, in a region west of Madrid, several officers complained that Law's actions revealed inexperience and cowardice. Yet three days later, on the morning of July 9, he demonstrated great bravery as he led the Lincolns in an attack on nearby Mosquito Ridge. He was seen in the lead, waving his pistol and ordering the men forward. "He was the first man over the top," said the battalion's runner. "There is absolutely no doubt of the courage of Oliver Law."

That morning there was a sudden burst of machine-gun fire from the enemy, and Law fell, wounded and bleeding profusely. A medic attempted to stop the flow of blood with an anticoagulant and moved Law to a first aid base where he died, one of the day's more than 135 American casualties.

The cause for which Oliver Law fought and died was a noble one, but it failed. Spain fell to Franco's army on March 28, 1939.

Further Reading

Carroll, Peter N. *The Odyssey of the Abraham Lincoln Brigade.* Stanford, Calif.: Stanford University Press, 1994.

Collum, Danny Duncan, ed. *African Americans in the Spanish Civil War: "This Ain't Ethiopia, but It'll Do."* New York: G. K. Hall and Co., 1992.

Eby, Cecil D. *Comrades and Commissars: The Lincoln Battalion in the Spanish Civil War.* University Park: Pennsylvania State University Press, 2007.

"Oliver Law." Spartacus Educational. Available online. URL: http://www.spartacus.schoolnet.co.uk/SPlawO.htm. Downloaded on September 4, 2008.

Lawrence, Robert Henry, Jr.

(1935–1967) *U.S. Air Force major, first African American chosen for astronaut training*

When selected for astronaut training in 1967, Major Robert H. Lawrence, Jr., insisted that race had not been an obstacle to him as a candidate. "I feel this is the culmination of a lot of effort that people put into preparing me for this. . . ." he said. Had a plane crash not cut short his life, he might have become the first African American in space.

Robert Henry Lawrence, Jr., was born in Chicago on October 2, 1935. His mother, Gwendolyn Lawrence, was a civil servant, and his father, Robert Henry Lawrence, Sr., was a disabled veteran. His parents divorced when he was small, and his mother remarried. Although young Robert and his older sister, Barbara, lived with their mother and stepfather, Charles Duncan, the children remained close to their father.

As a child, Robert enjoyed building model airplanes, playing chess, and dabbling in science, especially chemistry. He attended Haines Elementary School and predominantly African-American Englewood High School, where he participated in track and excelled academically. He graduated near the top of his class and was voted one of the 10 students most likely to succeed.

Robert Lawrence won a scholarship to Indiana University, but he instead enrolled at Bradley University in nearby Peoria. He majored in chemistry and worked part-time to pay his tuition. He joined the school's air force ROTC program and rose quickly to the rank of lieutenant colonel, thus becoming the cadet with the second-highest ranking in the corps.

Lawrence graduated from Bradley University in 1958 and was commissioned a second lieutenant in the air force. After completing pilot training at Craig Air Force Base in Alabama, he was stationed in Fürstenfeldbruck, West Germany, as a flight instructor and fighter pilot with the Mili-

U.S. Air Force major Robert H. Lawrence, Jr., was accepted for astronaut training in 1967, but he died before he had a chance to fly in space. *(National Aeronautics and Space Administration)*

tary Assistance Advisory Group. On July 1, 1958, while in Germany, he married Barbara Cress, whom he had begun dating in college. The couple's only son, Tracey, was born in 1960.

After returning to the United States in 1961, Lawrence enrolled in a program offered cooperatively by the Air Force Institute of Technology at Wright-Patterson Air Force Base in Dayton, Ohio, and Ohio State University. This led to a doctoral degree in physical chemistry in 1965. He maintained a grade point average of 3.5 or higher in graduate school and impressed his professors with his diligence and intellectual courage. In a tribute to those African Americans who were denied educational and professional opportunities, he dedicated his doctoral dissertation, on the chemical conversion of tritium rays to methane gas,

> to those American Negroes who have spent their lives in the performance of menial tasks struggling to overcome both natural and man-made problems of survival. To such men and women, scientific investigation would seem a grand abstraction. However, it has been their endeavors which have supplied both the wherewithal and motivation that initiated and helped sustain this effort.

Lawrence was a highly educated chemist who had accumulated more than 2,500 flight hours. These accomplishments qualified him for the astronaut program, but his first two applications for training were turned down. After a course of study at the Air Force Aerospace Research Pilot School in 1967, however, he became the first African American chosen for astronaut training when he was one of four pilots selected for the Manned Orbiting Laboratory Program, the precursor to the space-shuttle program.

In September 1967, Major Robert H. Lawrence, Jr., and the other three candidates reported to Edwards Air Force Base in California, where they joined 12 more who had been previously selected. Training involved practicing steep-descent landings in the F-104 Starfighter jet to simulate maneuvers of a shuttle-like craft.

On December 8, 1967, Lawrence was instructor and copilot in an F-104 piloted by Major Harvey Royer when the jet crashed on the runway during an attempted landing. Royer survived with serious injuries, but Lawrence was killed. Not only did the air force lose an outstanding officer, but the timetable for African-American achievement in space exploration was set back considerably. In was not until 1983 that GUION S. BLUFORD, JR., became the first African American in space.

Recognition of Lawrence's contributions came belatedly. In 1991, the Astronaut Memorial Foundation dedicated the Space Mirror Memorial, a monument to those astronauts who gave their lives to further the space program, at the Kennedy Space Center in Florida. The name Robert H. Lawrence, Jr., was omitted from the memorial due to a technicality: The military had specified that no one could be called an astronaut who had not flown 50 miles above Earth. Lobbying by space historian James Oberg, Congressman Bobby L. Rush of Chicago, and others persuaded the air force to review its policy and in 1997 grant Lawrence astronaut status so that his name could be added to the Space Mirror.

On January 21, 2000, Ohio State University dedicated the main lecture hall of its newly renovated chemistry building to Lawrence. Also, Bradley University established the Robert H. Lawrence, Jr., Memorial Scholarship to assist African Americans studying chemistry there.

Further Reading

Burns, Kephra and William Mills. *Black Stars in Orbit: NASA's African American Astronauts.* San Diego: Harcourt, Brace and Co., 1995, pp. 24–27.

Oberg, James. "The Unsung Astronaut: Robert Lawrence's Sacrifice, and Why It Took So Long to Be Honored." MSNBC.com. Available online. URL: http://www.msnbc.com/id/7018497/. Downloaded on September 6, 2008.

Phelps, J. Alfred. *They Had a Dream: The Story of African-American Astronauts.* Novato, Calif.: Presidio Press, 1994, pp. 47–59.

Phelps, Shirelle, ed. *Contemporary Black Biography.* Vol. 16. Detroit: Gale Research, 1998, pp. 128–130.

Lew, Barzillai

(1743–1822) *Revolutionary War fifer*

Most of the African Americans who served as regimental musicians through the time of the Civil War have been lost to history. The fact that the Lew family of Massachusetts has preserved knowledge of its early heritage allows present-day

Americans to learn about the life of Barzillai Lew, a Revolutionary War fifer who was present at the Battle of Bunker Hill.

Barzillai Lew was born in Groton, Massachusetts, on November 5, 1743, the son of Primus Lew, a free black from Haiti, and Margaret Lew. As a youth, Barzillai was trained as a cooper, but he put down his tools on March 10, 1760, to enlist as a private in a militia company formed in Groton under the leadership of Captain Thomas Farrington, and to take part in the French and Indian War. The colonies fought on the side of England in this war to eliminate French demands for land in the West. Farrington's company marched north to Canada and is thought to have been present for the surrender of Montreal to the British in September 1760.

The British victory in this war created tension between the colonies and their mother country. Not only did Parliament tax the colonists to pay for the war, but with the French no longer a threat, the colonies were less able to depend on British military protection.

Lew, had returned to civilian life on December 1, 1760, and in 1768, he married Dinah Bowman. It is thought that she was born in 1744 and that Lew purchased her freedom from an owner named Abraham Blood. Their first of 13 children, a son named Zadock, was born in 1768, the year of their marriage. By 1772, the Lews were living in Chelmsford, Massachusetts.

Barzillai Lew returned to military service with the outbreak of the Revolutionary War. On May 6, 1775, he joined a company from Chelmsford commanded by Captain John Ford. Ford described Lew as "big and strong with an extraordinary talent as a musician." This talent earned Lew the position of company fifer; his music would rally the soldiers' spirits and help them keep track of their company in battle.

Lew played his fife during the first large-scale engagement of the war, the Battle of Bunker Hill, which was fought in Boston on June 17, 1775. The Americans and British fought this battle for pos-

session of Bunker Hill and Breed's Hill, two strategic heights overlooking Boston Harbor. Among the 1,500 Americans defending the hills were a number of African Americans, including former slaves SALEM POOR and PETER SALEM. The latter is remembered for fatally shooting British major John Pitcairn during the battle. The Americans repelled two assaults by British naval units and 2,400 red-coated infantry soldiers, but they ultimately were forced to retreat.

Barzillai Lew was with Ford's company in northeast New York State from July through December 1776, and was discharged at Albany, New York, on January 1, 1777. He then lived with his family in Dracut, Massachusetts, before enlisting briefly as a fifer in a Dracut company led by Captain Joseph Varnum. In September 1777, Varnum's militia was sent to Fort Ticonderoga, New York, to confront the army of British general John Burgoyne.

After the war, his earnings as a soldier allowed Lew to buy a tract of farmland near the Merrimac River in what is now Lowell, Massachusetts. Lew and his sons raised crops, and between 1793 and 1805, they helped to build the Middlesex Canal, which connected Lowell and Boston. Like their father, the Lew children exhibited musical talent, and the family was often hired to perform at dances from Boston to Portland, Maine.

Barzillai Lew died in 1822, leaving his farm to his sons Zadock and Zimri. His descendants have fought in every American war, and they have also included several generations of professional musicians. In addition, Lew was an ancestor of Harry "Bucky" Lew, who became the first African American in professional basketball when he played for Lowell in the New England Basketball League in 1902.

Further Reading

Dorman, Franklin A. *Twenty Families of Color in Massachusetts: 1742–1998.* Boston: New England Historic Genealogical Society, 1998, pp. 271–274, 276–278, 280, 476.

"Negroes Who Fought at Bunker Hill." *Ebony* 19, no. 4 (February 1964), pp. 44–53.

"Profiles in Courage: African Americans in Lowell." University of Massachusetts Lowell Libraries. Available online. URL: http://library.uml.edu/clh/Prof/Pro3.Html. Downloaded on November 22, 2008.

Purcell, L. Edward. *Who Was Who in the American Revolution.* New York: Facts On File, 1993, p. 292.

Louis, Joe
(Joseph Louis Barrow)
(1914–1981) *heavyweight champion boxer, army private who broke racial barriers during World War II*

Known affectionately as the "Brown Bomber," boxer Joe Louis was world heavyweight champion from 1937 until 1949. As a soldier during World War II, he improved conditions for African Americans in the armed forces and in so doing furthered the cause of civil rights.

Joseph Louis Barrow was born on May 13, 1914, in Lafayette, Alabama, the seventh of eight children in a farming family. His father, Monroe Barrow, had epilepsy and was periodically committed to an asylum for African Americans in Mt. Vernon, Alabama. While Joseph was a child, his mother, Lily Reese Barrow, received news that her husband had died; she subsequently married Patrick Brooks, a man with eight children.

Members of the large, blended family began moving to Detroit, and Joseph joined them in this northern city when he was 12 years old. He attended public schools in Detroit for a few years before dropping out to take a job in an automobile plant. He also spent an increasing amount of his free time at the Brewster Recreational Center, honing his boxing skills. Before long, he left his job to train full-time as a boxer and began fighting under the name Joe Louis. In 1935, he married Marva Trotter, a secretary and photographer.

Joe Louis gained national attention on June 19, 1936, when he entered the ring with Max Schmeling, a German boxer who symbolized the Nazi "master race" to many Americans. In the 12th round of the match, Schmeling became the first boxer to knock Louis out. Louis again made headlines on June 22, 1937, when he defeated James Braddock to win the world heavyweight championship. In 1938, Louis fought a much-publicized rematch with Schmeling and knocked the German fighter out in the first round.

Louis became a sports hero, especially to black Americans. On January 9, 1942, a month after the United States entered World War II, he defended his title against Buddy Baer and donated his $50,000 purse to the Navy Relief Society, an organization that provided aid to the families of navy personnel killed in battle. The act earned Louis the Edward J. Neil Award from the Boxing Writers Association of New York, presented each year to the person "who had done the most to project a positive image for boxing." It also caused some criticism, because at the time African Americans were restricted to duty in the navy as cooks and stewards.

The next day, January 10, Louis volunteered for the army. Although offered a commission, he chose to enter the armed forces as a private and was assigned to Fort Dix, New Jersey. He had been in uniform only a short time when army leaders asked him to defend his title for charity again, this time for Army Relief. That fight, against Abe Simon, was held on March 27, 1942. It was a victory for Louis in the sixth round and generated $75,000 in relief funds. This time, Louis not only relinquished his winnings, but also spent $3,000 on tickets to the fight for soldiers who otherwise could not afford to attend.

For the remainder of the war, Louis fought only exhibition matches at army bases in the United States and overseas. Traveling with a group of boxers known as the Joe Louis Troupe, he refused to fight if black and white spectators were required to sit apart from one another. While visiting

Camp Silbert, Alabama, Louis defied the segregation rules imposed at the post bus station. When taken to the stockade, he told an officer, "Sir, I'm a soldier like any other American soldier. I don't want to be pushed to the back because I'm a Negro." The incident persuaded the army to end segregated busing at its forts and posts.

After Fort Dix, Louis was stationed at Fort Riley, Kansas, where he befriended fellow soldier Jackie Robinson, who in 1947 would become the first African American to play major league baseball. Robinson told Louis that he and other African Americans were barred from playing on the post's baseball and football teams. As a celebrity sports figure, Louis had met influential people in government and the armed forces, and he used those connections to benefit Robinson and other black soldiers. In this instance, he appealed to Brigadier General Donald Robinson of the army and secured for African Americans the right to join teams on all army bases. When Louis learned that Jackie Robinson, a college graduate, had been denied admission to officer candidate school, he took the matter up with friends in the federal government, with the result that Robinson and 18 other African Americans attended officer candidate school.

In 1945, Sergeant Joe Louis received an honorable discharge from the army, was awarded the Legion of Honor, and returned home to a troubled personal life. His daughter Jacqueline had been born in 1943, but Marva sued for divorce in 1945 on grounds of desertion. In 1947, Joe and Marva had a son, Joseph Louis Barrow, Jr., and in 1948 they married and divorced again.

Joe Louis retired from the ring on March 1, 1949, having successfully defended his title 25 times and having lost only seven of 129 amateur and professional fights. In 1950, owing a substantial sum to the Internal Revenue Service, he returned to the boxing ring, but after being knocked out by Rocky Marciano in 1951, he retired again. He also worked briefly as a professional wrestler.

In 1954, Louis was elected to the Boxing Hall of Fame. In 1955, he married Harlem businesswoman Rose Morgan, but in 1957 the couple divorced. In 1959, Louis married attorney Martha Malone Jefferson. He ended his working years at Caesar's Palace in Las Vegas, where he greeted guests. In 1977, an aortic aneurysm left Louis dependent on a wheelchair, and on April 12, 1981, Joe Louis died. He was buried at Arlington National Cemetery.

Further Reading

Bak, Richard. *Joe Louis: The Great Black Hope*. Dallas: Taylor Publishing, 1996.

Barrow, Joe Louis, Jr., and Barbara Munder. *Joe Louis: Fifty Years an American Hero*. New York: McGraw-Hill, 1998.

Jakoubek, Robert. *Joe Louis: Heavyweight Champion*. New York: Chelsea House Publishers, 1990.

Louis, Joe, with Edna Rust and Art Rust, Jr. *Joe Louis: My Life*. New York: Harcourt Brace Jovanovich, 1978.

Wynn, Neil A. "Joe Louis," in *African American Icons of Sport: Triumph, Courage, and Excellence*, edited by Matthew C. Whitaker. Westport, Conn.: Greenwood Press, 2008.

M

Miller, Dorie
(Doris Miller)
(1919–1943) *ship's cook, third class, and hero of Pearl Harbor*

Known as Dorie to his friends and shipmates, Doris Miller had been trained by the navy to serve meals and handle laundry. He nevertheless stood on deck beside his white fellow sailors at Pearl Harbor, Hawaii, on December 7, 1941, to defend his ship and his nation from attack.

Doris Miller was born in Waco, Texas, on October 12, 1919. He was one of four brothers, all sons of Henrietta and Conery Miller. Doris attended Moore High School in Waco, where he was a fullback on the football team, and he worked on his family's farm.

On September 16, 1939, wanting to see more of the world and earn money to aid his family, Doris Miller enlisted in the navy as a mess attendant, third class, the only naval rank open to him as an African American. He completed training at Norfolk, Virginia, and was assigned to the USS *Pyro,* an ammunition ship. On January 2, 1940, he was transferred to the battleship USS *West Virginia.* He was the ship's heavyweight boxing champion, and he rose to the rank of ship's cook, third class.

On December 7, 1941, the *West Virginia* was docked at the U.S. naval base at Pearl Harbor. Miller awoke at 6 A.M. and was collecting laundry

when Japanese planes appeared in the brightening sky and launched a surprise attack. Suddenly, an aircraft torpedo struck the *West Virginia,* destroying the ship's antiaircraft battery magazine and severely wounding the captain. Miller carried his commander to a location protected by a bulkhead, where he could be treated by medics, and looked for a way to defend the ship from oncoming planes.

He spotted an unmanned .50-caliber Browning antiaircraft machine gun, and although he had never been trained in its use, he took hold of the gun, aimed at the sky, and fired. "It wasn't hard," he said. "I just pulled the trigger and she worked fine. I had watched the others with these guns. I guess I fired her for about fifteen minutes." Standing in the seawater that had begun to wash over the deck of the sinking battleship, Miller fired the machine gun until he ran out of ammunition and then abandoned ship with the rest of the surviving crew. He had destroyed at least four, and possibly as many as six, enemy planes. Altogether, five torpedoes and two armor-piercing bombs struck the *West Virginia.*

The historic Sunday-morning attack on Pearl Harbor sank or crippled 18 U.S. naval vessels, destroyed some 200 military planes on the ground, and killed or wounded approximately 2,300 members of the armed forces. It marked the entrance of Japan into World War II on the side of Ger-

Admiral Chester W. Nimitz presented the Navy Cross to ship's cook Dorie Miller on May 27, 1942. *(Library of Congress)*

many and Italy, and of the United States on the side of the Allies.

On April 1, 1942, Secretary of the Navy Frank Knox commended Miller for his actions during the attack; on May 27, 1942, Admiral Chester W. Nimitz presented him with the Navy Cross in a ceremony at Pearl Harbor aboard the USS *Enterprise*. Nimitz said, "This marks the first time in this conflict that such a high tribute has been made in the Pacific Fleet to a member of his race and I'm sure that the future will see others similarly honored for brave acts."

Miller had been reassigned to the USS *Indianapolis* on December 13, 1941. In the spring of 1943, he reported for duty aboard the USS *Liscome Bay*, an escort carrier. On November 24, 1943, the *Liscome Bay* was in the central Pacific, supporting operations in the Gilbert Islands, which had been occupied by Japan since 1941.

The carrier was struck by a torpedo launched from a Japanese submarine and sank within minutes. Although 272 sailors survived, 646 died, including Dorie Miller.

In 1973, the navy christened a frigate, the USS *Miller*, in his honor.

Further Reading

Bielakowski, Alexander. *African American Troops in World War II.* Oxford, U.K.: Osprey Publishing, 2007, pp. 27–29.

"Cook Third Class Dorie Miller, USN." Naval Historical Center. Available online. URL: http://www.history.navy.mil/faqs/faq57-4.htm. Downloaded on September 8, 2008.

"Doris (Dorie) Miller, American Hero." Pearl Harbor.org. Available online. URL: http://www.pearlharbor.org/dorie-miller.asp. Downloaded on September 8, 2008.

Moore, Christopher. *Fighting for America: Black Soldiers—The Unsung Heroes of World War II.* New York: Ballantine Books, 2006, pp. 31–34.

Smith, Jessie Carney, ed. *Notable Black American Men.* Detroit, Mich.: Gale Research, 1999, pp. 814–815.

Smith, Jessie Carney, and Joseph M. Palmisano, eds. *The African American Almanac.* 8th ed. Detroit, Mich.: Gale Research, 2000.

Mulzac, Hugh Nathaniel
(1886–1971) *first African American to command a U.S. merchant marine vessel*

"A West Indian in the United States quickly learns that he is meant for menial labor," Hugh Mulzac observed. An accomplished seaman qualified for positions of responsibility, the West Indian–born Mulzac worked for more than 20 years in the galleys of merchant ships. Not until 1942, when the United States was at war and needed his expertise, did he become the first African American to command a U.S. merchant marine vessel, and only because he stood in a rare position of strength did he demand—and receive—an integrated crew.

Born on March 26, 1886, on tiny Union Island in the British West Indies (now part of St. Vincent and the Grenadines), Hugh Mulzac grew up fascinated by the sea and whaling ships. He attended primary school on Union Island and high school on its larger neighbor, St. Vincent. In 1907, after graduating from high school, he joined the crew of a ship with a Norwegian commander. Voyages on this ship and others took him to distant ports, to Norway, Britain, Turkey, and Chile. Meanwhile, he completed the requirements for a mate's license from Swansea Nautical Institute in Wales and rose to the rank of mate aboard British ships.

Mulzac immigrated to the United States in 1911 and became a U.S. citizen in 1918. He continued his training in New York, through the U.S.

Hugh Mulzac, shown here in a portrait by Betsey Graves Reyneau, briefly triumphed over racism in the U.S. merchant marine when he commanded SS *Booker T. Washington* during World War II. *(National Portrait Gallery, Smithsonian Institution)*

Shipping Board, a government agency that existed between 1917 and 1934 to regulate maritime commerce and oversee the merchant marine, the fleet of civilian-owned merchant vessels that serves as an auxiliary to the U.S. Navy in wartime. Within two years, Mulzac had earned a master's certificate—the first ever issued to an African American. Only prejudice prevented him from doing anything other than galley work aboard ships in the merchant marine.

Opportunities existed, however, with the Black Star Line, a shipping concern established in 1917 by Marcus Garvey, a proponent of social, political, and economic independence for blacks. Mulzac served as mate aboard the SS *Yarmouth*, a ship with an African-American captain and crew, but in 1922, when the Black Star Line folded, he found shipboard employment only as a steward. He made the best of this unjust situation by learning all he could about food-service management and attaining the position of chief cook. In May 1937, he was a founding member of the National Maritime Union (NMU), which secured for African Americans the right to work in the engine rooms of merchant ships.

Mulzac's prospects changed when the United States entered World War II, and the U.S. military depended on merchant mariners to transport troops and supplies overseas. Liberty ships—cargo vessels newly built for use in war—increased the merchant marine fleet, but there remained a shortage of qualified personnel. The navy therefore in 1942 offered Mulzac the command of the SS *Booker T. Washington*, the first liberty ship named for an African American. Mulzac had waited more than 20 years for the chance to command a ship, but he turned the offer down when he learned that the crew was to be all black. "Under no circumstances will I command a Jim Crow vessel," he stated.

Needing his service, the navy relented and gave Mulzac an integrated crew. Mulzac wrote of his pride while watching the launching of his ship. "Everything I ever was, stood for, fought for, dreamed of, came into focus. . . . Now at last I could use my training and capabilities fully. It was like being born anew." Under his command, the *Booker T. Washington* made 22 round-trip voyages and carried 18,000 fighting men to Europe and the South Pacific.

In 1947, the government turned the *Booker T. Washington* over to the U.S. Maritime Commission, the agency that replaced the Shipping Board, and Mulzac was again denied a position of command. His experiences had awakened in him a willingness to work for equal treatment for himself and others, so in 1948 he fought back against this discriminatory treatment with a lawsuit. "One of the advantages of sea life is that you have plenty of time to think," he said. "It is impossible for any reasonably sensitive human being to stand at a ship's wheel for two hours a watch, three times a day . . . without giving some thought to the world around him, his own past and the future of both it and himself."

Mulzac's lawsuit was unsuccessful, but he strengthened his commitment to the labor movement and joined political organizations such as the Council for West Indian Federation. In 1950, he ran for borough president in Queens, New York, on the American Labor Party ticket, but lost, receiving 15,500 votes. His political activism attracted the attention of the House Committee on Un-American Activities, and he was called to testify in Congress. His statements before the committee led to his blacklisting and loss of professional credentials, and it was not until 1960 that a federal judge restored his seaman's papers and license. He subsequently found employment aboard ship as a night mate.

In 1963, Mulzac published a memoir, *A Star to Steer By*. He lived on St. Vincent after his retirement and died while visiting the United States in 1971, at age 84.

Further Reading

"Captain Hugh Mulzac." National Portrait Gallery. Available online. URL: http://www.npg.si.edu/exh/harmon/mulzharm.htm. Downloaded on September 8, 2008.

Horne, Gerald. *Red Seas: Ferdinand Smith and Radical Black Sailors in the United States and Jamaica.* New York: New York University Press, 2005, pp. 61, 97, 196–197, 200.

Mulzac, Hugh, as told to Louis Burnham and Norval Welch. *A Star to Steer By.* New York: International Publishers, 1963.

Palmer, Colin A., ed. *Encyclopedia of African-American Culture and History.* Vol. 4: M-P. Detroit, Mich.: Thomson Gale, 2006, pp. 1,503–1,504.

"World War II and Hugh Mulzac." Maritime Administration. Available online. URL: http://www.marad.dot.gov/EDUCATION/history/Black History/world_war_ii_and_high_mulzac.htm. Downloaded on September 8, 2008.

N

Newton, Lloyd W.
(1943–) *U.S. Air Force general, first African American to fly with the Thunderbirds*

Lloyd W. "Fig" Newton achieved the dream of his youth in 1974, when he was selected to join the Thunderbirds, the air force's precision flying team, as the group's first African-American member. In 1997, he attained the highest rank in the air force, that of four-star general.

Lloyd Warren Newton was born in Ridgeland, South Carolina, in 1943. He was the fourth of seven children born to Annie and John H. Newton, who were farmers. Although his parents had only a few years of schooling, they instilled in their children a love of knowledge. All of the children completed high school, and some graduated from college. Young Lloyd worked hard at his studies and hoped as an adult to emulate an older cousin in uniform, whom he admired.

After graduating from Jasper High School in Ridgeland, Newton entered Tennessee State University in Nashville as a mechanical engineering student, but the school's air force ROTC program reinforced his desire for a military career. (A fellow ROTC cadet began to call him Fig, and the nickname stuck: From then on, Lloyd Newton would be Fig Newton to his friends.) As a student in 1964, Newton saw a demonstration by the Thunderbirds, the air force's aerial demonstration squadron, and vowed one day to join the team although there never had been an African-American Thunderbird. In 1966, as a distinguished ROTC graduate, he received a bachelor's degree in aviation education from Tennessee State and was commissioned a second lieutenant in the air force.

Then he was off to Williams Air Force Base in Arizona for 53 weeks of pilot training. Becoming accustomed to air force life was, Newton said, "the most difficult thing, up to that time, that I had ever done. . . . From a small town, an all black high school, to a 98 percent black college, and then to a 99 percent white class in pilot training, was quite an adjustment—especially in 1966."

Newton adapted well to the air force and on December 12, 1967, he was promoted to first lieutenant. On April 4, 1968, the day the Reverend Martin Luther King, Jr., was assassinated, he left the United States to begin a year's tour of duty in South Vietnam. As a pilot and systems operator aboard the F-4D Phantom II, a supersonic long-range fighter-bomber, he flew 269 combat missions from Da Nang Air Base, including 79 over North Vietnam. Reflecting on the experience in 2002, he said, "There were missions I was scared on, but that's combat, and the things that help mature a young American, no matter who you are."

In 1969, Newton was promoted to captain and assigned to the 523rd Tactical Fighter Squadron at

Clark Air Force Base in the Philippines. At Clark, he served for a year as equal opportunity and treatment officer and as base race-relations officer. He welcomed the chance to help solve the nation's racial problems, even in the limited setting of a military base. "There were 10,000 airmen at Clark at the time, with 19 percent of them a minority," he said. "With the outstanding staff I had to work with, we managed to enhance the racial harmony around the base."

Newton first applied to join the Thunderbirds in 1972, but it was not until he made his third application, in 1974, that he was accepted and became the first African American in the elite squadron. Between November 1974 and December 1978, he held three positions: squadron narrator, describing maneuvers to audiences during flight demonstrations; slot pilot, flying number four, or rear position, in the diamond formation; and right wingman, piloting the number-two jet in the same formation.

Having been promoted to major, Newton next served as air force liaison officer to the U.S. House of Representatives. Beginning in June 1982 he held command positions at Hill Air Force Base in Utah. He attained the rank of colonel before returning to Washington to study at the Industrial College of the Armed Forces from August 1984 through August 1985. In 1985, he also earned a master's degree in public administration from George Washington University.

In August 1985, Newton joined the staff at Air Force Headquarters in Washington, D.C., first as assistant deputy director for operations and training and then as assistant director of special projects in the Directorate of Plans. Beginning in July 1988, he held a series of command positions. First, he commanded the 71st Air Base Group and later the 71st Flying Training Wing at Vance Air Force Base in Oklahoma. Then in May 1990, he assumed command of the 12th Flying Training Wing at Randolph Air Force Base in Texas. In August 1991, the air force sent him to Holloman Air Force Base in New Mexico, where he commanded

the 833rd Air Division and, later, the 49th Fighter Wing. In July 1993, he became director of operations, J-3, U.S. Special Operations Command at MacDill Air Force Base in Florida. Meanwhile, he moved up the chain of command, being promoted to brigadier general on August 3, 1991, to major general on August 10, 1993, and to lieutenant general on May 25, 1995.

In March 1997, General Newton took charge of the Air Education and Training Command at Randolph Air Force Base. The command consisted of 13 bases, more than 43,000 active-duty military personnel, and 14,000 civilian employees. At the time he was himself a command pilot who had logged more than 4,000 flying hours in a variety of military aircraft, including the T-37, T-38, F-4, F-15, F-16, C-12, and F-117 stealth fighter. On April 1, 1997, Newton was promoted to general and received a fourth star. He retired from active duty on August 1, 2000, and joined Pratt and Whitney Military Engines, the nation's largest manufacturer of engines for military aircraft, in September 2000 as a vice president.

In his free time, General Newton visited schools to encourage the nation's children to pursue higher education. "That's the one medium that helps to level the playing field," he said. "My point to youngsters is, they can grow to be anything and anybody their capabilities will allow them to be."

President George W. Bush appointed Newton to the 2005 Base Realignment and Closure Commission, which made recommendations for reorganizing the system of military bases in the United States and its territories to increase efficiency and readiness and better support forces. In December 2006, after retiring from Pratt and Whitney as an executive vice president, Newton became a director at the Goodrich Corporation in Charlotte, North Carolina. He served as well on the boards of directors of the Sonoco Products and Torchmark Corporations and on the boards of the National Air and Space Museum, National Museum of the U.S. Air Force, and Air Force Association.

General Lloyd W. Newton and his wife, the former Elouise M. Morning of St. Petersburg, Florida, raised five children.

The general's major awards and decorations include the Defense Distinguished Service Medal, Distinguished Service Medal with Oak Leaf Cluster, Legion of Merit with Oak Leaf Cluster, Distinguished Flying Cross with Oak Leaf Cluster, Meritorious Service Medal with Oak Leaf Cluster, Air Medal with 16 Oak Leaf Clusters, Air Force Commendation Medal, Air Force Outstanding Unit Award with "V" device and two Oak Leaf Clusters, Vietnam Service Medal, Philippine Presidential Unit Citation, and Republic of Vietnam Campaign Medal.

Further Reading

"A Jet Pilot's Dream Come True." *Ebony* 30, no. 7 (May 1975), pp. 82–90.

"Lloyd W. Newton." Forbes.com. Available online. URL: http://www.forbes.com/finance/mktguideapps/personinfo/FromPersonIdPersonTearsheet.jhtml?passedPersonId=894103. Downloaded on September 8, 2008.

Williams, Rudi. "Thunderbirds' First African American Pilot Becomes Four-Star General." *Real African American History*. Available online. URL: http://www.raahistory.com/military/airforce/newtonarticle.htm. Downloaded on September 8, 2008.

O

Olive, Milton Lee, III

(1946–1965) *army private, Medal of Honor winner*

Private First Class Milton L. Olive III was just 18 years old when he sacrificed his life in a South Vietnamese jungle to save his fellow soldiers. His bravery earned him the Medal of Honor.

Milton Lee Olive III was born in Chicago on November 7, 1946. Within a few hours of his entering the world, his mother, Clara Lee Olive, died of complications of childbirth. Young Milton, or "Skipper," therefore spent his early years in the care of his father and extended family and sometimes stayed with his paternal grandparents on their Lexington, Massachusetts, farm.

After Milton Lee Olive, Jr., remarried, Skipper settled with his father and stepmother in a middle-class neighborhood on the South Side of Chicago. Skipper showed talent as a singer, so his stepmother, Antoinette Olive, arranged for him to have voice lessons, and he often sang in church and at school. Photography was another of his boyhood interests, and he once printed business cards that identified him as "Chicago's Only 12-Year-Old Photographer."

Milton Olive III left high school after his junior year and, at age 17 and with his father's permission, on August 17, 1964, enlisted in the army for three years. He completed basic training at Fort Knox, Kentucky, and advanced training at the Artillery School at Fort Sill, Oklahoma, before qualifying for further training as a paratrooper. In April 1965, the army sent him to the Airborne School at Fort Benning, Georgia. Upon completion of that course, he joined Company B, 2nd Battalion (Airborne), 503rd Infantry, a unit that was already deployed in Vietnam.

As a paratrooper in South Vietnam, Olive took part in intense fighting and was awarded a Purple Heart in July 1965. In letters to his family, however, he never mentioned his combat experiences or battlefield injury.

On October 22, 1965, Company B was ordered to patrol a region near Phu Cuong, about 35 miles northwest of Saigon. As the paratroopers moved through the jungle, they came under enemy fire that was at some times light and at other times heavy. More than once, the shooting became intense enough to keep the men pinned down, but they always managed to fight off the Viet Cong and move forward.

It was late in the day when an enemy grenade landed near the paratroopers. There was no time to get away, because movement through the dense tropical foliage was slow. Without hesitating, Olive reached for the grenade, held it close to himself, and dropped to the ground so that his body absorbed the explosion and his comrades' lives were spared. "It was the most incredible display of selfless bravery that I ever witnessed," said Olive's platoon commander, First Lieutenant James Sanford. Olive's body was returned to the United States and buried in his family's plot in Lexington, Massachusetts, with military honors.

On April 12, 1966, President Lyndon B. Johnson presented a posthumous Medal of Honor to Private First Class Milton L. Olive III. The Olive family, friends, and military and civilian officials gathered in the White House rose garden for the noon ceremony. "Words can never enlarge upon acts of heroism and duty, but the nation will never forget Milton Lee Olive III," the president said. "Those who have earned this decoration are few in number. But true courage is very rare. This honor we reserve for the most courageous of all of our sons."

Johnson said that Olive had been compelled by "an instinct of loyalty which the brave always carry into conflict. In that incredibly brief moment . . . in which he decided to die, he put others first and himself last. I have always believed that to be the hardest, but the highest decision, that any man is ever called upon to make." Johnson handed the medal to Olive's father along with a second Purple Heart.

Milton L. Olive III received honors both private and public. In July 1967, his parents welcomed Medal of Honor recipient LAWRENCE JOEL into their home for a visit. Joel had come to Chicago to attend a military reunion and could not leave without paying his respects to Olive's family. In 1970, the city of Chicago named Olive-Harvey College for two Chicagoans who received the Medal of Honor posthumously, Olive and infantryman Carmel B. Harvey. The city also established Milton Lee Olive Park along its waterfront and placed there a bronze monument to the fallen hero.

Further Reading

"'For Valor Beyond the Call of Duty.'" *Sepia* 15, no. 7 (July 1966), pp. 8–12.

"Heroes and History." *Ebony* 21, no. 8 (June 1966), p. 160.

"Milton L. Olive III." African-American Involvement in the Vietnam War. Available online. URL: http://www.aavw.org/special_features/speeches_speech_lbj_miltonolive.html. Downloaded on September 8, 2008.

Murphy, Edward F. *Vietnam Medal of Honor Heroes.* New York: Ballantine Books, 1987, pp. 36–38.

"PFC Milton L. Olive III, U.S. Army." Special Operations.com. Available online. URL: http://www.specialoperations.com/MOH/olive.html. Downloaded on September 8, 2008.

O'Reilly, Salaria Kee

(1913–1991) *nurse, first African-American woman to volunteer in the Spanish civil war*

Salaria Kee O'Reilly's desire to help others inspired her to pursue a nursing career. In 1937, she became the first African-American woman to serve in the Spanish civil war when she traveled to Spain to nurse soldiers fighting for the Loyalist cause.

Salaria Kee was born in Akron, Ohio, on July 13, 1913. Her father died when she was very young; shortly thereafter, her mother either died or abandoned her children, leaving Salaria and her siblings to grow up in a series of foster homes.

Salaria finished high school and, wanting to be a nurse, applied to three nursing schools near Akron. All three rejected her because of her race, but she persisted and was eventually accepted into the Harlem Hospital School of Nursing in New York City. She graduated in 1934 and went to work at New York's Seaview Hospital. Immediately she discovered that working conditions for black and white nurses differed significantly. For example, it was the black nurses who cared for patients in the tuberculosis ward, a section of the hospital that white supervisors refused to enter. Kee knew several nurses who contracted the disease as a result of working in the ward.

In the early spring of 1936, Kee was working as an obstetrics nurse at Harlem Hospital when flooding affected the Midwest. She volunteered to work with the Red Cross aiding victims, but the organization declined the services of African-American nurses.

Soon, however, she found another way to donate her skills to a worthwhile cause. Hundreds of African-American men were sailing for Europe to take part in the Spanish civil war. General Francisco Franco of the Spanish army was leading a revolt against his country's leftist government with military support from Nazi Germany and fascist Italy, and African Americans saw a link between racism in the United States and the ethnocentric ideologies of Nazism and fascism. African-American men therefore fought for the Loyalist forces in support of the Spanish government, drove ambulances, and carried stretchers, while African-American doctors treated the wounded.

On March 27, 1937, Salaria Kee sailed to Spain aboard the SS *Paris* as part of a Catholic medical mission. She was the only African American among the 12 doctors and nurses traveling together and the first African-American woman to serve in Spain. Her group was assigned to the International Medical Unit at Villa Paz, which had been established in a former summer home of King Alfonso XIII that had been abandoned since his abdication in 1931. Because enemies of fascism had come from all over the world to fight for the Loyalists in this bloody war, Kee treated men from European countries, the United States, Mexico, Cuba, Japan, Ethiopia, and other nations. She

befriended one of her patients, John P. O'Reilly, who had been wounded while serving with a British international unit. Kee and O'Reilly were married in the hospital at Villa Paz.

The war was dangerous even for medical personnel, and Kee was wounded three times. Her third and most serious injury occurred in March 1938, when an exploding bomb buried her under several feet of rock and earth.

Salaria Kee O'Reilly returned to the United States aboard the *Queen Mary* in late 1938 to solicit medical aid and food for Spain. Until Franco achieved total victory on April 1, 1939, and established a dictatorship, she spoke about the Spanish cause at churches, schools, and NAACP gatherings. In the years that followed, she trained practical nurses and nurses' aides. She also served in the Army Nurse Corps in the final months of World War II. Salaria and John O'Reilly retired to Akron in the 1970s, and Salaria Kee O'Reilly died in Akron in 1991.

Further Reading

A Negro Nurse in Republican Spain. New York: Negro Committee to Aid Spain, n.d.

Carroll, Peter N., Michael Nash, and Melvin Small, eds. *The Good Fight Continues: World War II Letters from the Abraham Lincoln Brigade*. New York: New York University Press, 2006, pp. 26–28.

Collum, Danny Duncan, ed. *African Americans in the Spanish Civil War*. New York: G. K. Hall and Co., 1992, pp. 19–20, 81–82, 102, 123–124.

P

Penn, Robert

(1872–1912) *the only African-American sailor serving in the Spanish-American War to win the Medal of Honor*

Fireman Second Class Robert Penn became a hero in 1898 when an explosion threatened his ship in foreign waters. His quick action, with little regard for his own safety, saved the vessel and the lives of everyone aboard and earned him the Medal of Honor.

Robert Penn was born on October 10, 1872, in City Point, Virginia. He grew up in a time and place in which most African Americans were kept in poverty and ignorance. As a result, he worked as a field hand as a boy and had very little schooling. Hoping for "a better life," he enlisted in the navy upon reaching maturity.

By April 25, 1898, when the U.S. government declared war on Spain, Penn was serving as a fireman second class aboard the battleship USS *Iowa*. Commissioned June 16, 1897, the *Iowa* was the newest battleship sent into action in the Spanish-American War. On May 28, 1898, the *Iowa* was ordered to the waters off Santiago de Cuba, on the Spanish-held island of Cuba, to be part of a naval blockade.

On July 3, the *Iowa* fired the first shot in the battle of Santiago de Cuba, a confrontation in which the U.S. Navy destroyed a Spanish naval squadron that attempted to cross the blockade. The sailors aboard the *Iowa* exchanged fire with two Spanish cruisers, set them on fire, and drove them onto the beach. Their gunfire also helped to sink a Spanish destroyer and chased two other enemy ships aground.

On July 18, the Spanish government asked for a settlement with the United States. The *Iowa* was heading back to the United States when, just before 7 A.M. on July 20, there was an explosion in the ship's boiler room number two. Robert Penn and coppersmith Philip B. Keefer hurried from the nearby compartments where they had been stationed and discovered that a manhole gasket had blown off one of the boilers that supplied the ship with steam power.

It was nearly impossible to see into the steam-filled room, but Penn made out the form of the coal passer, who had been injured and was about to fall into the boiling water that covered the floor. Himself a man of average size and strength, Penn lifted the muscular, 140-pound coal passer over his shoulder and carried him to safety. Keefer, meanwhile, had removed the coal fires from the two furnaces in the room in order to avoid a second explosion that might have destroyed the ship.

While others treated the passer's scalded feet and lacerated forehead, Penn went back into the boiler room to aid Keefer. Balancing a foot above the boiling water on a makeshift bridge consisting of a board placed across coal buckets, Penn made several trips into the vapor-filled room, returning each time with a shovel full of flaming coals.

The *Iowa* left Cuban waters and reached New York on August 20, 1898. On December 11, 1898, Penn was awarded the Medal of Honor for his heroic act. Keefer received the Medal of Honor as well.

Further Reading

"Fireman First Class Robert Penn, USN (1872—1912)." Naval Historical Center. Available online. URL: http://www.history.navy.mil/photos/pers-us/uspers-p/r-penn.htm. Downloaded on September 8, 2008.

Greene, Robert Ewell. *Black Defenders of America, 1775–1973*. Chicago: Johnson Publishing Co., 1974, pp. 147, 377.

Lee, Irvin H. *Negro Medal of Honor Men*. New York: Dodd, Mead and Co., 1967, pp. 53–55.

Petersen, Frank Emmanuel, Jr.

(1932–) *first African-American marine aviator, first African-American general in the Marine Corps*

Frank E. Petersen, Jr., fought for his country in Korea and Vietnam as a Marine Corps officer and pilot. In 1952, he was the first African American to fly for the marines. Twenty-seven years later, he made history again by becoming the first African-American general in the corps.

Frank Emmanuel Petersen, Jr., was born in Topeka, Kansas, on March 2, 1932, the second of four children. His father, Frank E. Petersen, Sr., was a native of St. Croix, Virgin Islands, who repaired radios for a living; his mother, Edythe Southard Petersen, had been born and raised in Kansas. Frank Petersen, Jr., graduated from Topeka High School in 1949 and spent a year at Washburn University in Topeka. He was eager to see more of the world than Kansas, though, so he joined the U.S. Navy Reserve as a seaman apprentice in June 1950.

Petersen was serving as an electronics technician in California in December 1950, when he learned that Ensign JESSE L. BROWN, the first African-American naval aviator, had been shot down over Korea. Brown's example as a black military pioneer inspired Petersen to apply for the Naval Aviation Cadet Program. Upon being accepted in 1951, he reported to the naval air station at Pensacola, Florida, for flight training.

An African-American aviation cadet was a rarity on the base, and Petersen perceived that one instructor had singled him out for harassment because of his race. He received encouragement from air force captain CHAPPIE JAMES, who would become the nation's first African-American four-star general, and toughed it out. On October 22, 1952, when he was commissioned a marine second lieutenant, Petersen was designated a marine aviator, becoming the first African American to fly for the marines.

In 1953, after further training at the Marine Corps Air Station at El Toro, California, Petersen was ordered to active duty in the Korean War and assigned to Fighter Attack Squadron 212, known as the Devil Cats. This historic squadron had fought with valor in the South Pacific in World War II and had supported the American invasion of Okinawa. Like the rest of the armed forces, Squadron 212 was newly integrated. Petersen, the lone African American among the Devil Cats, flew 64 combat missions and earned six Air Medals and the Distinguished Flying Cross.

Petersen returned to El Toro in July 1954, and in February 1955 formally transferred from the U.S. Navy Reserve to the Marine Corps. He continued his education while in the armed forces, earning a bachelor's degree in 1967 and a master's degree in international affairs in 1973, both from George Washington University in Washington, D.C. He also completed Amphibious Warfare School at Quantico, Virginia, and the Aviation Safety Officers Course at the University of Southern California. In addition, he was the first African-American marine to attend the National War College in Washington, D.C.

In 1968, Petersen was ordered to Vietnam to command Marine Attack Squadron 314 (VMFA-314), thus becoming the first African American to lead a tactical air squadron in the Marine Corps or navy. Under his leadership, in 1969 VMFA-314 won the Robert M. Hanson Award, which the Marine Corps Aviation Association presents annually to the year's most outstanding Marine Corps fighter squadron.

Petersen flew 290 missions in Vietnam, including one over North Vietnam in August 1968 in which his F-4 Phantom was hit by fire from the ground. Knowing that landing in enemy territory would mean internment in a North Vietnamese prison camp, Petersen and his copilot flew the burning jet over safe ground before ejecting. Petersen was awarded the Purple Heart for wounds received in the incident.

Frank Petersen's military career also included regular promotions. On April 27, 1979, Petersen's wife, Alicia Petersen, and the commandant of the Marine Corps, General Louis H. Wilson, presented him with his stars as brigadier general, making him the first African-American general in the corps.

Petersen retired in 1988, after 38 years in the Marine Corps. At the time of his retirement, he headed Marine Corps Combat Development Command at Quantico, Virginia. He was a marine Silver Hawk, which means that he had been honored as the active-duty marine aviator with the earliest designation date. He had also received the Gray Eagle trophy, which honors long years of dedicated service to the navy or Marine Corps.

From 1990 to 1992, General Petersen served on the board of directors of the National Aviation Research and Education Foundation. Beginning in 1999, he served two years as chair of the National Marrow Donor Program. In 1999, he joined DuPont Aviation in New Castle, Delaware, as a vice president, overseeing DuPont's corporate flight programs worldwide and responsible for pilot training.

Among General Petersen's military decorations are the Defense Superior Service Medal, Legion of Merit with "V" device, Meritorious Service Medal, Navy Commendation Medal with "V" device, and Air Force Commendation Medal.

Further Reading

"Frank Petersen." National Visionary Leadership Project. Available online. URL: http://www.visionary project.org/petersenfrank/. Downloaded on September 9, 2008.

Hawkins, Walter L. *Black American Military Leaders.* Jefferson, N.C.: McFarland Co., 2007, p. 336.

Petersen, Frank E., with J. Alfred Phelps. *Into the Tiger's Jaw: America's First Black Marine Aviator.* Novato, Calif.: Presidio Press, 1998.

Smith, Jessie Carney, and Joseph M. Palmisano, eds. *The African American Almanac.* 8th ed. Detroit: Gale Research, 2000, pp. 1,239–1,240.

Pinchback, Pinckney Benton Stewart

(1837–1921) *captain of the Corps d'Afrique, first African-American governor*

Because his efforts to serve effectively as an army officer during the Civil War were repeatedly blocked by racism, P. B. S. Pinchback resigned his commission in 1863. In 1872 and 1873, when he briefly occupied the Louisiana governor's office, he was the first African-American governor in U.S. history. He was the only one until 1990, when C. Douglas Wilder was sworn in as governor of Virginia.

Pinckney Benton Stewart Pinchback was born in Macon, Georgia, on May 10, 1837. He was the son of William Pinchback, a white Virginia plantation owner, and Eliza Stewart, an enslaved woman whom William Pinchback had taken to Philadelphia in 1836 or 1837 to be manumitted. At the time of Pinckney's birth, the family was en route to Holmes County, Mississippi, where William Pinchback had purchased property and where Pinckney would spend his first years.

In 1846, when Pinckney was nine and his brother Napoleon was 16, the boys were sent to Gilmore's High School in Cincinnati to begin their formal education. Their schooling ended two years later when they were called to the bedside of their ill and dying father. Although the elder Pinchback had five children, his estate went to his white relatives following his death. Lacking money or property and fearful of re-enslavement, Eliza Stewart fled with her children to Cincinnati, and Pinckney reached maturity working as a cabin boy and steward on boats steaming along the Mississippi, Missouri, and Red Rivers.

At the mouth of the Mississippi River lay the city of New Orleans, which at the outbreak of the Civil War became an important Confederate military center and port. The Confederates defended the city with naval vessels and a heavy chain cable suspended across the lower Mississippi, but the blockade failed to prevent Pinckney Pinchback from slipping into New Orleans; it also failed to stop the Union from occupying the city on May 1, 1862.

On May 16, 1862, for an unknown reason, Pinchback fought with his sister's husband, John Keppard, on a New Orleans street corner, inflicting on him a superficial stab wound. Pinchback began serving a two-year sentence in a workhouse on May 23, but he was released on July 28, after a little more than two months. Then, eager to join the Union cause, the light-skinned Pinchback enlisted in the First Louisiana Volunteer Infantry, a white regiment.

That summer, the Militia Act of 1862 permitted the president to call African-American soldiers into military service. By August, African-American regiments, known as the Corps d'Afrique, were being assembled in Louisiana. Two of the regiments formed in New Orleans were to have African-American officers. Pinchback applied to serve with the corps, and on August 27, 1862, was authorized to recruit a company. When his regi-

Pinckney Benton Stewart Pinchback, a captain with the Corps d'Afrique during the Civil War, was governor of Louisiana for five weeks in 1872 and 1873. *(Library of Congress)*

ment went into service on October 12, Pinchback was captain of Company A. The reality of black regiments commanded by black officers was short-lived, however. The officers had received only temporary commissions and were gradually replaced by whites. Before long, Pinchback was the sole African-American officer with the Corps d'Afrique.

Segregation was the rule in the Union-held city of New Orleans, but as an officer of the U.S. Army, Pinchback refused to conform to local custom. When he insisted on riding in streetcars designated for whites he rode alone, because the conductors barred any other passengers from boarding. Pinchback also raised objections to unfair treatment of African Americans in the army, specifically to inequality in the pay that black and white soldiers received and to the slurs from white officers that he and his men endured.

His protests achieved no results, so on September 10, 1863, he resigned his commission. He wrote to his commanding general, "I find nearly all the officers inimical to me, and I can foresee nothing but dissatisfaction and discontent, which will make my position very disagreeable indeed."

After the Civil War, Pinchback served as a delegate to the convention that drafted a new constitution for Louisiana and wrote a provision guaranteeing all citizens equal treatment as users of public transportation and as patrons of businesses. A Republican, he was elected to the state Senate in 1868 and acted as president pro tempore. In 1871, he replaced Oscar J. Dunn as lieutenant governor following Dunn's death. Then, for five weeks beginning December 9, 1872, he acted as governor while the Louisiana House of Representatives conducted impeachment proceedings against Governor Henry Clay Warmoth. Thus, Pinchback became the first African American to serve as governor of a state.

P. B. S. Pinchback was both idealistic and opportunistic. He often spoke in favor of African-American rights and worked as a politician to secure those rights, and he published an African-American newspaper, the *Louisianian.* At the same time, he used his position as an elected official to grow wealthy through such corrupt methods as selling real estate to the state government at inflated prices and speculating in state bonds.

Pinchback was elected to Congress from Louisiana in 1872, but his Democratic opponent contested the election and won the seat. He was elected to the U.S. Senate in 1873, but was again refused his seat. In 1875, he became chairman of the Convention of Colored Newspaper Men, forerunner of the Associated Negro Press, and in 1882 he was appointed surveyor of customs in New Orleans.

In 1887, at age 50, Pinchback undertook the study of law at Straight College in New Orleans; he was later admitted to the bar. In 1897, he moved with his wife, the former Nina Hawthorne, to Washington, D.C., where he involved himself in politics. He died in Washington on December 21, 1921.

Further Reading

Foner, Eric. *Freedom's Lawmakers: A Directory of Black Officeholders during Reconstruction.* Baton Rouge: Louisiana State University Press, 1996, pp. 171–172.

Foner, Eric, and Olivia Mahoney. *America's Reconstruction.* New York: HarperPerennial, 1995, p. 101.

Haskins, James. *The First Black Governor: Pin[c]kney Benton Stewart Pinchback.* Trenton, N.J.: Africa World Press, 1996.

Palmer, Colin A., ed. *Encyclopedia of African-American Culture and History.* Vol. 4: M–P. Detroit, Mich.: Thomson Gale, 2006, p. 1,782.

Pitts, Riley Leroy

(1937–1967) *first African-American commissioned officer to be awarded the Medal of Honor*

The commitment to the safety of the men under his command that Captain Riley L. Pitts displayed in 1967, in a Vietnam jungle, earned him a place in history, as the first African-American commissioned officer in the U.S. armed forces to be awarded the Medal of Honor. "What this man did in an hour of incredible courage will live in the story of America as long as America endures," said President Lyndon B. Johnson, upon presenting the medal to Pitts's widow. "He was a brave man and a leader of men. No greater thing could be said of any man."

Pitts, who was born in Fallis, Oklahoma, earned a degree in journalism in 1960 from the Municipal University of Wichita (now Wichita State University) in Kansas. A distinguished military graduate, he was commissioned a second lieutenant in the army through the Reserve Officers Training Corps (ROTC). Pitts remained in the army reserve while he worked for the Boeing Corporation, married, and began to raise a family.

By December 1966, he had attained the rank of captain in the reserves; in that month he was placed on active duty and sent to Vietnam, where he served as an information officer until being transferred to combat duty, as captain of C Company of the 2nd Battalion, 27th Infantry, in the 25th Infantry Division.

The U.S. troops in Vietnam frequently relied on helicopter, or airmobile, transport to launch assaults for the purpose of seizing critical terrain in conjunction with larger ground operations. On October 31, 1967, Pitts's company participated in such an airmobile assault at Ap Dong in the Mekong Delta region. As C Company landed, the men immediately came under fire from Viet Cong machine gunners.

It was a time for fast action, and Pitts led his soldiers in an assault on the enemy positions before being ordered to move north, to aid another unit that was barely holding its own against a powerful enemy force. Reaching the outnumbered soldiers was a challenge in itself, because intense gunfire coming from three directions made it all but impossible for C Company to move forward. The Americans knew that some of the bullets came from two enemy bunkers that lay within 15 meters of their position, but the thick jungle growth prevented them from effectively returning fire. A grenade could have done the job, so Pitts picked up a Chinese grenade that had been seized from a captured Viet Cong soldier and lobbed it at the forward bunker. The grenade sailed high and arced toward its target, but Pitts had aimed low, with the result that the grenade bounced off a tree and landed near the spot from which it had been launched, where he and his soldiers had taken cover. Pitts again acted quickly, throwing himself on top of the grenade to protect the others, but it never exploded.

Pitts's next strategy was to maneuver the company into position to employ artillery, which weakened the enemy enough to allow the men to move toward the Viet Cong positions, and Pitts himself killed at least one more enemy sol-

dier. C Company remained in danger, however, and the thick foliage continued to present an obstacle. With no thought for his own safety, Pitts moved to an exposed site, from which he could fire with accuracy on the enemy. As he urged his men on, he was shot and killed, just two weeks after his 30th birthday and a month before he was scheduled to be sent home.

Captain Riley L. Pitts was honored posthumously for his heroism on this day with the Medal of Honor. The citation accompanying his medal stated that his "conspicuous gallantry, extraordinary heroism, and intrepidity at the cost of his life, above and beyond the call of duty, are in the highest traditions of the U.S. Army and reflect great credit upon himself, his unit, and the Armed Forces of his country."

Further Reading

America's Medal of Honor Recipients: Complete Official Citations. Golden Valley, Minn.: Highland Publishers, 1980.

"Riley L. Pitts." African-American Involvement in the Vietnam War. Available online. URL: http://www.aavw.org/served/homepage_pitts.html. Downloaded on October 5, 2008.

"Riley L. Pitts: A Kansas Portrait." Kansas State Historical Society. Available online. URL: http://www.kshs.org/portraits/pitts_riley_l.htm. Downloaded on October 5, 2008.

Sutherland, Jonathan D. *African Americans at War: An Encyclopedia.* 2 vols. Santa Barbara, Calif.: ABC-CLIO, 2004, pp. 305–306, 634, 765–766.

Plummer, Henry Vinton

(1844–1905) *first African American commissioned as a regular army chaplain*

The case of Captain Henry V. Plummer was controversial in the 1890s and remained so for more than a century. Initially, white commanders praised Plummer, the first black chaplain commissioned in the regular army, yet when he attempted to change conditions on his base and address larger racial issues, he was court-martialed and discharged. An army review of the case resulted, in 2005, in an honorable discharge for Plummer.

On June 30, 1844, Henry Vinton Plummer was born into slavery in Prince George's County, Maryland. He toiled in the fields of the Calvert plantation until the spring of 1864, when he escaped from bondage and enlisted in the Union navy. He was assigned to a gunboat, the USS *Coeur de Leon*, one of 25 vessels in the Potomac Flotilla. This small fleet provided the Union military campaigns in northeast Virginia with men, munitions, and supplies and also served as a blockade squadron, preventing replacements and provisions from reaching Confederate units in the area.

Plummer was honorably discharged from the navy in August 1865 and found a job as a night watchman at a Washington, D.C., post office. On June 22, 1867, he married Julia Lomax. Having learned to read and write while in the navy, and aspiring to have a career, he enrolled in the Wayland Seminary in Washington as soon as he could afford the tuition. During his years as a student at Wayland, he preached to Baptist congregations in the District of Columbia and Maryland.

Henry Plummer graduated from Wayland in 1879, and in 1881 began a campaign to become an army chaplain. He repeatedly sent letters of entreaty to Secretary of War Robert T. Lincoln, and he enlisted Frederick Douglass as a character reference. Douglass wrote to President Chester A. Arthur that Plummer was "an honest man, well fitted by character and attainment" for the position.

The campaign was at last successful, and on July 1, 1884, Plummer became the first African American commissioned as a regular army chaplain. He was assigned to the 9th Cavalry, an African-American regiment, at Fort Riley, Kansas, where he performed the duties of chaplain, school superintendent, and bakery manager.

A year later, Plummer and the 9th Cavalry were stationed in the Department of the Platte, which stretched the length of the Platte River in Nebraska and Wyoming Territory and encompassed Iowa and Utah. Plummer was posted at Fort Robinson, Nebraska, headquarters of the department, where he proved to be an energetic and popular chaplain. He led services on Sundays and on Thursday evenings, held periodic revival meetings, and conducted Sunday school for 21 children living on the post. He was promoted to captain and received praise from his superiors, including Lieutenant Colonel George Sanford, who noted the "efficient manner in which the chaplain carries out his work." Mary Gerrard, an officer's wife who played the organ in the post chapel, viewed Plummer as "energetic, faithful & devoted to his duties."

An advocate of temperance, Plummer delivered the first in a series of lectures on the evils of drink in March 1892. He organized the post children into the Loyal Temperance Union and extended his crusade into the nearby town of Crawford. Not content to limit himself to these activities, he convinced the Department of the Army to ban the sale of alcoholic beverages at Fort Robinson. Thus, for the first time he earned the disapproval of his superiors, who perceived that he had made them look bad to the top brass.

Soon, Plummer lodged more complaints that further antagonized the post command. He objected, for example, to use of the chapel for dancing in off-hours. He also protested that his quarters were damp and too small for his family, which included his wife, four of their six children, and his sister, and that he was required to live alongside the black enlisted men rather than near the white officers.

When both an anonymous letter to the *Omaha Progress* and a privately printed pamphlet threatened the white community with violence by blacks, the white officers at Fort Robinson suspected Plummer of writing them. They became more alarmed in April 1894, when he wrote to the War Department in Washington, D.C., proposing to lead between 50 and 100 volunteers from the 9th Cavalry on a mission of conquest and Christian conversion in Africa.

Three months later, Plummer faced a court-martial, charged with "Conduct Unbecoming an Officer and a Gentleman." He was accused of fraternizing with enlisted men, using vulgar language in the presence of a woman, and, ironically, drunkenness. He tried to resign from the army for medical reasons, but the post physician pronounced him healthy, and his trial began in October 1894.

The case against Plummer depended largely on the testimony of Sergeant Robert Benjamin of the 9th Cavalry and his wife, although Benjamin held a grudge, insisting that Plummer had disciplined him unfairly years earlier. Despite testimony from organist Mary Gerrard, who said that she had never seen Plummer "even to the smallest degree, show any evidence of being under the influence of alcohol," and others who claimed that Plummer was sober on the night in question, on November 2 he was convicted on two counts, and on November 10 he was dismissed from the army.

Plummer moved with his family to Kansas and ministered to Baptist congregations in Kansas City and Wichita. He involved himself in local Republican politics and tried unsuccessfully to be reinstated as an army chaplain. He died in Kansas City on February 10, 1905.

In February 2004, a group of Plummer's relations and supporters petitioned the Army Board for Correction of Military Records, seeking his exoneration. In 2005, the board announced its decision to grant Plummer a posthumous honorable discharge. The army upheld his court martial, however, stating that it appeared to have been properly conducted. The board was reluctant to apply 2005 legal standards to a case more than a century old.

Further Reading

Glasrud, Bruce A., and Michael N. Searles, eds. *Buffalo Soldiers in the West: A Black Soldiers Anthology.* College Station: Texas A & M University Press, 2007, pp. 70–73.

Lamm, Alan K. *Five Black Preachers in Army Blue, 1884–1901: The Buffalo Soldier Chaplains.* Lewiston, N.Y.: Edwin Mellen Press, 1998.

"New Status for a Black Pioneer: Army Revises Record of First Black Chaplain." MSNBC.com. Available online. URL: http://www.msnbc.msn.com. id/6948815/. Downloaded on September 9, 2008.

Rich, Eric. "A Fallen Chaplain's Second Judgment." *Washington Post,* March 1, 2004, p. B1.

Schubert, Frank N. *Buffalo Soldiers, Braves, and the Brass: The Story of Fort Robinson, Nebraska.* Shippensburg, Pa.: White Mane Publishing Co., 1993, pp. 91–92, 99, 127–134.

Stover, Earl F. "Chaplain Henry V. Plummer, His Ministry and His Court-Martial." *Nebraska History* 56, no. 1 (spring 1975): 20–50.

Poor, Salem

(1747–unknown) *Revolutionary War soldier*

Praised by his commanding officers as a "brave and gallant soldier," Salem Poor spent five years in the Continental Army. He distinguished himself at Bunker Hill and was present at other significant events of the American Revolution.

In 1747, an infant African-American male named Salem was baptized in the North Parish Congregational Church in Andover (now North Andover), Massachusetts. He spent his childhood and youth as an enslaved worker on the farm of John and Rebecca Poor of Andover. On July 22, 1769, at age 22, he purchased his freedom from John Poor, Jr., with 27 British pounds that he had managed to save. His manumission was entered into the Andover court records in February 1772. Meanwhile, in August 1771, Salem Poor had married Nancy Parker, a servant of Captain James Parker and his family.

Poor's name entered the historical record again on April 24, 1775, when he enlisted in the 5th Massachusetts Regiment. Days earlier, on April 19,

British troops and American militiamen had met in the first armed engagement of the American Revolution. The early-morning exchange of gunfire at Lexington, Massachusetts, had left eight Americans dead, but it was followed by an encounter at Concord, about six miles distant, in which a numerically inferior American force used small-unit tactics to compel 800 British soldiers to retreat.

Poor was among the American fighting men who on June 16, 1775, built a fortification on Breed's Hill in the Charlestown section of Boston, overlooking the harbor. The British attacked Breed's Hill and nearby Bunker Hill on June 17, and after three assaults captured both heights. Fourteen colonial officers were impressed enough by Poor's actions in the battle to submit a recommendation of recognition to the General Court of Massachusetts Bay on December 5, 1775. This document stated, in part, ". . . Wee declare that a Negro Man, called Salem Poor . . . behaved like an Experienced officer, as well as an Excellent Soldier, to set forth Particulars of his conduct would be tedious, Wee Would Only begg leave to say in the Person of this Negro Centers a brave and gallant soldier." The officers declined to describe Poor's deeds, but Poor has been credited with fatally shooting British lieutenant colonel James Abercrombie.

The official Revolutionary War Militia Rolls place Salem Poor at the indecisive Battle of White Plains, fought on October 28, 1776, between armies led by General George Washington and General William Howe. He was also among the soldiers who survived the brutal winter of 1777–78 with Washington at Valley Forge, Pennsylvania.

History lost track of Salem Poor when his service with the Continental army ended on March 20, 1780. Where he went to live, how he earned his living, when and where he died, and where he is buried remain unknown. Salem and Nancy Poor had a son, Jonah, who was baptized in the North Andover Congregational Church on September 29, 1776, but whether they had other children is unknown as well.

In 1975, the U.S. Postal Service honored Salem Poor with a commemorative 10-cent stamp.

Further Reading

Palmer, Colin A. *Encyclopedia of African-American Culture and History.* Vol. 4: M-P. Detroit, Mich.: Thomson Gale, 2006, p. 1,823.

"Salem Poor." Celebrate Boston. Available online. URL: http://www.celebrateboston.com/biographies/patriots/poorsalem.htm. Downloaded on September 9, 2008.

"Salem Poor: 'A Brave and Gallant Soldier.'" Boston National Historic Park. Available online. URL: http//www.nps.gov/bost/bulletins/Salemp~1.pdf. Downloaded on September 9, 2008.

Smith, Jessie Carney, ed. *Notable Black American Men.* Detroit: Gale Research, 1999, pp. 947–949.

Powell, Colin Luther

(1937–) *army general, first African-American chairman of the Joint Chiefs of Staff, first African-American secretary of state*

General Colin Powell became a familiar figure to millions of Americans during the Persian Gulf War of 1991, when as chairman of the Joint Chiefs of Staff he conducted televised news briefings. Powell was not only the first African American to hold the highest job in the U.S. military, but also in 2001 he became the first African-American secretary of state.

Colin Luther Powell was born on April 5, 1937, in Harlem, in New York City, to Jamaican-immigrant parents. His father, Luther Powell, was a shipping clerk, and his mother, Maud Powell, worked as a seamstress. Colin and his older sister, Marilyn, were raised in the ethnically diverse Hunts Point neighborhood of New York City among a large extended family.

Recalling his youth, Powell said, "I grew up in a time of wars." As a child during World War II, he read about Colin Kelly, an American pilot who shared his first name, who died when his plane was shot down during an attack on a Japanese battleship. As a teenager, Powell followed the events that unfolded in the Korean War.

Powell entered the City College of New York in 1954, when he was 18. An indifferent student at Morris High School, he majored in geology in college, although he had no special interest in that subject. He discovered his life's direction when he joined the college's army ROTC program. He was commander of the Pershing Rifles, a precision marching team, and he graduated in June 1958 at the top of his ROTC class and as a second lieutenant in the army.

He headed for Fort Benning, Georgia, where he completed the Infantry Officer Basic Course, Ranger Course, and Airborne Course before being assigned as a platoon leader in Germany. He was stationed at Fort Devens in Massachusetts in 1960, when he met Alma Johnson, a student from Birmingham, Alabama. The couple married on August 25, 1962; several months later, Colin Powell went to Vietnam, where he received a severe foot wound when he stepped on a trap containing a sharpened bamboo stick while patrolling a rice field. His service in Vietnam earned him the Purple Heart and the Bronze Star. A son, Michael, was born in 1963, while Powell was in Vietnam.

In 1964, Powell attended the Army Command and Staff College at Fort Leavenworth and graduated second in a class of 1,244 officers. The Powells' first daughter, Linda, was born in 1965.

Colin Powell stood on the sidelines during the Civil Rights movement of the 1960s, but he felt that his accomplishments as an African-American military officer made others aware of opportunities for achievement. "I didn't have a chance to participate in that struggle in an active way," he said. "I did it in my own way, by my own example and by helping other people who were coming along as best I could."

The army sent Colin Powell back to Vietnam in 1968, first as an infantry battalion executive officer and later as assistant chief of staff, G-3, 23rd Infantry Division. In the latter role he survived a helicopter crash and rescued his commander and an aide from the burning craft—an act of heroism that earned him the Soldier's Medal.

Home again from Vietnam in July 1969, Powell enrolled in George Washington University in Washington, D.C., to study business administration. He earned an MBA in 1971, the year his daughter Annemarie was born. In 1972, Powell was promoted to major and was one of 17 candidates chosen from a pool of more than 1,500 to be White House Fellows. These special assistants gain experience in high government offices; Powell was assigned to the Office of Management and Budget.

Although Powell would later put his management skills to use in the upper levels of government, he next applied them in Korea in 1973, as commander of the 1st Battalion, 32nd Infantry. Powell eliminated problems of fighting and drug abuse from the troubled unit and turned it into a source of pride for the army.

From Korea, Powell went back to Washington in 1974 to be operations research analyst in the office of the secretary of defense. In 1976, he took command of the 2nd Brigade, 101st Airborne Division, at Fort Campbell, Kentucky. He also graduated with distinction from the National War College at Fort McNair in Washington, D.C. The college offers a course of study in national security policy and strategy to prepare leaders for the armed forces, the State Department, and other government agencies. The War College course qualified Powell to serve in the office of the secretary of defense in 1977 and as executive assistant to the secretary of energy in 1979. Also in 1979, he was promoted to brigadier general.

General Colin Powell was named assistant commander for operations and training of the 4th Infantry Division at Fort Carson, Colorado, in 1981, deputy commander of Fort Leavenworth, Kansas, in 1983, and senior military assistant to the secretary of defense, also in 1983. In 1986, he

General Colin Powell poses with President Bill Clinton, Secretary of Defense Les Aspin, and the Joint Chiefs of Staff in 1993 (left to right: Admiral Frank Kelso, General Gordon Sullivan, Powell, Clinton, Aspin, Admiral David Jeremiah, General Merrill McPeak, and General Carl Mundy). *(Library of Congress)*

assumed command of the U.S. Fifth Army in Frankfurt, West Germany.

In 1987, President Ronald Reagan appointed Colin Powell to be the first African-American national security advisor. It was a time for reflection, and Powell acknowledged his debt to those African Americans who had come before him, people who had labored and sacrificed to create openings for others. He called them "men and women of enormous potential who, because of prejudice and intolerance, were not allowed to make their full contribution to this great country." As national security advisor, Powell kept the president informed about the nation's military preparedness, advised him on foreign policy, and helped to plan summit meetings between Reagan and Soviet president Mikhail Gorbachev.

Powell's stint as national security advisor ended in 1989, when George H. W. Bush was sworn in as president, but he continued to achieve and break

barriers. In early 1989, he was promoted to the highest military rank in the United States and pinned a fourth star to his uniform. He next served as commander in chief of the army's largest combat unit, U.S. Forces Command at Fort McPherson, Georgia.

Within a few months, however, Colin and Alma Powell returned to Washington, where Colin Powell was sworn in as the first African-American chairman of the Joint Chiefs of Staff. At age 52, he was the youngest person to hold the highest military position in the country. The Joint Chiefs of Staff, a group of six military leaders representing the army, navy, air force, and Marine Corps, formulate the nation's defense strategy and supervise military operations.

On December 20, 1989, Powell ordered the start of Operation Just Cause, a surprise nighttime invasion of Panama with the goal of arresting dictator Manuel Noriega, who had been profiting from the shipment of drugs to the United States. Noriega surrendered on January 3, 1990, after U.S. forces destroyed his headquarters and key military posts. He was indicted in the United States on racketeering and drug charges, and in 1992 he was convicted on eight counts of racketeering, drug trafficking, and money laundering and was sentenced to 40 years in prison.

Powell next oversaw U.S. operations in the Persian Gulf War of 1991, which was fought to free Kuwait from an Iraqi invasion. This brief war began on January 16, 1991, with massive air and missile attacks launched from bases in Saudi Arabia on targets in Iraq and Kuwait. Powell employed what he called a "very, very simple" strategy to defeat Iraq's army. "First, we're going to cut it off," he said. "Then we're going to kill it." The strategy worked: By late February, Iraq was in full retreat, and on February 27, as Kuwaitis raised the emirate's flag in Kuwait City, Bush suspended offensive combat and laid out conditions for a permanent cease-fire.

General Colin Powell retired from the army on September 30, 1993, and accepted the chairmanship of the Alliance for Youth, a nonprofit organization dedicated to building character and competence in the young. He pursued a busy speaking career, and in 1995 he published a best-selling autobiography, *My American Journey*. On December 16, 2000, president-elect George W. Bush nominated Powell to be the first African-American secretary of state. The Senate approved the nomination, and Secretary Powell was sworn in on January 20, 2001.

As secretary of state, Powell traveled widely. In 2002 alone, he made 16 trips overseas, visiting 41 countries. On February 5, 2003, Iraq's failure to comply with UN Resolution 1441 brought Powell to New York City, where he went before the UN Security Council to lay out the U.S. case against Iraq. (Resolution 1441 required Iraq to disarm itself of weapons of mass destruction and disclose the locations of its weapons program.) Powell described in detail Iraq's continuing development

of biological, chemical, and other weapons, and its efforts to hide weapons sites from UN inspectors. "Leaving Saddam Hussein in possession of weapons of mass destruction for a few more months or years is not an option, not in a post-September 11th world," Powell said.

Whether to wage war or allow the Iraqi president more time to comply with the resolution was a controversial question among UN member nations, and when the United States and other nations took military action against Iraq in March and April 2003, it was without UN support. By April 25, U.S. forces had secured control of Baghdad, and Bush declared the war to be over.

Powell soon resumed his diplomatic travels. After flying to Paris to attend the G-8 foreign ministers meeting of May 22 and 23, 2003, he accompanied Bush on a trip to Europe and the Middle East. From June 8 through 10, he was in Chile and Argentina to attend the General Assembly of the Organization of American States.

Although Powell continued to fulfill his diplomatic obligations, conflicts arose within the rest of the Bush administration over the War on Terror and the War in Iraq. Tensions escalated in 2004, when U.S. forces found no weapons of mass destruction in Iraq, and Powell admitted that the information he had given the UN was based on faulty intelligence. Powell stepped down as secretary of state after Bush's reelection in 2004. In 2005, he joined Kleiner, Perkins, Caufield and Byers, a Silicon Valley venture capital firm, as a limited partner.

Powell's military awards include the Defense Distinguished Service Medal with three Oak Leaf Clusters, Army Distinguished Service Medal with Oak Leaf Cluster, Defense Superior Service Medal, and Legion of Merit with Oak Leaf Cluster. Among his civilian awards are two Presidential Medals of Freedom, the President's Citizen's Medal, Congressional Gold Medal, Secretary of State Distinguished Service Medal, and Secretary of Energy Distinguished Service Medal.

Further Reading

De Young, Karen. *Soldier: The Life of Colin Powell.* New York: Knopf, 2006.

Krim, Jonathan. "Powell to Join Storied Venture Capital Firm." *Washington Post,* July 13, 2005, p. D1.

Lusane, Clarence. *Colin Powell and Condoleezza Rice.* Westport, Conn.: Praeger Publishers, 2006.

Powell, Colin L., with Joseph E. Persico. *My American Journey.* New York: Random House, 1995.

Prioleau, George Washington

(1856–1927) *chaplain with the 9th Cavalry*

Unlike his predecessor, HENRY V. PLUMMER, whose ambition angered his commanding officers and led to his court-martial, George W. Prioleau served long and peaceably as chaplain of the 9th Cavalry. In his writings he spoke eloquently about racial inequality in the United States.

George Washington Prioleau was born into slavery in Charleston, South Carolina, in 1856, to L. S. and Susan Prioleau. After the Civil War, L. S. Prioleau became a minister in the African Methodist Episcopal (AME) Church, and his son George went to school in Charleston. George continued his education in Orangeburg, South Carolina, at Claflin University, the oldest historically black college in the United States, which was founded in 1869.

During his four years at Claflin, George Prioleau taught school in Lyons Township in Orangeburg County. He graduated in 1875 and joined the Columbia, South Carolina, Conference of the AME Church. He also performed a variety of duties, including those of choir leader, Sunday school teacher, and occasional preacher at the AME church in St. Matthews, South Carolina, where his father was pastor.

In 1880, the Columbia Conference sent Prioleau to Wilberforce University, a traditionally black school in Ohio, to further his studies. While enrolled in Wilberforce, Prioleau supported himself by doing agricultural work, and he ministered to an AME mission in Selma, Ohio.

Prioleau graduated from Wilberforce in 1884 with a bachelor of divinity degree. He then served as pastor to churches in Hamilton, Troy, and other Ohio towns, taught at a public school in Selma, and married Anna L. Scovell of New Orleans, another Wilberforce graduate. In 1888, he became professor of ecclesiastical history and homiletics at Wilberforce, and in 1890, when the university's theology department became Payne Theological Seminary, he was named chair of historical and pastoral theology. He continued to serve the AME Church as chair and secretary of the Northern Ohio Conference, delegate to the General Conference in Philadelphia, and editor of the church publication *Lesson Leaf.*

George Prioleau's career took a new turn on April 25, 1895, when President Grover Cleveland

Chaplain George W. Prioleau of the 9th Cavalry spoke out in the press about unfair treatment of his regiment. *(Library of Congress)*

commissioned him a chaplain in the U.S. Army. He was assigned to the 9th Cavalry at Fort Robinson, Nebraska. By the 1890s, the army had defeated the Native Americans of the West and forced them onto reservations, and the cavalrymen served primarily as peacekeepers.

A devout man, Prioleau found a calling among the African-American soldiers, who were openly engaging in behavior he viewed as immoral: drinking, gambling, and visiting houses of prostitution. "Who is to help by precept and example,—to lift the almost wrecked life above its surrounding, and point the wandering eye back to Calvary?" he asked, and answered, "Who, but the Chaplain." During his three years at Fort Robinson, Prioleau preached on the post and in a Congregational church in the neighboring town of Crawford. He labored to raise morale, and he presided over the post school. In 1898, he conducted a memorial service for the American military personnel killed when the USS *Maine* exploded in Havana Harbor on February 15 of that year. More than 400 people listened as Chaplain Prioleau eulogized the dead and Anna Prioleau sang.

With the start of the Spanish-American War in April 1898, the government ordered its four African-American regiments—the 9th and 10th Cavalry and the 24th and 25th Infantry—to Cuba. Prioleau accompanied the 9th Cavalry to Tampa, Florida, the embarkation point. Although he had grown up in the South, after an absence of 18 years he was alarmed at the racial hatred and segregation that the black soldiers encountered on their southern journey. On May 13, 1898, he wrote in a letter to the *Cleveland Gazette,*

'Talk about fighting and freeing poor Cuba of Spain's brutality; of Cuba's murdered thousands, and starving reconcentradoes. Is America any better than Spain? . . . Has she not subjects in her own borders whose children are half-fed and half-clothed, because their father's skin is black. . . . Yet the Negro is loyal to his country's flag. . . . [H]e sings

'My Country 'Tis of Thee, Sweet Land of Liberty,' and though the word 'liberty' chokes him, he swallows it and finishes the stanza 'of Thee I sing.'

Prioleau contracted malaria in Tampa and stayed behind when the 9th Cavalry shipped out for Cuba. Upon recovering he went on a recruiting mission for his regiment and rejoined the men in August 1898, after the war, when the Buffalo Soldiers reached Montauk Point, New York. In October, he accompanied the 9th Cavalry to Fort Grant, Arizona Territory, with a stop in Kansas City. The valor of the Buffalo Soldiers in Cuba had matched that of the white regiments, yet as Prioleau observed, the black fighting men returned to a nation reluctant to thank them for their sacrifices. Recalling their treatment in Kansas City, he wrote, "[T]hese black boys, heroes of our country, were not allowed to stand at the counters of restaurants and eat a sandwich and drink a cup of coffee, while the white soldiers were welcomed and invited to sit down at the tables and eat free of cost."

Anna Scovell Prioleau died in 1903. In 1905, George Prioleau married Ethel G. Stafford of Kansas, with whom he would have four children. He served two tours of duty with the 9th Cavalry in the Philippines before being transferred in 1915 to the 10th Cavalry, which was posted on the Mexican border. In 1917, Prioleau was promoted to major and transferred to the 25th Infantry at Schofield Barracks near Honolulu. He worked energetically in behalf of all African Americans and raised $3,200 from the men of the 25th to support the NAACP and to aid victims of a race riot that occurred in East St. Louis, Illinois, on July 2, 1917. On that date, a white mob, angered by the employment of black workers in a factory with government contracts, had destroyed more than 200 homes in the black community of East St. Louis. Thirty-nine blacks and nine whites had died in the accompanying violence, and hundreds had been injured.

Major George Prioleau retired from the army in 1920. He settled in Los Angeles, where he helped to found the Bethel AME Church. He died in 1927.

Further Reading

Gatewood, Willard B., Jr. *"Smoked Yankees" and the Struggle for Empire: Letters from Negro Soldiers, 1898–1902.* Urbana: University of Illinois Press, 1971, pp. 26–29, 74–76, 82–84, 300–303, 306–309.

Glasrud, Bruce A., and Michael N. Searles, eds. *Buffalo Soldiers in the West: A Black Soldiers Anthology.* College Station: Texas A & M University Press, 2007, pp. 72–75.

Lamm, Alan K. *Five Black Soldiers in Army Blue.* Lewiston, N.Y.: Edwin Mellen Press, 1998.

Schubert, Frank N. *Buffalo Soldiers, Braves, and the Brass: The Story of Fort Robinson, Nebraska.* Shippensburg, Pa.: White Mane Publishing Co., 1993.

Steward, T. G., ed. *Active Service: or, Gospel Work Among U.S. Soldiers.* New York: United States Army Aid Association, 1898.

R

Reason, Joseph Paul

(1941–) *first African American to earn four-star rank in the navy, first African-American commander in chief of the U.S. Atlantic Fleet*

J. Paul Reason, the first African-American four-star admiral, has called himself a "navigator." He has said that he followed in the wake of every African-American sailor who came before him, from those blacks who enlisted in the Union navy in 1861 to SAMUEL L. GRAVELY, JR., the first African-American rear admiral.

Joseph Paul Reason was born in Washington, D.C., on March 22, 1941. As a child, he loved "anything to do with the water," he said. On family outings to the Chesapeake Bay, he swam, fished, caught crabs, or sat and simply looked out to sea. He also grew up in an academically oriented home and from early life valued education. "With it, many things are possible," he said as an adult. "Without it, life gets much harder very quickly." Reason's father, Joseph Reason, was a professor of Romance languages and director of libraries in the course of a long career at Howard University. His mother, Bernice Reason, taught science in the District of Columbia public schools.

Joseph Paul Reason, called Paul, thought about a naval career while in high school, but after graduation he entered Howard University. During his third year at Howard, Representative Charles Diggs of Michigan appointed him to the United States Naval Academy at Annapolis, Maryland. Reason was accepted and chose to go to the academy although he was required to enter in June 1961 as a plebe, or freshman.

While a midshipman, Reason hoped to continue his education in the navy and sought admission to the Naval Nuclear Propulsion Program, which would give him expertise in the technology used in the growing number of nuclear-powered vessels in the navy's combatant fleet. As an applicant he was required to undergo an interview with Admiral Hyman Rickover, the engineer who had supervised construction of the *Nautilus*, the first nuclear-powered submarine. Rickover insisted that Reason improve his grades as a condition of acceptance; in fact, he demanded a promise from the cadet that he would improve his class standing by 20 before graduation. Reason refused to make that promise, explaining that he had no control over the study habits and grades of the students ahead of him. He returned to the academy certain that he had forfeited his chance to enter the elite training program and was surprised the next day to learn that he had been accepted.

Reason graduated from the naval academy on June 9, 1965, with a bachelor's degree in naval science and was commissioned an ensign in the U.S. Navy. Three days later, he married Dianne Lillian

Fowler of Washington, an elementary school teacher who was the daughter of an army officer. They would have two children, Rebecca and Joseph Paul, Jr.

Reason's first shipboard assignment after completing his training was as operations officer aboard the USS *J. D. Blackwood*, a destroyer escort. In 1968, he was promoted to lieutenant and stationed on the USS *Truxtun*, a guided missile cruiser and the nation's fourth nuclear-powered surface ship. The crew of the *Truxtun* supported Task Force 77, the main striking arm of the U.S. Seventh Fleet, in the Gulf of Tonkin, off South Vietnam, by maintaining continuous positive identification of all aircraft in nearly 50,000 square miles of ocean area and the air space above it.

In 1970, Reason earned a master's degree in computer systems management from the Naval Postgraduate School in Monterey, California, and in 1971, he took on the duties of electrical officer aboard the nuclear-powered aircraft carrier USS *Enterprise*. He was with the *Enterprise* when it was deployed twice to Southeast Asia and once to the Indian Ocean. He was promoted to lieutenant commander on July 1, 1973.

After a brief return to the *Truxton* and a stint as an assignment officer with the Bureau of Naval Personnel, Reason became naval aide to the White House under President Gerald Ford in 1976 and President Jimmy Carter in 1977. On September 1, 1978, he attained the rank of commander.

Reason left Washington in 1979 to command the USS *Coontz,* a guided missile frigate that was part of NATO's Standing Naval Forces Atlantic, the world's first multinational naval squadron. He then proceeded to Norfolk, Virginia, to take command of the USS *Bainbridge*, a destroyer. In Norfolk he met Admiral Jeremy Michael "Mike" Boorda, who was later to become chief of naval operations. The two men formed a friendship during a cruise to West Africa, the Mediterranean, and the Black Sea, and Reason learned a great deal professionally from Boorda. "He was the most

capable naval officer I ever went to sea with," Reason said.

On October 1, 1983, Reason was promoted to captain. In 1986, he was named commander of Naval Base Seattle and oversaw all naval activities in waters off Oregon, Washington, and Alaska. Following his elevation to flag rank on October 1, 1987, Reason took on assignments of increasing responsibility. In 1988, he assumed command of Cruiser-Destroyer Group One, which consisted of an aircraft carrier, air wing, and small contingent of ships providing escort for cruisers and destroyers.

Reason took pride in his career and in his grown children. His daughter, Rebecca, had become an accountant, and his son, Joseph, had graduated from the U.S. Naval Academy in 1990 and embarked on a naval career. Admiral Reason and his son are thought to be the first African-American father and son to graduate from the Naval Academy.

In 1994, after earning his third star, J. Paul Reason served as deputy chief of operations for the U.S. Navy. Then in December 1996, he became the first African-American four-star admiral in the navy and was given command of the U.S. Atlantic Fleet, which remains prepared to send combat-ready forces to regions of conflict in support of the United States and NATO. Admiral Reason's area of responsibility included the Atlantic Ocean from the North Pole to 28 degrees north latitude as well as the Norwegian, Greenland, and Bering Seas.

Admiral J. Paul Reason retired from the navy in November 1999 and worked in private industry. In October 2007, he became chairman of the board of directors of the U.S. Navy Memorial, and in 2008 he accepted a four-year appointment to the secretary of the navy's Advisory Subcommittee on Naval History.

Reason's military awards include the Distinguished Service Medal, Legion of Merit, Navy Commendation Medal, Republic of Vietnam Honor Medal, Navy Unit Commendation, Navy Meritorious

Unit Commendation, Navy "E," National Defense Service Medal, Armed Forces Expeditionary Medal, Republic of Vietnam Meritorious Unit Citation, and Republic of Vietnam Campaign Medal. He received the Naval Almirante Luis Brion Medal from the government of Venezuela.

Further Reading

Hawkins, Walter L. *Black American Military Leaders.* Jefferson, N.C.: McFarland and Co., 2007, pp. 384–385.

"Our Leadership." United States Navy Memorial. Available online. URL: http://www.navymemorial. org/About/OurLeadership/tabid/71/Default.aspx. Downloaded on October 25, 2008.

Phelps, Shirelle, ed. *Contemporary Black Biography.* Vol. 19. Detroit: Gale Research, 1999, pp. 185–87.

Williams, Rudi. "Reason Is Navy's First Black Four-Star Admiral." DefenseLINK News. Available online. URL: http://www.defenselink.mil/news/ Feb1998/n02191998_9802198.html. Downloaded on September 14, 2008.

Rivers, Prince

(1824 or 1825–unknown) *Civil War veteran, South Carolina legislator and trial judge*

After serving as a sergeant in the first African-American regiment formed in the Union army following passage of the Militia Act of 1862, the 1st South Carolina Volunteers, Prince Rivers was active for 10 years in Reconstruction politics.

Prince Rivers was born into slavery in Beaufort, South Carolina, in 1824 or 1825, and worked for his master as a coachman. Intelligent and literate, he perceived the Civil War to be "a new day," the crisis that would lead to the end of slavery.

In 1862, he stole his master's horse and managed to ride through the Confederate line to Edgefield, South Carolina, where he enlisted in the 1st South Carolina Volunteers, the first African-American regiment established in the Union army. In late 1862, the army sent Rivers north to recruit African-American soldiers, but he was attacked by a white mob in New York City. Returning to his regiment, he made himself generally useful by performing the duties of color sergeant, carrying the regimental flag into battle; and provost sergeant, policing the camp and having charge of all prisoners. His competence inspired his white commander, Colonel Thomas Wentworth Higginson, to write, "There is not a white officer in this regiment who has more administrative ability, or more absolute authority over the men; they do not love him, but his mere presence has controlling power over them. . . . [I]f his education reached a higher point, I see no reason why he should not command the Army of the Potomac."

Rivers's regiment was stationed on Folly Island, off the South Carolina coast, in June 1864, and remained in the region throughout the siege of Charleston. On November 30, 1864, the 1st South Carolina Volunteers took part in the Battle of Honey Hill, South Carolina, in which Confederate troops, firing from fortified entrenchments, surprised a larger Union force, inflicted many casualties, and caused the federal soldiers to withdraw. Beginning in February 1865, the regiment performed provost and guard duty in Charleston, Savannah, and other cities. It was disbanded and its soldiers mustered out of service on February 9, 1866, at Fort Wagner, South Carolina.

Prince Rivers was active in local and state politics during the Reconstruction era. In 1867, he served as registrar of Edgefield County, South Carolina; he also represented Edgefield in the Constitutional Convention of 1868.

Rivers was a trial judge during the brutal South Carolina gubernatorial campaign of 1876. Followers of the Democratic candidate, former slave owner Wade Hampton, formed a paramilitary organization called the Red Shirts to terrorize black and white Republican supporters, with the goal of ridding the state of Republicans and Reconstruction platforms. The worst violence occurred in the town of Hamburg, where six blacks and one white were killed. The rioting whites ransacked Rivers's home and forced him to flee.

Prince Rivers ended his working life as a coachman, doing the job he had performed while enslaved. The date of his death is unknown.

Further Reading

Foner, Eric. *Freedom's Lawmakers: A Directory of Black Officeholders During Reconstruction.* Baton Rouge: Louisiana State University Press, 1996, pp. 183–184.

Higginson, Thomas Wentworth. *Army Life in a Black Regiment.* East Lansing, Mich.: Michigan State University Press, 1960.

Holt, Thomas. *Black over White: Negro Political Leadership in South Carolina During Reconstruction.* Urbana: University of Illinois Press, 1977, pp. 47, 62, 78–80, 199.

Poole, W. Scott. *South Carolina's Civil War: A Narrative History.* Macon, Ga.: Mercer University Press, 2005.

Rivers, Ruben

(1918–1944) *staff sergeant with the 761st Tank Battalion during World War II, posthumously awarded the Medal of Honor*

"Come Out Fighting" was the motto of the 761st Tank Battalion, the only unit of African-American tankers to fight the Germans during World War II. One member of this intrepid battalion, Staff Sergeant Ruben Rivers, sacrificed his life to spare the rest of his company; more than 50 years later, he was awarded the Medal of Honor.

Ruben Rivers was born in Tecumseh, Oklahoma, on October 30, 1918, the third of 15 children born to a cotton farmer and his wife. After entering the army at Oklahoma City on January 15, 1942, he proceeded to Camp Hood, Texas, to train with the 761st Tank Battalion.

The battalion was rated superior by Lieutenant General Ben Lear, commander of the Second Army, yet it remained stationed in the United States while white tank units entered the war, because army leaders doubted that African Americans could handle the large armored vehicles. At last, on June 9, 1944, three days after D-day and the start of the Normandy invasion, the 761st was ordered overseas. Its six white officers, 30 black officers, and 676 black enlisted men landed on Omaha Beach in France on October 10, 1944.

The 761st "Black Panther" Battalion was attached to the 26th Infantry Division, XII Corps, and assigned to General George S. Patton's Third Army, which was pushing east across France toward Paris. Although privately Patton had expressed misgivings about employing the black tankers, he greeted them by saying, "I would never have asked for you if you weren't good. . . . Everyone has their eyes on you. Most of all, your race is looking forward to you. Don't let them down, and damn you, don't let me down."

On November 7, 1944, while leading an infantry column, Staff Sergeant Ruben Rivers's company, Company A, was stalled by a German roadblock. Braving enemy fire, Rivers climbed out of his tank, attached a cable to the obstacle, and pulled it from the road, enabling the column to proceed and earning the Silver Star for his valor.

On November 16, 1944, as the 761st was heading toward the French town of Guebling, Rivers's tank was at a railroad crossing when it hit a mine that blew apart its undercarriage and propelled it to the side of the road. Rivers emerged with a leg torn so severely that the bone was exposed. The wound was grave enough for Rivers to be evacuated for treatment and sent home, but he chose to stay and fight, refusing even a shot of morphine. "You need me," he said, and he took command of another tank and advanced with Company A. He received several evacuation orders over the next few days, as the army fought for control of Guebling, but he refused them all.

On November 19, while heading for the town of Bourgaltroff, the company was stopped by enemy fire. Spotting the German guns, Rivers radioed the company commander, Captain David

J. Williams, to report, "I see 'em. We'll fight 'em." Rivers fired on the German position, giving the rest of the company time to retreat, until his own tank was hit. Rivers was killed, and the other members of the tank's crew were wounded. Sergeant Ruben Rivers was buried in the American Battle Monument Cemetery in France.

Williams recommended Rivers for the Medal of Honor, but for more than 50 years, no African American who fought in World War II was to receive the nation's highest military award. In the 1990s, the Defense Department investigated whether any deserving African Americans had been overlooked and determined that a number of black military personnel had indeed performed actions making them worthy of consideration for the medal. As a result, on January 13, 1997, President Bill Clinton bestowed the Medal of Honor on seven African-American World War II veterans, including Ruben Rivers. Only one of those heroes, VERNON J. BAKER, was still alive. Clinton presented Rivers's medal to his family.

Further Reading

Hanna, Charles W. *African American Recipients of the Medal of Honor.* Jefferson, N.C.: McFarland and Co., 2002, pp. 131–132.

Moore, Christopher Paul. *Fighting for America: Black Soldiers—The Unsung Heroes of World War II.* New York: Ballantine Books, 2006, pp. 233–236.

Ruane, Michael E. "Half-Century Late, Seven Heroes Receive Highest Tribute: Black GIs of World War II Awarded Medal of Honor." *San Diego Union Tribune,* January 13, 1997, p. A-1.

Robinson, Hugh Granville

(1932–   ) *first African-American military aide to the president of the United States, first African-American general from the Army Corps of Engineers*

Hugh G. Robinson overcame significant racial barriers twice in the course of nearly 30 years in the army. In 1965, he was selected to be the first African-American military aide to a U.S. president. He later called this job "one of the most challenging and rewarding assignments of my military career." In 1978, he distinguished himself further by becoming the first African-American general in the Army Corps of Engineers.

Robinson was born in Washington, D.C., to Colonel James H. Robinson of the U.S. Army and his wife. After graduating from Washington's Dunbar High School, he enrolled in the U.S. Military Academy at West Point, New York. He earned his degree from West Point in June 1954, was commissioned a second lieutenant, and began his career with the Army Corps of Engineers. The corps serves the nation by managing water resources and developing and overseeing other civil works projects. Its engineers also design and construct military facilities and support design and construction projects undertaken by government agencies.

After completing the Engineer Officer Basic Course at Fort Belvoir, Virginia, Robinson went to Fort Benning, Georgia, to attend the Basic Airborne Course, which provides training in the use of parachutes for combat deployment, and the Jumpmaster Course, for officers supervising the jumping of paratroopers. He was a platoon leader and company commander in South Korea from April 1955 to July 1956 and was promoted to first lieutenant on December 4, 1955.

Robinson spent a year as a branch chief in the Corps of Engineers' St. Louis District before earning a master's degree in civil engineering from the Massachusetts Institute of Technology in 1957. He then completed the Engineer Advanced Course at Fort Belvoir.

In July 1960, Robinson began serving in Orleans, France, as chief of the Catalog and Authorization Division, Engineer Supply Control Agency. His promotion to captain occurred soon after his arrival, on August 11, 1960. While in France, Robinson played on an army championship basketball team. In 1963, he was transferred to Washington, D.C., to head the Combat Branch of the War Plans Division, Engineering Strategic Studies Group. On August 5, 1964, he was promoted to major.

Robinson was planning to attend the Army Command and General Staff College at Fort Leavenworth, Kansas, when he was asked by his superiors if he would be willing to accept an alternative assignment. Robinson replied that he preferred not to change his plans, and he remained firm in his commitment to furthering his training when the request was repeated. He changed his mind only after his father persuaded him that his repeated refusal might reflect poorly on his record. When he at last agreed to take on the new assignment, Robinson learned that he was to be a military aide to President Lyndon B. Johnson—and the first African American to fill such a role.

Major Robinson confessed to being surprised, honored, and humbled by the appointment. "To think that I had been chosen as the first Negro to become a military aide to a President of the United States, I was flabbergasted," he said. He would be one of four White House military aides; the three others represented the air force, marine corps, and navy.

In his new position, Robinson handled correspondence and documents concerning army affairs, supervised the military aspects of visits by foreign dignitaries, acted as an escort at White House social events, and made sure that the motor vehicles used by the president and his staff were maintained and ready. In addition to his regular duties, he accompanied Johnson to functions such as the funeral of politician and diplomat Adlai Stevenson in July 1965, and he planned the April 12, 1966, ceremony at which Johnson presented the Medal of Honor to the family of Pfc. MILTON L. OLIVE III. Robinson remained in his White House post until the end of Johnson's presidency, in January 1969, and found the experience to be invaluable. "I learned more in that tour [job] than

I could have ever learned in 50 years of college or university anywhere about the political process—how powerful people deal with powerful people," he said.

From the White House Robinson went to Vietnam. Having been promoted to lieutenant colonel, he served first as executive officer of the 45th Engineer Group and then as commander of the 39th Engineer Battalion (Combat). By 1970, he was back in Washington as chief of the Regional Capabilities Branch in the Office of the Deputy Chief of Staff for Operations, War Plans Divisions, in the Pentagon. In June 1972, he had the opportunity to train future army officers when he returned to West Point as executive officer, and then commanding officer, of the 3rd Regiment, U.S. Corps of Cadets.

Robinson was promoted to colonel on June 14, 1973; a year later, he was placed in command of the U.S. Army Engineer School Brigade at Fort Belvoir. He subsequently served as an army district engineer and as deputy director of civil works in the Office of the Chief of Engineers in Washington. On July 1, 1978, he was promoted to brigadier general, becoming the Army Corps of Engineers' first African-American general. In 1980, he was named division engineer for the U.S. Army Engineer Division Southwestern, headquartered in Dallas. He was promoted to major general on February 1, 1981, and retired from the army in 1983.

In retirement Robinson pursued a career in industry. In 1983, he joined the Southland Corporation as a vice president and supervised the construction of Southland's corporate office complex in Dallas. When Southland formed the subsidiary City Place Development Corporation, Robinson was named its president. In 1989, he became chairman and chief executive officer of the Tetra Group, a construction management and building services firm, and in 2003 he took on the same role with the Granville Construction and Development Company. He next was chief executive officer of Global Building Systems, Inc., a firm dedicated to building low- and moderate-income housing. Robinson also spent seven years as vice chairman, and then chairman, of the Federal Reserve Bank of Dallas.

Hugh G. Robinson's military decorations include the Distinguished Service Medal, Legion of Merit (with Oak Leaf Cluster), Bronze Star (with Oak Leaf Cluster), Meritorious Service Medal, Air Medal (with two Oak Leaf Clusters), Joint Service Commendation Medal, Army Commendation Medal (with Oak Leaf Cluster), Vietnamese Cross of Gallantry (gold star), Vietnamese Service Medal, and Vietnam Campaign Medal.

Further Reading

"The Corps of Engineers' First African American General Officer." U.S. Army Corps of Engineers. Available online. URL: http://www.hq.usace.army. mil/history/Vignettes/Vignette_80.htm. Downloaded on November 30, 2008.

Hawkins, Walter L. *Black American Military Leaders.* Jefferson, N.C.: McFarland and Co., 2007, pp. 395–396.

"Hugh G. Robinson." Forbes.com. Available online. URL: http://people.forbes.com/profile/hugh-g-robinson/15974. Downloaded on November 30, 2008.

"Military Aide to LBJ." *Ebony* 22, no. 1 (November 1966), pp. 96–97, 100–102, 104.

Robinson, Roscoe, Jr.

(1928–1993) *first African-American four-star general in the army*

On April 7, 2000, The United States Military Academy named one of its busiest lecture halls for Roscoe Robinson, Jr., class of 1951, who in 1982 became the first African-American four-star general in the army. According to Lieutenant General Daniel W. Christman, West Point superintendent, the dedication ensures that Robinson's "legacy will continue to inspire the next generation of Army leaders graduating from this academy he so cherished and entering the Army he so loved and faithfully served."

Roscoe Robinson, Jr., was born on October 28, 1928, in St. Louis, Missouri. He was educated in the St. Louis public schools and upon graduating from Charles Sumner High School was appointed to the U.S. Military Academy at West Point. He enrolled in the academy in July 1947 and graduated with a degree in military engineering in 1951.

Entering an army that had started to become integrated while he was a cadet, Second Lieutenant Robinson headed for Fort Benning, Georgia, to attend the Infantry Officers Course and the Basic Airborne Course. He then moved to Fort Campbell, Kentucky, to join the 11th Airborne Division as a platoon leader in the 3rd Battalion, 188th Airborne Infantry Regiment.

The Korean War was underway, and in October 1952 Robinson joined that conflict as a member of the 31st Infantry Regiment, 7th Division. He served the regiment as a platoon leader, rifle-company commander, and battalion S-2.

Upon returning to the United States in 1953, Robinson was again assigned to the 11th Airborne Division. In 1954, he became an instructor in the Airborne School at Fort Benning, and in 1957, he attended the Infantry Officers Advanced Course, also at Fort Benning. Two years later, Robinson, who was now a captain, completed a tour with the U.S. Mission to Liberia.

Robinson spent two years with the 82nd Airborne Division beginning in 1960, first as S-4 in the 2nd Battle Group, 504th Airborne Infantry Regiment, and then as commander of Company E in the same regiment. Always eager to further his education, he attended the Army Command and Staff College at Fort Leavenworth, Kansas, graduating in 1963. He also earned a master's degree in international affairs from the University of

Pittsburgh in 1964. During these years, Roscoe Robinson and his wife, the former Mildred E. Sims of Falls Church, Virginia, were raising two children, Carol and Bruce.

After three years with the Office of Personnel Operations, Department of Army Staff, Robinson was ordered to Vietnam to take part in the escalating conflict there. As a lieutenant colonel, he joined the staff of the 1st Air Cavalry Division (Airmobile) before becoming the first African American to command the 2nd Battalion, 7th Cavalry.

In 1969, Robinson completed a course of study at the National War College at Fort McNair in Washington, D.C. By 1972, he had been promoted to colonel and was in command of the 2nd Brigade, 82nd Airborne Division, at Fort Bragg, North Carolina. Steadily moving up in rank, Robinson was promoted to brigadier general in 1973. In 1975, he was placed in command of the U.S. Army Garrison, Okinawa; he subsequently was the first African American to command the 82nd Airborne Division. Later, he was commanding general of the U.S. Army's Japan/IX Corps.

In August 1982, Roscoe Robinson, Jr., became the army's first African-American four-star general. (He was the second African-American four-star general in U.S. history; the first was CHAPPIE JAMES of the Air Force.) Upon reaching four-star rank, he began his final army assignment, as the U.S. representative to NATO's Military Committee at NATO Headquarters in Brussels.

General Roscoe Robinson, Jr., retired from the army in October 1983, but like many retired military officers, he remained active professionally. He headed a panel that reevaluated the performance of African-American units in the Korean War—units that had been criticized at that time. He also served on the board of directors of the parent company of Northwest Airlines.

The Association of Graduates of the U.S. Military Academy honored Robinson with its Distinguished Graduate Award just months

before he died of leukemia at Walter Reed Army Hospital in Washington, D.C., on July 22, 1993. Robinson was buried at Arlington National Cemetery.

Robinson's military decorations include the Distinguished Service Medal, Silver Star with Oak Leaf Cluster, Legion of Merit with two Oak Leaf Clusters, Distinguished Flying Cross, and Bronze Star.

Further Reading

Hawkins, Walter L. *Black American Military Leaders.* Jefferson, N.C.: McFarland and Co., 2007, pp. 397–398.

"1993 Distinguished Graduate Award: Gen. Roscoe Robinson, Jr." West Point Association of Graduates. Available online. URL: http://www.westpointaog. org/NetCommunity/Page.aspx?pid=529. Downloaded on September 16, 2008.

"Roscoe Robinson, Jr." Arlington National Cemetery Website. Available online. URL: http://www. arlingtoncemetery.com/rrobinjr.htm. Downloaded on September 16, 2008.

"Roscoe Robinson Jr. Dies at 64; First Black to Be 4-Star General." *New York Times Biographical Service* 24, no. 7 (July 1993): p. 1,020.

Rogers, Charles Calvin

(1929–1990) *major general, highest-ranking African-American Medal of Honor winner*

In 1968, as a battalion commander in Vietnam, Charles C. Rogers risked his life helping his artillery unit defend itself from enemy attack, thus earning the Medal of Honor. With his promotion to major general in 1975, he became the highest-ranking African American to have received that honor.

Charles Calvin Rogers was born on September 6, 1929, in Claremont, West Virginia. His parents, Mr. and Mrs. Clyde Rogers, Jr., raised their children to love God and country. Charles earned a bachelor's degree in mathematics from West Virginia State College, a traditionally black school in Charleston, and entered the army in the town of Institute, West Virginia.

After completing the basic course at the U.S. Army Field Artillery School at Fort Sill, Oklahoma, he enrolled in the advanced course at the Army Artillery and Missile School. This program of study prepares officers to be battery commanders, fire support officers, and battalion fire direction officers. It qualified Rogers to serve as commanding officer of the 1st Battalion, 2nd Brigade, at Fort Lewis, Washington. In November 1967, the army sent Rogers to Vietnam.

On November 1, 1968, Lieutenant Colonel Rogers was commanding the 1st Battalion, 5th Artillery of the 1st Infantry Division, which was defending a forward fire-support base in the Fishhook region of South Vietnam, near the Cambodian border. Early in the morning, the position came under heavy artillery bombardment and attack by ground forces. As mortar shells and grenades fell around him, Rogers moved to the embattled position, encouraged his men, and directed their fire toward the enemy. Despite being wounded, he led a small counterattack. Rogers was wounded again, but he kept pushing forward and succeeded in killing several of the enemy and forcing the rest from their positions.

With a second enemy ground attack about to begin, Rogers refused medical treatment, strengthened his unit's defensive positions, redirected its fire, and led a second counterattack. Throughout the night, he moved from one soldier to another, rallying spirits and giving instruction. When the enemy launched a third assault at dawn, Rogers fought alongside his men, returning to action a howitzer that was standing inactive due to casualties. After being wounded a third time, he was injured too severely to lead another charge, but his orders and encouragement inspired his soldiers to defeat a larger force. For his valor, Rogers was awarded the Medal of Honor. President Richard M. Nixon presented the medal to him at the White House on May 14, 1970.

In January 1969, Rogers was named operations chief, J-3, U.S. Military Assistance Command in Vietnam. In August 1969, he was back in the United States to serve in the office of the deputy chief of staff for military operations, U.S. Army, in Washington, D.C. He and his wife, the former Margarete Schaefer, were raising two daughters, Jackie Linda and Barbara.

Rogers furthered his training and education as an army officer by attending the U.S. Army War College in Carlisle Barracks, Pennsylvania. He also earned a master's degree in vocational education from Shippensburg State College in Pennsylvania and, later, a master's degree in theology from the University of Munich.

In September 1971, Rogers held his first post in Europe, as assistant deputy commander of V Corps Artillery. He became deputy commander of that unit before being assigned, in January 1972, as commanding officer of the 42nd Field Artillery Group. His promotion to brigadier general came on July 1, 1973, and he was named commanding general of VII Corps in Europe.

Rogers attained the rank of major general in 1975, the year he returned to the United States to serve as deputy chief of staff at ROTC headquarters, Training and Doctrine Command, at Fort Monroe, Virginia. In 1978, he was back in Europe as deputy commanding general of V Corps. In 1980, he became commanding general of VII Corps Artillery, Europe.

Major General Charles C. Rogers retired in 1984; he was ordained a Baptist minister in Heidelberg in 1988, and spent his final years ministering to U.S. troops stationed in Germany. He died of prostate cancer on September 21, 1990, at his home in Munich; his cremated remains were buried at Arlington National Cemetery.

Further Reading

"Charles Calvin Rogers." African-American Involvement in the Vietnam War. Available online. URL: http://www.aavw.org/served/homepage_rogers.html. Downloaded on September 16, 2008.

"Charles Calvin Rogers." Arlington National Cemetery Website. Available online. URL: http://www.arlingtoncemetery.com/charlesc.htm. Downloaded on September 16, 2008.

Griffith, Stephanie. "Comrades Give Final Salute to Black Hero." *Washington Post,* October 17, 1990, p. D3.

Hanna, Charles W. *African American Recipients of the Medal of Honor.* Jefferson, N.C.: McFarland and Co., 2002, pp. 170–172.

Lang, George, Raymond L. Collins, and Gerard F. White, comps. *Medal of Honor Recipients, 1863–1994.* Vol. 2, *World War II to Somalia.* New York: Facts On File, 1995, p. 3,347.

Westheider, James E. *Brothers in Arms: The African American Experience in Vietnam.* Lanham: Md.: Rowman and Littlefield, 2008, pp. 128–129.

S

Salem, Peter

(ca. 1750–1816) *Revolutionary War soldier, hero of the Battle of Bunker Hill*

Peter Salem exchanged slavery for life in the colonial militia. An accomplished marksman, he is remembered for shooting Major John Pitcairn of the Royal Marines during the Battle of Bunker Hill on June 17, 1775.

Peter Salem was born into slavery in Framingham, Massachusetts, around 1750. He was named for Salem, Massachusetts, the birthplace of his first owner, Captain Jeremiah Belknap. He was later sold to Major Lawson Buckminster, a prominent resident of Framingham.

In 1775, Salem obtained his freedom upon enlisting in a 75-man company of Framingham Minutemen led by Captain Simon Edgell. This company was present at Concord, Massachusetts, on the morning of April 19, 1775, when 200 colonial militiamen stopped the advance of about 700 British soldiers who had been ordered to capture or destroy American supplies stored at Concord and forced the British to retreat.

On April 23, 1775, the colonial leaders of Massachusetts called for 13,500 men to volunteer for eight months of service in the war against Great Britain. The next day, Peter Salem enlisted as a private in the 5th Massachusetts Regiment.

He was the only African American in the company headed by Captain Thomas Drury and one of approximately 20 in all companies of the regiment.

On June 16, 1775, Americans commanded by Colonel William Prescott built fortifications on Breed's Hill and Bunker Hill on the Charlestown Neck, overlooking Boston Harbor, as a defense against British soldiers landing there. The next day, however, when British forces under General William Howe came ashore and attempted to take the peninsula, army commanders sent in the 5th Massachusetts Regiment to repel them.

With Salem's company fighting from a redoubt, or earthen enclosure, the Americans held their ground during the first and second British assaults. The third assault dislodged the Americans, and in anticipation of victory, Major Pitcairn mounted the redoubt and reportedly exclaimed, "The day is ours!" At that moment, Salem aimed his musket and fired, mortally wounding the hopeful British officer.

Salem reenlisted in January 1776, this time joining a company of the 5th Regiment led by his old commander, Captain Simon Edgell. He would remain with the 5th Regiment for the remainder of the war, serving under Captain Micajah Gleason, Captain Thomas Barnes, and Captain John Holden. He participated in the battles at Saratoga,

John Trumbull's painting of the Battle of Bunker Hill, which hangs in the rotunda of the U.S. Capitol, depicts an African American, perhaps intended to be Peter Salem. *(Library of Congress)*

New York, in the fall of 1777, and at Stony Point, on the Hudson River in New York, on July 15 and 16, 1779. The Battle of Stony Point was the last major military engagement of the Revolution to occur in the North. Americans led by Brigadier General Anthony Wayne wrested from British control a garrison at Stony Point, killing 20 British soldiers and taking the rest who were present as prisoners. Fifteen Americans died in the battle. The British returned to Stony Point and rebuilt their fort, but within months they abandoned it.

After the war, Peter Salem settled in Framingham and wove cane for a living. In 1783, he married Katie Benson. He moved to Leicester, Massachusetts, in 1793, and returned to Framingham in 1815. He died August 15, 1816.

Further Reading

Greene, Robert Ewell. *Black Defenders of America, 1775–1973.* Chicago: Johnson Publishing Co., 1974, p. 20.

"Peter Salem." Celebrate Boston. Available online. URL: http://www.celebrateboston.com/biographies/patriots/salempeter.htm. Downloaded on September 16, 2008.

Purcell, L. Edward. *Who Was Who in the American Revolution.* New York: Facts On File, 1993, p. 427.

Smith, Jessie Carney, ed. *Notable Black American Men Book II.* Detroit: Thomson Gale, 2007, pp. 581–582.

Toppin, Edgar A. *A Biographical Dictionary of Blacks in America Since 1528.* New York: David McKay Co., 1971, pp. 51–54.

Savary, Joseph

(unknown–unknown) *hero of the War of 1812*

A soldier by profession, Joseph Savary fought in turn for the French, the Americans, and the Mexicans. He earned his greatest glory as an officer in the army of the United States, serving under General Andrew Jackson in the War of 1812.

Joseph Savary was born in the French colony of Saint-Domingue in the West Indies. His parentage is unestablished, but if he was the brother of Battle-of-New-Orleans veteran Belton Savary, as historians think, then he was the son of Charles Savary and Charlotte Lajoie. As an officer in the army of Saint-Domingue, Joseph Savary aided the French government in its efforts to put down slave rebellions in the colony. The enslaved people of Saint-Domingue gained their freedom in 1793,

and in 1804 the colony was declared free of French rule and its name was changed to Haiti.

In 1809, the Savarys were among the whites and free blacks who fled Haiti to settle in New Orleans. Soon after arriving, Joseph Savary formed a close association with the pirate Jean Lafitte, who was preying on Spanish ships from a base at Barataria, south of the city.

During the War of 1812, General Andrew Jackson appealed to the Saint-Dominguans of New Orleans to join the fight against the British. Savary responded to the call and formed the 2nd Battalion of Free Men of Color, composed of volunteers from Saint-Domingue and Martinique. Savary's military rank cannot be determined; Jackson referred to him in dispatches as both Colonel Savary and Captain Savary. According to one historical account, Jackson promoted him to major on December 19,

Joseph Savary was among the African Americans who helped to win the Battle of New Orleans. *(The Historic New Orleans Collection)*

1814, the date on which the 2nd Battalion was mustered into service and supplied with muskets that had been deemed "unfit for use."

The 2nd Battalion played a key role in the Battle of New Orleans, which began on the night of December 23, 1814. Under the cover of darkness and fog, Jackson moved an army of 1,800 soldiers toward a Louisiana sugar plantation where British soldiers were encamped. Savary urged the men forward, calling out in his native French, "March on! March on, my friends, march on against the enemies of the country!" The surprise attack weakened the British force, and Jackson praised his black soldiers, telling them, "You surpass my hopes."

On January 8, 1815, the 2nd Battalion was one of two African-American units stationed behind the battle lines as the Americans fought British troops under the command of General Sir Edward Pakenham. Dissatisfied with being held in reserve, the African Americans conducted an "unauthorized sortie," breaking through to the front contrary to their orders and reaching the British. About the death of General Pakenham in this battle, Jackson wrote, "I have always believed he fell from the bullet of a free man of color. . . ." Belton Savary was fatally wounded as well, and on February 6, 1815, the Louisiana State Legislature awarded a pension to his father, Charles Savary.

With the end of the war in 1815, the black soldiers returned to New Orleans to encounter hostility and mistrust in the white population. In 1816, Savary left Louisiana and rejoined Lafitte, who had established a new base at the site of present-day Galveston, Texas. He later fought against Spain for Mexican independence.

Savary had returned to New Orleans by 1819, the year he petitioned the Louisiana House of Representatives for a pension. The legislators resolved that "the said Joseph Savary deserves a reward for the services by him rendered to this state under command of major general Jackson during the invasion of the British." *Paxton's New Orleans Directory of 1822* contains the last reference to Savary in the historical record, a listing for Colonel Joseph Savary at 158 Burgundy.

Further Reading

Buckley, Gail. *American Patriots*. New York: Random House, 2001, pp. 49–52.

Greene, Robert Ewell. *Black Defenders of America, 1775–1973*. Chicago: Johnson Publishing Co., 1974, pp. 37, 344.

Logan, Rayford W., and Michael R. Winston, eds. *Dictionary of American Negro Biography*. New York: W. W. Norton and Co., 1982, pp. 543–545.

Rothman, Adam. *Slave Country: American Expansion and the Origins of the Deep South*. Cambridge, Mass.: Harvard University Press, 2005, pp. 153–156.

Scott, Emmett Jay

(1873–1957) *special assistant for Negro affairs to the secretary of war*

Although best remembered for his work with Booker T. Washington at the Tuskegee Institute early in the 20th century, Emmett Jay Scott served as a special assistant in the War Department during World War I. In 1917, Professor Kelly Miller of Howard University called the choice of Scott for this post "the most significant appointment that has yet to come to the colored race."

Emmett Jay Scott was born in Houston on February 13, 1873, the son of Emma Kyle Scott and Horace Lacy Scott, who was a blacksmith and civil servant. He graduated from Houston's Colored High School in 1887, at age 14, and entered Wiley College, a small school for African Americans in Marshall, Texas, that was affiliated with the Methodist Church. To help cover the cost of his schooling, Scott performed odd jobs that included carrying mail, chopping wood, feeding the college's livestock, and doing clerical work. Despite his strong desire to learn, however, he left college in 1890, before graduating, so that others in his family could afford to be educated.

Hoping to be a journalist, Scott applied for a job with the *Houston Daily Post*. He was hired as a janitor and messenger because of his race, but his employers soon recognized that he had greater ability and promoted him to writing copy and classified ads. In time, he became a reporter. Meanwhile, inspired by the example of Norris Wright Cuney, an influential African-American political appointee, Scott worked on behalf of Republican politicians in his state.

On April 14, 1897, Scott married Eleanora J. Baker, with whom he would have five children. Also in 1897, he helped to found and publish an African-American weekly, the *Texas Freeman*, for which he regularly wrote columns extolling the philosophy of Booker T. Washington. Washington, who had established the Tuskegee Institute, a vocational school for African Americans in Alabama, advocated gradual advancement in society for the members of his race.

Scott persuaded Washington to address an audience of blacks and whites in Houston in June 1897. His able promotion of the event convinced Washington to offer him a job, and in September Scott moved with his wife to Tuskegee, to be Washington's private secretary. He would hold the position until Washington's death in 1915. Scott quickly became one of the well-known educator's closest advisers, prompting Washington to write this about him:

> Without his constant and painstaking care it would be impossible for me to perform even a very small part of the labor that I now do. Mr. Scott understands so thoroughly my motives, plans and ambitions that he puts himself into my own position as nearly as it is possible for one individual to put himself into the place of another. . . .

In 1901, Wiley College acknowledged Scott's achievements with an honorary master of arts degree. Scott gained increasing prominence in the decade that followed. Beginning in 1902, he was

Emmett Jay Scott was photographed on a New York pier in 1909, when he served on the Liberian Commission. *(Library of Congress)*

secretary of the National Negro Business League; in 1909, President William Howard Taft appointed him to the American Commission to Liberia, a group that advised the U.S. government on ways to aid the African nation diplomatically and economically. Scott served as secretary of the International Conference on the Negro, which was held at the Tuskegee Institute in April 1912; also in 1912, he was appointed secretary of the institute. In 1916, Scott published *Booker T. Washington: Builder of a Civilization*, a biography cowritten with Lyman Beecher Stowe.

On October 15, 1917, upon the recommendation of Robert R. Moton, Washington's successor at Tuskegee, President Woodrow Wilson named Scott to be a special assistant to Secretary of War Newton D. Baker. In announcing the appointment, Baker said that Scott would act as a "confidential advisor in matters affecting the interests of the ten million Negroes of the United States and the part they are to play in connection with the present war." As a special assistant, Scott served as a liaison between the African-American community and the government and worked to improve morale among African-American troops. He also sought to equalize the treatment of blacks and whites under existing Selective Service regulations. Especially in the South, some draft boards more readily exempted whites than blacks. In addition, Scott investigated numerous racial incidents in the armed forces. His experiences in wartime Washington aided him in writing *Scott's Official History of the American Negro in the World War*, which was published in 1919.

In 1918, Scott received honorary doctorates of law from Wiley College and Wilberforce University in Ohio. From 1919 until 1934, he was secretary-treasurer of Howard University in Washington, D.C. In 1920, he published his third and final book, *Negro Migration During the War*, concerning the movement of African Americans from the rural South to the industrial North, and in 1922 he again became active in Republican politics.

During World War II, Scott was in charge of personnel for the Sun Shipbuilding Company of Chester, Pennsylvania, a firm with government contracts that employed African Americans in one of its shipyards. He retired to the nation's capital after the war and died in Freedman's Hospital in Washington on December 11, 1957, after a long illness.

Further Reading

Logan, Rayford W., and Michael R. Winston, eds. *Dictionary of American Negro Biography*. New York: W. W. Norton and Co., 1982, pp. 549–551.

Palmer, Colin A., ed. *Encyclopedia of African-American Culture and History*. Vol. 5: Q–Z. Detroit, Mich.: Thomson Gale, 2006, p. 2,021.

Scott, Emmett Jay. "The Handbook of Texas Online." Available online. URL: http://tshaonline.org/handbook/online/articles/SS/fsc42.html. Downloaded on September 16, 2008.

Smith, Jessie Carney, ed. *Notable Black American Men*. Detroit: Gale Research, 1999, pp. 1,051–1,054.

Simmons, Bettye Hill

(1950–) *brigadier general, chief of the Army Nurse Corps*

During nearly 30 years in uniform, army nurse Bettye H. Simmons rose through the ranks from staff nurse to chief of the Army Nurse Corps. She retired from active duty in 2000, a brigadier general.

Bettye Hill was born in San Antonio, Texas, on February 15, 1950. The nurses who cared for her chronically ill grandmother were early role models for young Bettye, and they influenced her choice of career. After graduating from Highlands High School, Bettye Hill attended Incarnate Word College in San Antonio. She received assistance with tuition and living expenses through the Army Student Nurse Program, and after earning a bachelor of science degree in nursing, she entered the Army Nurse Corps. She completed the Army Medical Department's Officer Basic Course and in June 1971 began her first assignment, as a clinical staff nurse at Brooke Army Medical Center at Fort Sam Houston, Texas.

In June 1973, Hill became an instructor of practical nursing at Brooke Army Medical Center, and in 1975 she received a master's degree from the University of Texas School of Nursing at San Antonio. Her education and training qualified her to be an Army Nurse Corps counselor with the U.S. Army Recruiting Command at Fort Sheridan, Illinois. In June 1977, she traveled to Seoul, South Korea, to be head nurse at the 121 Evac Hospital.

Through her military career, Bettye Hill met her husband, Army Reserve officer Charles W. Simmons. In 1978, she took on the duties of head nurse in the Medical Intensive Care Unit at Walter Reed Army Medical Center in Washington, D.C.

In 1981, Bettye Simmons completed the Army Medical Department's Officer Advanced Course and assumed the directorship of the 91C20 Course, an educational program offered at Fitzsimons Army Medical Center in Denver. Moving away from hands-on patient care and into army healthcare administration, she continued her military education over the next two years, attending both the Inspector General Course and the Command and General Staff College at Fort

Leavenworth, Kansas. In July 1983, she was named assistant inspector general at Headquarters, U.S. Army Health Services Command, Fort Sam Houston.

Simmons was a student at the Army War College at Carlisle Barracks, Pennsylvania, from 1989 until 1991; in October 1991, she became chief of nursing administration at U.S. Army Medical Department Activity (MEDDAC) at Fort Polk, Louisiana. In August 1992, she was promoted to chief of the Department of Nursing, U.S. Army MEDDAC, at Fort Polk.

On September 12, 1995, Colonel Bettye H. Simmons was serving as chief nurse at Headquarters, U.S. Army Medical Command, Fort Sam Houston, when Secretary of Defense William Perry announced her impending promotion to brigadier general. In January 1996, General Simmons became deputy commander of the U.S. Army Medical Department Center and School, the largest military medical college in the world, with approximately 30,000 students on- and off-site. She was also selected by the army surgeon general to be the 20th chief of the Army Nurse Corps, which had 4,000 active personnel. As the first person to fill both jobs simultaneously, Simmons had a significant impact on the education and professional performance of the army's nursing staff. She was selected in April 1997 as U.S. Army Forces Command (FORSCOM) surgeon and stationed at FORSCOM Headquarters, Fort McPherson, Georgia. She continued to serve as chief of the Army Nurse Corps.

Brigadier General Simmons attributes her success to Martin Luther King, Jr.'s dream and the accomplishments of the Civil Rights movement. Yet she commented in 1999 that "racism still exists in America and we still have a long way to go. No matter what legislation changes, the hearts of people must also change." Simmons retired from the Army Nurse Corps on January 31, 2000. Believing that "we are all responsible for the next generation," she became director of the Leadership Institute at Hampton University in Hampton, Virginia. The institute emphasizes leadership skills, service, and discipline as it trains undergraduates to contribute to society.

Simmons's military decorations include the Legion of Merit, Meritorious Service Medal with four Oak Leaf Clusters, Army Commendation Medal with two Oak Leaf Clusters, the Army Achievement Medal, and the Army Good Conduct Medal. She has received the Army Medical Department's highest award for professional excellence, the "A" proficiency designator, and she is a member of the Order of Military Medical Merit.

Further Reading

Hawkins, Walter L. *Black American Military Leaders.* Jefferson, N.C.: McFarland and Co., 2007, pp. 423–424.

Nemeh, Katherine H., ed. *American Men and Women of Science.* 23rd ed. Vol. 6: *Q-S.* Detroit, Mich.: Thomson Gale, 2007, p. 851.

Pocklington, Dorothy B., ed. *Heritage of Leadership: Army Nurse Corps Biographies.* Ellicott City, Md.: ALDOT Publishing, 2004, pp. 120–125.

Additional biographical information provided by the Army Nurse Corps.

Sissle, Noble Lee

(1889–1975) *drum major with the 369th Infantry Regiment Band, professional musician*

Noble Sissle built a reputation as a singer, songwriter, and bandleader. He is remembered as well for triggering a racial confrontation while training in the South for military service in World War I and for buoying spirits in war-torn France as a member of the 369th Infantry Regiment Band.

Noble Lee Sissle was born on July 10, 1889, in Indianapolis, Indiana. He was the son of George Andrew Sissle, a Methodist minister, and Martha Scott Sissle, a teacher and juvenile probation officer. Noble had a fine voice even as a child, and he sang as a boy soprano in church and school choirs.

After the family moved to Cleveland in 1906, he was a tenor soloist with the glee club at Central High School, where he was one of six African-American students. Sissle interrupted his education in 1908 to begin singing professionally, and it was not until he was 21, in 1911, that he finished high school.

The Reverend Sissle died in 1913, and Noble moved back to Indianapolis with his family. He dabbled in college, briefly attending De Pauw University in Greencastle, Indiana, and Butler University in Indianapolis, and worked meanwhile as a singer and dancer. In 1915, he withdrew from college to devote himself to music. He formed a songwriting partnership with pianist Eubie Blake, and he sang at social gatherings with bands, including one led by JAMES REESE EUROPE.

Europe persuaded Sissle to join the 15th New York National Guard, an African-American regiment that was activated in June 1916. Foreseeing U.S. entry into the World War, the regiment's white commander, Colonel William Hayward, hoped to build an exemplary unit that would showcase blacks' ability and gain them the opportunity to fight. Hayward had enlisted Europe to put together a regimental band, and Europe in turn tapped musicians of his acquaintance.

When the United States entered the war in April 1917, many national guard units were incorporated into the Regular Army. Because its members were African American, however, the 15th was excluded from the Rainbow Division, commanded by Colonel Douglas MacArthur. MacArthur's 42nd Division was intended to span the country like a rainbow and included regiments from New York, Alabama, Ohio, and Iowa and soldiers from every region of the nation. The 15th was at last recognized as part of the army on July 15, 1917, and sent to Camp Spartanburg, North Carolina, for training.

Spartanburg's white population was openly hostile toward the northern black soldiers, and although the regiment's officers cautioned the enlisted men to maintain peaceful relations with civilians, trouble erupted. It began on a Sunday morning when Europe asked Sissle to buy a newspaper at a nearby hotel. Sissle's failure to remove his hat upon entering the lobby earned him kicks and verbal abuse from an irate hotel manager. Sissle asked, "Do you realize you are abusing a United States soldier and that is a government hat you knocked to the floor?" "Damn you and the government, too," the man responded.

News of Sissle's mistreatment incited several soldiers of his regiment to march toward Spartanburg seeking revenge, but Colonel Hayward persuaded them to return to camp. Nevertheless, EMMETT J. SCOTT, special assistant to the secretary of war, was concerned enough about the potential for violence to travel to South Carolina and appeal to the men to do nothing that might discredit their regiment or their race. The army defused the situation by sending the 15th overseas.

Renamed the 369th Infantry Regiment, the African-American unit reached Brest, on the west coast of France, on January 1, 1918. The soldiers were eager to enter battle, but American military leaders, unwilling to mix black and white combat troops, put them to work unloading ships and building dams. The French felt no such reluctance, however, and trained the men of the 369th to fight in the trenches alongside the 161st French Infantry. The 369th therefore became the first U.S. regiment to fight as part of a foreign army.

While the fighting men compiled an impressive combat record, the regimental band embarked on a tour to raise people's morale. The band's drum major, Sergeant Noble Sissle, observed that "all through France the same thing happened." French civilians, French and American soldiers, and even German prisoners of war "dropped their work to listen and pat their feet to the stirring American tunes." On February 22—Washington's Birthday—the band performed in the Nantes Opera House, a majestic columned structure built in the 18th century. On that night, men and women in evening clothes swayed to African-

American rhythms, which they were hearing for the first time.

Upon returning to the United States after the war, the musicians toured their own country. Posters announcing their performances called Sissle "The Greatest Singer of His Race." The American tour ended abruptly on May 9, 1919, when a disturbed band member stabbed Europe to death.

Noble Sissle married Harriett Toye in 1919 or 1920 and enjoyed a long career in popular music. With Eubie Blake, he performed in vaudeville and created the popular musicals *Shuffle Along* (1921) and *Chocolate Dandies* (1924). In September 1925, Sissle and Blake toured London, Dublin, and Paris. Sissle returned to Europe in 1927 to perform with his own band and as a soloist. By 1933 he was back in the United States and with Blake produced *Shuffle Along of 1933*. Sissle continued to perform with his own band and between 1938 and 1942 frequently appeared at Billy Rose's Diamond Horseshoe, a New York City nightclub. During this period he married Ethel Harrison, with whom he had two children. (The date of his divorce from his first wife is unknown.)

During World War II, Sissle performed for U.S. troops stationed overseas and produced an updated version of *Shuffle Along* as part of a USO tour of Italy in 1945. At war's end he appeared again at the Diamond Horseshoe, and in 1950 he opened his own nightclub, Noble's. Noble Sissle retired to Tampa, Florida, in 1970, and died at home on December 19, 1975.

Further Reading

Buckley, Gail. *American Patriots.* New York: Random House, 2001, pp. 193, 197–198, 202–203, 220, 226.

Garraty, John A., and Mark C. Carnes, eds. *American National Biography.* Vol. 20. New York: Oxford University Press, 1999, pp. 50–52.

Kimball, Robert, and William Bolcom. *Reminiscing with Sissle and Blake.* New York: Viking Press, 1973.

"Noble Sissle, 1889–1975." *Library of Congress: Performing Arts Encyclopedia.* Available online. URL: http://lcweb2.loc.gov/diglib/ihas/loc.natlib. ihas.200038853/default.html. Downloaded on September 16, 2008.

Slide, Anthony. *The Encyclopedia of Vaudeville.* Westport, Conn.: Greenwood Press, 1994.

Smalls, Robert
(1839–1915) *Civil War hero, first African-American ship's captain in the U.S. Navy*

In 1862, when enslaved steamboat pilot Robert Smalls delivered the *Planter*, a Confederate vessel, and its cargo of weaponry to the Union navy, *Harper's Weekly* called his deed "one of the most daring and heroic adventures since the [Civil War] commenced." Smalls piloted the *Planter* and other vessels in battle and became the first African American to serve as a ship's captain in the U.S. Navy.

Robert Smalls was born in Beaufort, South Carolina, on April 5, 1839. His mother, Lydia Smalls, was an enslaved woman belonging to a family named McKee. His father was a white man whose identity is uncertain. Robert was raised in the McKee home on Prince Street. When their master, John McKee, died in 1848, Robert and Lydia Smalls became the property of his son Henry. Henry McKee was an avid sportsman who put young Robert to work as his personal servant. Robert cared for McKee's horses, rowed his boat, and carried his bow and arrows on hunts. Robert was fortunate to have escaped slavery's greatest cruelties, but his mother made sure that he did not grow up ignorant of them. Lydia Smalls brought him to sites where slaves were being beaten or sold at auction.

In 1851, Henry McKee bought a plantation near Charleston and went there to live, bringing 12-year-old Robert Smalls. Smalls and McKee made an agreement whereby Smalls hired himself out to other employers in the city and paid McKee

$15 a month from his earnings. In this way Smalls became a lamplighter and a hotel worker. He also spent a year in the employ of John Simmons, a rigger, from whom he learned not only how to stitch heavy canvas to a ship's rigging but also how to sail a boat and navigate the inland waterways.

When he was 17, Smalls married Hannah Jones, an enslaved hotel maid 14 years his senior. Their first daughter, Elizabeth Lydia Smalls, was born on February 12, 1858. Robert Smalls hoped to purchase the freedom of his wife and daughter but managed to save only $700 of the $800 that their owner demanded. Then son, Robert Smalls, Jr., was born in 1861.

With the start of the Civil War in 1861, the Confederates pressed slaves into service to aid the military. Robert Smalls was forced to pilot the *Planter*, a 150-foot cotton steamer that had been converted into a dispatch boat. Smalls and the *Planter's* black hands gave the appearance of being loyal servants, but they secretly devised a plan for stealing the vessel and sailing to freedom.

The opportunity for escape came on the night of May 12, 1862, when the white captain, chief engineer, and mate went ashore on an unauthorized leave. Smalls and his seven African-American shipmates brought aboard several women and children, including his family. At approximately 3:00 A.M. on May 13, Smalls freed the *Planter* from its mooring and sailed into Charleston's harbor. It was a dangerous move, because discovery by the Confederate forces would have meant certain death. Wearing the captain's hat, Smalls gave the appropriate signals as he passed the five Confederate forts lining the harbor. As he steamed past Fort Sumter, he uttered a prayer that no lookout would question the vessel's activity at such an early hour. Smalls and his crew had agreed to blow up the *Planter* rather than be taken captive.

The *Planter's* movement attracted no notice, however, and once Smalls had navigated out of range of Confederate guns, he raised a bed sheet as a white flag and sailed toward the Union fleet that was blockading the harbor. He surrendered the *Planter* and its cargo of Confederate ammunition and guns to Lieutenant J. Frederick Nickels, commander of the USS *Onward*.

Robert Smalls and his gunboat, the *Planter,* were sketched for *Harper's Weekly* in 1862. *(Library of Congress)*

Smalls's act of bravery gained him national recognition. A report in the *New York Tribune* stated, "A slave has brought away under the very guns of the enemy, where no fleet of ours has yet dared to venture, a prize whose possession a commodore thinks worthy to be announced in a special dispatch." A free man, Smalls settled his family in the North; his second daughter, Sarah Voorhees Smalls, was born there on December 1, 1863.

The Union wanted to make use of Smalls's navigational skill, but navy pilots were required to be graduates of naval schools. Smalls therefore was commissioned a second lieutenant in the 33rd Regiment, U.S. Colored Troops, and detailed to the *Planter*. An army officer serving the navy, he piloted the *Planter* and other ships in the southern waters he knew so well. In December 1863, he was steering his craft along the Stono River near Folly Island, South Carolina, when it came under fire. The captain ordered his pilot to beach the boat and surrender, but Smalls refused to obey, knowing that, if captured, his African-American crew would be killed. While the captain panicked and hid in a coal bunker, Smalls took command of the situation and brought the *Planter* to safety. For this act of bravery, he was promoted to captain of the *Planter*.

On April 7, 1863, Robert Smalls piloted the *Keokuk*, an ironclad warship that was one of nine U.S. vessels attacking Charleston. Negotiating the seven miles of water from the harbor entrance to the city was difficult and dangerous. Hidden below the surface were obstructions and explosives, and guns mounted at the mouth of the harbor fired continuously, battering the Union fleet. Approximately 90 Confederate projectiles pierced the *Keokuk*'s wood and iron armor, forcing the ship to withdraw from the assault and anchor out of firing range. The *Keokuk* sank on the morning of April 8, soon after the crew was rescued.

Robert Smalls again gained national attention in 1864, when he and a companion were ordered to give their seats on a Philadelphia streetcar to white passengers, and Smalls exited the car rather than ride on an open platform. The local press reported the incident, and the resulting publicity and pressure from citizens caused the state legislature in 1867 to integrate public transportation in Pennsylvania.

The navy no longer needed Smalls's service when the Civil War ended, and he was discharged on June 11, 1865. On September 30, the *Planter* entered the service of the Freedmen's Bureau, the government agency that helped former slaves make the transition to life as free Americans. Smalls continued to pilot the *Planter* to bring food and supplies to African Americans left homeless by the war.

In 1866, Congress compensated Smalls and the crew that helped deliver the *Planter* with payments of $1,500 to Smalls and $500 to each of the others. The amount of compensation was blatantly unfair, because by law the men were entitled to half the vessel's appraised value, but the navy appraised the steamer at $15,000—far less than its true worth. In 1883, John F. Dezendorf, chair of the House Committee on Naval Affairs, introduced a bill in Congress that would have corrected the injustice, but it failed to become law.

Smalls meanwhile spent nine months learning to read and write under the guidance of a teacher named Miss Cooley. In 1867, convinced that education was necessary for the success of his race, he purchased a two-story building in the town of his birth for use as a school for African-American children. He also bought the Beaufort home of Henry McKee, where he had been raised. He was a director of the Enterprise Railroad, which was owned by African Americans, and he helped publish the *Beaufort Standard,* an African-American newspaper. In 1868, as a delegate to the South Carolina Constitutional Convention, he led an effort to make free, compulsory schooling available to all children in the state. His resolution was drafted into the state constitution with some modifications.

Robert Smalls entered politics in 1868, when he was elected to the state House of

Representatives as a Republican. He was elected to the state Senate in 1870 and served as an officer in the South Carolina militia until 1877. He was elected to the U.S. House of Representatives in 1875 for the first of five terms. In 1877, he was convicted of accepting a bribe in connection with the awarding of a government contract but was later pardoned.

Hannah Smalls died in 1883. After leaving Congress in 1887, Robert Smalls was a customs collector and worked on behalf of the Republican Party. In 1890, he married Annie Elizabeth Wiggs, a teacher, with whom he had a son, William Robert Smalls, in 1892. Annie Smalls died in 1895.

Also in 1895, Robert Smalls attended a convention for the revision of the South Carolina state constitution at which the delegates debated the fitness of African Americans to vote. Addressing the assembly, he said, "My race needs no special defense, for the past history of them in this country proves them to be the equal of any people anywhere. All they need is an equal chance in the battle of life." Smalls lived another 20 years; ill with malaria and diabetes, he died at home on February 23, 1915.

Further Reading

Billingsley, Andrew. *Yearning to Breathe Free: Robert Smalls and His Families.* Columbia: University of South Carolina Press, 2007.

McLaughlin, J. Michael, and Lee Davis Todman. *It Happened in South Carolina.* Guilford, Conn.: TwoDot, 2004, pp. 81–85.

Miller, Edward A. *Gullah Statesman: Robert Smalls from Slavery to Congress, 1839–1915.* Columbia: University of South Carolina Press, 1995.

Poole, W. Scott. *South Carolina's Civil War: A Narrative History.* Macon, Ga.: Mercer University Press, 2005.

"A Thumbnail Sketch of Robert Smalls." The Robert Smalls Foundation. Available online. URL: http://www.robertsmalls.org/about.htm. Downloaded on September 16, 2008.

Stance, Emanuel

(1843–1887) *sergeant of the 9th Cavalry, Medal of Honor winner*

While stationed with the 9th Cavalry in Texas, Sergeant Emanuel Stance took part in five armed conflicts with Native Americans, all of them counted as successes for the army. During one of those engagements, on May 19 and 20, 1870, Stance rescued two settler children and earned the Medal of Honor.

Emanuel Stance was born in Carroll Parish, Louisiana, in 1843. When he enlisted in the army, on October 2, 1866, he identified himself as a farmer. Stance was small in stature, just five feet, one and a half inches tall. His height might have kept him out of the army, but his ability to read and write counted in his favor. Within 10 months of his enlistment he had been promoted to sergeant.

Stance was assigned to Troop F of the 9th Cavalry, one of four African-American regiments formed after the Civil War for service on the western frontier whose men were known as Buffalo Soldiers. In 1870, he was stationed at Fort McKavett, on the San Saba River in Texas. The Kickapoo people of the region, resentful of settlers encroaching on their land, had been attacking soldiers and ranchers, killing and kidnapping, and stealing horses.

On May 19, Stance led a detachment of 10 privates toward a Native American village approximately 14 miles from the fort, where the Kickapoo were holding two children captured during a raid on a white settlement. En route the rescue party surprised a band of Indians leading a herd of stolen horses. Stance formed his men into a line, and upon his order they raised their weapons and charged. The Indians scattered, and the soldiers recaptured nine horses.

The Buffalo Soldiers camped for the night and in the morning set out again. Soon, however, they encountered a band of Kickapoo warriors and engaged them in combat. The soldiers fought the

Indians off, not just at this time but also later in the day when the same band caught up with them to retaliate. Stance also confiscated six more horses, and before the day was over, he led his men to the Kickapoo village and rescued the two boys held there.

Because of his actions on May 19 and 20, Sergeant Emanuel Stance became the first African American to win the Medal of Honor after the Civil War and the first African American to be so honored for service in the Indian Wars. Stance expressed his gratitude for the medal in a letter to the adjutant general, stating, "I will cherish the gift as a thing of priceless value and endeavor by my future conduct to merit the high honor conferred upon me."

Stance's subsequent conduct was less than exemplary, however. On January 3, 1873, he was convicted by general court-martial of biting off a piece of another soldier's lip while drunk. He was sentenced to six months' confinement without pay and reduced in rank to private.

By 1887, Stance had regained his sergeant's stripes and was serving at Fort Robinson, Nebraska. The fort was the scene of frequent discord between noncommissioned officers and enlisted men, with a number of incidents involving Stance, who had a reputation as a strict disciplinarian. On one occasion, Stance punished a private who was persistently careless about watering the horses by jailing the man for 10 days. Another private was fined five dollars and locked up for 10 days after clashing with Stance over orders.

When Emanuel Stance was found shot to death on the morning of December 25, 1887, beside the road linking Fort Robinson and the town of Crawford, authorities immediately suspected that the murderer was one of his own men. The sheriff of Dawes County arrested Private Milton Milds of Troop F, but the federal government had jurisdiction in the case and showed little interest in prosecuting. After spending a year in jail and in the post hospital, Milds received a dishonorable discharge and was never convicted of Stance's murder.

Further Reading

Glasrud, Bruce A., and Michael N. Searles, eds. *Buffalo Soldiers in the West: A Black Soldiers Anthology*. College Station: Texas A&M University, 2007, pp. 89, 91.

Lang, George, Raymond L. Collins, and Gerard F. White. *Medal of Honor Recipients, 1863–1994*. Vol. 1, *Civil War to 2nd Nicaraguan Campaign*. New York: Facts On File, 1995, p. 1,883.

Logan, Rayford W., and Michael R. Winston, eds. *Dictionary of American Negro Biography*. New York: W. W. Norton and Co., 1982, pp. 568–569.

Michno, Gregory, and Susan Michno. *A Fate Worse Than Death: Indian Captives in the West, 1830–1885*. Caldwell, Idaho: Caxton Press, 2007, p. 413.

Schubert, Frank. *Buffalo Soldiers, Braves, and the Brass: The Story of Fort Robinson, Nebraska*. Shippensburg, Pa.: White Mane Publishing Co., 1993.

Schubert, Irene, and Frank N. Schubert. *On the Trail of the Buffalo Soldier II: New and Revised Biographies of African Americans in the U.S. Army, 1866–1917*. Lanham, Md.: Scarecrow Press, 2004, pp. 272–273.

Stowers, Freddie

(1896–1918) *sole African American to win the Medal of Honor for service in World War I*

Freddie Stowers sacrificed his life on a battlefield in France in 1918, displaying unusual courage to carry out an order. Nearly three-quarters of a century later, in 1991, President George H. W. Bush awarded him the Medal of Honor.

Freddie Stowers was born in Sandy Springs, South Carolina, in 1896. During World War I, he entered the army in Anderson County, South Carolina, and was assigned to Company C of the 371st Regiment, an African-American unit.

On September 28, 1918, Corporal Freddie Stowers was in the Champagne-Marne Sector of northeastern France with orders to lead an assault on Hill 188, a strategic position held by the

Germans. Protecting the hill were enemy gunners in trenches who pointed their machine guns at the Americans. As the attack began, however, the Germans left their trenches and climbed onto the surrounding parapets, holding up their weapons. Observing this apparent gesture of surrender, the Americans ceased firing, came out into the open, and fell into a trap. As they moved to within 100 meters of the trench line, the Germans leaped back into their dugouts and commenced shooting.

Enemy machine-gun and mortar fire was creating heavy casualties as Corporal Stowers took the lead. Ignoring the danger to himself, Stowers crawled forward, guiding his squad toward a trench sheltering the machine gunners responsible for many of the casualties. Fierce fighting broke out when the Americans reached the site, but the African-American soldiers destroyed the trench and killed all the soldiers within. Stowers then urged his men to move toward a second line of trenches. He was seriously wounded but called out words of encouragement until he died.

The capture of Hill 188 enabled the Allies to seize key territory from the Germans, take prisoners, and confiscate weapons and supplies. For their heroism, 10 African-American officers and 12 enlisted men of the 371st Infantry received the Distinguished Service Cross. In addition, the French Croix de Guerre went to 34 of the regiment's officers and 89 of its enlisted personnel.

Freddie Stowers's contribution went unacknowledged until 1988, when the army launched an investigation to determine why no African Americans who served in World War I had received the Medal of Honor. The army researchers discovered that Stowers's commanding officer had recommended him for the award but that the recommendation had never been processed. Congress waived the statute of limitation on the medal, and on April 24, 1991, President George Bush presented a posthumous Medal of Honor to Corporal Freddie Stowers. The citation read in part: "Cpl. Stowers' conspicuous gallantry, extraor-

dinary heroism, and supreme devotion to his men were well above and beyond the call of duty, follow the finest traditions of military service, and reflect the utmost credit on him and the United States Army." Stowers's two surviving sisters attended the White House ceremony to accept the award.

Further Reading

"Black Hero of World War I Is Posthumously Awarded Medal of Honor 72 Yrs. Late." *Jet* 80, no. 4 (May 13, 1991), p. 9.

"Freddie Stowers." Arlington National Cemetery Website. Available online. URL: http://www.arlingtoncemetery.com/fstowers.htm. Downloaded on September 18, 2008.

Lang, George, Raymond L. Collins, and Gerard F. White. *Medal of Honor Recipients, 1863–1994.* Vol. 1, *Civil War to 2nd Nicaraguan Campaign.* New York: Facts On File, 1995, p. 428.

Lengel, Edward G. *To Conquer Hell: The Meuse-Argonne, 1918.* New York: Henry Holt and Co., 2008, p. 194.

Sweeney, Robert Augustus

(1853–1890) *the only African-American two-time Medal of Honor winner*

Armed forces personnel can display bravery above and beyond the call of duty in times of peace as well as during war. Robert Sweeney served in the peacetime navy, from 1881 to 1884, yet twice he risked his life to rescue a fellow sailor. He became one of 19 people to receive two awards of the Medal of Honor and the only African American to be so honored.

Robert Sweeney was born on the island of Montserrat in the West Indies on February 20, 1853. He immigrated to the United States and in 1881 entered the U.S. Navy in New Jersey as an ordinary seaman. He was assigned to the USS *Kearsarge*, a vessel built in 1861 and powered by steam and sail.

The *Kearsarge* is remembered most for defeating the Confederate raider *Alabama* off the coast of France in 1864. When Sweeney came aboard, the *Kearsarge* was performing peacetime duty, patrolling the Atlantic coastline from Newfoundland south to Panama. Its mission took it through Hampton Roads, a channel in southeastern Virginia that carries the waters of the James, Nansemond, and Elizabeth Rivers into Chesapeake Bay. Hampton Roads was the site of the battle between the *Monitor* and the *Merrimack,* the famous ironclads of the Union and Confederacy, on March 9, 1862.

When the *Kearsarge* entered Hampton Roads on October 28, 1881, the current was running swiftly due to a brewing storm. Suddenly, a crewman fell overboard. As he struggled to keep his head above water, he shouted for help, calling out that he could not swim. Sweeney, standing 5 feet, 10 inches tall, had developed into a strong swimmer growing up on the shores of the Caribbean, but even he had trouble staying afloat in such a rough tide. He went under more than once before he reached the sailor in distress, and then he stayed with the man for several minutes until the crew of the *Kearsarge* located and rescued them. For risking his life to save a fellow sailor, Robert Sweeney was awarded the Medal of Honor.

On September 6, 1883, Sweeney was transferred to the USS *Yantic,* a steam frigate that had spent the summer in the waters of Greenland searching unsuccessfully for a missing exploratory team led by Lieutenant Adolphus Greely of the U.S. Army. After returning from the Arctic, it was cruising along the eastern seaboard. On December 20, 1883, the *Yantic* was approaching the New York Navy Yard (now the New York Naval Shipyard), on the Brooklyn side of the East River, in dense fog. As the *Yantic* sailed close to the USS *Jamestown,* despite reduced visibility, Sweeney saw a man fall from the deck of the other ship. Sweeney plunged into the frigid water, and as his head emerged he looked around and saw nothing. The fog obscured the drowning man, the two ships, and everything else. Sound travels well in fog, though, so Sweeney located the man by following his cries for help. Knowing that he and the other sailor would never be spotted by shipboard rescuers, Sweeney again relied on his ears, swimming toward the foghorn sounding on one of the vessels. At last he and the other man reached the side of the ship, and they shouted for ropes to be lowered for them. For this second selfless act, Sweeney received another Medal of Honor.

Sweeney completed his period of enlistment and was discharged from the navy at the end of August 1884. The events of his civilian life are obscure, but he is known to have died on December 19, 1890, and to have been buried in Calvary Cemetery in Woodbury, New York.

Further Reading

America's Medal of Honor Recipients: Complete Official Citations. Golden Valley, Minn.: Highland Publishers, 1981, p. 631.

Lang, George, Raymond L. Collins, and Gerard F. White. *Medal of Honor Recipients: 1863–1994.* Vol. 1, *Civil War to 2nd Nicaraguan Campaign.* New York: Facts On File, 1995, p. 330.

Tassin, Ray. *Double Winners of the Medal of Honor.* Canton, Ohio: Daring Books, 1986, pp. 116–122.

T

Taylor, Susie Baker King
(1848–1912) *Civil War nurse*

During the Civil War, Susie King Taylor served the army as a nurse, laundress, cook, and teacher. She was not the only African-American woman to donate her time and energy to the Union cause, but she was the only one to write about her life and wartime experiences.

Susie Baker was born on August 5, 1848, on a coastal island near Savannah, Georgia. She was the first of nine children (six surviving) born to Hagar Ann and Raymond Baker. Hagar Ann Baker was a housekeeper owned by a family named Grest; whether Raymond Baker was free or enslaved is unknown.

When Susie was seven, she and two siblings went to live in Savannah with their grandmother, Dolly Reed, who was hired out there as a servant. Reed enjoyed unusual freedom for an enslaved person. She often attended meetings or took part in political discussions with other African Americans, and in violation of the law she arranged for Susie and her brother to have lessons in reading and writing. Because any African American out past 9:00 P.M. in Savannah was required to carry a written pass, Susie used her skill with a pen to forge passes for her grandmother and others.

On April 1, 1862, nearly a year after the Civil War began, Reed was arrested for her political activities. Susie returned to her mother on the Grest farm. Days later, on April 11, the Yankees captured nearby Fort Pulaski, at the mouth of the Savannah River, and Susie, an uncle, and several other relatives sought refuge on Union-held St. Catherine's Island, Georgia. Two weeks later, they were among a group of African Americans transported to St. Simon's Island, where the Union army was distributing confiscated land to former slaves for cotton farming. There, 14-year-old Susie operated a school, giving lessons to approximately 40 children during the day and to a smaller number of adults at night.

The school closed in late 1862, when the army moved the African Americans to Camp Saxton in Beaufort, South Carolina, for their safety. Stationed at Camp Saxton was the first African-American regiment formed in the Union Army, the 1st South Carolina Volunteers, commanded by Colonel Thomas Wentworth Higginson, a white abolitionist from Massachusetts. Company E of the 1st South Carolina Volunteers recruited Susie Baker as a laundress, but she soon took on other duties as well, cooking for the soldiers and teaching them to read and write. She also learned to handle a musket.

In January 1863, the 1st South Carolina Volunteers conducted a successful raid along the St. Mary's River, which serves as a boundary between Georgia and Florida. In March, it was one of two regiments that captured and occupied Jacksonville, Florida. These and other encounters with the enemy resulted in many casualties, and the shorthanded military surgeons called on Baker to assist them. As the numbers of wounded and sick soldiers rose, nursing eclipsed her other duties. She gave generously of her time to all of the regiment's dying and convalescing soldiers, not just those of Company E, telling the men, "You are all doing the same duty, and I will do just the same for you."

Sometime in 1863, Baker married Sergeant Edward King of the 1st South Carolina Volunteers, who had escaped slavery in Georgia to join

Susie King Taylor served as an army nurse during the Civil War. *(Schomburg Center for Research in Black Culture, New York Public Library)*

the army. After the war, the Kings settled in Savannah, where Edward King worked as a longshoreman. Observing that there was no school for African Americans in the community, Susie Baker King opened one, charging 20 children and several adults $1 per month to attend.

Edward King died in an accident on the Savannah waterfront on September 16, 1866. A 20-year-old widow, Susie Baker King found it impossible to support herself and her infant son teaching school, so she applied for and received her husband's army pension. She deposited much of it in the Freedmen's Bank, an institution chartered by the federal government to encourage African Americans to save, but the bank's collapse in 1874 left her destitute once more. (Because she served the 1st South Carolina Volunteers without pay and was never officially recognized as an army nurse, Susie Baker King was not entitled to a pension of her own.)

King became a domestic servant and made her home in Boston, far from the cruel treatment that African Americans received in the South. She married Russell L. Taylor, a Union army veteran, in 1879, and continued to do patriotic work. In 1886, she founded a branch of the Women's Relief Corps, an organization created in 1883 to serve the nation's veterans. Corps members decorated graves, cared for disabled veterans, and aided soldiers' widows and orphans. Taylor was guard, secretary, and treasurer of the local corps, and in 1893 she was its president. In 1898, during the Spanish-American War, she packed supplies for wounded men in military hospitals.

Also in 1898, Taylor received word that her son, an actor, had fallen ill and died while performing in Louisiana. She traveled by train to Shreveport and again encountered the bitter racism of the South, even witnessing a lynching in Mississippi. She spoke out eloquently against racial hatred in her autobiography, *Reminiscences of My Life in Camp,* published in 1902. "In this 'land of the free,'" she wrote, we are burned, tortured, and denied a fair trial, murdered for any imaginary wrong conceived in the brain of the Negro-hating white man. . . . They say, "One flag, one nation, one country indivisible." Is this true? Can we say this truthfully, when one race is allowed to burn, hang, and inflict the most horrible torture weekly, monthly on another?

As its title implies, the book also described Taylor's experiences as a teenager with the 1st South Carolina Volunteers during the Civil War.

Nothing is known about Taylor's activities during the last decade of her life. She died alone in a rooming house on October 6, 1912.

Further Reading

Encyclopedia of World Biography. 2nd ed. Vol. 15. Detroit: Gale Research, 1998, pp. 127–128.

Hine, Darlene Clark, ed. *Black Women in America: An Historical Encyclopedia.* Brooklyn, N.Y.: Carlson Publishing, 1993, pp. 1,145–1,147.

Page, Yolanda Williams. *Encyclopedia of African American Women Writers.* Vol. 2. Westport, Conn.: Greenwood Press, 2007, pp. 550–551.

Smith, Jessie Carney. *Epic Lives: One Hundred Black Women Who Made a Difference.* Detroit: Visible Ink Press, 1993, pp. 501–507.

"Susie King Taylor (1848–1912)." The New Georgia Encyclopedia. Available online. URL: http://www.georgiaencyclopedia.org/nge/Article.jsp?id=h-1097. Downloaded on September 18, 2008.

"Susie King Taylor Assists the First South Carolina Volunteers, 1862–1864." History Matters. Available online. URL: http://historymatters.gmu.edu/d/6599/. Downloaded on September 18, 2008.

Taylor, Susie King. *Reminiscences of My Life in Camp.* Athens: University of Georgia Press, 2006.

Williams, Heather Andrea. Self-Taught: *African American Education in Slavery and Freedom.* Chapel Hill: University of North Carolina Press, 2005, pp. 19, 22, 49–50.

Theus, Lucius

(1922–2007) *third African-American general in the U.S. Air Force*

In a 36-year career, Lucius Theus used his administrative skills to increase efficiency in the air force and improve life for military and civilian personnel. The third African-American general in the air force, he was promoted to major general on May 1, 1975.

Lucius Theus was born in Madison County, Tennessee, on October 11, 1922, and raised in Robbins, Illinois. He graduated from Community High School in Blue Island, Illinois, and in December 1942 entered the Army Air Corps as a private. He completed basic training and served out World War II at Keesler Field (now Keesler Air Force Base) in Biloxi, Mississippi, where the Army Air Corps trained 142,000 aviation mechanics and 336,000 recruits. Theus carried out in turn the duties of administrative clerk, chief clerk, and first sergeant of pre-aviation cadet and basic training squadrons.

Theus elected to remain in the military at war's end. In January 1946, he graduated from Officer Candidate School second in his class and was commissioned a second lieutenant. He spent a year as squadron adjutant at Tuskegee Army Air Field before attending the Statistical Control Officers School at Lowry Air Force Base in Colorado. The training he received at Lowry qualified him to serve as base statistical control officer at Lockbourne Air Force Base, Ohio. In August 1949, the air force assigned him to Erding Air Depot, West Germany, as analysis and depot statistical control officer. Then, beginning in August 1952, Theus was chief of the Materiel Logistics Statistics Branch in the office of the deputy chief of staff, comptroller, at Air Force Headquarters in Washington, D.C. While stationed in the national capital region he earned a bachelor of science degree from the University of Maryland and a master's degree in business administration from George Washington University.

Subsequent air force assignments took Theus and his wife, the former Gladys Marie Davis of

Chicago, to bases overseas and across the United States. In October 1957, he took on the responsibilities first of statistical services staff officer and then of technical statistical adviser to the comptroller at Headquarters, Central Air Materiel Forces Europe, at Chateauroux Air Base in France. In January 1959, he was named chief of management services in the Eastern Air Logistics Office in Athens, Greece. In 1960, Theus attended the Armed Forces Staff College in Norfolk, Virginia. From there the air force sent him to Headquarters, Spokane Air Defense Sector, at Larson Air Force Base in Washington state. In December 1962, Theus was named base comptroller, or chief accounting officer, at Kingsley Field in Oregon.

After graduating with distinction from the Air War College at Maxwell Air Force Base in Alabama in 1966, Theus served in Vietnam as comptroller of Cam Ranh Air Base. In addition, for five months he was acting deputy base commander. Theus returned to Washington, D.C., in July 1967, when the air force was beginning to make use of computer technology, to be a data automation staff officer in the office of the comptroller of the air force. At the same time, he chaired the Inter-Service Task Force on Education in Race Relations for the office of the secretary of defense. The task force determined that racial tensions and conflicts were harming the military's mission and recommended education as a key method for solving racial problems in the armed forces. The recommendations of the task force resulted in an educational program in race relations for military personnel and civilian workers at all levels in the Department of Defense and the establishment in 1971 of the Defense Race Relations Institute, which educates personnel on the military's policy of equal opportunity, fair treatment, and zero tolerance for unlawful discrimination.

Theus continued his education in 1968 by attending the Department of Defense Computer Institute. In 1969, he was the first African American to graduate from the Advanced Management Program of the Harvard Graduate School of Business Administration. He held increasingly important administrative positions in the air force, beginning in June 1971, when he was named director of management analysis in the office of the comptroller of the air force. In June 1972, he became special assistant for social actions in the Directorate of Personnel Plans, Office of the Deputy Chief of Staff, Personnel, at Air Force Headquarters. On June 10, 1974, Theus took command of the Air Force Accounting and Finance Center in Denver and was responsible for air force financial and accounting activities throughout the world.

On May 1, 1975, Theus attained his highest rank in the air force, major general. He was the third African-American general in the air force and the first African-American air force support officer to be promoted to general. He retired from active duty on July 1, 1979, and settled in Bloomfield, Michigan. In retirement Theus joined the board of directors of the Wellness Group, a provider of employee-assistance programs. In 1985, he was elected to the board of trustees for Embry-Riddle Aeronautical University, a school that prepares students for careers in aviation and the aerospace industry on its campuses at Daytona Beach, Florida, and Prescott, Arizona. He gave of his time to other institutions of higher learning, including Madonna College in Livonia, Michigan, and Lane College in Jackson, Tennessee. He was active as well in charitable organizations, especially those benefiting youth.

General Theus received the Distinguished Service Medal, Legion of Merit, Bronze Star, and Air Force Commendation Medal with Oak Leaf Cluster. He was also the recipient of the Distinguished Federal Service Award of the Denver Federal Executive Board and the Harvard Business School Distinguished Alumni Achievement Award. On October 19, 1996, he was inducted into the Michigan Aviation Hall of Fame. He died on October 15, 2007.

Further Reading

"Black Armed Forces Brass." *Crisis* 80, no. 10 (December 1973): 341–346.

Hawkins, Walter L. *Black American Military Leaders.* Jefferson, N.C.: McFarland and Co., 2007, pp. 454–455.

"Major General Lucius Theus." Air Force Link. Available online. URL: http://www.af.mil/bios/bio.asp?bioID=7368. Downloaded on September 19, 2008.

Rossiter, Joe. "Maj. Gen. Lucius Theus: He Trained Tuskegee Airmen." Tuskegee Airmen. Available online. URL: http://www.tuskegeeairmen.org/uploads/Theus.pdf. Downloaded on September 19, 2008.

Thomas, Charles Leroy

(1920–1980) *officer with the 614th Tank Destroyer Battalion, Medal of Honor winner*

When Charles L. Thomas died in 1980, newspapers in the Detroit area, where he had spent most of his life, declined to print his obituary. His heroism in World War II was all but forgotten until 1997, when he was posthumously awarded the Medal of Honor.

Charles Leroy Thomas was born on April 17, 1920, in Birmingham, Alabama, but his family soon moved north to Detroit, where his father found work in an automotive plant. Charles was a studious boy whose interest in aircraft and electronics led him to attend Cass Technical High School. After graduating in 1938, he worked with his father at the Ford Motor Company's River Rouge Plant and studied mechanical engineering at Wayne State University.

On January 20, 1942, just weeks after the United States entered World War II, Charles Thomas was drafted into the army. He completed basic training at Camp Wolters, Texas (renamed Fort Wolters in 1963), and then trained to be an officer at Camp Carson, Colorado (renamed Fort Carson in 1954). On March 11, 1943, he was commissioned a second lieutenant and placed in command of Company C of the 614th Tank Destroyer Battalion, 103rd Infantry Division.

The African-American battalion remained in the United States, practicing maneuvers, until August 1944, when it was sent to France, where General George S. Patton was leading the Third Army toward the German border. By December, the 614th had reached Alsace-Lorraine, and on the morning of December 14, the army began its attack on Climbach, a town held by the enemy that was five miles from the German border. Because the only way reach the town was over an open road passing through a wooded valley, it was impossible for the Americans to enter Climbach without exposing themselves to enemy fire.

Despite the obvious danger, Thomas volunteered Company C to lead the assault. "I knew that if the job could be done these men could do it," he said, "because they could and would fight; they were proud and they were good. Training and discipline were the key and they had plenty of both." Thomas rode in front in an armored M20 Scout Car, hoping to draw the Germans' fire and identify their positions.

The German defense, when it began, was sudden and merciless. Shards of glass and shrapnel sliced Thomas's skin as German mortar and artillery fire disabled the M20 and smashed its windshield. Ignoring his pain, Thomas climbed onto the vehicle and began shooting at the German infantry with a .50-caliber machine gun. Bullets struck him in the arms, chest, abdomen, and legs, but he kept on firing. He then crawled under the car and from that protected spot positioned his men to defend themselves and directed the fire of their antitank guns. He said later that one thought was running through his mind: "Deploy the guns and start firing or we are dead." Thomas refused to be evacuated until he made sure his men were well positioned and he had briefed a junior lieutenant to take over.

The bravery displayed by First Lieutenant Thomas and his platoon enabled the army to achieve its objective by nightfall. Thomas's commanding officer, Colonel John Blackshear, called the actions of the 614th "the most magnificent display of mass heroism I have ever witnessed." Casualties, however, were high. More than half the soldiers of the 614th were wounded or killed. Blackshear recommended Thomas for the Distinguished Service Cross, and the award was announced in 1945, when Thomas was promoted to captain. Thomas also received the Purple Heart, European-African-Middle Eastern Medal, and World War II Victory Medal. The 614th became the first African-American battalion to win a distinguished unit citation, and, overall, its members received eight Silver Stars, 28 Bronze Stars, and 79 Purple Hearts.

The African-American press hailed Charles Thomas as a hero when he returned to Detroit in March 1945. Thomas was discharged from the army on August 10, 1947, with the rank of major, and although his right arm was permanently disabled, he put his combat experiences behind him and got on with his life. In July 1949, he married Bertha Thompson, a waitress, with whom he would have two children, Linda and Michael.

He worked as a missile technician at Selfridge Air Force Base (now Selfridge Air National Guard Base) in Mt. Clemens, Michigan, and continued to take courses in mechanical engineering at Wayne State University. He later became a computer programmer for the Internal Revenue Service. He died of cancer on February 15, 1980, and was buried in West Lawn Cemetery in Wayne, Michigan.

It was not until the 1990s, when the public and the Defense Department expressed concern that no African Americans who served in World War II had received the Medal of Honor, that his country gave Charles Thomas his due recognition. A team of historians commissioned by the Pentagon to study the matter concluded that seven African-American veterans deserved the nation's highest military award. The seven included VERNON J. BAKER; EDWARD ALLEN CARTER, JR.; RUBEN RIVERS; GEORGE WATSON; and Major Charles L. Thomas, the man who humbly insisted in 1945, "I was just trying to stay alive out there." President

Bill Clinton presented the medal to Thomas's niece, Sandra Johnson, on January 13, 1997.

Further Reading

"African American World War II Medal of Honor Recipients." U.S. Army Center of Military History. Available online. URL: http://www.history. army.mil/html/moh/mohb.html. Downloaded on September 19, 2008.

Cohen, Warren. "Recognizing Valor." *Michigan History* 81, no. 1 (January/February 1997): 52–54.

Hanna, Charles W. *African American Recipients of the Medal of Honor.* Jefferson, N.C.: McFarland and Co., 2002, pp. 132–135.

Moore, Christopher Paul. *Fighting for America: Black Soldiers—The Unsung Heroes of World War II.* New York: Ballantine Books, 2006, p. 238.

Motley, Mary Penick, comp. *The Invisible Soldier: The Experience of the Black Soldier, World War II.* Detroit: Wayne State University Press, 1987, pp. 167, 170, 172–175.

Thompson, William Henry
(1927–1950) *army private, first African American awarded the Medal of Honor in the 20th century*

On August 6, 1950, a young man who had grown up in poverty in New York City sacrificed his life to save the rest of his platoon and was awarded a posthumous Medal of Honor. Private William Thompson was the first African American in the 20th century and one of only two from the Korean War to be so honored.

William Henry Thompson was born to a single mother in Brooklyn, New York, on August 16, 1927. He spent some of his childhood in his grandmother's care, but when he entered the army in 1945, he gave as his address a shelter for homeless boys in the Bronx.

Thompson found a secure, stable way of life in the peacetime army. He completed a tour of duty in Adak, Alaska, and he reenlisted in 1948, the year President Harry S. Truman ordered an end to segregation in the armed forces. He was assigned to the 6th Infantry Division, which was stationed in South Korea, in the southern half of the U.S. zone of occupation. When the unit was deactivated on January 20, 1949, the army transferred Thompson to Company M of the 24th Infantry Regiment in Japan.

On June 25, 1950, the North Korean army invaded South Korea, starting the military conflict that would become known as the Korean War. Within days, Truman ordered U.S. armed forces into action to repel the invaders, and among the first American units to reach Korea were elements of the 24th Infantry, including Company M.

On the night of August 6, 1950, Thompson's platoon was settling in near Haman, South Korea, when suddenly it was attacked by a large enemy force. Outnumbered and unfamiliar with the mountainous terrain, the men nevertheless rapidly prepared to defend themselves. Private Thompson showed unusual courage, setting up his machine gun in the path of the oncoming North Korean and Chinese soldiers and spraying them with bullets. Thompson halted the enemy's approach temporarily and willingly exposed himself to enemy fire as he made it possible for the rest of the platoon to withdraw to a safer position.

As bullets and fragments of grenades struck Thompson's body, his comrades called on him to retreat and warned that he would be killed. "Maybe I won't get out," Thompson reportedly shouted back, "but I'm going to take a lot of them with me." He continued to fire his machine gun with deadly accuracy until an enemy grenade took his life. Several days later, Company M secured the area and retrieved Thompson's body.

Thompson's remains were returned to the United States for burial in the Long Island National Cemetery at Farmingdale, New York. For distinguishing himself "by conspicuous gallantry and intrepidity above and beyond the call of duty," Private First Class William H. Thompson was awarded the Medal of Honor in death. Just

one other African American who fought in Korea, Sergeant CORNELIUS CHARLTON, was so honored. On June 21, 1951, General Omar N. Bradley presented the medal to Thompson's mother, Mary Henderson, in a ceremony at the Pentagon. An aide to the general read the citation that accompanied the medal, noting, "Pfc. Thompson's dauntless courage and gallant self-sacrifice reflect the highest credit on himself and uphold the esteemed traditions of military service."

Further Reading

Lang, George, Raymond L. Collins, and Gerard F. White. *Medal of Honor Recipients, 1863–1994*. Vol. 2, *World War II to Somalia*. New York: Facts On File, 1995, p. 650.

Lee, Irvin H. *Negro Medal of Honor Men*. New York: Dodd, Mead and Co., 1967.

Murphy, Edward F. *Korean War Heroes*. Novato, Calif.: Presidio Press, 1992, pp. 21–23.

Trowell-Harris, Irene

(1939–   ) *first African-American female general in the National Guard*

Irene Trowell-Harris once summed up her career as "an uncharted flight from the cotton fields of South Carolina to the pinnacle of success as a registered nurse, mentor, role model and military officer." She simultaneously pursued careers in nursing and in the Air National Guard and excelled in both. In 1987, she became the first African-American woman general in the National Guard.

Irene Trowell-Harris was born in Aiken, South Carolina, on September 20, 1939, into a family of cotton farmers. The entire family—mother, father, and 11 children—worked together in the fields. One day in the 1950s, Irene astonished her siblings by pointing to a plane passing overhead and vowing, "[O]ne day I will fly and work on an airplane." The other children laughed because Irene's dream seemed impossible, but looking back, Trowell-Harris said, "Ten years later, I proudly walked upon the stage and accepted my silver flight nurse wings. . . ."

Trowell-Harris took that walk thanks to a caring community. Her church and high school combined their resources to send her to the Columbia Hospital School of Nursing in Columbia, South Carolina. In 1959, she received a diploma in nursing and went to work as a staff nurse in obstetrics and gynecology at Talmadge Hospital in Augusta, Georgia. In 1960, she moved north to be head nurse in obstetrics at the New York Hospital–Cornell Medical Center (now the New York Weill Cornell Medical Center) on the Upper East Side of Manhattan.

In 1964, Trowell-Harris joined the Air National Guard. National Guard units support the nation's security objectives and protect life and property at the state and community levels. Their members are civilians who aid their country on a part-time basis and in times of emergency. Trowell-Harris completed flight-nurse training at the Aerospace School of Medicine at Brooks Air Force Base in San Antonio, Texas, learning how to evacuate and transport critically ill and acutely injured patients. In her 38 years with the National Guard, she would also perform the duties of flight-nurse examiner and chief nurse executive. As assistant to the director of the Air National Guard for resources and readiness, she developed a program for facilitating the career progression of the 107,000 men and women in the Air National Guard. In addition, for six years she was military representative to the Defense Advisory Committee on Women in the Services. This committee of civilians appointed by the secretary of defense makes recommendations to the Defense Department on ways to improve the recruitment, employment, and well-being of women in uniform.

As a civilian nurse, Trowell-Harris became pediatric supervisor at Brookdale Hospital in Brooklyn in 1964, and assistant home health agency administrator at Maimonides Medical Center in Brooklyn in 1966. She also furthered her education, earning a bachelor's degree in health education with honors from Jersey City State College (now New Jersey City University) in 1971, a master's degree in public health from Yale University in 1973, and a doctorate in education from Columbia University in 1983. In 1986, she became the first Air National Guard nurse to command a medical clinic when she was placed in charge of the 105th U.S. Air Force Clinic at Newburgh, New York. With responsibility came promotions, and the following year, she became the first African-American woman general in the National Guard.

Trowell-Harris joined the Department of Veterans Affairs (VA) in 1993. As director of Patient Care Inspections and Program Evaluation in Washington, D.C., she supervised the quality of care and facilities at 163 hospitals, 650 clinics, 130 nursing homes, and 40 domiciliaries operated by the VA nationwide.

General Trowell-Harris continued to work on behalf of armed forces personnel. In 1997, she represented the air force on the Committee on Women at the NATO Forces Conference in Istanbul. This committee works to improve opportunities and conditions for military women in every nation of the alliance.

In September 2001, Trowell-Harris retired from the Air National Guard with the rank of major general. On October 2, 2001, she was appointed director of the VA's Center for Women Veterans in Washington, D.C. It became her job to see that the nation's 1.3 million female veterans received the health, burial, and other benefits to which they were entitled. She worked to ensure that women veterans—especially those in rural areas—had access to VA services, and she developed programs to meet the women's special needs, such as counseling services for those who suffered sexual trauma while in the armed forces. Trowell-Harris was also an adjunct graduate faculty member at the Uniformed Services University of the Health Sciences in Bethesda, Maryland.

General Irene Trowell-Harris has received the Distinguished Service Medal and the Legion of Merit. From the Department of Veterans Affairs she has received the Outstanding and Invaluable Service to the Community Award, Office of Inspector General performance awards, and special recognition from the Central Office Federal Women's Program Committee. In 1998, she became the first African-American woman to have a chapter of the Tuskegee Airmen, Inc., named in her honor. She has been inducted into Columbia University's Nursing Hall of Fame and Yale University School of Medicine's Honor Roll.

Further Reading

Butler, Mary Ellen. "Former USAF General Appointed Director of VA's Center for Women Veterans." *U.S. Medicine.* Available online. URL: http://www.usmedicine.com/dailyNews.cfm?dailyID=73. Downloaded on September 19, 2008.

"Irene Trowell-Harris, R.N., Ed.D." Department of Veterans Affairs. Available online. URL: http://www1.va.gov/womenvet/docs/ITHNewBioJune06.pdf. Downloaded on September 19, 2008.

"Major General Irene Trowell-Harris Keynotes WVA National Convention in Nashville." Clarksville Online. Available online. URL: http://www.clarksvilleonline.com/2008/08/04/women-veterans-national-convention-keynote-speaker-is-woman-of-national-achievement-pinnacle/. Downloaded on September 19, 2008.

Tubman, Harriet Ross

(ca. 1820–1913) *Civil War spy, scout, nurse*

Harriet Tubman's courage defined her life. Known as "the Moses of her people," she led hundreds of enslaved men, women, and children to freedom in the promised land of the North. During the Civil War, she ventured into the Confederacy to gather information for the Union army. She also nursed the sick and wounded.

Harriet Ross was born around 1820 on a plantation near Cambridge in Dorchester County, Maryland. She was one of 11 children born to Benjamin and Harriet Green Ross, an enslaved couple. Although christened Arminta, she used her mother's name, which she preferred. Young Harriet was unschooled, like nearly all enslaved children. Instead of learning to read and write, she worked on the plantation for her owner and was hired out to clean houses for others. Harriet exhibited unusual bravery even in her youth. When she was 13, for example, she stood up to a plantation overseer who was preparing to whip another slave and was struck with a two-pound weight. The blow left her with a permanent head injury that made her prone to sudden sleeping spells.

Around 1844, Harriet Ross married John Tubman, a free African American. In 1849, after learning that the plantation on which she lived was to be sold and its enslaved residents sent to the Deep South, she fled to the North on the Underground Railroad. This secret network of antislavery activists and safe houses enabled thousands of people to find freedom in the northern states or Canada. Harriet Tubman settled initially in Philadelphia and soon began returning to the South to help others escape bondage. She made 15 trips south and rescued approximately 300 people, including her parents and siblings. John Tubman remained in Dorchester County, however, and although the Tubmans never formally divorced, he remarried. Harriet Tubman's activities had such a severe economic impact on Maryland slaveholders that at one time they offered a $40,000 reward for her capture.

During the 1850s, Tubman and her parents lived in St. Catherines, Ontario. Toward the end of the decade, they moved to Auburn, New York, a town that was home to abolitionists, woman suffragists, and other progressive thinkers, and Tubman began speaking at abolitionist rallies.

Tubman's participation in the Civil War began in 1862, when Governor John Andrew of Massachusetts issued papers of introduction that allowed her to aid the Union army, which had gained a foothold on the South Carolina coast. Knowing of her familiarity with the southern terrain, Brigadier General David Hunter, who commanded the army's Department of the South, comprising South Carolina, Georgia, and Florida, had requested her services. Tubman joined Hunter at Beaufort, South Carolina, and rolled up her sleeves to nurse the many ill and malnourished African Americans who had fled slavery and sought protection from the federal forces.

In February 1863, she was attached as a scout to the 2nd South Carolina Volunteers, an African-American unit led by Colonel James Montgomery, a white officer. In that role Tubman ventured behind enemy lines to set up a spy network among enslaved African Americans. She posed as a slave herself, and through careful observation learned the location and strength of Confederate positions. She displayed "remarkable courage, zeal and fidelity," said Union general Rufus Saxton. Thanks to information she provided, on June 2, 1863, Montgomery led a successful raid along the Combahee River of South Carolina during which his regiment destroyed Confederate supplies and brought 756 slaves to freedom.

Tubman was present as an army nurse on July 18, 1863, when 600 African-American soldiers of the 54th Massachusetts Infantry led the attack on Fort Wagner, a Confederate installation on Morris Island, South Carolina, near the entrance to Charleston's harbor. She described the battle poetically, comparing it to a summer storm. "We saw the lightning, and that was the guns," Tubman said. "And then we heard the thunder, and that was the big guns; and then we heard the rain falling, and that was the drops of blood falling; and when we came to get in the crops, it was dead men we reaped." The battle was a loss for the Union, but it made heroes of men such as WILLIAM H. CARNEY, the first African American awarded the Medal of Honor.

Harriet Tubman, shown here in her old age, selflessly and courageously helped her fellow African Americans before, during, and after the Civil War. *(Schomburg Center for Research in Black Culture, New York Public Library)*

Harriet Tubman returned to Auburn in 1864. John Tubman died in 1867, and in 1869, Harriet Tubman married Nelson Davis, a disabled veteran. Slavery had ended with the U.S. victory in the Civil War, but Tubman continued to help her people by caring for the orphaned and the aged. She repeatedly sought financial compensation from the government for her war service, but her requests were denied. After Nelson Davis died in 1888, she received a widow's pension of $8 a month.

Tubman spent her last years working on behalf of women's rights, raising money for schools for African Americans, and promoting the growth of the African Methodist Episcopal Zion Church in upstate New York. In 1903, she donated 25 acres to the church for the construction of a shelter for impoverished African Americans, and the Harriet Tubman Home for Indigent and Aged Colored People opened in 1908. Tubman died there of pneumonia on March 10, 1913.

Further Reading

Hall, Richard. *Patriots in Disguise: Women Warriors of the Civil War.* New York: Paragon House, 1993, pp. 164–166.

Lowry, Beverly. *Harriet Tubman: Imagining a Life.* New York: Doubleday, 2007.

McGuire, William, and Leslie Wheeler. *American Social Leaders.* Santa Barbara, Calif.: ABC-CLIO, 1993, pp. 452–453.

Sernett, Milton C. *Harriet Tubman: Myth, Memory and History.* Durham, N.C.: Duke University Press, 2007.

Smith, Jessie Carney. *Epic Lives: One Hundred Black Women Who Made a Difference.* Detroit: Visible Ink Press, 1993, pp. 529–537.

Turner, Henry McNeal
(1834–1915) *first African-American army chaplain*

As a pastor in Washington, D.C., during the Civil War, Henry McNeal Turner established an African-American regiment and served as its chaplain, becoming the first African-American chaplain in the U.S. Army. Although the war ended slavery, it failed to bring racial equality, and Turner became so disillusioned with the United States that in 1906 he called its flag a "dirty rag."

The son of free parents, Henry McNeal Turner was born near Abbeville, South Carolina, on February 1, 1834. His father, Hardy Turner, died while Henry was very young, so the child was raised by his mother, Sarah Green Turner. In childhood, Henry worked in nearby cotton fields and was apprenticed to a blacksmith. He became literate by the time he was 15, through both his own ingenuity and lessons from whites who were willing to break the law against teaching blacks to read. Later, when he had been hired to sweep out a law office, he learned to write and do arithmetic.

Turner joined the Methodist Episcopal Church, South, in 1851. (Following a disagreement among church leaders over the appropriateness of clergymen owning slaves, the Methodist Episcopal Church had split in two in May 1845.) Turner was licensed to preach in 1853, and he traveled throughout the slaveholding states leading prayer services for blacks and whites. In 1856, he married for the first time. (He would marry again in 1893, in 1900, and for a fourth time some years later. He would father several children, only two of whom would outlive him.)

In 1858, Turner transferred his allegiance to the African Methodist Episcopal (AME) Church, which was formally organized in 1816 so that Afri-

This engraving of the Reverend Henry McNeal Turner, chaplain of the 1st U.S. Colored Troops, appeared in *Harper's Weekly* on December 12, 1863. *(Schomburg Center for Research in Black Culture, New York Public Library)*

can Americans might worship in settings that were free of discrimination. He was ordained a deacon in 1860 and assigned to the AME mission in Baltimore. After studying English grammar, Latin, Greek, Hebrew, and Scripture, he was appointed pastor of Israel AME Church in Washington, D.C.

From the start of the Civil War in April 1861, Turner advocated the enlistment of African Americans. Once the Emancipation Proclamation opened the armed forces to African Americans, he used his pulpit to recruit soldiers for the Union army. Turner, together with his assistant, Thomas H. C. Hinton, and others, organized the 1st Regiment of the U.S. Colored Troops. On November 6, 1863, Turner was commissioned as a chaplain in the army and attached to the regiment he had helped to assemble. He is thought to have been the first African-American chaplain in the U.S. armed forces.

The 1st U.S. Colored Troops fought in nine battles, including the 10-month siege of Petersburg, Virginia, which began on June 15, 1864, and led to the fall of Richmond. The regiment also took part in the capture of Fort Fisher, an imposing earthen fortress that kept the port of Wilmington, North Carolina, open to blockade runners. The fort fell to the Union following an amphibious assault that began on January 15, 1865.

Turner accompanied the men into battle and liked to brag that although Confederate bullets had torn through his coat and hat and taken the heel off his boot, he never suffered a scratch. Illness was another matter, though. Contagious diseases spread easily through army camps and caused more deaths than did battlefield wounds. In February 1864, Turner fell ill with smallpox and nearly died. He took a three-month leave from the regiment to regain his health.

During lulls in the fighting, Turner conducted prayer meetings nightly and three services on Sundays. He performed weddings and funerals, and he ministered to the sick and wounded, Union and Confederate alike. Turner considered it his mission

to teach the many illiterate soldiers in his regiment to read and write, and he appealed to charitable friends for reading matter such as Bibles, hymnals, religious tracts, newspapers, and especially spelling books, which were in great demand among the soldiers. Turner's lessons made it possible for some of the men to receive promotions.

After the regiment was dissolved in September 1865, President Andrew Johnson appointed Turner to be a chaplain in the Regular Army and assigned him to the Freedmen's Bureau in Georgia. Turner soon resigned, however, preferring to establish churches in the South and participate in Reconstruction politics. In 1867, he was elected to the Georgia Constitutional Convention and to the Georgia state legislature. In September 1868, the legislature declared African Americans ineligible to hold seats, so Turner served instead as a customs inspector and as postmaster of Macon, Georgia. In March 1869, after Georgia rejected the Fifteenth Amendment to the Constitution, Congress subsequently placed the state under military rule to require ratification of the amendment and restore African-American legislators to their elected offices.

Turner was therefore able to complete his legislative term in 1870. He then returned to clerical duties, and in 1876 he became manager of the AME Book Concern in Philadelphia; in 1880, he was named a bishop. He served for 12 years as president of Morris Brown College in Atlanta, a school affiliated with the AME Church that opened formally in 1885, and in 1885 he wrote *The Genius and Theory of Methodist Policy*. He compiled a catechism and hymn book, and he founded three AME publications: the *Southern Christian Recorder* (1889), *Voice of Missions* (1892), and *Voice of the People* (1901).

Perhaps Turner is remembered best, though, for promoting African-American emigration. By 1874, having become convinced that African Americans would never achieve equality in the United States, he advocated a return to Africa. Between 1891 and 1898, he made four trips to

Liberia, the West African nation founded by blacks from the United States, to observe missionary work and generate interest in immigration, yet he remained a lifelong resident of North America. Bishop Henry McNeal Turner died in Windsor, Ontario, on May 8, 1915.

Further Reading

Anderson, Gerald H., ed. *Biographical Dictionary of Christian Missions.* New York: Macmillan Reference, 1998, p. 685.

Angell, Stephen Ward. *Bishop Henry McNeal Turner and African-American Religion in the South.* Knoxville: University of Tennessee Press, 1992.

Encyclopedia of World Biography, 2nd ed. Vol. 15. Detroit: Gale Research, 1998, pp. 351–352.

Logan, Rayford W., and Michael R. Winston, eds. *Dictionary of American Negro Biography.* New York: W. W. Norton and Co., 1982, pp. 608–610.

Williams, Heather Andrea. *Self-Taught: African American Education in Slavery and Freedom.* Chapel Hill: University of North Carolina Press, 2005, pp. 45, 53–55, 66, 126, 230.

Tye

(Colonel Tye, Titus)

(ca. 1753–1780) *former slave who fought for the British in the American Revolution*

A promise of freedom led a New Jersey slave named Titus to transform himself into the guerrilla warrior Tye and fight for the Loyalists in the American Revolution. For most of his brief career as a fighting man, Tye operated outside the law and military chain of command, exacting revenge against the whites who had enslaved him as he aided the British cause.

From birth, the slave named Titus belonged to a thriving Monmouth County, New Jersey, Quaker named John Corlies. Although by the 1760s the Quakers of New Jersey were following the example of their Philadelphia brethren and giving up the ownership of slaves, often educating them and

granting them freedom at age 21, Corlies kept his adult African Americans enslaved and treated them cruelly.

As Titus reached maturity, colonists desiring independence had begun clashing with their English rulers in the first confrontations of the American Revolution. Titus saw an opportunity for escape when John Murray, the fourth Earl of Dunmore and governor of Virginia, offered freedom to any enslaved man able to bear arms who joined the royal forces. Adopting the name Tye and posing as a free African American, Titus worked his way south along the Atlantic coast to Norfolk, Virginia, supporting himself by doing odd jobs. Corlies, meanwhile, offered a reward for the return of the slave he described as "about 21 years old, not very black and about six feet high."

Tye eluded capture and became a captain in Lord Dunmore's Ethiopian Regiment. Wearing uniforms embroidered with the words "liberty to slaves," the men of this African-American fighting force furthered the British cause not only militarily, but also psychologically, by causing slave-owning Patriots to fear that the people laboring under their whips might violently turn against them. The Ethiopian Regiment enjoyed an initial victory against the colonial militia at Kemp's Landing, Virginia, in November 1775, successfully defending a large store of gunpowder, only to suffer a defeat a month later in the Battle of Great Bridge, near Chesapeake, Virginia. The British counted heavy losses in this battle; afterward, plagued by hunger and smallpox, Dunmore's forces retreated to British-held New York City, where the Ethiopian Regiment disbanded.

From New York, Tye made the short trip to New Jersey, where he enlisted in the Black Brigade, an independent guerrilla band that became associated with the Queen's Rangers, a white Loyalist unit. Tye is first known to have fought with the Black Brigade in the large but indecisive Battle of Monmouth, in which the Continental army, under General George Washington, attacked the British column led by Sir Henry Clinton. During this battle, Tye captured Captain Elisha Shepard of the Monmouth Militia and transferred him to the Sugar House, the grim stone building in New York City that the British used as a prison. With his knowledge of Monmouth County geography and flair for leadership, he was an effective Loyalist commander and became known as Colonel Tye. The title was an informal one that indicated respect.

Beginning in summer 1779, from Refugeetown, their base on the barrier peninsula called Sandy Hook, Colonel Tye and his men, both black and white, went out on nighttime raids, approaching in silence and launching surprise attacks. They burned the houses of Patriots, took prisoners, freed slaves, and seized food, firewood, and livestock for the British troops. They targeted Shrewsbury, in Monmouth County, on one of their first raids and returned with 80 head of cattle, 20 horses, two prisoners, clothing, and furniture. Tye became a principal supplier of cattle and firewood to the British soldiers in the region, and he was generously paid. As an added reward, he had the satisfaction that came from depriving the Americans of needed food and fuel.

In late March 1780, Tye and his followers murdered John Russell, a Patriot marauder who conducted raids on Staten Island, New York, where the British regular and irregular forces were headquartered. They also looted and burned Russell's house and wounded his son. In June 1780, they killed Private Joseph Murray of the Monmouth militia in his home, because Murray had executed several Tories. Deeds such as these caused Patriots throughout the region to fear the name Tye and encouraged many slaves to flee their masters. In July, Monmouth County Patriots formed the Association for Retaliation, to protect and defend themselves from Tye's attacks. The governor of New Jersey also proclaimed martial law in an attempt to curb the violence, but these measures had no effect on Tye and his men, who continued to raid, often targeting former masters.

On September 1, 1780, Tye's band attacked the Colt's Neck, New Jersey, home of Captain Josiah Huddy, a man famed for raiding Loyalist positions on Staten Island and Sandy Hook whom the British had been trying for years to capture or kill. Incredibly, Huddy and a female friend, Lucretia Emmons, managed to hold off the siege for two hours by firing muskets from windows. The black Loyalists eventually set fire to the house and smoked the pair out, but a musket ball had passed through Tye's wrist, and although the wound appeared small he developed tetanus, which killed him. (Josiah Huddy escaped after the skirmish by jumping from the boat that was carrying him to Refugeetown and swimming to safety.)

Further Reading

"Colonel Tye." Africans in America. Available online. URL: http://www.pbs.org/wgbh/aia/part2/2p52. html. Downloaded on September 19, 2008.

Gilje, Paul A., and William Pencak, eds. New York in the Age of the Constitution, 1775–1780. Rutherford, N.J.: Fairleigh Dickinson University Press, 2007.

Papas, Philip. That Ever Loyal Island: Staten Island and the American Revolution. New York: New York University Press, 2007, pp. 97–98.

Schama, Simon. Rough Crossings: Britain, the Slaves and the American Revolution. New York: HarperCollins, 2006, pp. 111–116.

V

Vashon, John Bathan

(1792–1853) *seaman imprisoned during the War of 1812, abolitionist*

John Bathan Vashon, a Pittsburgh abolitionist and businessman, was a veteran of the War of 1812 who spent two years as a prisoner of the British.

Vashon was born in Norfolk, Virginia, in 1792, but his exact date of birth is unknown. His father, George Vashon, who was white, earned his living as a merchant. John's mother, Fanny Vashon, had been one of a small number of slaves owned by George Vashon's father and received her freedom shortly before John's birth. George Vashon's level of involvement in his son's upbringing cannot be determined. Fanny Vashon maintained her own household and even owned a slave, and George Vashon married a white woman in 1819.

At age 20, John Vashon joined the navy as a common seaman. He was stationed aboard the USS *Revenge*, a warship that patrolled the Caribbean Sea and the Atlantic coast of South America. Vashon's enlistment coincided with the start of the War of 1812, a conflict waged largely at sea. He was captured following a battle off the coast of Brazil and held in the infamous British prison ship *Jersey*, the same hulk in which JAMES FORTEN had been confined during the American Revolution. Vashon spent two years aboard the *Jersey*, surviving on too little food and amid filth and disease. When the British at last released him in exchange for one of their officers who was being held by the Americans, he felt gratified not just to be obtaining his freedom but also to be recognized as equal in value to a white man.

John Bathan Vashon settled in Leesburg, Virginia, after the war. Along with other free African Americans living in the area, he volunteered for the land service, the militia group charged with protecting the region from any further British attack. He married a woman named Anne Smith, and in 1822 their first child, Mary Frances, was born.

Preferring to live in a state where slavery was outlawed, the Vashons relocated in 1822 to Carlisle, Pennsylvania, where a second child, George Boyer Vashon, was born on July 25, 1824. In 1829, the family moved to Pittsburgh, and John Bathan Vashon went into business. He operated a barbershop, and in 1834 he opened the first public bath in the city.

Vashon also was active in the anti-slavery movement and contributed funds to buy the freedom of African Americans being held by slave catchers. The notorious slave catchers earned a tidy profit by kidnapping African Americans in the North and delivering them to slavery in the South. In one instance, Vashon gave shelter and employment to a young man after purchasing his freedom. Vashon was a friend of the abolitionists MARTIN R. DELANY and William Lloyd Garrison, and he sold subscriptions to Garrison's newspaper, *The Liberator,* in Pittsburgh. In 1833, he helped to establish the Pittsburgh Anti-Slavery Society; he also made his home available to African Americans traveling north on the Underground Railroad.

John Vashon aided the free African-American population as well. Regretting his own lack of formal education and wanting younger generations to have opportunities that had been denied to him, in January 1832 he was a founder and first president of the Pittsburgh African Education Society, which operated a school in the basement of an African Methodist Episcopal Church. Vashon's son, George B. Vashon, was among its students. (Mary Frances Vashon attended a private girls' academy.)

Upon reaching adulthood, George B. Vashon joined his father in the abolitionist cause. In 1853, father and son traveled to Rochester, New York, to attend a Colored National Convention organized by Frederick Douglass to demand justice and equality under the law for African Americans.

John Bathan Vashon served as vice president of the convention while George B. Vashon wrote the keynote address for the Committee on Declaration of Sentiments.

On December 29, 1853, John Vashon was in the Pittsburgh railroad station waiting to board a train to Philadelphia, site of a convention of the Veterans of the War of 1812, when he died of heart failure. A friend stated that "he fell with his harness on, and died in the last act of service to his brethren, and in obedience to the summons of his country, in the person of one of her delegated warriors."

Further Reading

Haskins, Jim. *African American Military Heroes.* New York: John Wiley and Sons, 1998, pp. 24–26.

"Noted Abolitionists in Pittsburgh: John Bathan Vashon." University of Pittsburgh Library System. Available online. URL: http://www.library.pitt.edu/freeatlast/abolition.html. Downloaded on February 13, 2010.

Thornell, Paul N. D. "The Absent Ones and the Providers: A Biography of the Vashons." *Journal of Negro History* 83, no. 4 (fall 1998): pp. 284–301.

W

Waddy, Harriet West
(Harriet M. Hardin, Harriet West)
(1904–1999) *first African-American major in the Women's Army Corps*

Harriet West Waddy believed that serving in an army that discriminated against African Americans was a way to work for equality. She served well, and in 1943 she became the first African-American major in the newly established Women's Army Corps.

Harriet M. Hardin was born in Jefferson City, Missouri, on June 20, 1904, the child of a black mother and white father. When her mother died, she lost both her parents, because her father took her brother, who was blond and blue eyed, to live with him, and left dark-skinned Harriet with her maternal grandmother. The little girl never saw her father again.

Harriet Hardin graduated from the Kansas State College of Agriculture and Applied Science (now the College of Engineering at Kansas State University) in Manhattan, Kansas. In the 1930s, she worked for Mary McLeod Bethune, who was then director of the Division of Negro Affairs for the National Youth Administration (NYA). The NYA was a New Deal program that gave work to women between the ages of 16 and 25 and to young men unfit for hard physical labor. This federal agency also employed students and thus permitted many

young people to finish high school or college. Some 12 percent of those helped were black; they received the same training and pay as white participants.

By early 1942, the unemployment of the Great Depression had decreased, the United States was fighting World War II, and the NYA was training youth for war work. On May 15, 1942, President Franklin Delano Roosevelt signed legislation establishing the Women's Army Auxiliary Corps (WAAC) to give official status to women serving the army in wartime apart from the Army Nurse Corps. The government would provide WAAC volunteers with food, lodging, medical care, uni-

Harriet West Waddy's military career spanned a quarter of a century. *(Library of Congress)*

232

forms, and pay in return for noncombat service. The corps was organized militarily, with officers and enlisted personnel, but WAAC officers were not permitted to give orders to men.

Harriet Hardin had married Charles West, M.D., the first of her four husbands, and was known during the years of World War II as Harriet West. Patriotic throughout her life, in 1942 she enlisted in the WAAC. Because she had completed college, she was sent to Officer Candidate School at Fort Des Moines, Iowa. Black and white WAAC officer candidates ate and slept apart at Fort Des Moines, but they trained together under white male officers. When her training was complete, West returned to Washington, D.C., to work under WAAC director Major Oveta Culp Hobby.

Black and white WAAC officers might have been trained without regard for race, but black and white enlisted women, or "auxiliaries," performed very different duties. While white women typed critical communications and operated switchboards, the majority of black auxiliaries cleaned officers' clubs or performed other janitorial tasks. In April 1943, West spoke on the radio and urged African-American women to enlist in the corps despite this discrimination. "[A]ccepting a situation which does not represent an ideal of democracy is not a retreat from our fight [for equality]," she said, "but our contribution to its realization." At the time, she held the auxiliary rank of first officer, which was comparable to the Regular Army rank of captain.

In July 1943, the WAAC became the Women's Army Corps (WAC), part of the Regular Army. Harriet West completed a course at the Adjutant General's School and was placed in command of 50 typists in the Casualty Branch. These women typed letters to families throughout the nation to inform them that loved ones in uniform had been killed or wounded or were missing in action.

On August 21, 1943, West became the first African-American major in the Women's Army Corps. She would be one of two to serve in World War II. (The other was CHARITY ADAMS EARLEY.).

She subsequently served as chief of planning for the Bureau of Control Division at WAC Headquarters in Washington, D.C.

In 1944, the army sent West on a tour of the South to investigate the grievances of African-American WACs. Traveling by train from Atlanta to Fort McClellan in Anniston, Alabama, she endured insults from a white conductor. On another official trip, to Fort Des Moines, she recommended that "all references to white and colored personnel be completely eliminated" from notices posted on the fort's bulletin boards to spare the feelings of African Americans and convey "that a forward step has been made toward democracy."

Harriet West was promoted to lieutenant colonel in 1948, and she retired from the armed forces in 1952. Making her home in Eugene, Oregon, she worked for the Federal Aviation Administration and counseled girls at a Job Corps Center. She and her fourth husband, Major Edward Waddy, eventually divorced.

In 1998, in failing health, Harriet West Waddy went to live with a friend in Las Vegas. She died in that city on February 21, 1999, at age 94.

Further Reading

Commire, Anne, ed. *Dictionary of Women Worldwide: 25,000 Women through the Ages.* Detroit, Mich.: Thomson Gale, 2007. Vol. 2: M–Z, pp. 1,947–1,948.

Goldstein, Richard. "Harriet M. Waddy, 94, Officer in Women's Army Corps, Dies." *New York Times Biographical Service* 30, no. 3 (March 1999): p. 420.

Patrick, Bethanne Kelly. "Lt. Col. Harriet West Waddy." Military.com. Available online. URL: http://www. military.com/Content/MoreContent?file=ML_ waddy_bkp. Downloaded on September 21, 2008.

Waller, Calvin Agustine Hoffman
(1937–1996) *lieutenant general, deputy commander of Operation Desert Storm*

A career army officer, General Calvin Waller was deputy to the commander-in-chief of the

U.S. Central Command during the Persian Gulf War.

Calvin A. H. Waller was born in Baton Rouge, Louisiana, on December 17, 1937. He attended Prairie View A & M University, a historically black college in Texas, and earned a bachelor of science degree in agriculture in 1959. Having completed the Reserve Officers Training Program in college, he entered the army in August 1959 and attended the Infantry Officer Basic Course at the U.S. Infantry School, Fort Benning, Georgia.

Waller began to develop expertise in chemical warfare in June 1961, when he was placed in command of the 247th Chemical Platoon at Fort Lewis, Washington. He was promoted to first lieutenant on July 30, 1962, shortly before entering the U.S. Army Chemical Center and School at Fort McClellan in Anniston, Alabama.

On July 29, 1963, Waller received his promotion to captain; the following December, he was made chief of the Chemical, Biological, and Radiological Center in the office of the assistant chief of staff, 7th Logistics Command, Eighth U.S. Army in Korea. In February 1965, after returning to the United States, he was stationed at Fort Bragg, North Carolina, as a chemical officer, first with Headquarters Company and then with the 2nd Brigade, 82nd Airborne Division. In July 1968, Waller, who had been promoted to major, entered the Army Command and General Staff College at Fort Leavenworth, Kansas. He and his wife, Marion, were raising two sons, Michael and Mark. Waller was separated from his family temporarily in 1969 and 1970, when he served in Vietnam.

As time progressed, Waller held positions of greater responsibility and continued to rise in rank. In April 1971, he was appointed training staff officer in the Policy and Programs Branch of the army's office of the deputy chief of staff for personnel in Washington, D.C. On June 1, 1975, he was promoted to colonel, and in August 1975 he took command of the 1st Battalion, 77th

Armor, 4th Infantry Division (Mechanized) at Fort Carson, Colorado.

Waller furthered his education as well. In August 1977, he entered the U.S. Army War College at Carlisle Barracks, Pennsylvania, and in 1978, he earned a master's degree in public administration from Shippensburg State University in Pennsylvania. He was therefore well qualified in July 1980 to serve as senior military assistant in the office of the assistant secretary of defense for manpower, reserve affairs, and logistics, in Washington. He attained the rank of colonel on August 1, 1980, and in August 1983 was chief of staff of the 24th Infantry Division (Mechanized) at Fort Stewart, Georgia. In December 1983, he returned to Fort Bragg as chief of staff of XVIII Airborne Corps, the army's largest warfighting organization. In that position, Waller exercised control over more than 88,000 soldiers stationed at various army bases. He later served as assistant commander of the 82nd Airborne Division at Fort Bragg.

On November 1, 1984, Waller was promoted to brigadier general, and in July 1986, he was named deputy commanding general of I Corps and Fort Lewis, Washington. A year later he was in Europe, commanding the 8th Infantry Division of V Corps and the Seventh Army. On November 1, 1987, while overseas, he moved up in rank to major general. His final promotion, to lieutenant general, took place in August 1989, when he was named commanding general of I Corps and Fort Lewis.

General Calvin Waller entered the media spotlight in November 1990, when General COLIN L. POWELL, chairman of the Joint Chiefs of Staff, appointed him deputy to General H. Norman Schwarzkopf, commander of the American forces in Saudi Arabia. With Iraqi soldiers stationed across the border with Kuwait, the United States was gearing up for probable action in the Middle East. Powell chose Waller for his expertise as much as for his even temperament, which Powell hoped would be a moderating influence on the more mercurial Schwarzkopf.

The United States and the United Nations gave Iraqi leader Saddam Hussein until January 15, 1991, to withdraw his troops from Kuwait or face attack. Waller meanwhile caused controversy by telling reporters that U.S. forces would be unprepared to fight by the deadline. Although Waller's statement was arguably accurate, supporters of a military solution to the Iraqi crisis, including Powell, accused Waller of undermining President George H. W. Bush's strategy, and the general received a private reprimand. Yet Powell later praised Waller's organizational skill and patriotism. "Cal was the one [Schwarzkopf] and I looked to to make sure all of the pieces were coming together on that desert floor as we built up the force from nothing to 540,000 troops," Powell said. "It was Cal who watched the training, the logistics . . . who inspired the troops."

Saddam Hussein refused to back down, so on January 17, the Coalition forces launched Operation Desert Storm, beginning with a 38-day air campaign that destroyed Iraq's military infrastructure. During that assault and the brief ground war that followed it, U.S. troops showed themselves to be prepared. From February 15 through February 23, Waller replaced Lieutenant General John Yeosock, who was responsible for army combat operations and logistical support within the Kuwaiti theater of war, while Yeosock underwent surgery.

Lieutenant General Calvin Waller retired from the army on November 30, 1991, as one of the highest-ranking African Americans in the armed forces. He and Marion Waller made their home in Colorado, where he was president and chief executive officer of RKK, Ltd., a corporation that develops technology for hazardous-waste sites. In July 1995, he joined the environmental contractor Kaiser-Hill as senior vice president for Department of Energy programs. Between 1995 and 2005, Kaiser-Hill managed the cleanup of radioactive and hazardous materials, including 12.9 metric tons of plutonium and sizeable quantities of beryllium, asbes-

tos, and lead, from Rocky Flats, a former nuclear-weapons plant outside Denver.

Calvin Waller died of a heart attack on May 9, 1996, while visiting Washington, D.C., with his wife, and was buried in Arlington National Cemetery. Waller left "a legacy of leadership, professionalism and a genuine love for the men and women in uniform," said General John Shalikashvili, former chairman of the Joint Chiefs of Staff.

Further Reading

"Calvin A. H. Waller." Arlington National Cemetery Website. Available online. URL: http://www.arlingtoncemetery.com/cawaller.htm. Downloaded on September 26, 2008.

Hawkins, Walter L. *Black American Military Leaders.* Jefferson, N.C.: McFarland and Co., 2007, pp. 478–479.

"Lieut. Gen. Calvin Waller, 58, Deputy Commander in Gulf War." *New York Times Biographical Service 27,* no. 5 (May 1996), p. 683.

Schwartz, Richard Allen. *Encyclopedia of the Persian Gulf War.* Jefferson, N.C.: McFarland and Co., 1998, pp. 12, 160, 163–164, 173.

Walley, Augustus

(1856–1938) *Buffalo Soldier, Medal of Honor winner*

Service in the 9th and 10th Cavalry Regiments took Augustus Walley, a former slave, to the western frontier, Cuba, and the Philippines. Twice he risked his life to save wounded comrades, but it was his bravery in the mountains of New Mexico in 1881 that earned him the Medal of Honor.

Augustus Walley was born into slavery on March 10, 1856, in Reisterstown, Maryland, and gained his freedom at the end of the Civil War. He was a laborer until November 26, 1878, when he traveled to Baltimore and enlisted in the army. He was assigned to Company I of the 9th Cavalry, one of the African-American regiments formed

Soldiers of Augustus Walley's regiment, the 9th Cavalry, drill on the parade ground at Fort Davis, Texas, ca. 1875. *(National Archives)*

after the Civil War whose men became known as Buffalo Soldiers.

Walley had been in the West nearly three years when, at noon on August 16, 1881, a distraught Mexican ranch hand rode to the spot near the Cuchillo Negro Mountains of New Mexico where Company I was camped. The hand reported that a band of Apache had attacked the Chavez ranch, two miles away, and tortured and killed the Chavez family and two of their hired men. The Apache had been led by Nana, a chief intent on exacting revenge against the United States for driving his people from their homeland. Nana was 70 years old, but he had the strength and stamina of a much younger man.

The company's white commander, Lieutenant Gustavus Valois, sent Lieutenant George Burnett and 12 black soldiers, including Augustus Walley, in pursuit. Burnett's force rode to the Chavez ranch and, with a group of armed Mexican Americans, followed Nana's trail into the mountains. They spent the afternoon pursuing the Apache—who numbered between 40 and 60—from one ridgeline to another. Soon after 4 P.M., the Apache encountered Lieutenant Valois and the rest of Company I, and fiercely attacked them.

Burnett's band rode toward the sounds of gunfire and came upon Valois and his men desperately trying to repel the Apache assault. Most of Valois's soldiers' horses had been killed, and several of the men had been wounded. Burnett's men charged and drove the Indians back; then they dismounted and kept up a steady fire, giving the other soldiers time to retreat. Once the wounded had been moved to safe ground, Burnett, Walley, and Sergeant Moses Williams formed the rear guard, holding the Apache back while Burnett's soldiers also retreated.

The cavalrymen thought they had escaped a dangerous situation until shouts told them that three of their own were stranded, trapped behind prairie-dog mounds and unable to run 200 yards to safety because of heavy enemy fire. Unwilling to abandon the three, Burnett asked for volunteers to retrieve them. Walley and Williams answered the call and took positions from which they could shoot to provide cover while the trapped men crawled away.

Two of the men got out, but the third was wounded and needed assistance to move. At this moment, Walley displayed the heroism that earned him the Medal of Honor. With Burnett's permission, he mounted his horse and rode through a rain of Apache bullets to reach the wounded man. Ignoring the danger to himself, he lifted the soldier onto his saddle and carried him back to the company.

Lieutenant Burnett recommended Walley for the Medal of Honor, and the regimental commander, Colonel Edward Hatch, recommended that he also be presented a Certificate of Merit for "extraordinary exertion in the preservation of human life." Walley received both awards on October 1, 1890. (Nana remained free and continued to wage war until March 1885, when he surrendered to the army. He was one of 77 Apache who were loaded onto a train and sent to Fort Marion, Florida, to end their days as prisoners of war.)

Augustus Walley was discharged from the army at Fort Reno, Arizona, on November 25, 1883, with a character rating of "excellent," only to enlist the following day in the 10th Cavalry. He served in Cuba with Company I of the 10th Cavalry during the Spanish-American War. Walley again displayed great courage on June 24, 1898, when, along with Colonel Theodore Roosevelt's Rough Riders, his company took part in the Battle of Las Guasimas, the first important land battle in this war with Spain. The exchange of gunfire in this battle was intense, and many Americans became casualties, including Major Bell of the 1st Cavalry, who lay in the field unable to move because a bullet had shattered his leg. Walley and Captain Charles Greenlief Ayers, a white officer with the 10th Cavalry, dragged Major Bell to safety. This act of heroism earned Walley a second Medal of Honor recommendation, but the award was not approved. Walley's unit also fought alongside Roosevelt and the Rough Riders on July 1, in the Battle of San Juan Hill, and helped to achieve another important victory in the war.

Beginning in 1899, Walley served for two years with the 10th Cavalry on occupation duty in the Philippines. When he retired as a sergeant on February 1, 1907, he was stationed at Fort Washakie, Wyoming. Having spent his life around horses, he earned his living as a farrier and lived successively in Butte, Montana; Prague, Oklahoma; Cleveland, Ohio; and Baltimore, Maryland. He returned to active duty during World War I and was stationed at Camp Beauregard, Louisiana, from May 1, 1918, until March 7, 1919. He died in Baltimore on April 9, 1938, and was buried in St. Luke's Cemetery in Reisterstown, the place where he was born.

Further Reading

Department of the Army. *The Soldier's Guide: The Complete Guide to U.S. Army Traditions, Training, Duties, and Responsibilities.* New York: Skyhorse Publishing, 2007, pp. 2–25.

Hanna, Charles W. *African American Recipients of the Medal of Honor.* Jefferson, N.C.: McFarland and Co., 2002, pp. 85–89, 93.

Leckie, William H. *The Buffalo Soldiers: A Narrative of the Negro Cavalry in the West.* Norman: University of Oklahoma Press, 1967, pp. 232–233.

"Pvt. Augustus Walley." Buffalo Soldiers: Lawton-Fort Sill Chapter. Available online. URL: http://www.buffalosoldiers-lawtonftsill.org/walley.htm. Downloaded on September 26, 2008.

Schubert, Irene, and Frank Schubert. *On the Trail of the Buffalo Soldier II.* Lanham, Md.: Scarecrow Press, 2004, pp. 306–307.

Ward, William Edward

(ca. 1949–   ) *fifth African-American four-star general in the army, first commander of U.S. Africa Command*

William E. Ward's logistical skills and talent for diplomacy enabled him to attain the highest rank in the U.S. Army, that of four-star general. As the first commander of U.S. Africa Command (AFRICOM), he cooperates with the governments and armed forces of African nations to promote economic, social, and political stability as Africa assumes greater importance in global affairs.

Ward was born in Baltimore and raised in nearby Ruxton, Maryland. His father, Richard Ward, a World War II combat veteran, managed an apartment complex. William Ward, whose nickname is Kip, attended Morgan State University in Baltimore, where he was enrolled in the Amy ROTC program. On April 3, 1971, he married classmate Joyce Lewis in the campus chapel, and on June 6, 1971, he graduated with a degree in political science. He was also commissioned a second lieutenant in the U.S. Army. Upon seeing him in uniform, Ward's father greeted him with the prophetic words "Hello general!"

Ward began his army career at Fort Bragg, North Carolina, where he was an antitank platoon leader and later a motor officer with the 3rd Battalion, 325th infantry, 82nd Airborne Division. He was promoted to second lieutenant on October 9, 1972. His promotion to captain came on June 9, 1975, while he was serving as a rifle platoon leader in South Korea.

Like many career military officers, Ward continued his education. He completed the Infantry Advanced Course at the U.S. Army Infantry School, Fort Benning, Georgia, and in 1979 earned a master's degree in political science from Pennsylvania State University. He was an instructor and assistant professor of social sciences at the U.S. Military Academy at West Point, New York, from 1978 until 1982, and in June 1983, he graduated from the U.S. Army Command and General Staff College at Fort Leavenworth, Kansas.

In August 1983, Ward, who had attained the rank of major, went to Germany to serve with U.S. Army Europe and the Seventh Army. He returned to the United States in July 1987 to assume the duties of staff officer in the army's Office of the Deputy Chief of Staff for Logistics in Washington, D.C. Beginning in October 1988, he served with the 6th Infantry Division (Light) at Fort Wainwright, Alaska. After graduating from the U.S. Army War College in Carlisle Barracks, Pennsylvania, in June 1992, he was promoted to colonel.

Ward was a commander in Operation Restore Hope, a multinational effort conducted in 1992

President George W. Bush selected General William E. "Kip" Ward to be the first director of U.S. Africa Command (ARFICOM). *(Courtesy of the Department of Defense)*

and 1993, led by the United States and sanctioned by the United Nations, to ensure the delivery of food and other humanitarian aid to starving refugees in Somalia, where civil war had led to a breakdown of authority. Factions controlled separate territories, and warlords were commandeering supplies and shooting at relief workers. The UN considered this intervention a success, although it brought U.S. troops into armed conflict with the forces of coup leader General Mohamed Farrah Aidid, which led to 18 American deaths.

Beginning in July 1994, Ward again served in Washington, D.C., as executive officer to the vice chief of staff for the U.S. Army and as deputy director for operations in the National Military Command Center, J-3, Operations Directorate in the Office of the Joint Staff in the Pentagon. The directorate puts into action the various plans and policies of the Joint Staff, moving military forces throughout the world, briefing the nation's leaders, and providing a link between commanders in the field and the National Command Authority. After returning to Fort Bragg in 1996, as assistant divisional commander of the 82nd Airborne Division, Ward moved in 1998 to Cairo, Egypt, where he was chief of the Office of Military Cooperation in the U.S. Embassy. He was promoted to brigadier general on April 1, 1996, and to major general on February 1, 1999.

By the time Ward took over the command of the 25th Infantry Division (Light) at Schofield Barracks, Hawaii, he had gained a reputation for interacting closely with his soldiers and was known to participate alongside them in drills. In doing so, he was following the example set by his father. "I think probably the greatest thing that my dad taught me was that every individual has value and worth," he explained. "I just watched him treat people with dignity and respect." In Hawaii Ward also put Ben Affleck, Josh Hartnett, and other actors through the army's basic training as they prepared for roles in the 2002 film *Pearl Harbor.* He believed the experience would give the actors

a better understanding of what it means to be a soldier and make them goodwill ambassadors for the army.

In 2002, Lieutenant General Kip Ward commanded an international stabilization force in Bosnia and Herzegovina that was there to implement the 1995 peace agreement negotiated at Wright-Patterson Air Force Base in Dayton, Ohio, ending more than three years of war. He also safeguarded U.S. interests in the region in the aftermath of the September 11, 2001, terrorist attacks in the United States.

Ward again put his diplomatic skills to use in February 2005, when he assumed the duties of U.S. security coordinator in the Middle East. He played a key role in stabilizing relations between Israelis and Palestinians after Ariel Sharon, prime minister of Israel, and Mahmoud Abbas, chair of the Palestinian Authority, resolved to end their ongoing conflict. Israel agreed to withdraw from some occupied regions, and the Palestinians pledged to end militant attacks on Israelis. Ward's first task was to ensure a peaceful transition, in part by equipping and training the Palestinian security forces that would keep order in their territory. He also helped Israelis and Palestinians work together on the demolition of homes abandoned by Israelis in Gaza after the withdrawal. The process was completed by August 23, and Ward reported to the House International Relations Committee, "Disengagement did occur, and I think we all should take note of the fact that it occurred in an organized manner and very substantially not under fire as many feared that it would."

When Ward received his fourth star, on May 1, 2006, he remarked that his father, who died in 1999, would have been proud. Ward became the fifth African-American four-star general in the history of the U.S. Army, and with the promotion came his appointment as deputy commander of U.S. European Command (EUCOM), headquartered in Stuttgart, Germany. EUCOM maintains readiness to conduct military operations unilaterally or with partner nations in support of NATO, to promote regional stability, or to advance U.S. interests overseas. In his new position Ward represented the United States in meetings with heads of state and senior officials in foreign governments.

On October 1, 2007, when he became the first commander of AFRICOM, a new subcommand of EUCOM, Ward was the only serving African-American four-star general in the army. His goal as commander, he said, was "to build an enduring organization with regular and sustained engagement that benefits both the citizens of the United States and the citizens of the nations of Africa."

Ward's military decorations include the Distinguished Service Medal, Defense Superior Service Medal with Oak Leaf Cluster, Legion of Merit with two Oak Leaf Clusters, Defense Meritorious Service Medal, Meritorious Service Medal with six Oak leaf Clusters, Joint Service Commendation Medal, Army Commendation Medal with three Oak Leaf Clusters, and Army Achievement Medal with Oak Leaf Cluster.

Further Reading

"General William E. 'Kip' Ward." Headquarters United States Africa Command. Available online. URL: http://www.africom.mil/ward.asp. Downloaded on October 5, 2008.

"Morgan Alumnus to Head Africa Command." Morgan State University. Available online. URL: http://www.morgan.edu/Stories/tos_ward.htm. Downloaded on October 5, 2008.

"Statement of General William 'Kip' Ward, Commander, United States Africa Command, Before the House Armed Services Committee on 14 November 2007." House Armed Services Committee. Available online. URL: http://armedservices.house.gov/pdfs/FC111407/Ward_Testimony111407.pdf. Downloaded on October 5, 2008.

Thompson, Clifford, ed. *Current Biography Yearbook 2005*. New York: H. W. Wilson Co., 2005, pp. 593–595.

Watson, George
(1914–1943) *private with the 29th Quartermaster Regiment, Medal of Honor recipient*

All soldiers serving in wartime know that they might one day be required to act heroically, even those in labor battalions. Private George Watson, who was assigned to quartermaster duty in the South Pacific in World War II, saved several American servicemen when their ship was attacked by the Japanese, but he lost his own life in the effort. His actions earned him the Medal of Honor.

George Watson was born in Birmingham, Alabama. Desiring to serve his country in World War II, he enlisted in the army on September 11, 1942, and was assigned to the 2nd Battalion of the 29th Quartermaster Regiment, an African-American unit that was unloading ships and delivering supplies to white combat troops in the Far Eastern Theater.

On March 8, 1943, Private Watson and other members of his battalion were aboard the USAT *Jacob*, a Dutch steamer being used for U.S. Army transport, near Porloch Harbor, New Guinea. Much of New Guinea was under Japanese occupation, and Japan was eager to expand its defensive perimeter in the Pacific. Any ship being used by Americans was a target for Japanese bombers, including a defenseless one such as the *Jacob*. When the attack came, there was nothing the soldiers and sailors aboard could do except hope to survive.

At last the planes flew off, leaving the *Jacob* on fire and about to sink. The captain had no choice but to order the crew to abandon ship. In the smoke and panic, some crew members inflated the few life rafts that the *Jacob* carried, while other men, including George Watson, plunged into the sea.

Watson saw men swimming desperately toward the rafts or floundering in the water and in danger of drowning. Putting aside any concern for his own safety, he took hold of a soldier who could not swim, pulled him through the water to a raft, and helped him get aboard. He then swam away to rescue someone else and managed to save several lives, exhausting himself in the process. The life rafts moved away in order to avoid being pulled underwater by the *Jacob* when it sank, but Watson and the other men left in the sea were not so fortunate. The force of the ship going down carried them far below the surface, and Watson, who was just days away from his 29th birthday, was among those drowned.

George Watson became the first African American who served in World War II to be awarded the Distinguished Service Cross, the highest decoration given to any African American in that war, but such heroism merited greater recognition. That was the conclusion of a panel commissioned by the Defense Department in the 1990s to investigate whether any African-American World War II veterans deserved the Medal of Honor. Watson was one of seven men whom the panel determined should have received the nation's highest military decoration and the only one recognized for action in the Far Eastern Theater. President Bill Clinton presented the medals during a White House ceremony on January 13, 1997, although only one of the honored veterans, VERNON J. BAKER, was still living. Because Watson had no known next of kin, Army Sergeant Major Eugene McKinney accepted the medal on his behalf. Today, the U.S. Army Quartermaster Museum at Fort Lee, Virginia, houses Watson's medal.

Also in 1997, the U.S. Navy christened a ship in honor of Private George Watson. The USNS *Watson* is a large, medium-speed roll-on/roll-off ship, capable of carrying an entire army task force, including 58 tanks, 48 additional track vehicles, and more than 900 trucks and other wheeled vehicles for combat and humanitarian missions.

Further Reading

Hanna, Charles W. *African American Recipients of the Medal of Honor.* Jefferson, N.C.: McFarland and Co., 2002, pp. 135–136.

"Private George Watson." U.S. Army Quartermaster Center and School. Available online. URL: http://www.quartermaster.army.mil/OQMG/professional_bulletin/2001/Spring01/Private_George_Watson.htm. Downloaded on September 26, 2008.

West, Togo Dennis, Jr.

(1942–) *secretary of the army, secretary of veterans affairs*

Having been an attorney in both the army and the Defense Department, Togo D. West, Jr., was well qualified to serve as secretary of the army and secretary of veterans affairs in the administration of President Bill Clinton. He was the second African American in each of those cabinet posts.

Togo Dennis West, Jr., was born on June 21, 1942, in Winston-Salem, North Carolina. He was the son of Togo D. West, Sr., a high school principal, and Evelyn Carter West. While growing up, Togo West, Jr., was active in the Boy Scouts of America and attained the rank of Eagle Scout.

West attended Howard University in Washington, D.C., and graduated in 1965 with a bachelor of science degree in electrical engineering. Upon graduation, he was commissioned a second lieutenant in the U.S. Army Field Artillery Corps. He worked briefly as an electrical engineer with the Duquesne Light and Power Company in Pittsburgh before entering Howard University Law School. He gained legal experience while he studied, first as a patent researcher with the law firm Sughrue, Rothwell, Mion, Zinn, and McPeak and later as a legal intern with the Equal Employment Opportunity Commission and as a law clerk with the firm of Covington and Burling. He also found time to edit the *Howard Law Journal.* In 1966, he married his classmate Gail Estelle Berry, with whom he would have two daughters.

In 1968, West graduated from law school cum laude and first in his class and began a judicial clerkship with the Honorable Harold R. Tyler, judge of the U.S. District Court for the Southern

District of New York. He was called to active duty in the army in 1969 and assigned to the Judge Advocate General's Corps, which provides legal services for the army and its soldiers.

West returned to civilian life in 1973 and was hired by Covington and Burling as an associate attorney. Washington, D.C., offers many opportunities to attorneys wishing to pursue government careers, and in 1975 West joined the U.S. Department of Justice as an associate deputy attorney general. In 1977, he put to use his experience with military law as a general counsel for the Department of the Navy. In 1979, he became special assistant to the secretary of defense, and in 1980 general counsel for the Department of Defense.

West, a Democrat, resumed the private practice of law in 1981, following the election of Ronald Reagan as president, becoming a managing partner at the Washington office of Patterson, Belknap, Webb, and Tyler. In 1990, he went to work for the Northrop Corporation, a defense contractor. As the senior vice president for government relations, he was Northrop's most influential lobbyist.

The next Democratic president, Bill Clinton, appointed West to be secretary of the army in September 1993. The nomination faced little opposition in the Senate, and in November West was sworn in as the 16th secretary of the army. He was the second African American to hold this cabinet post; the first was CLIFFORD ALEXANDER, JR. It was West's responsibility to ensure that the army fulfilled its role in the post–Cold War era, to remain ready to fight and win the nation's wars and to undertake peacekeeping and humanitarian missions.

West had been on the job a short time when female soldiers complained of sexual harassment by drill instructors at Aberdeen Proving Ground in Maryland. Under West's leadership, the Department of the Army operated a sexual abuse hotline at Aberdeen and received thousands of reports of sexual misconduct at army posts nationwide. West launched a broad investigation of army policies and procedures regarding sexual harassment. "Sexual misconduct is incompatible with our traditional values of professionalism, equal opportunity and respect for human dignity, to which every soldier must adhere," he said. There were also criminal investigations that resulted in 12 indictments at Aberdeen. In May 1997, Delmar Simpson, a staff sergeant at Aberdeen, was convicted of rape and sentenced to 25 years in a military prison.

Togo West next served in Clinton's cabinet as secretary of veterans affairs. He was acting secretary beginning on January 2, 1998, and was sworn in as the second African-American secretary of veterans affairs on May 5, 1998. (The first was JESSE BROWN.) West's performance in this position brought criticism from Congress and veterans groups, however. His detractors found fault with his failure to secure an adequate budget for his department and with his frequent and costly travel at government expense. On July 7, 1999, West informed the White House that he planned to leave the cabinet. In July 2000, he returned to Covington and Burling, where he specialized in cases involving government-business relationships.

As an army officer West received the Legion of Merit and the Meritorious Service Medal. His civilian honors include two awards of the Department of Defense Medal for Distinguished Public Service, the Department of the Army Decoration for Distinguished Civilian Service, the Department of the Navy Award for Distinguished Public Service, and the Department of Air Force Decoration for Exceptional Civilian Service.

From 2004 through 2007, West was president and chief executive officer of the Joint Center for Political and Economic Studies, a policy research institution that focuses on issues of concern to African Americans. In 2007, he cochaired with John O. Marsh, Jr., another former secretary of the army, the Independent Review Group, which was appointed by Defense Secretary Robert M. Gates to investigate facilities and services for veterans of the Iraq war at Walter Reed Army Medical Center in Washington, D.C. The group presented evidence of a deteriorating building; an undersized, overworked, and inadequately trained staff; and negligent leadership. Its recommendations included immediate repairs and acceleration of plans to close the facility.

Effective January 22, 2008, West joined the board of directors of Bristol-Myers Squibb Company, a manufacturer of biopharmaceuticals and related health care products. He was also chairman of TLI Leadership Group, a consulting firm specializing in national and homeland security issues, and Noblis, a nonprofit organization dedicated to scientific, technological, and strategic problem solving. In November 2009, Secretary of Defense Robert Gates appointed West and retired admiral Vernon Clark to lead an investigation of the November 5, 2009, mass shooting at Fort Hood, Texas, that left 13 people dead and 30 wounded.

Further Reading

"Bristol-Myers Squibb Names Togo D. West, Jr. to Board of Directors." Reuters. Available online. URL: http://www.reuters.com/article/pressRelease/idUS216334+22-Jan-2008+PRN20080122. Downloaded on September 27, 2008.

Phelps, Shirelle, ed. *Contemporary Black Biography.* Vol. 16. Detroit: Gale Research, 1998, pp. 226–229.

Vogel, Steve. "Panel Calls for Closing Walter Reed Sooner." *Washington Post,* April 12, 2007, p. A1.

"West Reveals Plan to Resign VA Post." *Washington Post,* July 8, 1999, p. A23.

White, William Andrew

(1874–1936) *chaplain with Canada's No. 2 Construction Battalion*

The Reverend William White enlisted in the No. 2 Construction Battalion, Canada's only black battalion, to serve his country in World War I. As the unit's chaplain and a captain, he was the sole black commissioned officer in the British Expeditionary Force during that war.

William Andrew White was born in Williamsburg, Virginia, in 1874. As a young man he went to Baltimore, where he met a Canadian schoolteacher whose loving descriptions of Nova Scotia inspired in him a desire to see the province. At the turn of the 20th century, White enrolled in Acadia University in Wolfville, Nova Scotia. In 1906, he became the first black to graduate from the school, receiving bachelor of arts and bachelor of divinity degrees. Also in 1906, he married Izie Dora White, a woman from Mill Village, Nova Scotia, who happened to share his last name. When World War I began in 1914, William White was an ordained minister serving the congregation of Zion Baptist Church in Truro, Nova Scotia.

Motivated by patriotism, black and white Canadians alike volunteered for military service in the war. Although it was the military's policy to accept recruits regardless of race, the army rejected many African Canadians. Some persistent blacks gained acceptance into the army only to be sent home when they reported for training. For example, in November 1915, 20 African-Canadian recruits from St. John, Nova Scotia, who arrived at Camp Sussex in New Brunswick were told by the officer second in command to leave immediately. Not only did a majority of white Canadian soldiers object to serving alongside blacks, but also it was widely believed that blacks lacked the necessary loyalty and ability to fight in France.

In December 1915, White appealed to Lieutenant Colonel W. H. Allen, commander of the 106th Battalion, Nova Scotia Rifles, to accept African-Canadian recruits. Allen suggested that White raise a black platoon and promised to take it into the battalion, but soon afterward he received word from Ottawa that there were to be no distinctions in enlistment based on color. He therefore integrated the 16 soldiers White had recruited into his battalion, with the result that a number of whites who had planned to enlist changed their minds.

In April 1916, Major General W. G. Gwatkin, chief of the general staff in Ottawa, proposed the formation of a black noncombat battalion. On

May 11, the British War Office agreed to accept such a unit, and on July 5, the Canadian army established the No. 2 Construction Battalion.

Despite their patriotism and willingness to fight, African Canadians were slow to join the new battalion. For one thing, they remained angry about the army's rejection of black volunteers; for another, they opposed being required to serve in a segregated labor battalion. William White spoke in favor of the unit to African-Canadian audiences and encouraged men to sign up. On February 1, 1917, White himself enlisted in the No. 2 Construction Battalion, and the army made him the unit's chaplain with the honorary rank of captain.

By March 17, 1917, when the black battalion was ordered overseas, it consisted of 605 soldiers. Although most were from Nova Scotia, they represented all parts of Canada. William White was the only black among the battalion's 19 officers, and he would be the only black officer in the British Expeditionary Force during World War I.

The men of No. 2 Construction Battalion embarked for Liverpool on March 28 aboard the SS *Southland*, a troop-transport ship. They arrived in France in May and were assigned to No. 5 District of the Canadian Forestry Corps. They served honorably and spent the war supplying lumber for trenches, laying railroad lines, and constructing roads and bridges. Some soldiers were killed or injured in construction accidents or after coming into contact with unexploded ammunition. When their work brought the men close to the front lines, artillery fire and poison gas also took a toll. Before the war ended, several of the battalion's soldiers transferred to combat units.

Following the armistice, William White served as pastor of the Cornwallis Street Baptist Church in Halifax, Nova Scotia, where he and Izie White raised 11 children. The No. 2 Construction Battalion was disbanded in 1920, and Canadian military personnel never again served in segregated units.

In the years of the Great Depression, William White organized concerts in a local theater to raise money for his church. His daughter Helen played the organ in these programs, and his daughter Portia, who would go on to have a successful career as a concert singer, acted as choir director. The Reverend William White died of cancer in 1936.

Further Reading

"Black Battalion." A Scattering of Seeds: The Creation of Canada. Available online. URL: http://www.whitepinepictures.com/seeds/iii/32/sidebar.html. Downloaded on September 27, 2008.

"Canada's Black Contribution and the Second Construction Battalion." Veterans Affairs Canada. Available online. URL: http://www.acc-vac.gc.ca/remembers/sub.cfm?source=feature/black_history/battalion. Downloaded on September 27, 2008.

Levitt, Fern, director. *Captain of Souls: Reverend William White*. Brooklyn, N.Y.: First Run/Icarus, 2000.

Ruck, Calvin W. *The Black Battalion, 1916–1920: Canada's Best Kept Military Secret*. Halifax, Nova Scotia: Nimbus Publishing, 1987.

Williams, Cathay
(Cathy Williams, Cathey Williams, William Cathey, William Cathay)
(1842–unknown) *female Buffalo Soldier*

Working as an army cook and laundress during the Civil War introduced Cathay Williams to military life. After the war, she disguised herself as a man to join the 38th U.S. Infantry as a private. In so doing, she became the only documented African-American woman to serve in the U.S. Army in the 19th century.

Cathay Williams was born in 1842 near Independence, Missouri. Her father was a free man, and her mother, Martha Williams, was the slave of a wealthy farmer named William Johnson. Johnson moved his household to Jefferson City, Missouri, when Cathay was a small child, and there she served him as a domestic worker. Johnson died sometime before the start of the Civil War.

During the first year of the war, Colonel William P. Benton of the 13th Army Corps pressed Cathay Williams into service as a cook. Although she protested that she knew nothing about cooking, the army brought her to Little Rock, Arkansas, where she learned to prepare meals for the officers. As a paid servant, Williams traveled with the army to the Battle of Pea Ridge, which was fought in northwest Arkansas, just a few miles from the Missouri line, on March 7 and 8, 1862. In this battle to determine whether Missouri would remain under Union control, 16,000 Confederates led by Major General Earl Van Dorn fought 10,250 federal soldiers commanded by Brigadier General Samuel R. Curtis. The battle was a victory for the North that left approximately 1,300 Union and 2,000 Confederate soldiers dead or wounded. In the spring of 1864, Williams witnessed the burning of an estimated 150,000 bales of southern cotton by Union troops at Shreveport, Louisiana, and the destruction of Confederate gunboats on the Red River.

The Civil War took Williams to New Orleans, to Savannah and Macon in Georgia, and then to Washington, D.C., and Virginia, where she cooked and laundered clothes for General Philip Sheridan and his officers while their army drove the Confederates out of the Shenandoah Valley. She spent the final months of the war at Jefferson Barracks, Missouri, a fort built in the 1850s.

On November 15, 1866, the five-foot, nine-inch Cathay Williams disguised herself as a man and enlisted as William Cathey in the 38th U.S. Infantry, a short-lived African-American army regiment formed after the Civil War. (The 38th became part of the 24th Infantry in 1869.) Many of the 12,500 black men who joined the army after the war sought jobs and living conditions better than those available to civilians, and Cathay Williams was of the same mind. "I wanted to make my own living and not be dependent on relations or friends," she told a reporter for the *St. Louis Daily Times* in 1876. She also wanted to be near a cousin and "a particular friend" who both belonged

to the regiment. These two soldiers kept her secret throughout her period of enlistment.

On February 17, 1867, Williams was one of 76 privates mustered into the newly formed Company A of the 38th Infantry. Her military service entailed long marches from one army post to the next. In the early spring of 1867, the soldiers of Company A marched to Fort Riley, Kansas, and stayed there until June, when they set out for Fort Harker, Kansas. They next marched to Fort Union, New Mexico, 536 miles away, arriving July 20. They spent the days from September 7 through October 1 marching to Fort Cummings, New Mexico, where they would be stationed for eight months. On June 6, 1868, they began the 47-mile trek to Fort Bayard, New Mexico. Between marches they drilled, trained, performed garrison duty, and scouted for warring Indians. There is no record of Company A engaging in combat while Williams was a member.

Although Williams kept up with the company on marches, she was chronically ill during her time of service. She was hospitalized five times for complaints ranging from rheumatism to "itch," and she later claimed also to have contracted smallpox while in uniform. Curiously, although she frequently sought medical treatment, army doctors failed to discover that she was a woman. On October 14, 1868, after serving less than two years of a three-year enlistment, William Cathey was discharged from the army on grounds of disability. The surgeon at Fort Bayard noted that Cathey was "feeble both physically and mentally, and much of the time quite unfit for duty." According to Williams's 1876 newspaper account, the army discovered her deception just prior to her discharge.

Cathay Williams resumed life as a woman and worked as a cook and laundress at locations in New Mexico and Colorado. In the 1870s she made Trinidad, Colorado, her permanent home. In June 1891, she applied to the U.S. Pension Bureau for an invalid's pension, claiming to suffer from deafness, rheumatism, and neuralgia resulting from her military service. A doctor employed by the Pension Bureau who examined Williams on September 8, 1891, reported that she was able to hear and showed no evidence of rheumatism or neuralgia. He did observe, however, that she walked with a crutch because all of her toes had been amputated. (The circumstances of these amputations are unknown.) In February 1892, the Pension Bureau rejected Williams's claim on the grounds that no service-related disability existed.

Nothing is known about Cathay Williams's life after 1892. Because her name is missing from the 1900 U.S. census records for Trinidad, Colorado, it is likely that she died before that year. In 2007, she was inducted into the National Cowboys of Color Museum Hall of Fame.

Further Reading

"Cathay Williams." Missouri Women's Council. Available online. URL: http://www.womenscouncil. org/cd_web/Williams.html. Downloaded on September 27, 2008.

"Cathay Williams, Female Buffalo Soldier." Buffalo Soldiers and Indian Wars. Available online. URL: http://www.buffalosoldier.net/CathayWilliams-FemaleBufalloSoldierWithDocuments.htm. Downloaded on September 27, 2008.

Tucker, Phillip Thomas. *Cathy Williams: From Slave to Buffalo Soldier.* Mechanicsburg, Pa.: Stackpole Books, 2002.

"2007 Hall of Fame Inductee: Cathay Williams." National Cowboys of Color Museum and Hall of Fame. Available online. URL: http://www.cowboys ofcolor.org/profile.php?ID=1. Downloaded on September 27, 2008.

Wilson, Johnnie Edward

(1944–) *four-star general, commander of U.S. Army Materiel Command*

In 1961, Johnnie E. Wilson was a 17-year-old army private hoping to attend college on the G.I. bill. Twenty-eight years later, he retired from active duty as the second African-American four-star general in army history and head of U.S. Army Materiel Command.

Johnnie Edward Wilson was born on February 4, 1944, in Baton Rouge, Louisiana. Soon after his birth, his family moved north to Lorain, Ohio, where his father found work in a steel mill. His mother worked part-time in a movie theater while Johnnie was growing up. The Wilson family—parents, four girls, and eight boys—lived in a three-bedroom unit in a housing project. Home was crowded and money was tight, but Wilson has fond memories of his early family life. "We respected each other. We paid attention," he said. "Paying attention meant listening and learning from others in the family."

As a teenager, Johnnie Wilson dreamed of going to college, but he knew his family could never afford the tuition. Military service offered a way to achieve his goal, so Wilson decided to enlist in the army, earn money, and get financial aid for his education. In August 1961, at age 17, he joined the army with his mother's consent, never imagining that he would pursue a military career, much less achieve four-star rank.

Wilson spent six years with the 7th Special Forces Group at Fort Bragg, North Carolina, and rose to the rank of staff sergeant. Soldiers in Army Special Forces, commonly known as "Green Berets," train in unconventional warfare, such as guerrilla tactics. Wilson entered Officer Candidate School and upon completing the course on May 31, 1967, was commissioned a second lieutenant in the Ordnance Corps. This branch of the army is responsible for the production and maintenance of weapons systems and munitions. It also disposes of unwanted explosives.

Wilson was assigned to Company A of the 782nd Maintenance Battalion, 82nd Airborne Division, at Fort Bragg, first as mechanical maintenance officer and then as commander. He was promoted to first lieutenant on May 31, 1968, and to captain exactly one year later. In October 1969, Wilson went to Vietnam with Company C of the

173rd Support Battalion (Airborne), 173rd Airborne Brigade, first as assistant brigade supply officer and then as commander.

From Vietnam, Wilson went to the U.S. Army Ordnance School at Aberdeen Proving Ground in Maryland, where in January 1971 he completed the Ordnance Officer Advanced Course. He continued his education at the University of Nebraska at Omaha, earning a bachelor's degree in business administration in December 1973. The following month, the army sent Wilson to Europe as commander of Company B, 123rd Maintenance Battalion of the 1st Armored Division. He later served as the battalion's technical supply officer.

Wilson was promoted to major on June 9, 1976, and in August 1976 completed studies at the Command and General Staff College at Fort Leavenworth, Kansas. In 1977, he earned a master's degree in logistics management from the Florida Institute of Technology in Melbourne, Florida. His knowledge acquired through education and years of military experience had prepared Wilson in November 1977 for positions in the Ordnance Assignment Branch, Combat Service Support Division, of the Army Military Personnel Center at Alexandria, Virginia. Starting as professional development officer, he moved up to personnel management officer and then chief.

On July 13, 1980, Wilson was promoted to lieutenant colonel; in December 1980, he was placed in command of the 709th Maintenance Battalion at Fort Lewis, Washington. In 1983, he attended the Industrial College of the Armed Forces at Fort McNair in Washington, D.C. This school offers a course at the postgraduate level in national security strategy, with emphasis on acquisition of resources.

Over the next several years, Wilson held command positions in Europe and the United States. He was promoted to colonel on November 1, 1984, and to brigadier general on September 1, 1989. In July 1990, he became commanding general of the U.S. Ordnance Center and School at Aberdeen Proving Ground, which provides mechanical

maintenance training to more than 20,000 U.S. and foreign personnel each year. Beginning in 1994, as deputy chief of staff for logistics, Wilson was responsible for army logistics all over the world.

In 1996, the army announced that General Johnnie E. Wilson was to head U.S. Army Materiel Command in Arlington, Virginia. This command, employing more than 60,000 people in 42 states and several foreign countries, acquires and distributes rations, weapons, and equipment to army personnel worldwide. Its staff develops and improves equipment and remains ready to support U.S. troops at any location.

The year 1998 marked the 50th anniversary of Executive Order 9981, the document with which President Harry S. Truman ended segregation in the U.S. armed forces. Reflecting on Truman's action and its impact, Wilson said, "We have come a long way." Without equal opportunity in the military, he added, "the nation wouldn't have people like Colin Powell."

As he moved from one army assignment to another, Johnnie Wilson made friends among his peers and gave guidance and advice to underlings. In 1999, when he retired from active duty as a four-star general, 1,200 people came together at Fort Myer, Virginia, to honor him. (Wilson was the second African-American four-star general in the army; the first was General ROSCOE ROBINSON, JR.) On the occasion of his retirement, Wilson said, "Soldiering requires respect, doing what is right and protecting all that our nation stands for. . . . There are few higher callings than to be able to follow in the footsteps of soldiers past. . . ." In civilian life, Wilson became president and chief organizational officer of Dimensions International, Inc., an international information technology company based in Alexandria, Virginia.

General Wilson's military decorations include the Legion of Merit, Bronze Star, and Meritorious Service Medal with two Oak Leaf Clusters. In 1996, he received the NAACP's Meritorious Service Award.

Further Reading

"General (Ret.) Johnnie Edward Wilson: Former Commander, U.S. Army Materiel Command." Redstone Arsenal, AL. Available online. URL: http://www.redstone.army.mil/history/integrate/wilson.htm. Downloaded on September 27, 2008.

Hawkins, Walter L. *Black American Military Leaders.* Jefferson, N.C.: McFarland and Co., 2007, pp. 519–520.

"President and Chief Operating Officer: General [Ret.] Johnnie E. Wilson." Dimensions International, Inc. Available online. URL: http://www.dimen-intl.com/about/jwilson.htm. Downloaded on September 27, 2008.

Woodward, Luther

(unknown–unknown) *decorated Marine Corps private*

Private Luther Woodward shows off his Bronze Star, which was later upgraded to a Silver Star. *(National Archives)*

Sent to Guam as part of a black service unit assisting white combat troops, Private Luther Woodward tracked down a group of Japanese soldiers, killed two, and wounded a third. He was awarded the Silver Star, the highest military decoration given to an African-American marine in World War II.

At the time the United States entered World War II, African Americans had never been permitted to join the Marine Corps. General Thomas Holcomb, commandant of the Marine Corps, was determined to keep them out, saying, "[T]he negro race has every opportunity now to satisfy its aspirations for combat in the Army. . . ." A presidential executive order soon led to a change in policy, however, and on August 26, 1942, the first African-American marine recruits arrived at the Montford Point, North Carolina, training center that had been built so that blacks might train apart from whites.

The Marine Corps formed two African-American combat units, the 51st and 52nd Defense Battalions, but prepared the majority of African-American recruits for non-combat duty. The marines needed an efficient way to bring supplies from factories and warehouses in the United States to men fighting in distant parts of the world, and created a workable system by assigning the incoming African Americans to depot and ammunition companies. Between March and September 1943, the marines formed and deployed 10 depot companies; the first ammunition companies were formed after that period. These companies loaded ammunition on and off ships, transported it to the dumps where it was stored, and delivered it to the troops on the front lines.

Ironically, the two African-American defense battalions never saw action, whereas the marines in depot and ammunition companies, who were armed with rifles, machine guns, or carbines, witnessed some intense battles and were often inserted into the front lines alongside their white peers. Their performance prompted Lieutenant General Alexander A. Vandergrift, who had succeeded Holcomb as Marine Corps commandant, to say, on January 1, 1944, "The Negro Marines are no longer on trial. They are Marines, period."

In civilian life, Luther Woodward had been a truck driver in Memphis, Tennessee, and had been born and raised in the bayou country of Mississippi. He joined the Marine Corps and after two months of training at Montford Point was assigned as a private to the 4th Ammunition Company, which was deployed to the western Pacific to assist in the recapture of the Mariana Islands from the Japanese.

On June 15, 1944, the marines and the army joined forces to launch an assault on Saipan, Tinian, and Guam, three principal islands in this group. Guam, a U.S. possession, had been under Japanese control since December 1941. On July 21, 1944, the 4th Ammunition Company assisted the 1st Provisional Marine Brigade, a white combat unit, on the southern beachhead of Guam. The men of Woodward's company set up the brigade's ammunition dump and took turns performing guard duty. Such vigilance was warranted: That night the African-American marines killed 14 Japanese soldiers armed with explosives who were attempting to destroy the dump. Three days later, three members of the company were wounded by fire from Japanese guns while working on the beaches.

By August 10, the U.S. forces had accomplished their objective on Guam. The fact that the Navy Unit Commendation awarded to the 1st Marine Provisional Brigade included the 4th Ammunition Company attests to the crucial role this company played. Brigadier General Lemuel C. Shepherd, Jr., commander of the 1st Provisional Brigade, commented that the 4th Ammunition Company "contributed in large measure to the successful and rapid movement of combat supplies in this . . . operation."

Guam had been declared safe and secure, but many Japanese remained on the island, hiding in the dense jungle vegetation. Private Woodward proved himself to be unusually adept at tracking them down. One afternoon, he spotted recent footprints around the ammunition dump and followed them into the jungle to a hut where six Japanese had found shelter. He opened fire, killing one enemy soldier and wounding another while the rest ran for safety. Woodward returned to camp and came back with five additional African-American marines to hunt down the four Japanese soldiers who remained at large. Woodward found and killed one of the four, and one of his companions killed another.

Woodward's actions earned him the Bronze Star, which was presented to him on January 11, 1945. The award was later upgraded to a Silver Star, making Private Luther Woodward the highest-decorated African-American marine to serve in World War II.

Luther Woodward survived the war. In all, nine African-American marines were killed in action or died of wounds received in World War II, 78 were wounded in action, and nine suffered combat fatigue. Nearly all belonged to service units.

Further Reading

Fischer, Perry E., and Brooks E. Gray. *Blacks and Whites—Together through Hell: U.S. Marines in World War II.* Turlock, Calif.: Millsmont Publishing, 1993, p. 32.

Shaw, Henry I., Jr. and Ralph W. Donnelly. *Blacks in the Marine Corps.* Washington, D.C.: U.S. Marine Corps, 1975, pp. 36–37.

Wilborn, Thom. "Montford Point Marines." *DAV Magazine* 47, no. 1 (January/February 2005), pp. 14–16.

Wright, Bruce McMarion

(1918–2005) *decorated World War II veteran, New York state supreme court justice*

Bruce M. Wright spent a lifetime fighting for what he believed was right. He battled the Nazis during World War II, earning decorations for valor, and protested an army that treated blacks and whites unequally. Later, as a judge, he generated criticism for allegedly displaying leniency toward African Americans who came before his bench. Ironically, Wright said in 1991, "All I ever wanted in life was to be a poet."

Bruce McMarion Wright was born in Princeton, New Jersey, on December 19, 1918, the son of A. Louise Thigpen Wright, who was white, and Bruce Alleyne Summers, a baker from the Caribbean island of Montserrat. Young Bruce was a bright student who hoped to become a poet and professor, but it took him a while to find his educational niche. In 1936, he enrolled in Virginia State University in Petersburg, Virginia, but he was expelled for expressing irreverent opinions in the college newspaper. He then had an opportunity to study at Princeton University on a scholarship but declined when he was made to feel unwelcome because of his race. Wright at last settled at Lincoln University and decided to pursue a career in law. Poetry would remain a lifelong avocation, however.

After graduating in 1942, Wright joined the army and was sent to Camp Rucker, Alabama, for basic training. A champion of justice and equality even in his youth, he was shocked at the unfair treatment of African Americans in the segregated army. On one occasion, officers awakened the black soldiers in camp at 2 A.M. and ordered them into the woods to extinguish a fire started accidentally by a white artillery unit. Wright spent 90 days in the stockade for protesting this blatantly unfair order. He also wrote letters to the *New York Times* describing the racism at Camp Rucker and to New York congressman Adam Clayton Powell, Jr., requesting a transfer, but the army made sure that these letters were never mailed.

In February 1943, his training complete, Wright was sent to Great Britain as a medical corpsman with an African-American quartermaster battalion. The African Americans sent to Britain encountered a population free of the racial prejudice that was so common at home. Wright befriended an English soldier with connections in publishing who arranged for the printing in 1944 of Wright's first poetry collection, *From the Shaken Tower,* which was edited by poet Langston Hughes.

Wright was in England when the army, needing combat troops, asked for black volunteers to fight with white units. General Dwight D. Eisenhower, commander of the U.S. forces in Europe, promised that any African American who volunteered for combat duty would never return to a service unit. Eager to fight for his nation's cause, demonstrate African Americans' abilities, and perhaps create opportunities for himself and others, Wright was among the volunteers. He was one of three African Americans assigned to Company K of the 26th Regiment, 1st Infantry. For the first time, African Americans were wearing the "Big Red One," the insignia of the 1st Infantry, the oldest continuously serving unit in the army.

As an infantryman, Wright was among the third wave of soldiers to hit Omaha Beach, on the Normandy Coast, during the D day invasion of June 6, 1944. As he waded ashore under a rain of artillery shells, he encountered a scene of horror. Around him panicking soldiers drowned in four feet of water. Ahead he saw tanks burning on the beach and bodies tossing in the surf. Wright was wounded seriously enough in the assault to require a 30-day stay in a British hospital. He was awarded the Purple Heart but, modest about his heroism, he declined to describe the actions that merited this or subsequent military decorations.

The 1st Infantry moved into Belgium and by December had reached the heavily wooded Ardennes region, on the border with Germany. There, the 1st took part in the Battle of the Bulge, the largest land battle of World War II, involving 500,000 U.S. soldiers, 55,000 British, and 600,000 Germans. It was January before the Allies forced the Germans to retreat. At one point during this long encounter, Wright crawled across a minefield, exposing himself to enemy fire, in an attempt to save the life of a wounded comrade. In so doing, he earned a Bronze Star and a second Purple Heart.

Following Germany's surrender, the 1st Infantry again became a segregated unit. The army posted the unit's white soldiers at the Nuremberg war crimes trials and sent its black volunteers to a relocation camp on the outskirts of Paris to dig sewage trenches with German prisoners, breaking

Eisenhower's promise. Wright was one of 30 African-American soldiers who protested the assignment by sleeping in foxholes outside the camp. Signing himself "Adgee Taitor," Wright posted open letters denouncing the injustice. "[These soldiers] volunteered for combat infantry at a time when they felt that their country needed them," he wrote. "Now they are being neglected and cast off, much in the manner of cheap shoes which are no longer serviceable." Wright was accused of inciting to riot and assigned to laundry detail but went AWOL. He was quickly apprehended and sentenced to a tour in an army prison.

The sentence served, Wright boarded a troop ship to return to the United States, wearing his uniform and medals, only to be insulted by a white navy officer. The slur was enough to send him AWOL again, and this time he disappeared into Paris, where he befriended Leopold Senghor, the future president of Senegal, who was living as a poet. The army caught up with Wright 18 months later and sent him to Fort Dix, New Jersey, in chains, making sure he had no chance to escape again.

Returning to civilian life, Wright attended New York University Law School. He graduated in 1950 and was admitted to the bar in New York. He practiced law privately until 1967, when he went to work for the New York City Human Resources Administration. In 1970, Mayor John V. Lindsay appointed him as a judge in the New York City criminal court. Wright served in that position through 1974 and again from 1978 until 1979. He was also a judge in the city's civil court system from 1974 until 1978 and from 1980 until 1982. Wright was a controversial figure on the bench who earned the nickname Turn-'Em-Loose Bruce for handing out light sentences and exercising leniency in setting bail when the accused was African-American. Wright insisted, however, that he was correcting a legal system "infested with racism." In 1983, he was appointed to the New York State supreme court. He retired 15 years later.

Wright's second poetry collection. *Repetitions*, was published in 1980. In 1987, he published a best-selling commentary on the criminal justice system, *Black Robes, White Justice*; in 1996, he published a memoir, *Black Justice in a White World*. Wright died in 2005, at age 86.

Further Reading

Bigelow, Barbara Carlisle, ed. *Contemporary Black Biography.* Vol. 3. Detroit: Gale Research, 1993, pp. 260–262.

Payne, Les. "Unequal Justice." *Essence* 22, no. 7 (November 1991), pp. 52–54, 110.

Smith, Michael Steven. "NLG Friend Judge Bruce M. Wright Dies at 86." *National Lawyers Guild New York City News* (fall 2005), p. 7.

Wright, Bruce McMarion. *Black Justice in a White World: A Memoir.* New York: Barricade Books, 1996.

———. *Black Robes, White Justice.* Secaucus, N.J.: L. Stuart, 1987.

Y

Young, Charles
(1864–1922) *army colonel, third African American to graduate from West Point*

Although the army made his race a formidable obstacle, Charles Young graduated from the U.S. Military Academy and over the course of a 29-year military career rose to the rank of colonel. He served in the western and eastern United States and in three foreign countries.

Charles Young was born on March 12, 1864, in Mays Lick, Kentucky, to Armintie and Gabriel Young, who were enslaved plantation workers. Gabriel Young fought in the Civil War as a private in Company F, 5th Regiment of Colored Artillery, and following his discharge from the army in February 1866, moved with his wife, child, and extended family to Ripley, Ohio.

There, encouraged by his grandmother, Charles excelled as a student and graduated with honors from Ripley High School. In 1882, he became a teacher at his former elementary school, but soon afterward, at the urging of his principal, he took the qualifying examination for the U.S. Military Academy when it was offered at Hillsboro, Ohio. He received the second highest grade and was accepted by the academy on May 20, 1884. At the time, only two African Americans had graduated from West Point: HENRY OSSIAN FLIPPER in 1877 and JOHN HANKS ALEXANDER in 1887.

Like those two soldiers and other African Americans who had entered the academy but left before graduating, Young endured insults and ostracism because of his race. He persevered for five lonely years, and on August 31, 1889, became the third African American to graduate from West Point. He began his army career as a second lieutenant at Fort Robinson, Nebraska, with the 9th Cavalry, an African-American regiment.

The lone black officer in the army continued to be snubbed by his white peers. An efficiency report from Fort Duchesne, Utah, where Young was stationed from 1890 until 1894, noted that he was "liked and respected but very much alone socially." Young next served as an instructor of military science at Wilberforce University, a historically black school in Ohio, and was promoted to first lieutenant in 1896.

In 1898, Young was assigned to Camp Algers in Virginia, where he had whites under his command. The white soldiers resented taking orders from a black officer, and one even refused to salute Young. In a particularly insulting incident, the camp commander placed Young's jacket on a chair and ordered the soldier to salute. The commander then explained that it was possible to show respect to the uniform and not the man wearing it.

Young continued to pursue an army career despite such humiliation and was promoted to captain in 1894. With his wife, the former Ada Barr, whom he had married in 1903, he traveled in 1904 to Port-au-Prince, Haiti, where he was to be his nation's first African-American military attaché. Young had an aptitude for languages and spoke French, the official language of Haiti, as well as Italian, Spanish, and German. He also had a reading knowledge of Latin and Greek. He impressed Haitian officials with his "distinguished bearing and charming manners," according to a contemporary press report.

Not only did Young perform his official duty as military attaché, which was to observe and assess the readiness of the Haitian armed forces, but also he produced maps of Haiti and neighboring Santo Domingo and reported on the culture of their shared island for the U.S. government. Young even wrote a play based on the life of the Haitian revolutionary leader, François-Dominique-Toussaint Louverture, and a book titled *Military Morale of Nations and Races* (1912), a study of military efficiency throughout the world in which he concluded that a soldier's effectiveness bears no relation to his race.

Young reported for duty with the War Department in Washington, D.C., in 1907, the year his son, Charles Noel, was born. A daughter, Marie, was born in 1909, while Young was in the Philippines commanding a squadron of the 9th Cavalry that was stationed there. In 1912, Young became military attaché to Liberia. Upon accepting the post, he wrote to Booker T. Washington, "I am always willing to aid in any work for the good of the country in general and our race in particular, whether the race be found in Africa or the United States."

With his customary zeal, he reorganized the Liberian army, explored remote regions of that African nation, reported to the U.S. government on the native people, and supervised road construction. His activities in Liberia earned him in 1916 the Spingarn Medal, which is presented annually by the NAACP for outstanding achievement by an African American.

Charles Young, shown here in a photograph taken between 1915 and 1920, graduated from the U.S. Military Academy in 1884 and attained the rank of colonel in 1917. *(Library of Congress)*

Young next went to Mexico with the all-black 10th Cavalry to take part in the Punitive Expedition of 1916, the unsuccessful mission undertaken to capture the Mexican revolutionary Pancho Villa. On April 12, 1916, he brought a squadron to the aid of Major Frank Tompkins of the 13th U.S. Cavalry who, although badly wounded, had been leading his men in repelling an attack by Mexican government forces near the town of Parral. Tompkins acknowledged that he won the battle only because of the help received from the African Americans, and he is reported to have said, "By God, Young, I could kiss every black face out there." Young allegedly replied, "Well, Tompkins, if you want to, you may start with me."

Young was promoted to lieutenant colonel in 1916 and to colonel in 1917, and served briefly as commander of Fort Huachuca, Arizona. He had become a hero to the African-American community. Writing to him on June 18, 1917, EMMETT J. SCOTT, secretary of the Tuskegee Institute, said, "All of us, in fact the whole race, are proud of you beyond measure because of the splendid record you have made. You are our one proof of what black soldiers can do in the way of accepting responsibilities as officers and of living up to the traditions of West Point if given a chance."

Young was eager to command forces in France during World War I. Rather than place an African-American officer in such a position of responsibility, however, and possibly make him eligible for promotion to general, the army ordered Young to undergo a physical examination and found him to have high blood pressure and the early signs of kidney disease—and to be unfit for service in the war.

Unwilling to accept the command offered to him of an African-American unit in the United States, Colonel Charles Young retired from the army after 29 years of service. He nevertheless set out to prove his fitness for European duty and over 16 days in June 1918 traveled 497 miles by foot and horseback from his home in Wilberforce, Ohio, to Washington, D.C. "I there offered my services gladly at the risk of life, which has no value to me if I cannot give it for the great ends for which the United States is striving," he said.

Colonel Young returned to active duty, and the army that had pronounced him too ill to serve in France sent him once more to Liberia as military attaché. It was to be his last overseas assignment: He died of kidney disease on January 8, 1922, while on an exploratory trip to Lagos, Nigeria.

Writing about Young in the February 1922 issue of *The Crisis*, W. E. B. DuBois noted, "Steadily, unswervingly, he did his duty. And Duty to him, as to few modern men, was spelled in capitals. It was his lodestar, his soul; and neither force nor reason swerved him from it." Young's body was returned to the United States and interred at Arlington National Cemetery.

Further Reading

Greene, Robert Ewell. *Colonel Charles Young: Soldier and Diplomat*. Washington, D.C.: R. E. Greene, 1985.

———. *The Early Life of Colonel Charles Young: 1864–1889*. Washington, D.C.: Department of History, Howard University, 1973.

"Roll Call: Colonel Charles Young: Black Cavalryman, Huachuca Commander and Early Intelligence Officer." Huachuca Illustrated. Available online. URL: http://www.lib.byu.edu/~rdh/wwi/comment/huachuca/HI1-19.htm. Downloaded on October 3, 2008.

Schubert, Irene, and Frank Schubert. *On the Trail of the Buffalo Soldier II*. Lanham, Md.: Scarecrow Press, 2004, pp. 344–345.

Shellum, Brian. *Black Cadet in a White Bastion: Charles Young at West Point*. Lincoln: University of Nebraska Press, 2006.

Z

Zimmerman, Matthew Augustus, Jr.
(1941–) *major general, first African-American chief of chaplains in the army*

His career as an army chaplain permitted Matthew A. Zimmerman, Jr., to serve God, his country, and his fellow human beings. In 1990, Major General Zimmerman became the first African-American chief of chaplains in the U.S. Army.

Matthew Augustus Zimmerman, Jr., was born on December 9, 1941, in Rock Hill, South Carolina. Young Matthew attended a Baptist church where his father, the Reverend Matthew A. Zimmerman, Sr., was pastor, and an elementary school where his father was principal. His mother, Alberta Zimmerman, taught his first-grade class. It is not surprising therefore that as an adult, Zimmerman credited his parents with inspiring him to succeed. "They taught me spiritual values and the importance of building good relationships," he said.

At 16, Matthew Zimmerman, Jr., graduated from Sims High School in Union County, South Carolina, as his class valedictorian. He then entered Benedict College in Columbia, South Carolina, a school founded in 1870 by the Baptist Church, planning to go on to medical school. After earning a degree in biology and chemistry in 1962, however, he took advantage of an opportunity to study at Duke University Divinity School

on a fellowship. The experience caused Zimmerman to change course and pursue a career in the ministry. In 1965, after becoming the first African American to earn a master of divinity degree from Duke University, he was ordained by the National Baptist Convention, Inc., USA.

Zimmerman entered the army on March 21, 1967, with a commission by direct appointment to first lieutenant. He completed the Chaplain Officer Basic Course at the U.S. Army Chaplain School, Fort Hamilton, New York, and was assigned as chaplain with the U.S. Army Training Center (Infantry) at Fort Gordon, Georgia. At Fort Gordon and later at other army posts, Zimmerman ministered to people of all faiths. His duties expanded in January 1968, when he was sent to Vietnam as assistant chaplain with the United States Military Assistance Command in Vietnam. There, Zimmerman, who had been promoted to captain, helped orphanages collect clothing and other needed supplies.

Between 1969 and 1974, Zimmerman ministered to soldiers and their families at Fort Hood, Texas, with the 1st Armored Division, and in West Germany with the 3rd Armored Division, U.S. Army, Europe, and the Seventh Army. His promotion to major came on October 3, 1974, while he was a student in the Chaplain Officer Advanced Course at the U.S. Army Chaplain Center and School, Fort Wadsworth, New Jersey.

In 1975, he received a master's degree in education from Long Island University in New York.

In June 1975, Zimmerman joined the office of the chief of chaplains, U.S. Army, in Washington, D.C., as operations training staff officer. In June 1976, he became staff parish development officer in the same office. Three years later, in June 1979, after completing studies at the U.S. Army Command and General Staff College at Fort Leavenworth, Kansas, he returned to Europe as a deputy corps chaplain with VII Corps and the Seventh Army. On August 6, 1979, he was promoted to colonel, and in July 1980 he was named division staff chaplain with the 3rd Infantry Division, U.S. Army, Europe, and the Seventh Army.

By June 1982, Zimmerman had returned to the United States to attend the U.S. Army War College at Carlisle Barracks, Pennsylvania. The following year, he took on the duties of assistant command chaplain, U.S. Army Training and Doctrine Command at Fort Monroe, Virginia. He was promoted to colonel on July 1, 1984, and appointed command staff chaplain at Forces Command (FORSCOM), Fort McPherson, Georgia, in December 1985. FORSCOM is the largest major command in the Department of the Army.

Zimmerman returned to Washington in August 1989 to serve as deputy chief of chaplains for the army. He continued to receive regular promotions, to brigadier general on October 1, 1989, and to major general on August 1, 1990. At that time he was named the first African-American chief of chaplains for the army. He oversaw 2,800 active-duty, reserve, and National Guard chaplains and an equal number of chaplain assistants, representing 92 denominations, who were stationed throughout the world.

In 1994, Matthew Zimmerman, Jr., retired from the army as a major general and began a two-year term as director of the Chaplain Service of the Veterans Health Administration in Hampton, Virginia. In 1995, Secretary of Defense William J. Perry appointed him to a task force studying ways to improve the quality of life of personnel, their families, and civilian employees of the Department of Defense.

General Zimmerman's military decorations include the Legion of Merit, Bronze Star, and Meritorious Service Medal with two Oak Leaf Clusters. His civilian honors include the 1990 Roy Wilkins Meritorious Service Award from the NAACP and the 1991 Distinguished Alumni Award from Duke University School of Divinity.

Further Reading

Hawkins, Walter L. *Black American Military Leaders.* Jefferson, N.C.: McFarland and Co., 2007, pp. 537–538.

"Matthew A. Zimmerman." The Coalition of Spirit-Filled Churches. Available online. URL: http://www.spirit-filled.org/zimmerman.htm. Downloaded on October 4, 2008.

BIBLIOGRAPHY AND
RECOMMENDED SOURCES

Astor, Gerald. *The Right to Fight: A History of African Americans in the Military.* Novato, Calif.: Presidio Press, 1998.

Barbeau, Arthur E., and Florette Henri. *The Unknown Soldiers: Black American Troops in World War I.* New York: Da Capo Press, 1996.

Berlin, Ira, ed. *Freedom's Soldiers: The Black Military Experience in the Civil War.* Cambridge: Cambridge University Press, 1998.

Bielakowski, Alexander. *African American Troops in World War II.* Oxford, U.K.: Osprey Publishing, 2007.

Buckley, Gail. *American Patriots: The Story of Blacks in the Military from the Revolution to Desert Storm.* New York: Random House, 2001.

Claxton, Melvin, and Mark Puls. *Uncommon Valor: A Story of Race, Patriotism, and Glory in the Final Battles of the Civil War.* Hoboken, N.J.: John Wiley and Sons, 2006.

Clinton, Catherine. *The Black Soldier: 1492 to the Present.* Boston: Houghton Mifflin, 2000.

Collum, Danny Duncan, ed. *African Americans in the Spanish Civil War: "This Ain't Ethiopia, but It'll Do."* New York: G. K. Hall and Co., 1992.

Culp, Ronald E. *The First Black United States Marines: The Men of Montford Point, 1942–1946.* Jefferson, N.C.: McFarland and Co., 2007.

Davis, Alphonse G. *Pride, Progress, and Prospects: The Marine Corps' Efforts to Increase the Presence of African-American Officers.* Washington, D.C.: History and Museums Division, Headquarters, U.S. Marine Corps, 2000.

Donaldson, Gary A. *The History of African-Americans in the Military.* Malabar, Fla.: Krieger Publishing Co., 1991.

Edgerton, Robert B. *Hidden Heroism: Black Soldiers in America's Wars.* Boulder, Colo.: Westview Press, 2001.

Field, Ron. *Buffalo Soldiers 1892–1918.* Oxford, U.K.: Osprey Publishing, 2005.

Fischer, Perry E., and Brooks E. Gray. *Blacks and Whites: Together Through Hell (U.S. Marines in World War II).* Turlock, Calif.: Millsmont Publishing, 1994.

Glasrud, Bruce A., and Michael N. Searles, eds. *Buffalo Soldiers in the West: A Black Soldiers Anthology.* College Station: Texas A & M University Press, 2007, pp. 70–73.

Hanna, Charles W. *African American Recipients of the Medal of Honor.* Jefferson, N.C.: McFarland and Co., 2002.

Haskins, Jim. *African American Military Heroes.* New York: John Wiley and Sons, 1998.

The History of Blacks in the Coast Guard from 1790. Washington, D.C.: Department of Transportation and U.S. Coast Guard, 1977.

Kaplan, Sidney, and Emma Nogrady Kaplan. *The Black Presence in the Era of the American Revolution.* Amherst: University of Massachusetts Press, 1989.

Kimbrough, Natalie. *Equality or Discrimination? African Americans in the U.S. Military during the Vietnam War.* Lanham, Md.: University Press of America, 2007.

Lanning, Michael Lee. *The African-American Soldier from Crispus Attucks to Colin Powell.* New York: Citadel Press, 2004.

———. *Defenders of Liberty: African Americans in the Revolutionary War.* New York: Citadel Press, 2000.

Latty, Yvonne. *We Were There: Voices of African American Veterans, from World War II to the War in Iraq.* New York: Amistad, 2004.

Leckie, William H., with Shirley A. Leckie. *The Buffalo Soldiers: A Narrative of the Black Cavalry in the West.* Norman: University of Oklahoma Press, 2003.

McPherson, James M. *The Negro's Civil War: How American Blacks Felt and Acted During the War for the Union.* New York: Vintage Books, 2003.

Moore, Christopher. *Fighting for America: Black Soldiers—The Unsung Heroes of World War II.* New York: Ballantine Books, 2006.

Motley, Mary Penick, comp. *The Invisible Soldier: The Experience of the Black Soldier, World War II.* Detroit: Wayne State University Press, 1987.

Murphy, Edward F. *Vietnam Medal of Honor Heroes.* New York: Ballantine Books, 2005.

Nalty, Bernard C. *The Right to Fight: African-American Marines in World War II.* Washington, D.C.: History and Museums Division, Headquarters, U.S. Marine Corps, 1995.

Ruck, Calvin W. *The Black Battalion, 1916–1920: Canada's Best Kept Military Secret.* Halifax, Nova Scotia: Nimbus Publishing, 1987.

Shaw, Henry I., Jr., and Ralph W. Donnelly. *Blacks in the Marine Corps.* Washington, D.C.: History and Museums Division, Headquarters, U.S. Marine Corps, 1975.

Sutherland, Jonathan D. *African Americans at War.* Santa Barbara, Calif.: ABC-CLIO, 2004.

Terry, Wallace, ed. *Bloods: An Oral History of the Vietnam War by Black Americans.* New York: Ballantine Books, 1992.

Westheider, James E. *The African American Experience in Vietnam: Brothers in Arms.* Lanham, Md.: Rowman and Littlefield, 2008.

RANKS IN THE U.S. MILITARY

Each branch of the U.S. armed forces has developed a system of issuing orders and delegating responsibility according to rank. The military distinguishes between commissioned officers, who have received their rank and authority by written order, and enlisted personnel, who receive no written commission.

ARMY

Officers
Second Lieutenant
First Lieutenant
Captain
Major
Lieutenant Colonel
Colonel
Brigadier General
Major General
Lieutenant General
General

Enlisted Personnel
Private (PV-1)
Private (PV-2)
Private First Class
Corporal/Specialist
Sergeant
Staff Sergeant
Sergeant First Class
Master/First Sergeant
Sergeant Major
Command Sergeant Major
Sergeant Major of the Army

AIR FORCE

Officers
Second Lieutenant
First Lieutenant
Captain
Major
Lieutenant Colonel
Colonel
Brigadier General
Major General
Lieutenant General
General

Enlisted Personnel
Airman Basic
Airman
Airman First Class
Senior Airman
Staff Sergeant
Technical Sergeant
Master Sergeant
Senior Master Sergeant
Chief Master Sergeant
Command Chief Master Sergeant
Chief Master Sergeant of the
    Air Force

MARINE CORPS

Officers	Enlisted Personnel
Second Lieutenant	Private
First Lieutenant	Private First Class
Captain	Lance Corporal
Major	Corporal
Lieutenant Colonel	Sergeant
Colonel	Staff Sergeant
Brigadier General	Gunnery Sergeant
Major General	Master/First Sergeant
Lieutenant General	Master Gunnery Sergeant
General	Sergeant Major
	Sergeant Major of the Marine Corps

NAVY AND COAST GUARD

Officers	Enlisted Personnel
Ensign	Seaman Recruit
Lieutenant Junior Grade	Seaman Apprentice
Lieutenant	Seaman
Lieutenant Commander	Petty Officer Third Class
Commander	Petty Officer Second Class
Captain	Petty Officer First Class
Rear Admiral Lower Half	Chief Petty Officer
Rear Admiral Upper Half	Senior Chief Petty Officer
Vice Admiral	Master Chief Petty Officer
Admiral	Master Chief Petty Officer of the Navy/Coast Guard

U.S. MILITARY DECORATIONS IN ORDER OF PRECEDENCE

Over time, the U.S. military has established decorations to honor personnel who serve the nation heroically in times of war or peace. The following is a list of the principal decorations for each branch of the armed forces in order of precedence, with their years of establishment.

ARMY

1. Medal of Honor (established 1862)
2. Distinguished Service Cross (1918)
3. Defense Distinguished Service Medal (1970)
4. Distinguished Service Medal (1918)
5. Silver Star (1918)
6. Defense Superior Service Medal (1976)
7. Legion of Merit (1942)
8. Distinguished Flying Cross (1926)
9. Soldier's Medal (1926)
10. Bronze Star (1942)
11. Meritorious Service Medal (1969)
12. Air Medal (1942)
13. Joint Service Commendation Medal (1963)
14. Army Commendation Medal (formerly Commendation Ribbon) (1945)
15. Purple Heart (1782)

AIR FORCE

1. Medal of Honor (established 1862)
2. Air Force Cross (1960)
3. Defense Distinguished Service Medal (1970)
4. Distinguished Service Medal (1918)
5. Silver Star (1918)
6. Defense Superior Service Medal (1976)
7. Legion of Merit (1942)
8. Distinguished Flying Cross (1926)
9. Airman's Medal (1960)
10. Bronze Star (1942)
11. Meritorious Service Medal (1969)
12. Air Medal (1942)
13. Joint Service Commendation Medal (1963)
14. Air Force Commendation Medal (1958)
15. Purple Heart (1782)

NAVY AND MARINE CORPS

1. Medal of Honor (1862)
2. Navy Cross (1919)
3. Defense Distinguished Service Medal (1970)
4. Distinguished Service Medal (1918)
5. Silver Star (1918)
6. Defense Superior Service Medal (1976)
7. Legion of Merit (1942)
8. Navy and Marine Corps Medal (1942)
9. Bronze Star (1942)
10. Meritorious Service Medal (1969)
11. Air Medal (1942)
12. Joint Service Commendation Medal (1967)
13. Navy Commendation Medal (formerly Navy Commendation Ribbon) (1944)
14. Purple Heart (1782)

ENTRIES BY BRANCH OF SERVICE

CONTINENTAL ARMY
Cromwell, Oliver
Dabney, Austin
Haynes, Lemuel
Hull, Agrippa
Lew, Barzillai
Poor, Salem
Salem, Peter

NATIONAL GUARD
Bryant, Cunningham C.
Denison, Franklin A.
Trowell-Harris, Irene

NOAA COMMISSIONED CORPS
Fields, Evelyn J.

U.S. AIR FORCE AND U.S. ARMY AIR CORPS
World War II
Archer, Lee A., Jr.
Brown, Roscoe Conkling, Jr.
Davis, Benjamin O., Jr.
Hall, Charles B.
Theus, Lucius

U.S. AIR FORCE
Vietnam War to Present
Anderson, Michael P.
Bluford, Guion S., Jr.

Cherry, Fred Vann
Gregory, Frederick Drew
Harris, Marcelite Jordan
James, Chappie
Lawrence, Robert Henry, Jr.
Newton, Lloyd W.

U.S. ARMY
War of 1812 to Civil War
Augusta, Alexander Thomas
Beaty, Powhatan
Cailloux, Andre
Carney, William Harvey
Delany, Martin Robison
Fleetwood, Christian Abraham
Gooding, James Henry
Pinchback, Pinckney Benton Stewart
Rivers, Prince
Savary, Joseph
Turner, Henry McNeal

Indian Wars to Spanish-American War
Alexander, John Hanks
Allensworth, Allen
Bivins, Horace Wayman
Flipper, Henry Ossian
Jordan, George

Plummer, Henry Vinton
Prioleau, George Washington
Stance, Emanuel
Walley, Augustus
Williams, Cathay

World War I
Europe, James Reese
Johnson, Henry
Sissle, Noble Lee
Stowers, Freddie
Young, Charles

World War II
Baker, Vernon Joseph
Carter, Edward Allen, Jr.
Cartwright, Roscoe Conklin
Davis, Benjamin O., Sr.
Davison, Frederic Ellis
Earley, Charity Adams
Louis, Joe
Rivers, Ruben
Thomas, Charles Leroy
Waddy, Harriet West
Watson, George
Wright, Bruce McMarion

Korean War
Becton, Julius Wesley, Jr.
Charlton, Cornelius H.
Robinson, Roscoe, Jr.
Thompson, William Henry

Entries by Year of Birth

Miller, Dorie
Rivers, Ruben
Wright, Bruce McMarion

1920–1925
Branch, Frederick C.
Brown, Roscoe Conkling, Jr.
Bryant, Cunningham C.
Doughty, Gene
Gravely, Samuel Lee, Jr.
Hall, Charles B.
James, Chappie
Theus, Lucius
Thomas, Charles Leroy
Woodward, Luther*

1926–1929
Becton, Julius Wesley, Jr.
Brown, Jesse Leroy
Brown, Wesley Anthony
Chambers, Lawrence
    Cleveland
Charlton, Cornelius H.
Cherry, Fred Vann
Joel, Lawrence
Johnson-Brown, Hazel
    Winifred
Robinson, Roscoe, Jr.

Rogers, Charles Calvin
Thompson, William Henry

1930–1939
Adams-Ender, Clara Leach
Alexander, Clifford Leopold, Jr.
Brashear, Carl Maxie
Cooper, J. Gary
Hacker, Benjamin T.
Lawrence, Robert Henry, Jr.
Petersen, Frank Emmanuel, Jr.
Pitts, Riley Leroy
Powell, Colin Luther
Robinson, Hugh Granville
Trowell-Harris, Irene
Waller, Calvin Agustine
    Hoffman

1940–1942
Bluford, Guion S., Jr.
Cadoria, Sherian Grace
Gaston, Mack Charles
Gorden, Fred Augustus
Gregory, Frederick Drew
Newton, Lloyd W.
West, Togo Dennis, Jr.
Zimmerman, Matthew
    Augustus, Jr.

1943–1949
Anderson, James, Jr.
Black, Barry C.
Bolden, Charles F., Jr.
Brown, Jesse
Fields, Arnold
Fields, Evelyn J.
Fishburne, Lillian Elaine
Harris, Marcelite Jordan
Olive, Milton Lee, III
Reason, Joseph Paul
Ward, William Edward*
Wilson, Johnnie Edward

1950–1959
Anderson, Michael P.
Austin, Lloyd James III
Brooks, Vincent K.
Brown, Erroll M.*
Cochran, Donnie L.
Gaskin, Walter E., Sr.
Goodman, Robert Oliver, Jr.
Simmons, Bettye Hill

1960–1973
Armour, Vernice
Howard, Michelle J.
Johnson, Shoshana Nyree

*The actual year of birth is unknown.

INDEX

Boldface locators indicate main entries. *Italic* locators indicate photographs. For a full list of references see an individual's main entry. Numbers precede letters.